Public Procurement in Europe:
Enforcement and Remedies

Public Procurement in Europe: Enforcement and Remedies

Edited by

Alan Tyrrell   QC, LLB, FCI Arb

of Gray's Inn

Becket Bedford   LLB

Barrister

With the assistance of InterAct Europe

Butterworths
London, Charlottesville, Dublin, Durban, Edinburgh,
Kuala Lumpur, Singapore, Sydney, Toronto, Wellington
1997

United Kingdom	Butterworths, a Division of Reed Elsevier (UK) Ltd, Halsbury House, 35 Chancery Lane, LONDON WC2A 1EL and 4 Hill Street, EDINBURGH EH2 3JZ
Australia	Butterworths, SYDNEY, MELBOURNE, BRISBANE, ADELAIDE, PERTH, CANBERRA and HOBART
Canada	Butterworths Canada Ltd, TORONTO and VANCOUVER
Ireland	Butterworth (Ireland) Ltd, DUBLIN
Malaysia	Malayan Law Journal Sdn Bhd, KUALA LUMPUR
New Zealand	Butterworths of New Zealand Ltd, WELLINGTON and AUCKLAND
Singapore	Reed Elsevier (Singapore) Pte Ltd, SINGAPORE
South Africa	Butterworths Publishers (Pty) Ltd, DURBAN
USA	Michie, CHARLOTTESVILLE, Virginia

A CIP Catalogue record for this book is available from the British Library.

ISBN 0 406 04783 9

Typeset by Kerrypress Ltd, Luton
Printed by Mackays of Chatham PLC, Chatham, Kent

Foreword

Professor A Mattera*

If the author of the Divine Comedy could be here to witness contemporary events and denounce the morals of our society, he would undoubtedly pay particular attention to the phenomenon of public contracts, reserving a special place in the lower circle of his inferno for the legion of corrupters and corrupted who have transformed public procurement into an instrument of pillage of taxpayers' money, whether with a view to personal enrichment or to swell the coffers of the political parties to which they belong.

This 'manipulation' is not something which has occurred only in our times. For the thrifty middle classes, public procurement today no more represents a means of furnishing goods and services under the most advantageous conditions offered on the market than it did in the last century. As the interference of public authorities in the economic and social life of our states has become more insistent, politicians have discovered in public procurement a favoured means of intervention which they have used sometimes as an instrument of trade cycle policy, sometimes as an instrument of structural or sectoral policy, sometimes even as an instrument of social or regional policy.

It is with every justification that informed observers consider that the phenomena of corruption, speculation, misappropriation, embezzlement and the like, to which we are witnesses, are not always the doing of a politico-economic class more corrupt than those which preceded it. Were this the case, changing the governments now in power would suffice to purge an unwholesome system. In reality, according to some observers, the phenomena in question are evidence of a continuing presence of the state, so inhibiting and with such ramifications in the economy, in banking and in the services, that it appears as an inexplicable interference and inconsistency in a free market context.

It is against this background that the Community has had to undertake and pursue action to open up public procurement – a background which explains both the accumulated delays in implementing legislative texts (30 years have passed since the start of work on the first Directive on public works and the adoption of the fourth, regulating public services contracts) and the undoubtedly inadequate degree of market liberalisation so far achieved.

While legislative action at Community level can be considered to be essentially complete, this in no way signifies that the opening up of public procurement is an objective achieved. Many are the observers who judge that

* Director in the European Commission, responsible for the free movement of goods and public procurement; Professor of Community Law at the College of Europe, Bruges, and the Free International University of Rome (LUISS).

little has changed in reality. Public contracts would remain a national fief, a private preserve jealously protected. So it is urgently necessary to attack this last bastion of state protectionism and this, with the twin objectives of:

(1) liberalising a market for products and services still largely closed, thus re-establishing the rules of competition in a priority sector of the European economy;
(2) giving the reforming forces of Member States the tools and support necessary to get rid of the dross of a corrupt political system and ensure healthier management of public finances.

Actions undertaken for this purpose must form part of a comprehensive strategy, developed on several fronts:

(1) first of all, it is essential to ensure correct implementation of the Community Directives in legal measures at national level and to reject any measure of implementation in domestic law (for example, administrative circulars) which does not guarantee to those for whom they were intended the full exercise of the rights which flow from the Community rules and the possibility of having them enforced in the national courts;
(2) next, it is advisable to ensure scrupulous respect for the Community rules concerned, setting up arrangements for increasingly vigilant surveillance. It is particularly necessary to see that the Remedies Directives generate the expected changes in national law, and that the 'political potential' of the Community procedure for which they make provision is fully exploited. To this end, it is fundamental that the authorities empowered at national and Community level are seized in time to use the procedures available to them to prevent the infringement complained of having legal effects. This is especially so in the case of the Commission. It will also be necessary for the services sector to be made subject to a similar Directive;
(3) it is of capital importance to ensure that all allocations from the Community funds and loans from the BEI, in connection with the purchase of goods and services or the execution of public works, are made conditional on compliance with the Community rules on the subject;
(4) greater firmness in enforcing compliance with the rules which have just been mentioned should not tend to lead to conflict in relations with Member States. Quite the contrary! A procedure involving dialogue and exchange of views will be put in place (after the fashion of the procedure followed in the 'package meetings' which deal with cases concerning free movement of goods),[1] offering Member States the necessary legal and technical assistance – particularly in implementing the Directives in national law – and, in currently contentious cases, seeking agreed solutions which are in conformity with Community law. In short, it is not enough to adopt new rules and modify existing ones; it is above all necessary to change mentalities and habits rooted in centuries of a culture of administrative autonomy. Such an objective will only be achieved at the cost of permanent effort and by persistent action to convince and interact with national administrations and contracting authorities;
(5) to achieve the objective sought, actions to raise awareness and provide

---

[1] See Article 30 of the EC Treaty, the Cassis de Dijon jurisprudence and the principle of mutual recognition in No 4/92, pp 64ff of this review.

information will have to be pursued with the actors concerned: public administrations, contracting authorities, firms (particularly small firms, since it is they which have most need of the law), so that they wake up to the obligations and rights flowing from the Community rules. Ignorance on the part of economic operators and firms of their rights and the remedies available to them, and resignation in the face of the continuance of abusive situations which are damaging to their interests, are a major contributory cause of the compartmentalisation of public procurement markets.

The present work fits precisely within this scenario. I congratulate the authors on the extent of their achievement.

A special effort will still need to be made, on the one hand, to improve the quality of the informative data on public procurement (for example, the tender notices in the OJEC) so that they are clear, complete and, as far as possible, uniformly presented, and, on the other hand, to have a more selective and rapid system for making them available to firms. The exchange of computerised data (EDI) is one means of meeting this last requirement. It would have to be completed by a system of information on public contracts (SIMAP) making it possible for all the actors who have a part to play in public contracting (contracting authorities, suppliers, service providers, national inspection authorities) to dispose in due time of all the information they need on a particular contract.

On 27 November 1996, the European Commission adopted a Green Paper on 'Public Procurement: the Way Forward'. This reflection paper is intended to launch a wide-ranging discussion on how the Union can best take advantage of the opening up of public procurement. As Professor Mario Monti, European Commissioner responsible for the single market, has said:

'The moment has come to take stock of what has been achieved and what remains to be done. The opening up of public procurement to competition must lead to significant savings for contracting authorities and new opportunities for economic operators.

The fundamental objectives of Union policy on public procurement are: rational use of public monies to obtain better quality public services at less cost, access of suppliers to a single market offering significant prospects and reinforcing the competitivity of European firms through transparency in contract procedures and the creation of the necessary conditions of competition to ensure the award of contracts without discrimination.'

Preface

Much has already been written about the substantive provisions of the EU Public Procurement Regime, the difficulties of implementation, interpretation and detailed application.

Previous works have rightly concentrated on matters of compliance and even though the Regime is now some 25 years old, that is as it should be, since the purpose of the Regime cannot be better served than by contracting authorities or entities adopting the tenets of transparency and non-discrimination when awarding public contracts.

With this book, we have sought to shift the focus of the literature onto the contractors themselves, their rights and remedies. Each chapter outlines in brief the existence, if any, of the various national public procurement regimes and the implementation of the EU Public Procurement Regime, before concentrating on the implementation of the Remedies Directives and, in particular, on the conditions governing the award of interim measures and the recovery of damages. The book does not obviate the need to instruct a lawyer in the Member State where action is being considered, but since decisions as to remedies have to be taken at very short notice, it will be valuable for lawyers in the Member State of the aggrieved party to have an overview of the system of enforcement in the Member State where the complaint is made. Our aim has been to provide a practical guide to any person contemplating legal action for an infringement of the Public Procurement Regime in any of the Member States.

The state, in its various central, regional, and delegated manifestations, is by far the biggest purchaser of supplies, works and services in every national territory. Taking all the Member States together, their purchasing power runs into many billions of ECUs. Historically, the power to award public contracts was used to support national or regional interests to the virtual exclusion of outsiders. In some Member States, this power was overtly used to advance a government's policy objectives. In others, there was no policy at all, the human nature of those with power in the awarding authorities being enough to achieve a similar result. This left a gaping hole in the construction of a common market.

Examples of this abound. No one Member State could tackle the problem alone without placing its own contractors at a major disadvantage. By common consent, European Community action was essential. Thus there came into effect the early Public Procurement Directives. They proved ineffective. Two striking cases in about 1980 come to mind. One, having lost its longstanding position as a supplier of stationery to a government department, found it could not retaliate in the successful bidder's home market because orders were placed in sufficiently small packages to escape the EC threshold. Another could not tender for a public works contract in a country it had traditionally supplied with a particular building material because the tender specification included a new standard which only home suppliers could meet. Yet there was no remedy.

Hence under the impetus of the Single European Act to complete the construction of the common market there came the Remedies Directives, the subject of this book.

The form of remedies for infringements of Community law is, and has always been, according to the jurisprudence of the European Court of Justice, a matter for national law. This is re-affirmed in *Brasserie du Pecheur SA v Germany* (Case C-46/93, judgment of 5 March 1996) at paragraph 67:

'... The State must make preparation for the consequences of the loss and damage caused in accordance with the domestic rules on liability, provided that the conditions for negotiation of loss and damage laid down by national law must not be less favourable than those relating to similar domestic claims and must not be such as in practice to make it impossible or excessively difficult to obtain reparation.'

The Remedies Directives, exceptionally, made some inroads into this principle, by setting out in somewhat broad terms, the type of remedies that should be available, and when. Procedures remain within the exclusive prerogative of Member States.

The substantive national chapters in this book show that most Member States have made a hash of it. None can don a completely white sheet. National authors have not forborne from pointing out the inadequacies of the attempts by their national legislatures or governments to achieve the objectives set out in the Directives.

In some Member States, the problems arise from placing remedies for public procurement infringements into an existing legal system not suited to it. Thus in some states where there are both administrative and judicial systems operating in parallel, jurisdiction is divided between the two, or one is followed by the other. Further, in some states the historical division of jurisdiction between central and regional authority has been preserved. In others, for historical reasons, jurisdictional distinctions are drawn between public supply, public works, and services; and in one between professional and other services.

Some Member States have had difficulty in deciding whether to allocate these remedies to public or private law. Some have drawn a distinction in the contract with utilities between those publicly owned and those privately owned: a distinction which is not necessarily easy to apply in practice. Some have applied the doctrine of 'detachable deeds' so that different legal principles are applied to pre-contract documents than to contractual documents.

So in some respects this book portrays a rather sad picture. One author writes that his national implementation:

'lacks the required cohesion to ensure an appropriate means of redress for the aggrieved contractor'. (Belgium)

Another writes that the method of implementation:

'caused several, and for outsiders incomprehensible, complications'. (Germany)

A third writes:

'the claim for compensation is very often dismissed while the illegality of the disqualification' (of a potential tenderer) 'is acknowledged by the Court'. (Greece)

One writer, defending the complex method of implementation in his country, remarks:

'Community law is not intended as a substitute for national law, even in cases where it is important to protect equality of treatment between all the jurisdictions of the Community'. (France)

This principle has been widely applied. The result is that most authors have felt constrained to give a mini-portrait of their national legal systems, sometimes complex, to demonstrate how the remedies prescribed by the Directives can be effected.

A further result has been that some Member States have set up a special authority to whom complaints should in the first instance be directed. Unfortunately these bodies typically have very limited powers and are mainly a stepping-stone to a court.

Some Member States originally took the view that the specified remedies were already available in their national jurisdictions. These were subsequently disillusioned either by the Commission or the European Court of Justice. Some enacted the Directives as they stood into their national legislation, overlooking the fact that the Directives do not provide for procedures.

For the EC Commission, the task of monitoring and enforcing the Public Procurement Directives has been formidable, and continues to be so. In its Thirteenth Annual Report on Monitoring Community Law (OJC303, 14 October 1996) it records (at paragraph 2.2.5 Public Procurement) serious delays in the implementation of some older Directives, specifying inter alia the Utilities Remedies Directive 92/13/EEC. It handled, during the year, 26 infringement cases concerning failure to notify national implementing measures. Of those that were notified, there were 14 new infringement cases for incorrect transposal, bringing the total number of cases pending to 30. It remarks:

'Some of these cases involve questions of principle which could undermine the liberalisation of public contracts awarded in the Member States concerned'.

The Commission has stepped up its monitoring of the practical application by the various awarding authorities in each Member State. Suspected infringements have increased by 50% in a year. Of the 238 cases processed in the year, including 97 new cases, the Commission was able to settle 38 without having to let Article 169 proceedings run their full course.

From the national chapters, it is seen that a majority of Member States have failed to set up the attestation procedure required by the Directive. Several have failed to set up a conciliation procedure. Three of the national authors draw attention to the 'Catch 22' apparent in the systems of several Member States: an aggrieved tenderer cannot obtain an injunction because damages would be an adequate remedy; but in order to recover damages it is necessary for him to prove at least a prospect that he would have won the contract but for the infringement, a burden very difficult to discharge, save in the rare cases where the sole criterion for success is price. In one Member State (Spain) no damages are recoverable unless the aggrieved contractor proves that he would have won the contract. In another (Austria) the damages recoverable excludes loss of profit. In some who have not implemented the Utilities Remedies Directive it is doubtful whether tender costs are recoverable, or whether in full or in part.

However, the reader of this book will find a lot of answers. In all Member States, damages or compensation is available in some jurisdiction or other (even though in one case it will take about ten years to get them!). In all Member States, some form of interim measures is available. In all Member States, it is possible to move for early relief. It will usually need the skill of a lawyer qualified in the relevant national jurisdiction to guide aggrieved contractors through the national procedures. Since there is usually urgency, such a lawyer needs to have advance familiarity with the subject.

In most (but not all) Member States, the number of complaints or actions has been small, sometimes minimal. Three national authors suggest that a contributory cause for this has been apprehension by aggrieved contractors that infringement proceedings could impede their prospects of securing future contracts. Probably such apprehension is misplaced. In any event it can be expected to diminish as more cases come forward. Ordinarily the infringements are due to ignorance rather than malice. Awarding authorities have their problems too, in abiding by the public procurement requirements. For them, the setting-up of the attestation procedure would provide welcome relief. It would also give confidence to prospective tenderers that the expense of preparing a tender is worthwhile.

It has taken two decades to reach this state of partial establishment of a fair and effective Public Procurement Regime. There is still a long way to go. Commonly, national courts are more stringent in granting interim measures than is the European Court of Justice, whose approach is exemplified in *Van Hool* (see p 79). It is an odd situation that the ECJ will suspend contract procedures at the request of the Commission but a national court will not do so at the request of an aggrieved contractor. In due course this may need further harmonisation legislation. The same may apply to ensure that national remedies include damages for loss of opportunity, and damages for loss of profit.

Meanwhile, better use can be made of what has been achieved. The existing body of law, Community and national, contains much of value to consumers and taxpayers, as well as to contractors.

Unfortunately our wants have not been quite equal to the immoderate demands of such a work. It is regrettable that we have not been able to secure national chapters from Italy, Portugal, Sweden and Luxembourg. We hope that this defect may be cured in the future.

For the present it is hoped that the shared experience of each of the national authors will serve to encourage and promote a greater awareness of the opportunities for legal redress for infringements of the Regime which we believe are not nearly so modest as is commonly thought.

Alan Tyrrell QC
Francis Taylor Building
Temple
London
EC4Y 7BY

Becket Bedford
5 Fountain Court
Steelhouse Lane
Birmingham
B4 6DR

InterAct Europe

InterAct Europe 1993 EEIG is an association of forward thinking law firms. Its aim is to extend the services and information available to their clients and enhance their knowledge of, and access to, an ever closer Europe. Founded in 1993, its membership has grown to include ten law firms representing seven European jurisdictions. It is expected that the network will expand so as to be representative of all the major jurisdictions in Europe while retaining the high quality of its membership.

For assistance with European projects and problems contact your local InterAct member. The members of InterAct Europe offer you access to a network of specialist legal firms with expertise in all aspects of national and European law.

Denmark
Flagstad Lawfirm
Amaliegade 42
DK-1256 Copenhagen K
Tel 00 45 33 11 33 99
Fax 00 45 33 12 13 98

France
D Angenieux, D Gilles, P Ceyrac &
C de Buhren
3 Rue de Turbigo
75001 Paris
Tel 00 33 1 44 76 13 00
Fax 00 33 1 40 26 11 59

Holland
De Vos & Steinz Advocaten
Prinses Irenestraat 41
1077 WV Amsterdam
Tel 00 31 (0)20 661 08 28
Fax 00 31 (0)20 661 36 15

Germany
Burger, Bohl, Meyer-Gutknecht &
Partners
Garmischer Str 8
80339 München
Tel 00 49 (0)89 5 40 94 90
Fax 00 49 (0)89 5 40 94 933

Lampestr 8
04107 Leipzig
Tel 00 49 (0)341 2 11 69 47
Fax 00 49 (0)341 2 11 69 48

Dr Weiland & Partners
Neuer Wall 86
20354 Hamburg
Tel 00 49 (0)40 36 13 07 0
Fax 00 49 (0)40 37 22 74

Mittelstrasse 2
10117 Berlin
Tel 00 49 (0)30 20 39 74 0
Fax 00 49 (0)30 20 39 74 222

Norway
Ro, Sommernes & Co DA
Øvre Slottsgt, 12 B
0157 Oslo
Tel 00 47 22 41 02 02
Fax 00 47 22 33 36 44

Spain
Coll-Navarro-Sanz-Villar &
Asociados Abogados SL
C/Alfonso XII 32
28014 Madrid
Tel 00 34 1 420 21 08
        and 420 21 09
Fax 00 34 1 420 22 35

United Kingdom
Pitmans
47 Castle Street
Reading RG1 7SR
Tel 00 44 (0)118 958 0224
Fax 00 44 (0)118 958 5097

Chambers of Alan Tyrrell QC
3rd Floor
Francis Taylor Building
Temple
London EC4Y 7BY
Tel 00 44 (0)171 797 7250
Fax 00 44 (0)171 797 7299

Contributors

Hubert Amiel
Maitre Hubert Amiel JEP (Paris), Doctor of Law, Avocat à la Court d'Appel
Aix-en-Provence, Maitre de Conference University of Aix-Marseille, specialist
in French public law.

Becket Bedford
Becket Bedford, barrister, Middle Temple 1989, LLB (Wales), practices EU
and commercial law at 5 Fountain Court, Birmingham and Francis Taylor
Building, London. Co-editor of forthcoming *European Travel Laws* (1997, John
Wiley & Sons).

Joseph Dalby
Joseph Dalby LLB (Hons), lic sp dr eur, is a practising English barrister,
writer, and academic lecturer. He specialises in European law and affairs,
concentrating on competition, trade, and procurement. He practices from
Winchester, England, and has offices in London, Brussels and Paris. E-mail
joseph.dalby@zetnet.co.uk.

Mogens Flagstad
Mogens Flagstad, member of the Bar of Danish High Court since 1981, partner
in Flagstad advokarterne, Copenhagen. Lectures at Danish General Council
of the Bar and University of Copenhagen, specialist in company and commercial
law.

Adrian Hardiman
Adrian Hardiman SC is a graduate of the National University of Ireland
and is a practising Senior Counsel in Dublin specialising in libel, criminal
and commercial law. He has appeared in many of the significant cases in
these areas in the past few years.

Karin I de Jong
Karin I de Jong, degree in law (Leiden), studied EC law at Poitiers. Advocate
at De Vos & Steinz, Amsterdam since 1993, practices in the company
commercial sector including public procurement law.

Laura Kalliomaa-Puha
Laura Kalliomaa-Puha, LLM, University of Helsinki, has been working as
a researcher both in the Institute of International Economic Law and the

Institute of Private Law at the University of Helsinki in various projects focusing on public procurement and competition law. She has published a book on both subjects in addition to some articles. At the moment she is writing her dissertation, 'Welfare State—Expectations, Privatization and Private Law'. E-mail laura.kalliomaa.@otdk.helsinki.fi.

José Maria Jiménez Laiglesia

José Maria Jiménez Laiglesia, abogado, Madrid Bar, degree in law (Madrid), LLM (London) in EC law. Partner G & J Abogados, Madrid, specialist in EU and competition law, formerly associate of J & A Garrigues, Brussels and Madrid. Lectures on EC law in Spain.

Reinhold Müller

Dr Reinhold Müller studied law at Innsbruck University from 1986–1991, practiced at the provincial court of Innsbruck until 1992 before studying EC law at Hannover University. Since 1995 he has practised at the firm of Dr Hauska & Dr Matzuski, Innsbruck.

Yvonne Murphy

Yvonne Murphy MBS is a graduate of the National University of Ireland (University College, Dublin) and a practising barrister in Dublin. She is joint editor of the Irish Times Law Reports and co-author of a book on insider dealing.

Vassiliki Papaioannou

Vassiliki Papaioannou, masters degree in law 1977 (Athens); DEA in business law 1984 (Paris II); masters degree in sociology 1983 (Paris X). Admitted to the Athenian and Parisian Bar in 1981 and in 1989 where she practices principally in the field of public construction law.

Thomas Schabel

Thomas Schabel, Rechtsanwalt since 1985, partner with Burgr Bohl Munich, has practiced in the field of public procurement, construction and architectural law since 1976. University law lecturer in Munich, Essen and Dusseldorf; author of *Public Procurement in One Market* (Munich, 7th edn, 1996), *Architect's Law from A to Z* (Munich, 2nd edn, 1996).

Christian Tang-Jespersen

Christian Tang-Jespersen, advokartern at Flagstad advokarterne, degree in law (Copenhagen), has published articles on EC competition law and the Danish Stock Exchange.

Alan Tyrrell

Alan Tyrrell QC is a practising English lawyer who has been deeply involved in legal problems arising from the construction of a common market for 20 years. He was a Member of the European Parliament from 1979–1984, was appointed Queen's Counsel in 1976 and is a Fellow of the Chartered Institute of Arbitrators.

Van Bael & Bellis

Van Bael & Bellis is a Brussels-based law firm that advises clients from around the world on doing business in Europe. Founded by two of the leading practitioners in the field of EU law, Van Bael & Bellis has long enjoyed a reputation as one of the pre-eminent firms in this field. As the firm has grown over the years, it has also established a reputation for excellence in the areas of commercial litigation and corporate transactions.

Contents

Table of National Legislation

Table of European and International Legislation

Table of Cases

In the following table those cases comprising part of the domestic law of a nation are listed according to the chapters in which such law is discussed. These are followed by decisions of the European Court of Justice listed alphabetically and then numerically.

CHAPTER 5. Remedies in Denmark

CHAPTER 6. Remedies in Finland

CHAPTER 7. Remedies in France

CHAPTER 11. Remedies in the Netherlands

CHAPTER 12. Remedies in Spain

CHAPTER 13: Remedies in the United Kingdom

Decisions of the European Court of Justice are listed below alphabetically. These decisions are
also listed numerically in the succeeding table.

Decisions of the European Court of Justice are listed below numerically. These decisions are also listed alphabetically in the preceding table.

CHAPTER 1

The EC Public Procurement Regime: the Remedies Directives

Becket Bedford

INTRODUCTION

As long ago as 1971 a system of rules was introduced at the Community level to enable contractors in the Member States to compete on an equal footing with domestic contractors for public contracts across the Community. The system of rules is described in this book as the EC Public Procurement Regime. The Regime was not enacted in one single piece of legislation. It began with a system of rules for public works contracts, followed by rules for public supply contracts. The rules created a standardised set of procedures to be adopted by bodies in the public sector, known as contracting authorities, when awarding public contracts. A different system, the Utilities Regime, was introduced for contracts let by utilities on account of their more commercial orientation and privatisation within the Member States. The utilities, known as contracting entities, have greater flexibility in their choice of contract award procedures under the Utilities Regime. Subsequently, the award of public service contracts was brought within the ambit of the public sector Regime, but they are not yet regulated under the Utilities Regime. The immense worth of public contracts awarded annually in the Member States ensured the Regime a vital role in assisting in the removal of continued barriers to cross-border trade within the Community. However, the mere creation of a standard set of procedures to be adopted by contracting authorities and utilities when awarding contracts would be ineffectual in achieving the aim of liberalising community trade unless there also existed the means of enforcing the Regime. So to complete the erection of a free-functioning public procurement regime the Community enacted the Remedies Directives with the avowed intention of enabling contractors to obtain effective and rapid remedies against contracting authorities and entities everywhere which infringe the Regime.

The purpose of this book is to provide an overview of the practice and procedures which govern the availability of remedies in the Member States against public bodies and utilities which infringe the Regime. It is not the purpose of this book to assess the extent to which the Community has been successful in increasing the numbers of cross-border tenders for public contracts. Nor is it intended to provide a detailed summary of the national measures by which the individual Member States have sought to implement the co-ordination of contract award procedures.

THE EFFECT OF THE EC PUBLIC PROCUREMENT REGIME

The EC Public Procurement Regime requires all public contracts and contracts awarded by utilities which exceed a certain monetary value to be advertised in the Official Journal and to be awarded according to uniform rules throughout the Community. The rules govern the choice of procedures which must be adopted when awarding contracts; the calculation of contract values; the form of advertisement; contractual and technical specifications; and selection criteria. They are both complex and mundane and they are subject to the overriding principle that undertakings throughout the Community should receive equal treatment.

In common with all EC directives the public procurement directives are addressed to the Member States which are obliged to give effect to the objects which the directives seek to achieve within the time period laid down.[1] The Member States have some degree of latitude over the precise manner in which they implement directives but they must implement the directives into national law. The directives have been implemented differently by the various Member States. Some have chosen to implement the Regime 'by reference', in other words by incorporating the directives straight into national law without attempting to expand or elucidate their meaning, whereas others have gone to great lengths to transpose directives into national law using national forms and terminology. For some Member States, implementation involved substitution or amendment of existing national rules on public procurement, whilst for others, rules governing the award of public contracts were entirely novel.

The distinctive feature of the directives was that in each case they created rights in individuals against the state, which comprises all contracting authorities and utilities. As a result their provisions were capable of being directly effective and thus of being enforceable by individuals in the national courts where the Member States had not implemented them within the period laid down as well as by the Commission and other Member States. However, it became apparent that in the absence of specific remedies, Community undertakings were being deterred from submitting tenders because existing arrangements at national and Community level were not adequate. In particular, what was required was to enable contractors to correct or prevent infringements of the Regime from affecting their chances of winning contracts prior to their being awarded and also to bring claims for damages to compensate them for any harm caused by infringements. To this end the Remedies Directives require that contractors should have the right to rapid and effective review of contract award procedures.

What follows in this introduction is a discussion of the individual provisions of the Remedies Directives themselves and of the powers ot the Commission to take action against the Member States for breach of the Regime.

THE REMEDIES DIRECTIVES

Once the Remedies Directives have been fully implemented, contractors everywhere across the Community should have the facility to take individual contracting authorities and utilities to task for infringements of the Regime.

---

[1] Article 189 of the EC Treaty.

They should have a remedy in damages, but perhaps more importantly, the right to seek interim measures to correct or suspend contract award procedures so as to preserve their right to tender for a contract before it has been awarded or concluded. In consequence the importance of the Remedies Directives to contractors, their legal and other advisers can hardly be overstated. They are a tool with which to penetrate public markets in other Member States and indeed to open up regional markets within their own Member States. It should not be overlooked that the directives give contractors remedies not only against foreign contracting authorities and utilities in foreign jurisdictions, but also against their own authorities and utilities in their own jurisdictions.

There are two Remedies Directives, one for each of the public procurement regimes, namely Directive 89/665/EEC[1] in respect of public works, supply and services contracts and Directive 92/13/EEC[2] in respect of utilities works and supply contracts.

Directive 89/665/EEC is the blue-print for the later directive. As such it will be as well to examine its detailed contents, comparing and contrasting its provisions with those in Directive 92/13/EEC where the latter provides alternative or additional remedies.

Article 1

Article 1(1) imposes an obligation on the Member States to provide contractors with an effective and rapid means of reviewing contract award procedures on the grounds of an infringement of the public procurement regime. The obligation is clear, precise and unconditional. Furthermore, the nature of the procedures for the review of public contract awards are not left to the discretion of the Member States. Article 1(1) requires that the system of review adopted in each of the Member States accords with the terms of the Directive and in particular that the decisions of review bodies must be capable of being effectively enforced.

By Article 1(2) the Member States are required to ensure that the conditions under which remedies will be made available to contractors pursuant to the system of review established in consequence of the Directives are not more onerous than the conditions which govern the award of other domestic remedies.

Article 1(3) specifies the class of persons to whom the system of review must be made available. The system of review must be open to 'at least any person having or having had an interest in obtaining a particular contract and who has been or risks being harmed by an alleged infringement'. The Member States are free to add to the class of persons who may apply for a remedy. Article 1(3) enables Member States to limit the right of review where a contractor has not previously notified a contracting authority of his intention to seek review.

Article 2

Article 2 sets out in detail the remedies, which include interim relief, the right to set aside unlawful decisions and damages, that review bodies must have at their disposal under any system of review set up in accordance with Article 1. It provides that the review procedures must be conducted before

[1]   OJ No L 395, 21 December 1989.
[2]   OJ No L 76, 23 March 1992.

the courts or some other review body, whose decisions in turn must be amenable to review by a court or independent tribunal.

Interim measures

By Article 2(1)(a), Member States are obliged to ensure that review bodies have the power to take, at the earliest opportunity and by way of interlocutory procedures, interim measures for the purpose of correcting an alleged infringement or preventing further damage. Such measures may include the power to suspend contract award procedures or the implementation of any decision taken by a contracting authority. The Directives do not require that an application for review should have the automatic effect of suspending a contract award procedure.[1]

It is important to note that Article 2(1)(a) requires that any review body seised of a claim on an interlocutory basis must have the power not only to restrain any further infringement of the regime, but to take positive steps to correct any infringement where necessary. It is submitted therefore that the review body must have the power not only to suspend a contract award procedure pending the substantive hearing, but also to permit the award procedure to continue on terms, for instance re-admitting an excluded tenderer to the bid process, or correcting a technical, economic or financial specification.

Article 2(4) sets out a general framework within which Member States are free to formulate the test to be applied when considering whether to grant interim measures. The Article is permissive and it allows any review to take into account the probable consequences of all interests likely to be harmed, including the public interest. Moreover, Article 2(4) envisages that interim measures may be refused at the national level where their negative consequences exceed their benefits. The single caveat is that the refusal of interim measures should not prejudice a contractor's application for final relief.

Power to set aside unlawful decisions and to award damages

Article 2(1)(b) sets out the powers which must be available to review bodies when granting final relief in public procurement cases. A review body must have the power to set aside decisions taken unlawfully, including the removal of discriminatory technical, economic or financial specifications in the invitation to tender, the contract documents or in any other document relating to the contract award procedure, and further it must have the power to award damages.

Although the directives give review bodies the power to set aside unlawful decisions made in the context of a contract award procedure, they do not set out the conditions in which unlawful decisions must be set aside. In fact they are silent on the question whether such decisions must be set aside when an infringement is proved. As a result it is submitted that the Member States are entitled to give review bodies complete discretion whether to set aside unlawful decisions or not.

Moreover, when a review body does exercise its power to set aside an unlawful decision in a contract award procedure, the effect on any contract concluded as a result of that procedure is expressly a matter for national law.[2]

---

[1]   Article 2(2).
[2]   Article 2(6).

Consequently, the Remedies Directives do not oblige Member States to set aside concluded contracts made following a contract awards procedure which has been conducted in breach of the public procurement regime. In fact the Remedies Directives specifically permit Member States the right to limit a contractor to a remedy in damages only, where a contract has already been concluded, depriving him of the right to apply to set aside the contract even though it may have resulted from a flawed bid process.[1]

The Directive is silent on the priority to be given to either the setting aside of unlawful decisions or the award of damages save that Member States are permitted to oblige contractors to apply to set aside decisions in order to make a claim for damages.[2] This provision is included in the Remedies Directives to take account of the procedures of those Member States whose national legal systems require unlawful decisions to be set aside as a precursor to the award of damages.

There is no obligation, even when an infringement has been proved, which requires the review body to grant contractors any remedy at all, since Article 2 does no more than require Member States to furnish review bodies with the power to set aside decisions or award damages. However, it is submitted that if a contractor is able to prove that there has been an infringement of the Regime and that he has suffered harm as a result, a subsequent refusal by a review body to grant any remedy may be a breach of the obligation imposed on Member States by Article 1 of the directive to ensure that decisions are reviewed effectively.

Penalty payments and damages awards under the Utilities Regime   The Remedies Directive[3] as it applies to the Utilities Regime permits Member States to authorise the imposition of penalty payments and to take other measures to correct infringements or prevent harm to contractors as an alternative to ordering interim measures and setting aside unlawful decisions or excising discriminatory specifications.[4] Such other measures must be effective to prevent injury to contractors.

Where the Member States adopt such an option the review bodies must still have the power to take action, at the earliest opportunity and if possible by way of interlocutory proceedings, with the aim of correcting any identified infringement and preventing injury to interests concerned. The directive contemplates that such measures will be available at an interlocutory stage as an alternative to the suspension of the contract award procedure. Where a Member State elects to equip a review body with the power to impose penalty payments such payments may be made dependent on a finding at the final hearing that there has been an infringement. The level at which the payments are set must be high enough to dissuade the entity from committing or persisting in an infringement.[5]

Furthermore, the Member States are free to limit the types of utilities which may be liable to penalty payments according to defined and objective criteria.

Whether the Member States opt for penalty payments under the Utilities Regime or not, review bodies must have the power to award contractors a remedy in damages for infringement of the regime. Whereas the first Remedies

[1]   Article 2(6) second paragraph.
[2]   Article 2(5).
[3]   92/13/EEC.
[4]   Ibid, Article 2(1)(c).
[5]   Ibid, Article 2(5).

Directive made no attempt to define the conditions under which damages should be recoverable, under the Utilities Regime it is expressly provided[1] that where a contractor claims damages in respect of the cost of preparing a bid or participating in a tender process, the contractor is required only to prove that there has been an infringement and that he would have had a real chance of winning the contract and that as a consequence of the infringement, the chance was adversely affected.

The omission of this significant provision from the earlier non-Utilities Remedies Directive may prevent contractors from obtaining damages in respect of their tendering costs where they cannot prove that but for the infringement they would have won the contract.

Review bodies

By Article 2(1), a Member State may establish more than one body to review contract award procedures, and separate bodies may be given the power to order interim measures, set aside decisions or award damages.

Article 9(8) contemplates that ordinarily review bodies will be judicial in character. However, they do not have to be nor must they be independent of the contracting authority conducting the contract award procedure. Where the review body is not a judicial organ it must give written reasons for its decisions, and further its decisions must be capable of review by a court or a tribunal within the meaning of Article 177 of the EEC Treaty which is independent of both the contracting authority and the initial review body. Where the body of second review, referred to as the 'independent body' in the Directives, is not a court its members must be appointed on the same basis as the appointment of the judiciary and the President of the independent body must have equivalent qualifications to a member of the judiciary. The independent body must hear both parties before reaching a decision and its decisions must be legally binding.

Powers of the Commission

The Remedies Directives both contain powers[2] which enable the Commission to intervene at the national level before a contract has been concluded, where it considers that there has been a clear and manifest infringement of the Regime. The procedure is known as the 'Corrective Mechanism' and its application is almost identical under both Regimes.[3] The corrective mechanism is analysed in detail in the next chapter which deals specifically with the powers of the Commission.

Additional procedures and remedies which are available only under the Utilities Remedies Directive

The Utilities Remedies Directive provides two important procedures which are unique to the Utilities Regime. They are known as 'Attestation' and

---

[1]   Article 2(7), 92/13/EEC.
[2]   Article 3, 89/665/EEC and Article 8, 92/13/EEC.
[3]   Under the non-Utilities Regime the Member States must respond to a Commission complaint within 21 days whereas under the Utilities Regime the Member States have 30 days.

'Conciliation' and they are contained in chapters 2 and 4 respectively of the Utilities Remedies Directive.

Attestation

By Article 3, the Member States are required to provide Utilities with recourse to a system of attestation in accordance with the directive. The purpose of attestation is to enable Utilities to advertise the fact that their contract award procedures are in conformity with the Regime and thereby give assurance to contractors across Europe that their tenders will receive equal consideration.

As such, attestation is not a remedy for contractors. It is intended for the benefit of Utilities and to engender confidence in contractors. It is conceivable that a recent attestation might assist a Utility in a defence to an infringement action, but it cannot in itself form the basis of a defence.

Article 4 provides that Utilities must be given the opportunity to apply to have their contract award procedures examined periodically with a view to obtaining an attestation that its award procedures and practices are in conformity with the public procurement regime.

By Article 5(1), once an attestor has been engaged by a Utility, he must report in writing the results of his examination. Before issuing an attestation, an attestor must satisfy himself that any irregularities identified in the report have been corrected and that measures have been taken to ensure that they will not be repeated.

Having obtained an attestation the Utility may publish a notice in the Official Journal in accordance with Article 5(2) to the effect that it has obtained an attestation that on a certain date its contract award procedures and practices were in conformity with the Regime.

By Article 6(1), attestors must be independent of the Utilities applying for attestation and they are required to be objective in their duties and they must be able to offer appropriate guarantees of relevant professional qualifications and experience. By Article 6(2) the Member States may establish a register of those persons, professions and institutions who may be regarded as suitably qualified attestors. The Member States have the right to insist that attestors have certain minimum qualifications if they are to receive professional recognition.

The importance that is attached to the establishment of attestation systems in each of the Member States is reflected in Article 7 which declares Articles 4, 5 and 6, namely those provisions which set out the framework for system of attestation, to be essential for the development of European standards on attestation.

Conciliation

By Article 9, any person who has standing to bring an infringement action may request the application of conciliation procedures in accordance with Articles 10 and 11, instead of applying for review. The contractor must address his request in writing either to the Commission or to the competent national authority which is in turn required to forward the request to the Commission.

In accordance with Article 10(1), if the Commission considers that the dispute concerns the correct application of Community law, it must ask the Utility whether it wishes to participate in the procedure. Unless the Utility agrees to conciliation the procedure cannot go further and the Commission must inform the contractor accordingly.

Where the Utility agrees to participate, the Commission is responsible for nominating as soon as possible a conciliator who must be drawn from a list of accredited and independent persons. The Commission is responsible for maintaining the list in consultation with the advisory committees for public contracts and telecommunications procurement. Both the contractor and the Utility must consent to the Commission's nominee and they are also permitted to designate one further conciliator each. Thereafter, each of the conciliators is free to chose two experts apiece in order to assist them, although both the parties and the Commission may reject any of the experts.

By Article 10(3), the conciliators must give each of the parties and any other person interested in the disputed contract the opportunity to make oral or written representations. Thereafter, the conciliators must try to reach an accommodation between parties as quickly as possible. However, any agreement which may be concluded must comply with Community law.[1]

The conciliators are obliged to report to the Commission both their findings and any result achieved. The parties are free to withdraw from the procedure at any stage. The parties are responsible for their own costs unless they otherwise decide, and they are both responsible for half of the costs of the procedure with the exception of the costs of any interveners.

By Article 11(1), whilst a conciliation is in progress, the Utility is under a duty to inform the conciliators if any other contractor initiates an infringement action in respect of the disputed contract. If the conciliators are notified of an infringement action, they must invite the contractor bringing the action to participate in the existing conciliation. If the contractor refuses to do so, the conciliators may decide that it is impossible to proceed with the conciliation and terminate it without reference to the parties. However, they must inform the Commission giving reasons for their decision.

Article 11(2) makes it clear that a request for conciliation cannot prejudice any action that the Commission or any Member State may bring under Articles 169 or 170 of the EEC Treaty, nor can it prejudice the right of the person who requests the procedure to bring an infringement action in the national court or the rights of the Utility or any other contractor.

Implementation dates

By Article 5 of the first Remedies Directive the Member States are obliged to bring into force the measures necessary to comply with the Directive before 1 December 1991. By article 13 of the Utilities Remedies Directive the Member States are obliged to implement its provisions before 1 January 1993, save for Spain and Greece which must comply with the directive no later than 30 June 1995 and 30 June 1997 respectively.

Failure to implement

A failure by a Member State to implement the Remedies Directives should leave a contractor with a plethora of options. In the first instance, there is

---

[1] Article 10(4).

the distinct possibility that the provisions of the substantive regime itself afford contractors with rights which are directly effective. A contractor may simply be entitled to rely on the provisions of the Remedies Directives on the grounds that they are clear, precise and unconditional. As a result, the national courts will be obliged to protect those rights by measures which are no less favourable than other domestic law remedies. Alternatively, a contractor may have remedies, including interim measures and damages, against the Member State for failing to comply with its Community obligations according to ECJ ruling in *Brasserie du Pêcheur; Factortame*.[1] Furthermore, whilst the Member States are free to set reasonable time limits for the bringing of public procurement actions, it is an irony of Community law that no such time limit can begin to run until such time as the Directive has been properly implemented by national law.[2]

[1] Joined cases C-46/93 and C-48/93 [1996] ECR I-1029.
[2] Case C-208/90 *Emmott* [1991] ECR I-4269.

CHAPTER 2

Powers of the EC Commission

Becket Bedford

POWERS OF THE COMMISSION

The Commission's powers in relation to the enforcement of the EU public procurement regime are in substance the same as its powers in relation to the enforcement of any other Community obligation. The Commission may bring proceedings against a Member State under Article 169 of the EEC Treaty and request interim measures under Article 186 of the EEC Treaty including the suspension of a contract that has already been concluded.[1] Further the Remedies directives[2] provide for a special corrective mechanism where the Commission considers that there has been a clear and manifest infringement of the regime.

INFRINGEMENT ACTION UNDER ARTICLE 169

As the guardian of the Treaties the Commission is responsible for ensuring that the Member States fulfil their Community obligations. Where a Member State does not do so the Commission may bring an infringement action in the ECJ under Article 169 of the Treaty. The first obligation of Member States in relation to the Remedies directives is properly to transpose them into national law. Failure to do so has given rise to a successful Article 169 action brought by the Commission against Germany.[3]

The peculiarity of the public procurement regime is that the Member States' duty in relation to the Community legal order does not end with the proper implementation of the directives. The directives impose continuing duties on the Member States to ensure that all public contracts are awarded in accordance with the regime. By definition public contracts are not awarded by individuals and the expansive concept of the state[4] in Community jurisprudence includes all of the bodies which award public contracts and may include privatised contracting entities[5] which fall within the utilities directives. Thus a failure to award a public contract in accordance with the regime is a failure by the Member State to comply with its Community obligations for which it may

---

[1] *Lottomatica* case C-272/91R: [1995] 2 CMLR 504.
[2] Article 3 and 8 of Directives 89/665/EEC and 92/13/EEC respectively.
[3] *Commission v Germany* case C-433/93 [1995] ECR I-2303.
[4] *Fratelli* case 103/88 [1989] ECR 1839, [1990] 3 CMLR 239.
[5] *Foster v British Gas* case C-188/89 [1990] 3 CMLR 833.

be liable to an infringement action brought by the Commission under Article 169 or by a Member State under Article 170.

Before the Commission can initiate court proceedings against a Member State under Article 169, it must first:

(1) notify the Member State of the alleged infringement;
(2) allow the Member State to submit its observations;
(3) deliver a reasoned opinion setting out a time limit for compliance with the opinion.

The period of time allowed to Member States for the submission of observations and compliance with the reasoned opinion is in the discretion of the Commission and may be as short as one week.[1]

If the Commission proves that a Member State has infringed the public procurement regime, the Court's only power is to give judgment in the form of a declaration that the Member State has failed to comply with its Community obligations, specifying the precise act or omission which is the cause of the infringement. The ECJ has no power on giving final judgment to order the Member State to pay damages to disappointed tenderers or to set aside the award of a contract.

However, by Article 171(1) and (2) of the Treaty the Member State is obliged to comply with the judgment. Failure to do so will amount to an additional failure on the part of the Member State to comply with its Community obligations and the Commission may renew proceedings against the Member State in the ECJ. If the ECJ finds that the Member State has failed to comply with its judgment it may impose a lump sum or penalty payment on it.

Furthermore once the ECJ has found that a Member State has infringed the public procurement regime disappointed tenderers may be entitled to seek a remedy in damages in their national courts quite independently of the Remedies directive. For the ECJ has ruled that Member States are bound to compensate individuals for damage caused by their failure to comply with directly effective Community obligations.[2]

INTERIM MEASURES UNDER ARTICLE 186

Once an infringement action pursuant to Article 169 has been brought by the Commission before the ECJ, the Court may grant the Commission interim measures against the Member State under Article 186 of the EEC Treaty. Such measures may include the suspension of a contract which has already been concluded.[3]

The power of the Court to order interim measures on the application of the Commission and in particular to order the suspension of concluded contracts is remarkable for two reasons. First, the Court has no power to order a Member State to take any action at all on the final hearing of an Article 169 action. It only has the power to grant declaratory relief. Thus, its interim powers under Article 186 would appear to be greater than its substantive powers under Article 169. Second, under the Remedies Directives, the Member States are not bound to give contractors the right to set aside

---

[1]   See *Storebaelt* case C-243/89 [1993] ECR I-3353, discussed below, p 19 et seq.
[2]   *Brasserie du Pêcheur SA* and *Factortame III* joined cases C-46/93 and C-48/93 [1996] ECR I-1029.
[3]   *Lottomatica* case C-272/91R: [1995] 2 CMLR 504.

contracts which have already been concluded. The Member States are permitted to limit contractors to a remedy in damages only in such circumstances.[1]

Article 186 of the EEC Treaty provides that the ECJ may prescribe 'any necessary interim measures' in 'any cases before it'. By Article 83(1) of the rules of procedure of the ECJ an application for interim relief is admissible 'only if it is made by a party to a case before the Court and relates to that case'. It follows that in the context of an infringement action, the ECJ has no power to award interim measures to the Commission unless and until it has first complied with the procedural steps required by Article 169 and subsequently proceedings have been lodged with the Court.

Once proceedings are lodged with the Court and a request is made for interim measures a date will be fixed for the interim hearing. Where necessary the ECJ may order interim measures prior to the interim hearing and in the absence of the Respondent.[2]

By Article 83(2) of the ECJ's rules of procedure an applicant for interim relief must state the subject matter of the proceedings, the circumstances giving rise to urgency and the pleas of fact and law giving rise to a prima facie case for the interim measures sought. In order to establish urgency an applicant must show that unless interim measures are ordered a subsequent finding by the Court at the substantive hearing in favour of the applicant would be of no effect because the damage suffered as a result of the breach would be serious and irreversible.

It was argued in *IBM v Commission*,[3] a case which did not concern an infringement of the public procurement regime, that there ought not to be a condition of urgency where the case is clear and manifest. The applicant did not satisfy the Court that its case was clear and manifest so the point did not arise. However, the Court stated, in reliance on its previous case law, that in addition to the requirements of a prima facie case and conditions of urgency, the interim measures sought 'must be provisional in the sense that they do not prejudge the decision on the substance of the case'.[4] It is suggested that if the Court were to abandon the condition of urgency the only remaining basis for determining the award of interim measures would be an assessment of the merits of the case and as such any decision would necessarily prejudge the final decision of the case and thereby transform the application for interim measures into procedure for summary judgment.

Although an applicant must establish both the cumulative conditions of a prima facie case and of urgency, it must follow equally that a Member State cannot oppose interim measures solely on the ground of urgency. If a Member State were to concede liability on an application for interim measures, the Court would not have to refrain from prejudging the decision on the substance of the case, so that it might be said that the condition of urgency would no longer apply. On the other hand, by conceding liability the Member State might argue that the proceedings are thereby transformed into the substantive hearing of the article 169 action, thus depriving the Court of its power to order interim measures and perhaps importantly the power of the Court to suspend a contract that has already been concluded.

---

[1]   Article 2(6) of Directives 89/665/EEC and 92/13/EEC permits Member States to limit contractors to a claim in damages only, where a contract has been concluded following its award. See also the *Van Hool* case C-87/94R, para 33.

[2]   *La Spezia* case. Case 194/88R [1988] ECR 4559.

[3]   Case 60 and 190/81R [1981] ECR 1857.

[4]   Para 4.

On each of the occasions when the Commission has sought interim measures for breach of the public procurement regime, the Court has insisted on the condition of urgency being met.[1] Further, the Court has stated that when examining the conditions of urgency, it must strike a balance between potential irreversible damage to the Commission and contractors and potential irreparable damage to the interests of the Member State.

In the case of *Dundalk*[2] the ECJ found that the factual and legal grounds giving rise to a prima facie case had been established, namely that Dundalk Urban District Council in Ireland proposed to discriminate unfairly in favour of an Irish contractor and to award a public contract in breach of Article 30 of the EEC Treaty. On the question of urgency the Commission argued that Community law and contractors excluded from the tendering process would suffer irreparable harm unless the contract award was suspended. The Irish government contended that excluded contractors might have an alternative remedy in damages. The President of the ECJ ruled that notwithstanding the damage to the Commission as the guardian of the interests of the Community, it was also necessary on an application for interim relief to weigh all the interests at stake. Interim measures were refused on the grounds that existing health and safety concerns would be aggravated if the contract were delayed and so the balance of interests was against the award of interim measures. However, the President indicated that the decision might have been otherwise but for the issue of public health and safety.

In the case of *La Spezia*,[3] the ECJ awarded the Commission interim relief where, prima facie, it appeared that an Italian public body proposed to conclude a public works contract for the construction of an incinerator for the disposal of solid waste in breach of the regime and without first publishing a notice in the Official Journal. On the question of urgency it was accepted by the Court that the Commission and, in particular, contractors would suffer serious and irremedial harm. The Italian government argued that local public health interests were so pressing other considerations were outweighed. The Court rejected the government's argument on the grounds that the public body was itself responsible for causing the delay which had brought about a situation in which the incinerator was urgently required.

In the *Lottomatica* case[4] the interim measures ordered by the Court included the suspension of a public contract for the concession of the Italian lottery which had already been concluded. Although the Court was content to hold on the first limb of the test that the Commission's case was not without substance, the Commission had claimed that the infringement was clear and manifest. The Court had previously rejected similar, if not identical, arguments tendered by the Italian government in its defence, on the substantive hearing of the earlier case of *Commission v Italy*.[5] On the question of urgency the Court ruled that in the light of its decision in case C-3/88, the Commission's interests outweighed the competing national interests which were stated to be the eradication of clandestine gambling and the preservation of significant state revenues. Damage to contractors was not even cited by the Court as a ground of urgency.

[1]   But see the *Lottomatica* case C-272/91R discussed below.
[2]   45/87: [1988] ECR 4929.
[3]   194/88R: [1988] ECR 4547.
[4]   C-272/91R: [1995] 2 CMLR 504.
[5]   Case C-3/88 [1989] ECR 4035.

In the *Van Hool* case[1] the Commission applied to suspend the execution of a contract for the supply of new public buses for the region of Walloon 5 months after it had learnt of its award. On the question of urgency the Court accepted that there might be irreparable damage to the Commission and to contractors if interim measures were not ordered. The Belgian government contended that the existing Walloonian bus fleet had to be urgently replaced because it posed a serious danger to public safety. The Court found that both the contracting authority and the Commission could have taken steps at an earlier stage which would have prevented the circumstances which gave rise to the urgency of both their pleas, but it ruled that since the Commission, as the party seeking the interim measures, had failed to display diligence, the balance tilted in favour of the Member State.

Conclusion

An analysis of the foregoing cases reveals that in addition to the twofold requirements of a prima facie case and the condition of urgency there is a third factor which proved decisive in the cases of *La Spezia* and *Van Hool*, namely diligence or the lack of it. Further, a Member State has not successfully opposed an application for interim measures on the grounds that contractors will not suffer irreparable harm because they have a remedy in damages at the national level.

Delay

In *La Spezia* the delay on the part of the public body related to the substance of the case. The Italians sought on the merits to argue reliance on the permitted derogation[2] from the obligation to advertise on the grounds that the incinerator was urgently required. The Court noted that the derogation from the requirement to advertise permitted by the regime applied only where the urgency was unforeseen. The Court took the view that the urgency was not unforeseen and the public body, if it had acted diligently, could have awarded the contract without seeking to rely on the derogation. It is suggested that by treating the question of the public body's delay as the decisive factor in determining whether interim measures ought to be granted, the Court prejudged the decision on the substance of the case.

In the much earlier case of *Dundalk* there was no question of whether the public body could rely on the derogation because it was accepted that at the time the public procurement regime did not apply to the contract. Thus on the question of urgency the President of the Court was faced with the stark choice of whether public health issues outweighed the interests of the Commission and excluded contractors. It may be that if *Dundalk* were to be decided today there would be a critical re-examination of the reasons which had brought about the urgent need for the contract to proceed unhindered. However, it is suggested that the reasons for a Member State's reliance on the permitted derogation in the case of unforeseen urgency should be irrelevant to the task of balancing the competing interests of the Member State against those of the Commission or of contractors.

---

[1] C-87/94R [1994] ECR I-1395; and see also case C-87/94, 25 April 1996.
[2] Article 9(d) of Directive 71/305/EEC.

Alternatively, the test which is applied on an application for interim measures should be re-cast so that in cases of clear and manifest breach of the regime the condition of urgency ought to be disregarded. Effectively this is what occurred in the *Lottomatica* case. The case is remarkable in that the Court set aside a concluded contract. The Italian government rehearsed arguments on the merits of the case which had been dismissed by the ECJ in its judgment in an earlier Article 169 action. There was tacit acceptance by the Court that if it did not grant interim measures, it would be powerless at the substantive hearing to correct a 'flagrant violation of Community law'. Hence the Court's summary refusal to accord any weight to matters which ordinarily would be of great importance, namely combating organised crime and preserving state revenues. The Court did not even cite irreversible damage to contractors as a factor giving rise to the condition of urgency.

In the case of *Van Hool* the Court examined the question of delay in relation to both the Commission and the Member State. Regarding the Commission's delay, the Court held that its failure to give notice of its intention to seek interim measures at the earliest opportunity and further its failure to apply for interim measures until five months after it had learnt of the contract's award were fatal to the application. The Court stated that as a matter of general principle a party seeking to rely on the urgency of interim measures must not itself be guilty of delay. Consideration of procedural delay on the part of the Commission clearly does not involve prejudging the final decision in the case. As a result, it is submitted that it is a matter that can properly be taken into account by the Court on an application for interim measures.

Regarding the delay on the part of the Member State, the Belgian government did not set up the derogation in respect of unforeseen emergencies as part of its substantive case, unlike the Italian government in *La Spezia*. As such its delay could properly be taken into account without prejudging the final decision in the case. Notwithstanding, the Court re-affirmed the reasoning in *La Spezia* and stated it to be a principle of general application that where a Member State claims urgency and where by due diligence on its part it could have prevented the urgency from arising, its opposition to interim measures is likely to fail. It appears that this principle is second only to the rule that the Commission should apply for interim measures in good time.

The relevance of a contractor's remedy in damages at the national level to an application for interim measures under Article 186

Strictly speaking, the Commission is only required to show that it will suffer irreparable harm as the guardian of the Treaties if interim measures are not granted. As a result, there is no necessity to establish the potential for irreparable harm to contractors. From the report of the interim application in the *Lottomatica* case, the Commission appear not to have relied on potential damage to contractors; certainly no such damage was cited by the Court in its reasoning when granting the interim measures sought.

However, the potential for harm to contractors clearly adds weight to an application by the Commission. The question which arises is whether a Member State can defeat an application for interim measures by holding out the possibility of a contractor's potential remedy in damages at the national level. If not, it begs the question whether the national courts or tribunals may be permitted to hold that the existence of a potential remedy in damages may preclude the award of national interim measures.

In *Dundalk*, *La Spezia* and *Van Hool*, in support of its argument that the condition of urgency was satisfied, the Commission argued that interim measures were required to prevent contractors suffering irreparable harm. On each occasion the Court accepted that damage to contractors was a relevant factor. Prior to the coming into force of the Remedies directives in December 1991, the availability of contractors' remedy in damages had not been spelt out. As a result the probability that contractors would suffer serious and uncompensatable harm was manifest. Yet as early as the decision in *Dundalk* in 1987, when the Irish government had canvassed the availability of a remedy in damages in the national courts, the ECJ rejected the notion that such would act as a bar to the award of interim measures in the ECJ.

As a result of the decision in *Van Hool*, which was made after the entry into force of the Remedies directives, it is submitted that the Court has put the matter beyond doubt. In *Van Hool* the Court stated at paragraph 31 of its judgment that:

> 'It should be noted that failure to comply with a directive applicable to a public contract constitutes a serious threat to the legality of the Community order and that the ensuing declaration by the Court on the basis of article 169 of the Treaty – usually after the contract has been performed – to the effect that the Member State in question has failed to fulfil its obligations, cannot reverse the damage suffered by the Community legal order and by all the tenderers who were either rejected or deprived of the opportunity to compete effectively in compliance with the principle of equal treatment. The Commission, in its capacity as guardian of the treaties, may therefore bring proceedings for the adoption of interim measures ...'

The Court expressly considered the effect of the Remedies directives and by implication the availability of a contractor's remedy in damages at the national level, but nonetheless found that the condition of urgency would have been satisfied by the Commission. Thus, it is suggested that the availability of a contractor's right in damages at the national level is not a ground on which the condition of urgency can be refuted by a Member State.

Consequently, it remains to be seen whether national procedures which preclude the award of interim measures to contractors, on the ground that they will not suffer irreversible damage if they can be compensated for breach in damages, are compatible with the Community legal order and in particular with Article 1 of the Remedies directives and the stipulation that national procedures for review should be effective.[1]

CORRECTIVE MECHANISM

The Remedies directives provide a corrective mechanism by which the Commission may seek a review of the award of a public contract by the Member State. The procedure is only available to the Commission prior to the conclusion of a contract and where the Commission considers a breach of the regime to be clear and manifest.[2] Under the procedure the Commission is required to notify both the contracting body and the Member State of

---

[1] See discussion of benefits of a complaint to the Commission, below, p 21 et seq.
[2] Article 3(1) and 8(1) of Directives 89/665/EEC and 92/13/EEC respectively.

the reasons which have led to its conclusion that there has been a clear and manifest infringement and request its correction by appropriate means.[1] Thereafter, depending on whether the infringement is in relation to the general or utilities regime the Member State has either 21 or 30 days respectively within which time it must respond to the Commission's notice.[2]

The Member State's response may take one of three forms: (a) confirmation that the infringement has been corrected; or (b) a reasoned submission as to why no correction has been made; or (c) a notice to the effect that the contracting body has suspended the contract award procedure or that the procedure has been suspended by the grant of interim measures in the Member State. A reasoned submission as to why no correction has been made does not have to dispute whether there has been a breach of the regime nor must it confirm that the award procedure has been suspended. It may simply state that a tenderer has begun infringement proceedings in the Member State and the outcome of the case is not yet known. Once the outcome is known the Member State is under a duty to inform the Commission of the result.[3] Where a Member State has given notice that the contract award procedure has been suspended, it is under a duty to notify the Commission when the suspension is lifted or another contract award procedure in relation to the whole or part of the original contract is begun.[4] The notice must confirm that the alleged infringement has been corrected or include a reasoned submission as to why no correction has been made.[5]

RELATIONSHIP BETWEEN ARTICLE 169 AND THE CORRECTIVE MECHANISM

The Commission's powers under Article 169 are separate and distinct from those under the corrective mechanism. The Commission can invoke Article 169 without reference to it at all as in the *Van Hool* case. Alternatively, it can invoke the procedure as a preliminary measure prior to commencing an infringement action as in the *Unix* case.[6] Otherwise, the corrective mechanism has no relation to Article 169 at all, save in so far as it gives precedence to review before conclusion of the contract.

The Court in *Van Hool*[7] considered the effect of the corrective mechanism and in consequence ruled that:

'the Commission must act at Community level so far as possible before the contract is concluded or at least inform the Member State concerned, quickly and unambiguously, that it is in the process of reviewing possible infringements of the rules applicable to the contract in issue, and that it intends to seek the suspension of the procedure for awarding the contract or the contract itself. That being so, the Member State may proceed with the award of the contract at its own risk.'

In the *Unix* case the Commission invoked the corrective mechanism and notified the Dutch government of an alleged breach of the regime prior to the conclusion

[1]   Articles 3(2) and 8(2), ibid.
[2]   Articles 3(3) and 8(3), ibid.
[3]   Articles 3(4) and 8(4), ibid.
[4]   Articles 3(5) and 8(5), ibid.
[5]   Ibid.
[6]   C359/93 [1995] ECR I-157.
[7]   Case C-87/94, 25 April 1996.

of the public contract. By Articles 3(1) and (2) of the Remedies directives, when invoking the procedure, the Commission must notify both the Member State and the contracting authority concerned. The Commission did not notify the contracting authority until just after the contract was signed. At the substantive hearing under Article 169, the Dutch government argued that the action was inadmissible because the Commission had failed to comply with the terms of the corrective mechanism. The argument was rejected by the ECJ which ruled that:

(1) according to the letter and the spirit of the corrective mechanism, notice ought preferably to be given prior to the conclusion of the contract so as to enable the Member State to both answer the complaint and if necessary correct the alleged infringement prior to the award of the contract; but
(2) the corrective mechanism is a preliminary measure which can neither derogate from nor replace the Commission's powers under Article 169 of the Treaty; and
(3) in any event a declaration by the Court under Article 169 does not depend on the existence of a clear and manifest infringement of the public procurement regime.

The summary of the judgment in *Unix* reads:[1]

'the procedure under directive 89/665 on the co-ordination of the laws regulations and administrative provisions relating to the application of review procedures to the award of public supply and public works contracts, which enables the Commission, where it considers that a clear and manifest infringement of Community provisions in the field of public procurement has been committed, to take up the matter with a Member State, constitutes a preventative measure which can neither derogate from or replace the powers of the Commission under Article 169 of the Treaty, so that the way in which the Commission uses the procedure is irrelevant in assessing the admissibility of an action against the Member State for failure to fulfil obligations brought by the Commission on account of an infringement by the Member State concerned of Community provisions in the field of public procurement.'

The Commission's powers under Article 169 are wider and potentially much more draconian, especially when coupled with an application for interim measures, than under the corrective mechanism. Article 169 can be invoked by the Commission irrespective of whether the contract has been concluded or of the nature of the infringement alleged. Further, it gives the Commission discretion to require Member States to submit their observations within a much shorter timescale than the 21-day or 30-day period which is allowed for a response to a Commission notice under the corrective mechanism. In *Storebaelt*[2] the Danish government was given seven days to submit its observations and only a further seven days to comply with the reasoned opinion that followed. Although *Storebaelt* was decided before the entry into force of the Remedies directive, as a result of the Court's statement in *Unix* to the effect that the Commission is not bound to observe the corrective mechanism, it is suggested that the Commission may depart from the normal time limits by shortening them under Article 169.

[1] C-359/93: [1995] ECR I-157.
[2] Case C-243/89: [1993] ECR I-3353.

The sole purpose of the corrective mechanism is to ensure that the Member State reviews the contract's award procedure prior to the conclusion of a contract where the Commission considers that there has been a clear and manifest breach of the regime. The corrective mechanism has no application in difficult cases or where the contract has been concluded. Although the purpose of Article 169 proceedings coupled with an application for interim measures is to remedy a breach of Community law it is not limited solely to achieving that end. By the time of the substantive hearing in the *Storebaelt* case,[1] the Danish government had accepted liability in part and further it purported to have remedied the breach. It therefore argued that the proceedings had lost their object and should no longer be admissible. The Court rejected the Danish argument and ruled that the proceedings continued to serve the essential function of establishing juridically that there had been an infringement of Community law.

The directives themselves do not specify what action the Commission may take if there is no or no satisfactory compliance by the Member State with the corrective mechanism, nor do they offer Member States immunity from an infringement action where ostensibly there has been compliance with the procedure. Theoretically, failure to comply with the corrective mechanism itself gives rise to liability on the part of the Member State under Article 169. However, it would make no sense for the Commission to begin Article 169 proceedings in respect of a failure to comply with the corrective mechanism, when it is already entitled to bring Article 169 proceedings against the Member State for failure to comply with the public procurement regime itself. If the Commission invokes the corrective mechanism and gives formal notice of a clear and manifest breach of the regime, it can by informing the Member State, treat it as a formal request to submit its observations as a precursor to Article 169 proceedings. If there is no response or the Commission considers the Member State's response to be unsatisfactory, it can proceed to deliver a reasoned opinion immediately. Subsequent failure to comply with the opinion within the period laid down will entitle the Commission to bring the matter before the Court directly and in respect of the original breach of the regime.

POTENTIAL FOR CONFLICT BETWEEN DECISIONS OF THE ECJ AND THE NATIONAL COURTS

Since the Commission's power to bring Article 169 proceedings for an infringement of the public procurement regime is quite independent of its power to cause the Member State to review awards procedures at the national level under the corrective mechanism and also of the rights of individual contractors to bring proceedings at the national level, there is the clear potential for conflict between the decisions of the courts and review bodies in the Member States and the rulings of the ECJ at the Community level. In fact there is the distinct possibility that the national courts and the ECJ may be seised of the same matter at the same time at both an interlocutory stage, on an application for interim relief, and at the final stage on the substantive hearing.

The case of *Van Hool* neatly illustrates the potential for conflict between the decisions of the national courts and the decisions of the ECJ. The Commission was castigated for bringing its application for interim relief some

---

[1]   C-243/89 [1993] ECR I-3353.

five months after it had learnt of the infringement. In that time the Belgian Conseil d'Etat had already granted and then refused interim measures at the national level. By implication, if the Commission had acted with proper diligence and applied for interim measures in conjunction with an Article 169 action as soon as it was able, the ECJ might well have granted interim measures within barely a month of the Belgian Conseil d'Etat's refusal to do so.

Thus, it is foreseeable that the ECJ may be called upon to exercise what will be in effect an appellate jurisdiction over the national courts on the issue of interim measures and over questions of infringement in public procurement cases. However, it should be noted that in the context of Article 169 proceedings there can be no overlap between decisions of the national courts and the ECJ on whether a particular contractor is entitled to damages and if so how much. The potential for conflict is not lessened by the existence of the corrective mechanism. Whereas the Commission may, after having invoked the corrective mechanism, choose to await the outcome of interlocutory or possibly substantive proceedings at the national level, no doubt it will take the precaution, in accordance with the Court's guidance in *Van Hool*, of informing the Member State that it will seek interim measures in the ECJ, if it does not agree with the results.

It is suggested, given the alarming potential for embarrassment which may be caused to a national court or review body if the ECJ were subsequently to overrule its decision, that where a national court or body is apprised of the Commission's interest or likely interest in a case of which it is seised, it should stay the proceedings on terms that the contract's award procedure is suspended pending a ruling from the ECJ under Article 177 of the Treaty. Alternatively, in view of the unpalatable delay which would be caused in seeking a ruling from the ECJ, the national court or review body should seek the advice of the Commission concerning its view of the merits of the case and of its likely intention to seek interim measures in the ECJ. In such circumstances, the national review body should exercise caution and only refuse interim relief or hold that there has been no infringement if there is no risk of the ECJ coming to a different conclusion.

ADVANTAGES AND DISADVANTAGES OF A COMPLAINT TO THE COMMISSION AND ARTICLE 169 ACTIONS OVER INDIVIDUAL ACTIONS IN THE MEMBER STATES

As the Commission has no power to bring actions in the national courts against individual public bodies, it must rely on the Member States to use their influence with the public body concerned in order to rectify any infringement. An individual contractor, on the other hand can bring direct pressure to bear on the public body by issuing proceedings in the national courts.

In most cases the indirect influence exercised by the Commission over contracting authorities by an Article 169 action or the threat of one, will be sufficient to correct infringements of the regime. However, there may be situations involving privatised utilities where the Member State cannot use its influence to secure compliance with the regime. In such circumstances, a contractor may have to look to its national courts or review bodies to exercise direct control over contracting entities.

Similarly, a consequence of the Commission's limited right of action against the Member State is that it has no power to win damages or compensation for contractors. However, the leverage that it exercises over the Member States may be sufficient to secure for disappointed contractors the costs they have incurred in participating in a flawed tendering process. In the *Storebaelt* case, the Commission withdrew its application for interim measures suspending the execution of the contract after winning a concession from the Danish government that each of the disappointed tenderers would receive at least compensation for the cost of tendering and consideration of their claims for lost profits.

Moreover, the case of *Storebaelt* illustrates another advantage for contractors over an individual action. The Commission can secure the removal of discriminatory provisions contained in the contract notice and other documents, without an individual contractor having to await the outcome of the final hearing of review proceedings at the national level. One of the complaints that was levelled at the Danish government was that the contract notice contained a clause which discriminated against non-Danish contractors. The clause was removed almost as soon as the Commission invited Danish observations on the point and prior to the award of the contract.[1]

By contrast to *Van Hool*, which showed that a complaint to the Commission and subsequent article 169 proceedings may prove to be too time-consuming and ultimately ineffective in preventing the award of an unlawful contract, *Storebaelt* is also instructive because it demonstrates that the Commission can take rapid effective action. The Commission commenced Article 169 proceedings on 21 June 1989 by requesting the Danish government to submit its observations within seven days. On 21 July 1989 the Commission delivered a reasoned opinion giving seven days for compliance. By 2 August 1989 the Commission had lodged an application for interim measures and by 22 September 1989, the date of the interim hearing, the Danish government had undertaken to compensate disappointed tenderers.

It is quite possible that a national court or review body might order the suspension of a contract's award procedure within days of a complaint being made to the contracting authority, but it is more doubtful whether compensation could be obtained in a mere three months with only the threat of interlocutory proceedings at the national level. Moreover, an application for interim measures at the national level may be fraught with risk and expense. There may be national rules of procedure which deny interim relief to contractors unless they can underwrite the costs of the proceedings or the potential damage to the contracting authority in the event that the complaint should prove unfounded, or where an alternative remedy in damages exists. It must be remembered that some Member States have exercised the option contained in the Remedies directives to limit a contractor only to a remedy in damages where the contract has already been concluded. The Commission is not so bound and it can apply to suspend the effect of an already concluded

---

[1]   Although the clause was removed prior to the Commission's reasoned opinion, the Danish Government was still found to be in breach of its Community obligations. The contract's award procedure had proceeded on an unlawful basis from the start, such that it may have affected the composition of the consortia which tendered for the contract. Thus, the Court held that by suppressing the discriminatory clause at the last moment just prior to the conclusion of the contract the Danish government had failed to put an end to its failure to fulfil its Community obligations.

contract at no cost to the whistleblower and without divulging his identity. A person who complains to the Commission about an infringement of the public procurement regime can do so anonymously, without expense and indeed without any locus standi. Under the Remedies directives the Member States are only obliged to entertain review proceedings at the national level commenced by a person with an interest in obtaining the contract. Thus, trade associations and environmental associations cannot usually insist on a review at the national level, but they can complain to the Commission.

Conclusion

There is a strong case for advising that in every case complaint should be made to the Commission as a first step and, thereafter for action at the Community level to run in parallel with national proceedings. This is especially so where a tenderer's main objective is to suspend the contract's award procedure and subsequently to participate in a renewed bids process. In cases of clear and manifest breach of the regime the case law of the ECJ suggests that ordinarily the condition of urgency will be satisfied and interim measures will be ordered. Consequently, when national courts or review bodies are aware of the Commission's intention to seek interim measures, it is arguable that they will have only very limited scope within which to exercise their discretion to refuse interim relief. For if they adopt national procedural requirements which run counter to the test for interim measures which is applied in the ECJ, they run the risk, de facto, of being overruled at Community level.

Equally, it is advisable for contractors to complain to the Commission where their only object is obtaining damages. Although the ECJ cannot order the payment of compensation to disappointed or excluded contractors, the national courts will be bound to take note of any judgment in which the ECJ finds that the regime has been infringed. If Article 169 proceedings are ongoing at the time when national proceedings come on for trial there is every likelihood that the national proceedings will be stayed pending the result or even a reference under article 177 which could then be heard by the ECJ simultaneously with the application under Article 169.

The only potential drawback of a complaint to the Commission is that action cannot be taken on every one. There are only a limited number of enforcement officers at the Commission dealing with infringements of the public procurement regime and they must compete with the other departments at the Commission for the resources of the Commission's legal service. As a result, a contractor cannot rely on the Commission to bring an action on its behalf.

Consequently, there is a perception that the Commission will not act save in cases involving the use of Community funds or in which important points of principle may be established. However, it should be borne in mind that after having taken a Member State to Court in the case of *La Spezia*[1] to establish that the Member States are only permitted to derogate from the requirement to advertise public contracts in cases of unforeseen emergency, it did so again in the case of *Commission v Spain*.[2] Similarly, after having

---

[1] Case 194/88R: [1988] ECR 4559.
[2] Case C-24/91: [1992] ECR I-1989.

established that a Member State cannot award a contract on the basis of information which is not stipulated in the contract notice in *Storebaelt*,[1] it did so again in *Van Hool*.[2]

[1] Case C-243/89 [1993] ECR I-3353.
[2] Case C-87/94R: [1994] ECR I-1395.

CHAPTER 3

Remedies in Austria

Reinhold Müller

AWARD OF PUBLIC CONTRACTS PRIOR TO THE IMPLEMENTATION OF EC DIRECTIVES

General

In Austria, the territorial authorities handle the award of contracts within the framework of private economy administration and the award of public contracts is therefore performed by private law. The public bodies accordingly establish contacts with the contractors who are subject of private rights.[1] A civil law contract is thus established between the public body and the contractor.[2] The private law freedom of disposition of the public authorities is however restricted by special regulations.[3] Thus, the award of public contracts is bound by the same legislation as any private economic activity of the Austrian state.[4] Until the implementation of the EC Directives on the award of public contracts, the legal situation was very disparate and not easy to grasp due to a variety of decrees on federal, provincial, and municipal levels and offered hardly any judicial relief, since the administrative decrees to be applied were only internal instructions without external effects. It has to be pointed out in particular that below the EC threshold values, the following administrative decrees are partly still valid.

Regulations already existing prior to the implementation of EC Directives

Until 1963, the 'submission decree' of 1909[5] was applied for public goods and services as far as the contract award by government agencies was concerned. Under certain conditions, the possibility already existed then to give preference to small-trade and local enterprises when awarding the contract. In principle, this decree provided for the award to the cheapest offeror. It did however already suggest other award criteria as well.

---

[1] Wenger, Karl *Fundamentals of Austrian Economic Law*, Vol II (Vienna, 1990), p 226.
[2] In Europe there are other systems as well. See Langer, Elisabeth 'European Systems of Contract Award', in: *Series of Publications of the Federal Economic Chamber* (Vienna, 1968).
[3] Compare in this connection Pernthaler, Peter, in: Funk/Marko/Pernthaler 'The National Implementation of EC Award Directives', *Series of Publications of the Institute for Federalism Research* (Vienna, 1992), Vol 52, pp 83ff.
[4] Korinek/Schwarzer *Administrative Law Fundamentals of Contract Award* (1982), pp 7ff.
[5] RGBl 61/1909 of 3.4.1909 (Imperial Law Gazette).

The Austrian Standards Committee for Industry and Trade, founded in 1920, worked out standards for the award of construction services. ÖNORM B 2001 as well as ÖNORM B 2060 of 1948 were replaced by the general ÖNORM A 2050 of 1957, providing no restriction for certain specialised fields, and were finally amended in 1993. It is a procedural standard of a recommendatory character, declared as compulsory only by the respective Federal Ministers by virtue of administrative decrees in 1963 and 1964. Almost all award regulations of the public authorities are derived from ÖNORM A 2050 and largely refer to it. The present contract award laws also additionally refer to the regulations of ÖNORM A 2050.

The 'Directives for the Placing of Services by Government Agencies' were replaced in 1978 by the 'Directives for the Award of Services by Government Agencies' and amended several times until 1990.[1] These regulations cover material services (for instance construction works, assemblies, transport, cleaning of buildings etc), supplies of goods (for example fuels, vehicles, pieces of equipment etc), as well as works and supplies of a non-material kind as long as their value is not in excess of 10 million Austrian shillings, for example planning, projects, calculations etc. This administrative decree, declaring ÖNORM A 2050 as binding and supplementing it, is obligatory for the agencies of the Federal Government only.

The Environment and Water Resources Award Directives of 1988 are applied for the invitation for tenders and for the contract award for services for the establishment, expansion, or improvement of water supply or sewage disposal installations, for which purpose the environment and water resources fund are called on. These directives also refer to and supplement ÖNORM A 2050.

In the field of the Federal Roads Administration and its special companies, the award decree for public construction contracts became effective in 1990; it is also an administrative decree without external effect. Its contents are essentially modelled on ÖNORM A 2050 and the regulations passed thereunder; it is however more precisely determined and suggests for the first time tendencies towards an adjustment of Austrian award law to EC Directives. For the first time a so-called 'Award Control Commission' was established at federal level,[2] which has to supply expert opinions and recommendations.[3]

The provincial and local authorities were recommended to pass analogous decrees in their areas. This recommendation has been complied with in part only.[4] Thus some of the provinces made ÖNORM A 2050 effective immediately. The regulations for the award of public contracts by the municipal authorities are different and not easy to grasp,[5] since in some cases local award rules have been made as well, and in some cases no award regulations exist at all.

---

[1]   Rulings of the Ministerial Council of 26.9.1978, 3.3.1981, 15.12.1981, 1.7.1986, 16.10.1990.
[2]   An Award Commission was already installed with the Office of the Salzburg Provincial Government in 1973, the task of which is standardised in § 30 of the Provincial Award Order for the award of services by the Province of Salzburg.
[3]   The Provincial Government of Carinthia enforced ÖNORM A 2050 by resolution for the Province of Carinthia in 1965.
[4]   In the province of Styria the local Provincial Award Regulation does not contain a hint of ÖNORM A 2050.
[5]   Compare also Wenger, Karl *Fundamentals of Austrian Economic Law*, Vol II (Vienna 1996), pp 230ff.

Judicial relief in case of award of public contracts prior to the implementation of EC Directives

Since the above-mentioned award regulations are largely administrative decrees, representing internal directives without external effect[1] which can be altered at any time by new directives,[2] the participants in public tenders had modest judicial relief only. In case of unlawful procedure by the administrative agencies there is the possibility of handing in a supervisory complaint with the superior administrative agency; this does not however imply that claims for damages can be maintained even if upheld.[3] Although such a complaint may lead to the suspension of the award procedure and to a new tender invitation, there does not exist any legal claim for dealing with such a supervisory complaint.[4] The complainant is not a party in the proceedings, since this supervisory complaint only results in disciplinary consequences.

Claims for damages

In some cases the Supreme Court ('OGH')[5] awards damages for breach of trust, on the legal principle *culpa in contrahendo*[6] by which, in the award procedure as well as at the pre-contract stage, common duties of care between the bidder and the tendering agencies have to be applied.[7] Thus for instance published award standards create a relationship of confidence with the bidders, which leads to compensation by way of damages caused by breach of trust[8] in case of culpable violation by the tenderer. In so far as the excluded bidder can prove however that he would have won the contract as best bidder, had the award regulations been complied with,[9] the OGH has stated over a long period of time that the expense of performance[10] would be reimbursed.[11] The proof that the bidder would have won the contract has to be supplied by the bidder himself; because of the principle of best bidder, prevailing in Austria, this will very likely be rather difficult to prove.[12] By a decision of the OGH of 19 October 1994, the performance expense was actually awarded in a case of a violation of the award regulation.[13] Since in case of the award of public

---

[1]   Ibid p 241; OGH 31.5.1988 WBI 1988, 433.

[2]   Gutknecht, Brigitte 'The liberalization of the award of public contracts in the EC and its importance for Austria', in: Griller/Lavric/Neck HG *European Integration from the Austrian Point of View* (1991), pp 280ff.

[3]   Wenger, Karl *The Law of Public Contracts* (1977), pp 126ff.

[4]   Aicher, Josef, 'The Award Control Commission and in its importance for the development of Austrian law and for the adjustment to EC law', in: Korinek/Aicher *Award Control Commission* (Vienna, 1991), p 22.

[5]   OGH of 29.11.1989 JBI 1990, p 520; OGH of 13.4.1988 WBI 1988, p 342; OGH of 31.5.1988 WBI 1988, 433.

[6]   This legal principle is a so-called 'judge's law' and not written law so that this basis for a claim could change at any time.

[7]   Krejci, ZWR 1982, 34; OGH 13.4.1988 WBI 342.

[8]   OGH 31.5.1988 WBI 1988, 433.

[9]   Wenger, Karl *Fundamentals of Austrian Economic Law*, Vol I (Vienna, 1989), p 153.

[10]   Here the damaged person is to be dealt with as he would be treated, had the contract been complied with.

[11]   Koziol/Welser *Fundamentals of Civil Law*, (8th edn), Vol 1, p 198; as well as OGH 13.4.1988 WBI 1988, 342 and OGH 10.10.1989 RdW 1990, 43 which does then promise compensation of performance interest.

[12]   Aicher, Josef, in: Korinek/Aicher *Award Control Commission* (Vienna, 1991), pp 25ff.

[13]   OGH 7 Ob 568/94, ecolex 1995, p 93ff.

contracts, private law contracts are signed, the ordinary courts have jurisdiction over these disputes.

IMPLEMENTATION OF EC DIRECTIVES FOR THE AWARD OF PUBLIC CONTRACTS INTO NATIONAL LAW

Because of the federal structure of the Republic of Austria, it was necessary for the implementation of the EC Directives for the award of public contracts to pass both a federal award law and special provincial award laws respectively for the nine federal provinces. Therefore the individual regulations of the federal provinces are considered below in detail.

Implementation on federal level

On 1 January 1994, Austria entered the 'European Economic Area' (EEA) and was therefore obliged to transpose the EC Award Directives, mentioned in appendix XVI of the EEA Agreement, into national law. Since Austria became a member of the European Union on 1 January 1995, however, the obligation resulting from the EEA Agreement is no longer applicable. As a member of the EU, Austria had to adopt the community law award system completely.

By virtue of the Federal Award Law[1] ('BVerG') which became valid on 1 January 1994 the Directives for supply contracts,[2] construction contracts,[3] contracts in the excluded sectors,[4] and the Remedies Directives for supply and construction contracts[5] have been enforced at the federal level. Not yet enforced at the federal level are the Services Directive 92/50/EEC, the Excluded Sectors Remedies Directive, as well as the amendments of the EC Directives, implemented since 1 July 1991. The draft for an amendment of the BVerG[6] contains provisions so that it is probable that missing Directives will be implemented in the autumn of 1996.

Scope of application

The BVerG is to be applied to public contracts the estimated contract value of which without turnover tax is above the EC threshold values. It is valid for public supply contracts, public construction contracts, and construction concession contracts[7] as well as for contracts in the field of the excluded sectors.[8]

---

[1] BGBl 1993/462.
[2] Directive 77/62/EEC ABl L 13 of 15.1.1977, amended by 80/767/EEC ABl L 215 of 18.8.1980 and by 88/295/EEC ABl L 127 of 20.5.1988.
[3] Directive 71/304/EEC ABl L 185 of 16.8.1971; 71/305/EEC ABl L 185 of 16.8.1971, amended by 89/440/EEC ABl L 210 of 21.7.1989.
[4] Directive 90/531/EEC ABl L 297 of 29.10.1990.
[5] Directive 89/665/EEC ABl L 395 of 30.12.1989.
[6] GZ 600.883/11-V/8/95 (reference number).
[7] Construction concession contracts are contracts where the counter-performance for works exists exclusively in the right of utilising the structure, or in this right plus payment of a compensation.
[8] § 1 BVerG 1993/462; it should be noted that the Remedies Directive is not yet to be applied in the field of the excluded sectors.

Public bodies as defined by the Federal Award Law are the federal government as well as foundations, funds and institutions, but only if they dispose of partial rights at least and if they are administered by government agencies or by persons who have been nominated for this purpose by government agencies. Also included are enterprises in which the government has a majority participation and which have been founded for the purpose of fulfilling tasks of general interest and are therefore subject to control by the Court of Auditors. The Austrian social insurance institutions and the integrated company of the electricity supply services as well as the special companies designated by the Second Nationalisation Law are subject to the Federal Award Law. Moreover, the BVerG applies to private and public bodies which exercise activities on the basis of special or exclusive rights in the field of the excluded sectors. For the latter, however, the judicial relief regulations of this BVerG do not yet apply.[1] An amendment according to which the judicial relief regulations will also apply to the excluded sectors is to be expected soon.

Exceptions from the scope of application

The BVerG is not to be applied for contract awards by provinces, local authorities and associations of local authorities nor to circumstances when it is necessary to protect the essential interests of national security. To contracts entered into on the basis of a special procedure of an international organisation or by an international agreement between a member of the European Economic Area and a third country relating to an objective to be realised, upheld, or utilised in common, the BVerG is also not to be applied.[2]

Implementation on provincial and municipal level

All provinces have passed provincial laws on the award of public supply, construction and construction concession contracts[3] as well as for contracts in the field of the excluded sectors. Thus the law of the EC award regime has been enforced on provincial and municipal level as well.

Scope of application

On the provincial and municipal level,[4] public supply contracts, construction contracts and construction concession contracts as well as contracts in the field of the excluded sectors are subject to the regulations of the respective Provincial Award Laws,[5] in so far as the estimated contract sum without turnover tax is above the EC threshold values. In the federal provinces of

---

[1] § 6 BVerG BGBl 1993/462.
[2] § 7 BVerG BGBl 1993/462.
[3] Construction Concession Contracts are contracts where the counter-performance for works exists exclusively in the right of utilising the structure, or in this right plus payment of a compensation.
[4] Also includes the Local Government Regional Authorities
[5] Vorarlberg LGBl 1994/24; Tyrol LGBl 1994/87; Salzburg LGBl 1995/1; Upper Austria LGBl 1994/59; Burgenland LGBl 1995/1; Carinthia LGBl 1994/55, 1994/72, 1994/89; Lower Austria LGBl 1995/84; Vienna LGBl 1995/36; Styria LGBl 1995/85.

Vorarlberg, Burgenland and Vienna, the Provincial Award Laws are already valid for public services contracts.[1]

The respective provincial laws are valid for the award of contracts by public provincial bodies. Public bodies in this sense are the provinces, the local authorities, the associations of local authorities, foundations, funds, institutions which are subject to control by the Court of Auditors, as well as enterprises which have been founded for the purpose of fulfilling non-commercial tasks of general interest and in so far as the province has a majority participation. For the purposes of the Provincial Award Law, provincial companies according to the Second Nationalisation Law,[2] and electricity supply companies according to the Electricity Supply Services Law,[3] are also public bodies.

Exceptions from the scope of application

The provincial laws do not apply to the award of contracts by the Federal Government. Moreover, the same exceptions from the scope of application as determined for the BVerG and as explained above have been standardised for the provincial laws. The Provincial Award Laws for Vorarlberg and Burgenland contain some additional regulations. Thus, among other things, the award of telephone services, satellite communication, arbitration and conciliation services, the commissioning of artistic services – to name the most important ones here – are excluded from the scope of application of the Provincial Award Laws.[4]

IMPLEMENTATION OF EC REMEDIES DIRECTIVE 89/665/EEC INTO NATIONAL LAW

Implementation on federal level

The Remedies Directive 89/665/EEC AB1 L 395 of 30 December 1989 has also been converted into national law on a federal level by virtue of the BVerG BGB1 (Federal Law Gazette) 1993/462, coming into force on 1 January 1994. The procedural sections of judicial relief according to the BVerG are subdivided into conciliation procedure, examination procedure, and damages procedure. In the fourth part of this law a legal basis was created for the installation of a 'Federal Award Control Commission' and a 'Federal Award Office' as examining bodies. These federal control bodies were instituted for the control of the award procedure. For better understanding it should be mentioned here that the Award Control Commission, already installed in 1990, acts within the framework of the supervision of the 'Award Decree for Public Construction Contracts' ('VOöB') only and was therefore responsible for public contracts in the field of the federal road administration and its special companies only. Before that, no comparable institutions existed on a federal level.

[1]   § 1, sub-cl 5 Award Law Vorarlberg; § 1, sub-cl 5, Award Law Burgenland.
[2]   Second Nationalisation Law, BGB1 1947/81 and BGB1 1987/321 and BGB1 1992/762.
[3]   Electricity Supply Services Law BGB1 1975/260 and BGB1 1979/131.
[4]   Compare § 8 Award Law Vorarlberg LGB1 1994/24 as well as § 8 Award Law Burgenland LGB1 1995/1.

Federal Award Control Commission ('VKK')

The members of the commission as well as its chairman are to be appointed by the Federal Government, taking into consideration the proposals of the pertinent bodies representing interests.[1] Since the VKK does not take any decisions but can only supply expert opinions and recommendations, it has no powers in the sense required by the Remedies Directives.[2] Prior to the contract award the VKK is responsible for the conciliation of differences of opinion in the enforcement of the BVerG or decrees issued thereto; within the award period it is responsible for the supply of an expert opinion on the question as to whether a proposal for the award of the contract is in agreement with the regulations of the BVerG and the decrees issued thereto. Following the contract award, it is responsible for the supply of expert opinions on the implementation of the order contract.

Federal Award Office ('VGA')

The chairman of the Federal Award Office has to be appointed for a period of five years by the Federal Government out of the circle of active judges. The Federal Government has to nominate further members, taking into consideration proposals made by pertinent bodies representing interests. A member of this commission must not at the same time be a member of the Federal Award Control Commission. The Federal Award Office is an independent authority with judicial functions, rights and privileges, which takes decisions in the first and in the last instance.[3] Thus the VGA qualifies as a 'Tribunal' according to Art 6 of the Convention on Human Rights and complies with all the criteria of Art 177 of the EEC Treaty.[4] This is of importance in so far as in case of disputes on the interpretation of the EC award law there is the power to refer to the European Court of Justice for a preliminary ruling.

The VGA is the organ required by the EC Remedies Directives, with powers both during the examination procedures and until the date of the contract award for granting interim injunctions, and declarations of nullity in cases of infringements on the part of the awarding agency of the public body. Following the contract award, the VGA is responsible for determining whether, because of a contravention of the BVerG or decrees issued thereto, the best bidder was not awarded the contract or[5] whether the respective bidder or competitor would have had a real chance to win the contract. Upon request of the public bodies it can also be determined however whether a bidder or competitor would in no event have been awarded the contract, even if the BVerG had been complied with. In the entire procedure, the VGA has to apply the General Administrative Procedure Law. Decrees passed by the VGA can only be contested before the Supreme Constitutional Court.

[1] Bodies representing interests are the Federal Chamber of Trade and Industry, the Federal Chamber of Workers, as well as the Federal Chamber of Architects and Engineering Consultants.

[2] Thienel, Rudolf '*Award Control Commission and Award Office according to the Federal Award Law*' ÖZW 1993, 71ff.

[3] § 78, sub-clause 2 BVerG.

[4] Compare Thienel, Rudolf '*Award Control Commission and Award Office according to the Federal Award Law*' ÖZW 1993, 71ff.

[5] Thus the Amendment Draft to § 91, sub-cl 3 of the BVerG, GZ 600.883/11-V/8/95.

Judicial relief prior to contract award

Conciliation procedure with the VKK   On the request of the awarding agency, or of a competitor,[1] a bidder, or a suitable body representing interests, a conciliation procedure is initiated.[2] This request must be received by the management of the VKK at the latest three weeks before expiry of the award period.[3] The VKK is responsible for the conciliation of disputes between the public bodies and the bidders with respect to compliance with the BVerG and the decrees issued thereto, but only up to the date of the contract award. The conciliation senate has to hear the litigant parties, to determine the facts, and to mediate between the litigant parties within two weeks. If one of the litigant parties is not prepared to negotiate, the draft for the amendment of the BVerG provides that the VKK has to record that an amicable settlement could not be achieved.[4] The parties may be granted inspection of the files with the exception of deliberation records, office lectures, and discharge drafts.[5] If no agreement is achieved, the senate is to supply a reasoned recommendation within the two-weeks term as to how the legal provision on which the dispute is based has to be applied. Such a recommendation is then judicial evidence in the examination procedure before the VGA. In so far as it has become active upon request of a competitor or bidder, the VKK has to inform the awarding agency without delay that it has taken up its activities. If the VKK is taking up activities upon request of a bidder or a competitor, the draft for the amendment of the BVerG provides for the important innovation that the awarding agency may not award the contract within three weeks from this notification.

Preparation of an expert opinion by the VKK   In addition, the VKK is responsible for the preparation of expert opinions on the question whether a proposal for a contract award is compatible with the regulations of the BVerG and whether the award rules have been complied with respectively. Here the possibility arises that the awarding agency may demand an expert opinion as to which bidder has to be awarded the contract. In this respect the VKK is to be active only on request of the awarding agency. This request is admissible only if the value of a contract amounts to at least ATS 200 million.[6] The VKK has to provide its expert opinion at the latest three months after having been called upon. If an expert opinion is not prepared, the requesting parties are to be informed within two months, indicating the grounds. Following the contract award, the VKK may however also prepare an expert opinion on the performance of the contract award on request of the awarding agency or the pertinent body representing interests.

Examination procedure with the VGA   An application for an examination procedure with the VGA until the contract is awarded is possible only if a conciliation procedure is taking place with the VKK and if no amicable

---

[1] By 'competitor' we have to understand a contractor who wants to participate in the tender procedure. As a rule, judicial relief will concern those contractors who have been excluded from the tender procedure.
[2] § 87, sub-cl 2 BVerG.
[3] § 87, sub-cl 5 BVerG.
[4] Amendment draft to § 88, sub-cl 1 BVerG, GZ 600.883/11-V/8/95.
[5] In § 88, sub-cl 2 BVerG reference is made to § 17, sub-cl 3 AVG (General Administrative Procedure Law).
[6] § 87, sub-cl 3 BVerG.

settlement has been achieved. The draft amendment to the BVerG provides that an application for an examination procedure is to be admissible also if the contractor can make it credible that the public body does not or did not stick to the amicable settlement.[1] An application for examination is to be admissible too, if the VKK has not become active within the two-week term, if it declared itself incompetent, or if it did not give its recommendation within the time limit.[2] An application for such an examination procedure with the VGA has to be filed at the latest after one week from having knowledge of the recommendation of the VKK. The applicant may then demand the examination of a decision in the award procedure because of illegality, in so far as the contractor has suffered or risks suffering damages due to the alleged illegality and in so far as an interest in the conclusion of a contract is being claimed.[3] Following the contract award, only the VGA is responsible for determinations; such an application is to be filed two weeks after having knowledge of the award at the latest. An application for an examination procedure is to contain the exact description of the procedure concerned, the decision contested, the identity of the public body, and a statement of the facts. The illegality of the contested decision has to be of 'essential influence' on the result of the award procedure.[4] According to the explanatory remarks with regard to this regulation, the decision is of 'essential influence' if another bidder or applicant would have won the contract if there had been no illegality. If this is not the case, the application is to be dismissed. Furthermore the application has to make a statement of its interest in concluding the contract, giving informations on the alleged actual or threatened damages, the grounds on which the assertion of illegality is based, as well as the relief sought. If a conciliation procedure has been performed previously, a copy of the records of this conciliation procedure is to be enclosed, in so far as the latter has been served upon the applicant. This application does not have suspensory effect.

The VGA has to apply the General Administrative Procedure Law ('AVG') and does therefore decide by virtue of a ruling which is however not subject to suspension or amendment by administrative channels.[5] In procedures before the VGA, the parties are to be heard and admissible evidence is admitted.

If the services of the authority in the examination procedure are obviously employed wantonly or if incorrect statements are made with the intention of delaying the matter, a fine of one per cent at most of the contract value, with a maximum of ATS 800.000, may be imposed.[6]

Declaration of nullity of the decision of the public body in the course of the examination procedure by the VGA As long as the contract has not been awarded, the VGA may declare a decision of a public body, made in a contract procedure, null and void under 'consideration' of the previously passed recommendation of the VKK, if this decision does not comply with the BVerG or the decrees made already and if it is of essential influence on the result

[1]   Amendment draft to § 92, sub-cl 2 BVerG, GZ 600.883/11-V/8/95.
[2]   Amendment draft to § 92, sub-cl 2 BVerG, GZ 600.883/11-V/8/95.
[3]   § 92, sub-cl 1 and 2 BVerG; compare also Directive 89/665/EEC, Art 1, sub-clause 3.
[4]   § 91, sub-cl 4 BVerG.
[5]   § 78, sub-cl 1 BVerG.
[6]   § 95, sub-cl 3 BVerG; compare in this connection Thienel, Rudolf *'The Examination Procedure according to the Federal Award Law'* WB1 1993, 380, who sees a constitutional law problem in this regulation because of too wide a scope of discretion.

of the procedure.[1] The recommendation of the VKK is admissible evidence in the examination procedure; its contents have to be dealt with by the VGA. It does not however result in any binding effect for the VGA.[2] Section 94, sub-clause 2 BVerG states in particular that a declaration of nullity relating to requirements in the tender documents or in other documents of the award procedure, which are discriminatory against the contractor with respect to technical performance characteristics or with respect to the economic or financial efficiency, have to be taken into consideration.[3] An application is to be filed within one week after having knowledge of the recommendation of the VKK. The VGA has to decide on an application for declaration of nullity within two months after receipt of the application, in so far as the contract has not been awarded yet.[4]

Interim injunctions in examination procedures by the VGA   According to the rules of the BVerG, the VGA has to take preliminary measures without delay upon application and after initiation of the examination procedure by means of an interim injunction, taking into consideration the previous recommendation[5] of the VKK. This measure has to appear necessary and apt to remove or prevent damage to the applicant's interests, originated by or threatened because of the alleged illegality. Such an application is to be filed within three weeks after having knowledge of the alleged illegality or of the threatened damage, indicating the interim measures with the VGA.[6] The VGA has to decide on an application for an interim injunction without delay, but at the latest within three days.[7] In this application, the required interim measure, the period of time over which the interim measure is to be valid, the alleged illegality, and the immediately threatened damage are to be described exactly. The facts founding the application are to be stated in accordance with the truth. The VGA may make the granting of an interim injunction dependent upon the performance of an adequate security.

Prior to the passing of an interim injunction, the VGA has to weigh the foreseeable consequences of the measure to be taken for all possibly damaged interests of the applicant, the other competitors or bidders, and the public body, as well as a possible special public interest[8] in the continuation of the award procedure. If this weighing of interests results in a majority of detrimental consequences, no interim injunction may be passed.[9] By virtue of an interim injunction, the entire award procedure or individual decisions of the public body may be suspended for the time being.[10] The most proportionate measure leading to the objective is to be taken, however.[11] Should the damage to the applicant's interests be temporarily removed by the interim injunction, the entire contract procedure must not be suspended. The interim measure must

---

[1]   § 94, sub-cl 1 BVerG.
[2]   Compare in this connection Thienel, Rudolf '*The Examination Procedure according to the Federal Award Law*' WB1 1993, 383ff.
[3]   Compare also Art 2(1) of the Remedies Directive 89/665/EEC.
[4]   § 95, sub-cl 2 BVerG.
[5]   Although recommendations are not binding for the VGA, it has to deal with its contents. Compare Thienel, Rudolf '*The Examination Procedure according to the Federal Award Law*' WB1 1993, 381.
[6]   § 93, sub-cl 2 BVerG.
[7]   § 95, sub-cl 1 BVerG.
[8]   This will be dealt with in the following section.
[9]   § 93, sub-cl 3 BVerG.
[10]   A prolongation of the tender term would also be conceivable.
[11]   § 93, sub-cl 4 BVerG.

not exceed one month.[1] The draft for the amendment of the BVerG provides that the interim injunction may be made for a period of two months at the most.[2]

According to Art 144 BVerG, interim injunctions can only be contested together with the final decision before the Supreme Constitutional Court; they are however immediately enforceable. For the enforcement the Administration Enforcement Law applies.

In a case where there are statements of facts in the application for an interim injunction which do not correspond to the truth, the applicant is liable to a fine of one per cent of the estimated contract value to a maximum of ATS 800.000.[3] According to a regulation which is not very much in favour with the judiciary, the applicant who has been granted an interim injunction is liable to claims for damages by competitors, bidders and public bodies, if the application for suspension or alteration was not permitted in the examination procedure in agreement with the previous decision of the conciliation senate.[4] But even if the application for interim measures was allowed, if the applicant does not make use of the consequential opportunity to participate in an award procedure, he has to pay damages to the public body and his competitors upon claim. Damages in the amount of the pecuniary loss caused by the interim injunction have to be paid.

Judicial relief following contract award

Declaratory administrative ruling of the VGA Following the contract award, the VGA may on application ascertain by virtue of a ruling whether, because of a contravention of the BVerG, the best bidder has not been awarded the contract. The VGA is therefore responsible for the examination of the ascertainment of the best bidder. It also has to determine on request whether an excluded competitor or bidder would have been awarded the contract in any event, had the BVerG been complied with.[5] According to the draft for the amendment of the BVerG, the VGA has to make the previously mentioned ruling or decide whether the competitor or bidder would have had a real chance to win the contract. An application for a declaratory administrative ruling must be handed in within two weeks after having knowledge of the contract award.[6] Here too the VGA has to examine previously whether the alleged illegality of the decision is of essential influence in the outcome of the procedure; if it is irrelevant, the application for a declaratory administrative ruling can be dismissed.[7] The 'Explanatory Remarks' to the BVerG make clear that of essential significance is the question whether the award would have gone to another bidder if the correct award procedures had been followed. Thus when determining whether there has been an infringement of the award procedures, the VGA will be concerned with the merits of the award itself. Very likely this is to be understood in such a way that the application is

---

[1] § 93, sub-cl 6 BVerG.
[2] Amendment draft to § 93, sub-cl 6 BVerG, GZ 600.883/11-V/8/95.
[3] § 95, sub-cl 3 BVerG; analogous regulations in the Provincial Award Laws, however partly with lower maximum limits.
[4] § 99, sub-cl 1 BVerG.
[5] § 91, sub-cl 3 BVerG.
[6] § 92, sub-cl 3 BVerG.
[7] § 91, sub-cl 4 BVerG.

to be dismissed in the case of obvious irrelevance.[1] A suspension of the award by the VGA is not provided for.

Expert opinion of the VKK   Following the contract award, the VKK has to prepare an expert opinion on the award of the contract upon request of the public body or of the body representing interests to be taken into consideration.[2] The expert opinions of the VKK have to be prepared within three months, to be notified to the agencies concerned, and to be published anonymously.

Implementation on provincial and municipal levels

In all federal provinces with the exception of Lower Austria[3] it is necessary to follow a preliminary procedure before filing an application for an examination procedure. Accordingly the contractor has to provide the public body before his application for examination with evidence of the alleged illegality within two weeks after having knowledge of the decision to be contested and to inform the latter that he therefore intends to initiate an examination procedure. Following that, the public body has to discontinue the alleged illegality without delay or to let the contractor have written information within two weeks explaining why, in its opinion, the alleged unlawfulness does not exist.

Different examination authorities have been installed in the nine Austrian federal provinces and different terms and procedures have also been determined. The most important differing regulations (as compared with the BVerG) will be shortly referred to below. It has to be stated that an amendment of the provincial laws can also be expected with respect to the Excluded Sectors Directives before long.

Federal province of Vorarlberg[4]

In Vorarlberg, the 'Award Control Senate', installed with the office of the provincial government, is the examination authority. It decides in the first and in the last instance.[5] After conduct of the preliminary procedure, the contractor may within two weeks after receipt of the public body's comment, or after expiry of the two-week term the public body had for its comment, file an application for examination with the Award Control Senate. Among other things, this application must be accompanied by evidence on the conduct of the preliminary procedure.[6] Within two months at the latest, the Award Control Senate has to take a decision on this application.[7] A declaratory administrative ruling following a contract award is to be filed with the Award Control Senate within two weeks after having knowledge of the award, at

---

[1]   Compare Thienel, Rudolf *'Award Control Commission according to the Federal Award Law'*
[2]   § 87, sub-cl 1, 3 BVerG.
[3]   In Lower Austria, a conciliation procedure is required before initiation of an examination procedure.
[4]   Award Law Vorarlberg, LGB1 1994/24.
[5]   § 88, sub-cl 2 Award Law Vorarlberg.
[6]   § 91, sub-cl 2 Award Law Vorarlberg.
[7]   § 91, sub-cl 5 Award Law Vorarlberg.

the latest within six months after the contract award.[1] A motion for the passing of an interim injunction has also to be filed within the term for the application for an examination procedure, and is admissible only if an examination procedure has been applied for at the same time.[2] A decision on an application for an interim injunction is to be taken immediately, at the latest however within seven days after receipt of the application.[3] The federal province of Vorarlberg has also enforced this examination procedure in the fields of the excluded sectors[4] and services.[5]

Federal province of Tyrol[6]

The Tyrolean award law largely refers to the regulations of the BVerG.[7] Here the Provincial Award Office[8] is the examination authority. Following the conduct of the preliminary procedure, the Provincial Award Office has to decide within two months of receipt of the application[9] for examination, to be filed at the latest two weeks after the preliminary procedure.

In case of a dismissed application, a motion for examination is to be filed with the Provincial Award Office within 20 days after receipt of the dismissal. With respect to the regulations in the public notice, in which enterprises are asked to participate in tenders or with respect to the tender rules, applications for examination are to be filed within half of the tender term. An application for examination following the contract award is to be filed within two weeks after publication of the contract award,[10] when it is being determined whether the competitor or bidder has not won the contract because of an illegality. A motion for an interim injunction can be filed at the earliest together with the examination application. The examination authority has to decide on it immediately, at the latest however within three days.[11]

Federal province of Salzburg[12]

In the federal province of Salzburg, the examination authority is the Award Control Senate. Following the preliminary procedure, the application for examination is to be filed with the Award Control Senate within two weeks after receipt of the public body's comment or two weeks after expiry of the term for the comment.[13] A proof that the public body has been informed is to be enclosed with the application. Before the contract award, the Award Control Senate has to suspend the contested decision, if it is in contradiction with the LVerG (Provincial Award Law) or the decrees issued thereto and if it can be of essential influence on the outcome of the award procedure. It decides in the first and in the last instance and has to determine the legality

---

[1] § 91, sub-cl 6 Award Law Vorarlberg.
[2] § 92, sub-cl 3 Award Law Vorarlberg.
[3] § 92, sub-cl 7 Award Law Vorarlberg.
[4] § 77, sub-cl 1 Award Law Vorarlberg.
[5] § 1, sub-cl 5 in connection with § 100, sub-cl 1, Award Law Vorarlberg.
[6] Tyrolean Award Law LGB1 1994/87.
[7] § 4 Tyrolean Award Law.
[8] § 6 Tyrolean Award Law.
[9] § 13, sub-cl 2 Tyrolean Award Law.
[10] § 9 Tyrolean Award Law.
[11] § 13, sub-cl 1 Tyrolean Award Law.
[12] Provincial Award Law Salzburg, LGB1 1995/1.
[13] § 15, sub-cl 3 Provincial Award Law Salzburg.

only after the contract has been awarded. A motion for an interim injunction is to be filed with the Award Control Senate within two weeks after the service of the public body's comment, if an application for examination is being filed at the same time.[1] A decision on this application is to be taken without delay, at the latest however within seven days.[2] An examination of the contract award can be requested immediately by virtue of an application to the Award Control Senate within two weeks after knowledge of the contract award. This application must contain a demand for determination of the unlawfulness of the contract award. In Salzburg, the examination procedures standardised in the fourth main part of the provincial award law are also valid for the excluded sectors.[3]

Federal province of Upper Austria[4]

In Upper Austria, the provincial government is the examination authority.[5] The essential difference with the BVerG is that an appeal against decisions of this examination authority to the Independent Administration Senate of the province of Upper Austria is admissible. Owing to these circumstances it will not be possible to deal with the examination procedure as quickly as on the federal level. The question arises as to how far the requirements for a quick examination procedure, as required by the Remedies Directive 89/665/EEC, Art 1, can be complied with in this respect. Discussion of this question, however, is outside the scope of this chapter.

Following the execution of the preliminary procedure, a decision on the declaration of nullity of an unlawful decision has to be taken upon request within two months after receipt of the application.[6] A motion for an interim injunction has to be filed as soon as possible together with the application for examination and at the latest three weeks after having knowledge of the alleged illegality;[7] it has to be dealt with by the authority without delay, at the latest however within a week.[8] Following the contract award, the application for examination has to be filed with the Upper Austrian provincial government at the latest two weeks after knowledge of the contract award,[9] when it is determined only whether an illegality does exist and whether the best bidder has therefore not been awarded the contract. The examination application is to be accompanied by a proof of the public authority's notification.

An action for damages before the ordinary courts is possible only if an appeal or a complaint to the Higher Administrative Court can no longer be brought against the ruling of the examination authority.[10] Here, however, a complaint against the decision is possible to the Higher Administrative Court. In the BVerG and in the individual regulations of the majority of the federal

---

[1]   § 17, sub-cl 1 Provincial Award Law Salzburg.
[2]   § 17, sub-cl 7 Provincial Award Law Salzburg.
[3]   § 3 sub-cl 2 Provincial Award Law Salzburg
[4]   Upper Austrian Award Laws LGB1 1994/59.
[5]   § 58, sub-cl 2 Upper Austrian Award Laws.
[6]   § 61, sub-cl 3 Upper Austrian Award Laws.
[7]   § 60, sub-cl 1 Upper Austrian Award Laws.
[8]   § 60, sub-cl 8 Upper Austrian Award Laws.
[9]   § 59, sub-cl 2 Upper Austrian Award Laws.
[10] § 67, sub-cl 3 Upper Austrian Award Laws.

provinces, the possibility of an appeal against decisions of the examination authority has been excluded explicitly.

Federal province of Carinthia[1]

The examination authority is the Independent Administrative Senate for Carinthia. If the public body has not pronounced upon the removal of the illegality within two weeks after receipt of the information, an application for an examination procedure can be filed within another two weeks after expiry of this term.[2] Upon request, the examination authority has to declare a decision of the public body null and void, if the latter is unlawful and if the award procedure would have led to a more favourable result for the applicant[3] had the rules been observed and had the contract not yet been awarded. A decision on such an application is to be taken within two months after receipt.[4] Following the award, the examination authority has to determine only whether the decision passed in the course of the award procedure was unlawful.[5] A motion for an interim injunction is to be filed together with the application for declaration of nullity of a decision as soon as possible, at the latest however within two weeks after expiry of the term the public body had for the information.[6] A decision on a motion for an interim injunction has to be taken immediately, at the latest however within seven days after receipt of the motion.[7] The period for which the interim measure was taken must not exceed one month.[8] It becomes ineffective with the decision on the application for declaration of nullity. Following the contract award, the Independent Administrative Senate is responsible for stating whether the decision passed in the procedure was unlawful. No term was determined for such an application in the provincial law. The Carinthian contract award law also does not contain any regulations according to which a declaratory administrative ruling would be a prerequisite for the assertion of claims for damages before the ordinary civil courts. It determines only that compensation claims become statute-barred after expiry of three years, calculated from the date the damage becomes known. Compensation for loss of profits is excluded here as well. There is no claim for damages if the public body can prove that the excluded bidder would not have been awarded the contract even if the violated rules had been complied with.[9] These judicial relief regulations do not yet apply for the excluded sectors.[10]

Federal province of Lower Austria[11]

The implementation of the examination procedure in Lower Austria lies with the Independent Administrative Senate. An application for examination is

---

[1]   Carinthian Contract Award Law, LGBl 1994/55.
[2]   § 60 Carinthian Contract Award Law.
[3]   § 63 Carinthian Contract Award Law.
[4]   § 63, sub-cl 2 Carinthian Contract Award Law.
[5]   § 61, sub-cl 2 Carinthian Contract Award Law.
[6]   § 52, sub-cl 2 Carinthian Contract Award Law.
[7]   § 62, sub-cl 9 Carinthian Contract Award Law.
[8]   § 62, sub-cl 7 Carinthian Contract Award Law.
[9]   § 64, sub-cl 1 and 2 Carinthian Contract Award Law.
[10] § 4, sub-cl 3 Carinthian Contract Award Law.
[11] Lower Austrian Award Law, LGBl 1995/84.

admissible only if a conciliation procedure has been carried out previously with the 'Lower Austrian Conciliation Agency for Public Contracts' and if no amicable settlement has been achieved.[1] This conciliation agency has to work towards an amicable settlement within two weeks without being bound to a formal procedure.[2] The bidder who is asking for conciliation has to inform the public body about this. As long as the contract has not been awarded, there is no term for the filing of an application for examination. Following the contract award, an application for determination is to be filed within four weeks after having knowledge of the award, at the latest however within six months after the contract award.[3] Upon request, the Independent Administrative Senate has to declare a decision null and void within two months,[4] if it is in contradiction with the award law and if it had essential influence on the outcome of the procedure. Following the contract award, the Independent Administrative Senate has only to determine whether the alleged contravention against the law does or does not exist. A motion for an interim injunction is to be filed at the latest one month after knowledge of the unlawfulness or the threatened damage and can be requested at the earliest after initiation of the examination procedure. Therefore the examination authority has to decide immediately, at the most however within a week.[5] The interim injunction may be made for a period of two months at the most.[6] The decisions of the Independent Administrative Senate can be contested in the Higher Administrative Court.

Federal province of Vienna[7]

With the Vienna provincial government the Award Control Senate has been set up, which is responsible for examination procedures in the first and in the last instance.[8] Only if the public body has not informed the contractor about the removal of the infringement in the preliminary procedure within two weeks, is an application for an examination procedure admissible. The application does not have any suspensive effect for the award procedure.[9] In case of the rejection of an application, an application for examination is to be filed at the latest within two weeks. Where accelerated procedures have been adopted, the application must be filed within three days of the rejection.[10]

Where the contract notice specifies restricted and/or negotiated procedures, or if accelerated procedures have been adopted, application for review must be lodged respectively within two weeks or one week of the request for the submission of tenders.[11] The Award Control Senate has to decide on applications for declarations of nullity at the latest one month after receipt of the application.[12] Following the contract award, an examination application

---

[1]   § 19 Lower Austrian Award Law.
[2]   § 17 Lower Austrian Award Law.
[3]   § 19, sub-cl 3 Lower Austrian Award Law.
[4]   § 22, sub-cl 2 Lower Austrian Award Law.
[5]   § 22, sub-cl 1 Lower Austrian Award Law.
[6]   § 20, sub-cl 6 Lower Austrian Award Law.
[7]   Viennese Provincial Award Law LGBI 1995/36.
[8]   § 94, sub-cl 2 Viennese Provincial Award Law.
[9]   § 97, sub-cl 4 Viennese Provincial Award Law.
[10] As provided for by § 52 of the Viennese Provincial Award Law for urgent reasons.
[11] § 98 Viennese Provincial Award Law.
[12] § 102, sub-cl 2 Viennese Provincial Award Law.

is to be filed within two weeks after the public notice of the contract award in the Official Journal of the European Community, with the Award Control Senate, which only has to determine whether the contract has not been awarded to the applicant as best bidder because of a contravention of the provincial award law.[1] If this publication has not been made, an examination application is to be filed six months after the contract award at the latest.[2] An interim injunction can be demanded at the earliest together with the examination application, at the latest however one week after having knowledge of the alleged illegality or of threatened damage.[3] How this regulation is to be handled in practice however seems to be a mystery, since an obligatory preliminary procedure, which may already require two weeks, has to be conducted. In the author's opinion it can be presumed therefore that the Award Control Senate will here assume knowledge of the infringement after expiry of the preliminary procedure only. An examination application would have to be submitted within a week so as to safeguard the possibility of a motion for an interim injunction. Decisions on motions for interim injunctions have to be taken immediately, in any case within a week.[4] Interim injunctions may be made for a period of one month at the most[5] and are enforceable immediately.[6] It is a special feature that in Vienna the contract award cannot be suspended by an interim injunction,[7] although in the author's opinion this regulation certainly contravenes Art 2 of the Remedies Directives. Interim injunctions can be contested in the Higher Administrative Court and in the Supreme Constitutional Court.

Federal province of Styria[8]

Examination authority in Styria is the Award Control Senate,[9] which has to decide in the first and in the last instance.[10] After a preliminary procedure has been conducted, an application for an examination procedure can be filed. The Award Control Senate has to decide on the request within two months in so far as the contract has not been awarded yet.[11] Following the contract award, the application for examination is to be filed with the Award Control Senate within two weeks from having knowledge of the award, but within six months from the actual contract award.[12] As in the other provinces, the application does not have any suspensive effect on the award procedure.[13] A motion for an interim injunction can be filed with the Award Control

---

[1] § 99, sub-cl 1, 2 Viennese Provincial Award Law.
[2] § 98, Viennese Provincial Award Law.
[3] § 100, sub-cl 5 Viennese Provincial Award Law.
[4] § 102, sub-cl 1 Viennese Provincial Award Law.
[5] § 100, sub-cl 4 Viennese Provincial Award Law.
[6] § 100, sub-cl 6 Viennese Provincial Award Law.
[7] § 100, sub-cl 2 Viennese Provincial Award Law.
[8] Styrian Award Law, LGBI 1995/85.
[9] § 81, sub-cl 1 Styrian Award Law.
[10] § 86, sub-cl 3 Styrian Award Law.
[11] § 90, sub-cl 2 Styrian Award Law.
[12] § 88, sub-cl 2 Styrian Award Law.
[13] § 88, sub-cl 4 Styrian Award Law.

Senate together with the examination application at the earliest, but three weeks after knowledge of the alleged illegality or the immediately threatened damage at the latest.[1] The peculiarity in Styria is that it is explicitly provided that following a required examination, an interim injunction can also be passed ex officio.[2] The period for which the interim injunction is made must not exceed one month.[3] On motions for interim injunctions decisions have to be taken immediately, at the latest however within seven days after receipt of the motion.[4] An action for damages is admissible only if the Award Control Senate has previously pronounced that there has been a violation of the law.[5]

Federal province of Burgenland[6]

Burgenland has passed its own comprehensive award law and does not for the most part refer to the BVerG as other provinces do. Here the examination authority is the 'Independent Administrative Senate Burgenland'. In Burgenland too a so-called preliminary procedure has to be observed, if a contract has not been awarded yet. A contractor has therefore to inform the public body within two weeks after having knowledge of the decision in a provable manner and indicating grounds why he considers the decision to be unlawful and that he intends to initiate an examination procedure in this respect.[7] The public body has to remove the illegality without delay or to inform the contractor within two weeks why the illegality does not exist.[8] The contractor can then file an examination procedure with the 'Independent Administrative Senate' within two weeks after the service of the public body's comment, or if no comment has been given, within two weeks after expiry of the term provided for it. A proof of the preliminary procedure adhered to is to be annexed to this application.[9] On applications for declarations of nullity of a decision, a ruling has to be passed two months after the receipt of the application at the latest.[10] A motion for an interim injunction has to be filed together with the application for an examination procedure within the same term.[11] The validity of an interim injunction must not exceed the period of one month. On this motion a decision is to be taken immediately, within a week at the latest however.[12] Following the contract award it has to be determined only whether the alleged illegality exists. An examination application following the contract award has to be filed within a week after having knowledge of the contract, at the latest however within six months after the contract award.[13] Burgenland has also extended the Remedies Directives to contracts in the field of the excluded sectors.

---

[1]   § 89, sub-cl 2 Styrian Award Law.
[2]   § 89, sub-cl 4 Styrian Award Law.
[3]   § 89, sub-cl 7 Styrian Award Law.
[4]   § 89, sub-cl 10 Styrian Award Law.
[5]   § 98, sub-cl 3 Styrian Award Law.
[6]   Burgenland Award Law, LGB1 1995/1.
[7]   § 94, sub-cl 1 Burgenland Award Law.
[8]   § 94, sub-cl 2 Burgenland Award Law.
[9]   § 95, sub-cl 3 Burgenland Award Law.
[10]   § 97, sub-cl 3 Burgenland Award Law.
[11]   § 96, sub-cl 1 Burgenland Award Law.
[12]   § 96, sub-cl 8 Burgenland Award Law.
[13]   § 95, sub-cl 2 Burgenland Award Law.

DAMAGES FOR EXCLUDED BIDDERS OR COMPETITORS

Competent courts

The BVerG and the provincial award laws do explicitly refer decisions on claims for damages to the civil courts.[1]

As before the implementation of the EC Directives, there is still the possibility in Austria for a bidder or competitor, violated in his rights, to claim damages by an action before the ordinary civil courts. Irrespective of the amount of the value in dispute, the law courts entrusted with the practice of general jurisdiction in civil cases for the district in which the public body has its registered office, are responsible in the first instance. If such a legal venue is not available in the interior, the Provincial Court for Civil Cases in Vienna is responsible.[2] In some cases, however, the provincial courts in the respective provinces are exclusively competent on a provincial level, irrespective of the domicile of the public body, as for instance in Vorarlberg, Salzburg and Burgenland.

Prerequisites

An action for damages with respect to claims resulting from the award laws is admissible only if a declaratory administrative ruling has previously been passed by the Federal Award Office or by the examination authorities at the provincial level,[3] and if no right of appeal is admissible against it any more. It should be noted in particular here that an action for damages is excluded when the usual two weeks' term for filing a motion for a declaratory administrative ruling is missed.[4] This is likely to be problematic from the point of view of constitutional law, since the decrees for public contracts are now as before valid for contracts below the EC threshold values and an action for damages can still be commenced in these fields until the general statutory period of limitation expires. In this respect therefore, contractors who are subject to the application of the BVerG or the provincial award laws are worse off.

Judicial evidence

On the basis of explicit provisions, the court is in principle bound by the determinations of the VGA or the examination authorities in the federal provinces. If the decision of the legal case depends on the question of the lawfulness of the declaratory administrative ruling and if the court considers the ruling to be unlawful, the current procedure is to be suspended and the determination of the lawfulness to be decided in the Higher Adminstrative Court by virtue of official complaint according to Art 131, sub-clause 2 BVerG. After receipt of a respective finding of the Higher Administrative Court, the

[1] § 102, sub-clause 1 Burgenland Award Law.
[2] § 102, sub-cl 1 BVerG; analogous regulations in the federal provinces.
[3] In Carinthia, an action for damages may also be filed without declaratory administrative ruling.
[4] Compare Thienel, '*The Examination Procedure according to the Federal Award Law*' WBl 1993, 385.

procedure is to be continued, the court being bound by the legal opinion of the Higher Administrative Court. The judicial evidence is also admissible before the ordinary civil courts.

Amount of damages

The situation for the aggrieved bidder who is founding his claims on the award laws has deteriorated considerably with respect to the amount of damages since the introduction of these regulations for the following reasons.[1]

Prior to the enforcement of the EC Directives, the Supreme Court upheld compensation for performance expenses in some of the decisions, if the excluded bidder could prove that he would have won the contract as best bidder, had the award regulations not been culpably contravened.[2] By a decision of 19 October 1994, the OGH has in fact awarded performance expenses for the first time in a case of a contravention of the administrative regulations.[3]

Since 1 January 1994, and also partly in the federal provinces since 1 January 1995, damages in the amount of performance expenses are expressly excluded for disregarded competitors or bidders[4] who are subject to the application of the BVerG or of the provincial laws on public contract award.[5] If organs of the awarding agency do therefore culpably contravene the BVerG or the provincial award laws or the decrees issued thereto, and if the declaratory administrative ruling does not state that the excluded bidder or competitor would in no event have won the contract, had the laws been complied with, the excluded bidder is only entitled to compensation of the costs for the submission of the tender and the remaining costs accruing in connection with the participation in the award procedure if he bases his claims on the damages clauses of the award laws. According to the author's opinion this also excludes compensation for other expenses made in expectation of an award. Bidders and competitors who submit a tender for public contracts below the EC threshold values are therefore better off with regard to damages, in so far as the legal damages regulations of the award laws are not extended to public contracts below the threshold values.

One problem is likely to arise due to the above reasons with respect to the implementation of the Excluded Sectors Remedies Directive 92/13/EEC, since Art 1 requires Member States to take care 'that the differentiation made in these directives between individual state regulations for the enforcement of community law and other national rules does not lead to discrimination between enterprises who could claim damages within the framework of an award procedure.' It remains to be seen how the legislator will solve this problem.

This problem arises also if the basis of the claim for damages of the aggrieved bidder or competitor is founded on the provisions of the General Civil Code[6]

---

[1] However different the provincial laws may be with respect to the public contract award and the appellate procedures, there seems to be an agreement on the limitation of damages.

[2] OGH 13.4.1988 WBI 1988, 342; OGH 10.10.1989, RdW 1990,43; with this opinion it is also in agreement with the prevailing doctrine.

[3] OGH 19.10.1994, 7 Ob 568/94 in: ecolex 1995, pp 93ff.

[4] By 'competitor' we understand a contractor who is interested in participating in a tender procedure in order to get a contract. A bidder is a contractor, a joint venture or a group of bidders who submitted an offer.

[5] On a federal level § 98, sub-cl 1 BVerG. Analogous regulations are also contained in the respective provincial laws.

[6] In short: ABGB.

and not on the award regulations and if the performance expense is therefore adjudicated. In the case of a violation of the award regulations one could found the claim on a contravention of the protective law within the meaning of § 1311, Art 2, 2nd case ABGB (General Civil Code). It will certainly be possible to classify the award laws as protective laws, since their primary objective is the securing of the bidders' competition; they have to protect bidders and competitors against unjustified discrimination.[1]

Lost chances

The amendment draft to the BVerG[2] provides that upon request, the VGA has to determine also whether an excluded bidder or competitor would in no event have been awarded the contract, had the regulations of the BVerG been complied with, or whether the bidder or competitor would have had a real chance of winning the contract. Thus the prerequisites are created on a federal level for a claim for damages according to the award laws for a lost chance to win a contract. The existence of a real chance will have to be judged by the VGA by a finding of fact whether the bidder or competitor would have belonged to the closer circle of candidates for the contract award, had the regulations of the contract award been complied with. It will therefore have to be decided upon consideration of the actual circumstances of each individual case whether the actual possibility of a contract award did exist. As far as the amount of damages is concerned, reference is made to the above explanations.

WITHDRAWAL FROM CONTRACT AWARD

In Austria, the setting aside of contracts on the basis of contraventions of the EC Directives for Public Contracts is not possible, under the award laws. The public body has the right to withdraw, if the contractor or a person he engaged for the contract procedure has committed a legally punishable act which was apt to influence the decision on the contract award.[3] Here therefore, the possibility of setting aside an already concluded contract in which a favoured bidder was involved is restricted to extreme violations of the law. The civil law rights to withdraw from a contract remain in force, however.

SIGNIFICANCE OF 'PUBLIC INTEREST' WHEN MAKING INTERIM INJUNCTIONS

General

Before making an interim injunction, the Federal Award Office and the examination authorities in the provinces have to weigh the consequences of the interim measure against the violated interests of the claimant. In the course

---

[1] Compare preamble to 92/13/EEC; Thienel *'Federal Award Law and Civil Law'*, ÖJZ 1993, 623.
[2] Amendment draft to § 91, sub-cl 3 BVerG, GZ 600.883/11-V/8/95.
[3] § 100 BVerG BGBl 1993/462; analogous regulations in the provincial award laws.

of this, a possible special public interest in the continuation of the award procedure has also to be taken into consideration. Owing to the use of the undefined legal concept of a 'special public interest', the authority is however not given the chance of selecting from various decision possibilities, but has to weigh various interests here by application of the principle of proportionality. In addition, the concept of public interest is qualified and restricted by the the adjective 'special'. If in the process of such a weighing the detrimental consequences of an interim injunction prevail, it must not be granted.

Because of the short time during which EC directives have been in force in Austria, no factual examples of the weighing of special public interests with interim injunctions in examination procedures are available. Since the public interest always has to relate to actual facts, a comparison with the weighing of administrative files in other fields would not be very helpful here.

Nevertheless, some relevant legal cases of violations of the directives and of the EEC Treaty will now be analysed and compared with Austrian law, dealing in particular with the weighing of interests. It has however to be stated in this connection that at the time of these cases, the Construction and Supply Contract Remedies Directives were not yet in force in the EU or had not yet been implemented into national law. These cases took place before the ECJ, which passed landmark decisions in this respect.

In the *Lottomatica* case,[1] the question arose as to what extent concluded contracts can be set aside by public bodies. Referring to Austrian law, private law provisions of the 'General Civil Code' would have to be applied here. Accordingly the contract with the contractor usually materialises at the time the bidder is informed of the acceptance of his offer, which is also the end of the award procedure. A withdrawal from this concluded contract can then take place only in accordance with the terms of the contract and the provisions in the 'General Civil Code'.[2] If the contract has already been awarded and an infringement of the award regulations has been determined in the examination procedure, this can only lead to claims for damages in Austria. The possibility of annulment of the contract was excluded in Austria, possibly for reasons of legal certainty.[3]

The second striking feature in the *Lottomatica* case when making the interim injunction was the weighing of the claimant's interests[4] against the interests of Italy. Italy alleged that by the making of an interim injunction and the delay in the contract award connected therewith, the state was losing 500 billion Lira in tax returns annually. These interests of Italy were weighed against the interests of the Commission for the prevention of infringements of the Rules of the EEC Treaty by the ECJ. The ECJ also weighed the judgment of the court of 5 December in the *Re Data Processing* case[5] and has thus on the whole given priority to the interests of the Commission.

The adjudication of the ECJ, by which the national examination authorities also have to abide, shows that comparatively high financial disadvantages to a public body, in particular if a violation of the contract has already been determined in a similar case, are given less significance when weighing the public interest in proceedings for the making of an interim injunction than

---

[1]   C-272/9R: [1995] 2 CMLR 504.
[2]   Also § 101 BVerG, BGBl 1993/462 as well as analogous regulations in the provincial laws.
[3]   With the exception of the right to withdraw of the contractor when committing a legally punishable act (§ 100 BVerG BGBl 1993/462).
[4]   The Commission in this case.
[5]   C-3/88: [1989] ECR 4035.

against the interests of the Community for observance and enforcement of the directives.

The tenor of the judgment in the *Re Data Processing* case is that contracts involving the equipment and operation of data processing systems which are to store or process confidential data, even data for crime prevention, do not call for the exercise of public authority. According to the ECJ, therefore, there does not exist any danger for public order, safety, and health, if these data processing systems are supplied and even operated by enterprises from other Member States. It appears that the concepts of public order, safety, and health are being interpreted by the ECJ in a very limited way.

In accordance with Art 6 of the Supply Contracts Directive 77/62/EEC, the provision of § 7, sub-clause 1, No 2 BVerG[1] was enacted in Austria. Accordingly the Federal Award Law is not to be applied to supply and construction contracts if the exemption is required for the protection of special interests of national security. In light of the above-mentioned ECJ ruling it becomes obvious that the concepts of public order, safety, and health are to be interpreted in a very limited way. Thus for example the VKK recommended and the VGA has determined in a ruling that supplies to the military at top security level, ie a prohibited military zone, are to be tendered publicly and are not subject to an exception within § 7, sub-clause 1, No 2 BVerG.[2]

The ECJ founded the suspension of the interim measure in the *Dundalk*[3] case on the fact that when weighing mutual interests, the interests of Ireland predominated in this particular case. Here, then, the interest for securing the water supply for the inhabitants of the city of Dundalk until 1990 and the risks to health and safety connected therewith were stronger than the interest of the Commission in complying with the Community law award regulations. By judgment of 22 September 1988, the ECJ decided that with regard to this tender, Ireland had contravened Art 30 of the EEC Treaty.

In Austria, the *Dundalk* tender would also contravene national regulations, since according to the also applying ÖNORM, named products may be required in certain exceptional cases only and even then one with the determinative of 'or of an equal kind'.[4] In any case, the service must not be circumscribed in such a manner that certain undertakings enjoy competitive advantages. In the *Dundalk* case the addition 'or equivalent' would have been required in the tender, following the specification of the standard demanded.

In Austria, the examination authorities have to weigh the consequences of an interim injunction for all possible damaged interests of the claimant and of the public body, when a possible special public interest in the continuation of the awards procedure is to be taken into consideration in the weighing process. In the *Dundalk* case, the ECJ gave more significance to the public interest in securing the water supply of the city until 1990 than to the interest of the Commission in the observance of Community law. It seems, however, that the ECJ in its ruling did make allowance for the long duration of the proceedings until the final decision when it saw a real danger to public safety and health in the resulting delay in completing the work. The ECJ also pointed out explicitly that in the case of construction contracts

---

[1] Analogous regulations in the provincial laws.
[2] VGA 26.4.1995, N-1/95 and N-2/95; recommendations of the VKK of 29.3.95 in: Connex 1996, 32.
[3] C-45/87: [1988] ECR 4929.
[4] ÖNORM A 2050 in the wording of 1.1.1993, item 2.1.3.

for another purpose and not involving health risks occasioned by a delay in the contract award, the ruling might be different. Since the examination authorities in Austria have to decide applications for declarations of nullity of decisions, made by a public body, within just two months,[1] it can hardly be imagined that a required interim injunction would not be granted, taking the facts of the *Dundalk* case as a basis. According to the BVerG, two-and-a-half months would pass at the most until the final ruling of the examination authority, including the obligatory conciliation procedure of two weeks. A maximum delay of that extent can therefore be assumed. This would however, in the author's opinion, not cause any danger to health in such a case. In practice however it might become a problem in that, according to the present legal situation,[2] an interim injunction can be made for a period of one month only.[3] If a decision is therefore suspended by an interim injunction, or if the award procedure is suspended only and the examination authority does not decide within a month of the filing of the motion, the interim injunction is without effect, since it is not in force for a period of more than a month.

According to § 58, sub-clause 4, No 3 BVerG 1993/462, construction contracts may be let using negotiated procedures without having to publicise the intended contract award on the condition that urgent and imperative reasons, which are to be attributed to the public body in connection with events unforeseeable to the latter, do not permit the observance of prescribed terms. Here, the Austrian legislator has fully adopted the provisions of Art 9(d) of Directive 71/305/EEC. The national examination authority would therefore have to make an interim injunction upon request of a bidder or competitor in a case with similar facts to the *La Spezia* case,[4] to the effect that the public body would have to suspend the award procedure or the decision, at the longest however for one month.[5] It has to be pointed out here that the federal provinces of Vorarlberg, Salzburg and Lower Austria may even grant interim injunctions until the ruling of the examination authority.

In the ruling on the *Van Hool* case,[6] the ECJ explained the prerequisites for the urgency of an interim injunction in detail. The claimant has to state the circumstances from which the urgency results. According to the adjudication of the ECJ, urgency is to be judged by the test whether an interim injunction is necessary in order to prevent serious and irreparable damage which would occur due to the immediate enforcement of the contested measure. The danger of serious and irreparable damage is therefore required and in addition, the applicant for an interim injunction has to credibly justify the Order he seeks. By Austrian law one only assumes irreparable damage, if compensation in money cannot put the damaged person back in the position in which he was before the occurrence of the damage. Since a contractor has a right to damages, albeit limited to the recovery of the cost of tender,[7] it may not be arguable that damages are irreparable.

According to the Austrian award laws, the examination authority has to take the steps asked for in the interim measure, which seem to be 'necessary

---

[1]   For instance § 95, sub-clause 1 BVerG BGBl 1993/462.
[2]   The amendment draft GZ 600.883/11-V/8/95 to the BVerG does already contain the regulation that the interim injunction can be granted for a period of two months at the most.
[3]   § 93, sub-cl 6 BVerG, BGBl 1993/462.
[4]   194/88R: [1988] ECR 4547.
[5]   According to the amendment draft GZ 600.883/11-V/8/95 to the BVerG for two months at the most.
[6]   C-87/94R: [1994] ECR I-1395, and see also C-87/94, 25 April 1996.
[7]   § 98, sub-cl 1 BVerG, analogous regulations in the provincial laws.

and apt' to remove or prevent damages to the applicant's interests, originating or threatened as a consequence of the alleged illegality.[1] In the author's opinion this may be understood in such a way that the interim measures to be taken must seem apt to the VGA and must not go beyond that.[2] It is the purpose of this interim measure to restore damage which has occurred or to prevent immediately threatened damages. In doing that, the VGA has to restrict itself to the most necessary interference with the public body's legal sphere. According to § 93, sub-clause 3 BVerG, the examination authority has to weigh the foreseeable consequences of the measures to be taken for all possibly violated interests of the claimant, the other competitors or bidders, and the public body, as well as a possible special public interest in the continuation of the award process. An interim injunction must therefore be made only if the detrimental consequences of these measures are not greater. According to the wording of the law, however, the danger of serious and irreparable damages for the applicants is not expressly required in Austrian award laws.

Apart from urgency, the ECJ also requires necessity for the making of an interim injunction. In this respect the ECJ decided in the *Muratori* case[3] that the necessity of an interim order did not exist, since even if realistic doubts exist against the conditions under which the winner of a tender has been selected, these are not sufficient to justify such a weighty measure. In addition, the applicant was the second only with respect to the tender price and not the best bidder. In the *Muratori* case, the ECJ adjudicated the urgency on the following grounds: the bidders are interested in asking for an interim order so as to prevent a contract being concluded, should the tender procedure prove faulty, and should its execution progress in such a way that an irreversible damage might develop.

It did not decide on the necessity for an interim order, since the interim measure, ie suspending the execution of the concluded contract by an obstruction of the means prepared, is a weighty one which the actual doubts in the conditions for the selection of the winner did not justify. Under these circumstances, taken with the fact that the applicant was not the lowest bidder, but only the second with respect to the price, the required necessity for the interim order did not exist and the application was therefore rejected.

Compare this with the legal situation in Austria: following the contract award, the VGA will have to dismiss a motion for an interim injunction, since this can be applied for successfully only as long as the contract has not been awarded.[4] A declaration of nullity of a decision of the awarding agency is also no longer possible when there is a concluded contract award. In this case, following the previous conciliation procedure, the examination authority would have to determine upon request only whether the lowest bidder was not awarded the contract because of a contravention of the rules[5] or if the contract would not have been awarded in any event, had the award regulations been complied with, or[6] whether the respective bidder or competitor would have had a real chance of winning the contract. As already mentioned

[1] § 93, sub-cl 1 BVerG.
[2] Compare also Konecny, Andreas *The Sphere of Application of an Interim Injunction* (Vienna, 1992), p 10.
[3] 118/83R: [1983] ECR 2583.
[4] § 91, sub-cl 2 BVerG; analogous regulations in the provincial laws.
[5] § 91, sub-cl 3 BVerG; analogous regulations in the provincial laws.
[6] As provided by the amendment draft GZ 600.883/11-V/8/95 to the BVerG.

above, this declaratory administrative ruling is a procedural requirement for a possible action for damages before the ordinary civil courts.[1]

IMPLEMENTATION OF THE EXCLUDED SECTORS REMEDIES DIRECTIVE 92/13/EEC INTO NATIONAL LAW

On the federal level, the Excluded Sectors Remedies Directive has not been implemented yet. A draft[2] for a respective amendment of the BVerG has already been produced, according to which the Remedies Directive is to be applied in the field of the excluded sectors as well.[3] In addition, the draft amendment contains regulations on the attestation procedure[4] and 'lost chances'. Accordingly, public bodies in the field of the excluded sectors can have their award procedures and award practices examined regularly by an examiner in order to get an attestation that their procedures and practices are in agreement with the requirements of Community law and with the national rules. Furthermore, regulations are provided for according to which every competitor or bidder who is or was interested in a contract in the field of the excluded sectors can avail himself of a conciliation procedure before the Commission, in so far as he is able to prove that he suffered or is liable to suffer damages because of a contravention of this law or of the Community law on contract awards.[5]

In the draft amendment, a variant, offered as a choice by the Excluded Sectors Remedies Directive, was not adopted. According to this variant, the public body in the field of the excluded sectors can be obliged to pay a penalty in case of a contravention of the award regulations, when the decision of the awarding agency is maintained. After enactment of the amendments, the above-mentioned general judicial relief regulations will therefore apply in the field of the excluded sectors. With respect to the conciliation procedure according to Art 9 of the Excluded Sectors Remedies Directive, no regulations have been passed so far.[6]

Only the federal provinces of Vorarlberg, Salzburg, Vienna, and Burgenland have introduced regulations in the provincial award laws, partly corresponding to the Excluded Sectors Remedies Directive, according to which the examination procedure, introduced as per Remedies Directive 89/665/EEC, is applied to contracts in the field of the excluded sectors as well. However, in the regulations for the attestation procedure and the conciliation procedure, reference is still made to the EEA Agreement and to the EFTA Supervision Authority, so that an amendment is required for application.

EFFICIENCY OF THE EXAMINATION PROCEDURE

The introduction of an accompanying award control in Austria for the first time is certainly to be valued positively. Because of the federal structure of

[1]   § 102, sub-cl 2 BVerG; analogous regulations in the provincial laws.
[2]   Amendment draft GZ 600.883/11-V/8/95 to BVerG.
[3]   After amendment: § 7, sub-cl 2 in connection with § 67, sub-cl 1 BVerG.
[4]   The amendment draft provides that respective regulations are to be contained in § 97a BVerG which will have to be inserted.
[5]   The amendment draft provides that respective regulations are to be contained in § 97b BVerG which will have to be inserted.
[6]   State as per 30.4.1996.

the Republic of Austria and the situation existing with regard to constitutional law, respective regulations for the federal government and for the individual nine federal provinces had to be passed for the implementation of the EC Directives. As shown above, these regulations on award control are however not uniform at the federal and the provincial level.[1] The large variety of regulations, valid in the public contract award sector, makes this difficult to grasp and will, in the author's opinion, frequently prevent contractors from initiating examination procedures.

Because of the compulsory preliminary procedures which may last up to two weeks, the efficacy of interim injunctions is considerably reduced and serves practically only to secure that a contract must not be awarded within the examination procedure and that decisions may be suspended, however not within the preliminary procedure.[2] According to the actual legal situation not even that is secured, however, since on the federal level, as well as in the different provinces with a few exceptions, interim injunctions and interim measures respectively may only be granted for a period of one month at the most,[3] whereas the examination authorities on the other hand are permitted up to two months to take their decisions. The draft for the amendment of the law[4] on the federal level makes allowance for this criticism; it is planned to increase the maximum duration of a permitted interim injunction to two months. In addition, it was provided in the amendment draft that the VKK has to inform the awarding agency immediately on taking up its activities and that the awarding agency must not award the contract within a term of three weeks from this information, other than by way of nullity, in so far as the conciliation procedure is in effect.

In the European Union, the past has shown that contractors do rather refrain from pursuing contraventions of award procedures. This might be due to the fact that contractors are afraid that the public bodies might be resentful with respect to future contract awards and will therefore more likely refrain from awarding a contract.[5] In Austria the BVerG has been in force since 1 January 1994 and approximately 90 proceedings have taken place before the examination authorities since then. At the provincial level, very few proceedings have been conducted so far. It remains to be seen however how the respective behaviour of Austrian contractors will develop.

COSTS OF PROCEEDINGS

The costs of proceedings on the one hand depend on the amount of the value in dispute and the scope of taking evidence, and on the other hand on whether representation by a lawyer is called for. Whilst in conciliation or examination procedures, being represented by a lawyer is at the discretion of the party, the representation by a lawyer is compulsory in proceedings before the Supreme Constitutional Court and the Higher Administrative Court, as well as in

---

[1] In addition, other regulations have to be applied for public contracts below the EC threshold values, as represented above.

[2] These problems do of course arise only in case of short award terms.

[3] The amendment draft to the BVerG provides that the interim injunction may be granted for a period of two months.

[4] GZ 600.883/11-V/8/95.

[5] Compare Stolz, Kathrin, 'Public Procurement Regime in the EC: Possibilities and Limits of a Liberalization', *Series of Publications* (ed Schwarze, Jürgen), *European Law, Politics, and Economy*, (Baden-Baden 1991), pp, 138 ff with further evidence.

proceedings before civil courts of the first instance. In view of the complicated legal situation it is however recommended in any event to call in a lawyer for conciliation and examination procedures as well.

Whereas, in conciliation and examination procedures, claims for the reimbursement of costs and expenses do not exist and a global reimbursement, which as a rule by no means covers the costs which accrued, is possible only in proceedings before the Supreme Constitutional Court and the Higher Administrative Court, the party completely defeated in civil proceedings before ordinary courts has to reimburse the opponent all costs occasioned by the conduct of the case. In case of partial success only, each party has to pay its own costs, or costs are divided proportionally. The costs to be reimbursed by the losing party are to be calculated according to the court fees law and according to the lawyers' tariff. The amount of the fee depends on the value in dispute and the kind of services performed as well as on the duration of the trials before the courts. The higher a legal case is assessed, the higher is the respective cost item. Furthermore, the cost items and the court fees are higher in the appellate instances than in first instance proceedings. A lawyer's fee can however also be calculated by the time spent, if this has been agreed upon, but it is inadmissible to agree on a payment by result.

The court fees also depend on the value of the object at issue, when the liability to charges starts in principle with the presentation of the action or other written pleadings, initiating proceedings. At present, the lump-sum fees for a civil proceeding with a value at issue of ATS 5 million amount to ATS 67.620 irrespective of the duration of the proceeding. With a value in issue of above ATS 5 million, the fees amount to 1.2% of the value in issue plus ATS 6.760. Apart from lawyers' fees and court fees, the additional costs for obtaining expert opinions particularly have to be taken into consideration. Since in the case of public contracts higher values in issue are involved, considerable expenses have to be calculated.

DURATION OF PROCEEDINGS

Conciliation and examination proceedings are of a limited duration; the maximum duration is several months.

For proceedings before the Higher Administrative Court and the Supreme Constitutional Court, a duration of approximately one to two years has to be reckoned with.

The duration of civil proceeedings before the ordinary courts strongly depends on the individual cases and cannot be indicated generally. One has to reckon on a long duration of up to several years, if expert opinions are prepared and if the proceedings do not only go through the first instance but through the second and third instance, ie the last instance (Supreme Court), as well. To give one example: proceedings at first instance, which is the factual and legal instance, require one to two years in cases involving an expert opinion and average other evidence.

LIST OF ADDRESSES

(1) **Federal Award Control Commission and Federal Award Office**
1. Bundes-Vergabekontrollkommission   Telephone: (222)   711000–5363
Dampfschiffstraße 4   Fax: (222)   7182393
A-1030 Wien

    2. Bundesvergabeamt   Telephone: (222)   711000–5363
Dampfschiffstraße 4   Fax: (222)   7182393
A-1030 Wien

(2) **Vorarlberg**
Amt der Vorarlberger Landesregierung   Telephone: (5574) 511–2333
Vergabekontrollsenat   Fax: (5574) 511–2320
Landhaus
A-6901 Bregenz

(3) **Tyrol**
Amt der Tiroler Landesregierung   Telephone: (512)   508–2282
Präsidialabteilung 4   Fax: (512)   508–2285
Landesvergabeamt
Wilhelm-Greil-Straße 17
A-6020 Innsbruck

(4) **Salzburg**
Amt der Salzburger Landesregierung   Telephone: (662)   8042–4335
Landesbaudirektion Referat 602   Fax: (662)   8042–4160
Vergabekontrollsenat
Michael-Pacherstraße 36
A-5020 Salzburg

(5) **Upper Austria**
1. Amt der Oberösterreichischen   Telephone: (732)   7720–1313
Landesregierung   Fax: (732)   7720–1767
Finanzabteilung
Klosterstraße 7
A-4020 Linz

    2. Unabhängiger Verwaltungssenat des   Telephone: (732)   7720–5681
Landes Oberösterreich   Fax: (732)   7720–4853
Fabrikstraße 32
A-4020 Linz

(6) **Carinthia**
Unabhängiger Verwaltungssenat für   Telephone: (463)   54350
Kärnten   Fax: (463)   54350–29
Völkermarkterring 25
A-9020 Klagenfurt

(7) **Lower Austria**
  1. Niederösterreichische   Telephone: (2742) 357500–2109
    Schlichtungsstelle für   Fax: (2742) 357500–2370
    Auftragsvergabe – Abteilung 1 AV
    Landhausplatz
    A-3100 St Pölten

  2. Unabhängiger Verwaltungssenat für Telephone: (2742) 357500–5530
    Niederösterreich   Fax: (2742) 357500–5540
    Neu-Gebäudeplatz 1
    A-3100 St Pölten

(8) **Vienna**
  Geschässtelle des   Telephone: (222) 4000–82742
  Vergabekontrollsenates   Fax: (222) 4000–9982701
  Rathaus – Stiege 5 – Zimmer 201 F
  A-1082 Wien

(9) **Styria**
  Vergabekontrollsenat   Telephone: (316) 877–3469
  Palais Trauttmansdorff   Fax: (316) 877–2164
  Trauttmansdorffgasse 2
  A-8010 Graz

(10) **Burgenland**
  Unabhängiger Verwaltungssenat   Telephone: (2682) 66811
  Burgenland   Fax: (2682) 66811–90
  Neusiedlerstraße 35–37/8
  A-7000 Eisenstadt

CHAPTER 4

Remedies in Belgium

Van Bael & Bellis

INTRODUCTION

The implementation in Belgian law of the European Directives related to
remedies in public procurement matters does not considerably affect the
remedies which were or are currently available. Since the Belgian legislator
is of the opinion that its current regulatory framework provides for an effective
means of redress for any aggrieved party, a transformation of the whole Belgian
procurement regime was thought to be almost superfluous. The major
amendments to Belgian public procurement relate to the regime itself rather
than to the remedies available.

Below we analyse to what extent the Belgian regulatory framework may
be deemed to comply with the Directives offering a relief in public procurement
matters.

Following a general overview of the structure of the Belgian regulatory
framework of public procurement, we will examine if and how the Belgian
legislator has implemented the said Directives. In order to illustrate the outlined
remedies we will briefly discuss two important Belgian procurement cases.

REGULATORY FRAMEWORK OF THE BELGIAN PUBLIC
PROCUREMENT REGIME

General rules

The award of a public contract does not necessarily fall within the scope of
the public procurement regime. The applicability of the public procurement
regime is only required in specific circumstances. When no particular provisions
apply, public entities are free to decide to whom they will award a public
contract. In such circumstances, Belgian contract law governs this specific area.

The freedom to award public contracts is nonetheless limited to a certain
extent. Regulatory and judge-made rules, both on the national and international
level, seek to regulate the award procedure to make sure that applicants are
treated equally with regard to the principle of non-discrimination.

For example, the general principles of proper administration are general
principles of Belgian administrative law which also govern the award procedure.
Especially the equal opportunity principle and the principle of the mandatory
reasoning of public decisions have to be taken into account. Furthermore,
public interest considerations will be important when deciding whether the
public entity has to organise a public procurement procedure.

Before discussing the remedies available under Belgian law which enforce the public procurement regime, it is useful to outline which contracts are subject to this regime. This area is currently governed by the Law of 1976 on the award of public works, supplies and services contracts[1] (hereinafter referred to as 'the Law of 14 July 1976') and by a number of implementing Royal Decrees, primarily by the Royal Decree of 22 April 1977 on the award of public works, supplies and services contracts (hereinafter referred to as 'the Royal Decree of 22 April 1977').[2]

Specific legislation: the Law of 14 July 1976

Although a subsequent Law has been adopted in December 1993, the Law of 14 July 1976 still remains in force, which in turn succeeds the former Law of 4 March 1963 regarding the Conclusion of Contracts on behalf of the State.[3]

Scope – ratione personae

The Law of 14 July 1976 applies to public contracts awarded by the 'state or any other public entity' (Article 1, para 1). Furthermore, the Law of 14 July 1976 is also applicable to universities which are subsidised by the State and legal entities in which the awarding authorities have a preponderant interest. Finally, the Law of 14 July 1976 can be made applicable by Royal Decree to private entities receiving subsidies from public entities with regard to public contracts (Article 2, para 2).

Although the Law of 14 July 1976 to a certain extent clarifies the term 'state or any other public entity', certain criteria defining the entities covered by the Law remain vague. Indeed, the gradual full or partial privatisation of a range of public entities calls for a clarification of the scope of application of the Law of 14 July 1976. As we will see below, the same holds true for the Law of 24 December 1993. Furthermore, several regulations specifically exclude certain entities from the scope of the Law of 14 July 1976. For example, although the *Algemene Spaar- en Lijfrentekas/Caisse Générale d'Epargne et de Retraite* may be perceived as a public entity, Article 7 of the Royal Decree no 1 of 24 December 1980 exempts this entity from the obligation to issue public tenders. On the other hand, the Law of 14 July 1976 is also applicable to legal entities in which public entities have a preponderant interest. A list of such entities should have been provided by Royal Decree but has never been issued.

Scope – ratione materiae

Article 1, para 1 of the Law of 14 July 1976 provides that public works, supplies and services contracts are concluded at a fixed price and are awarded on the basis of competition.

---

[1]   *Belgian Official Journal*, 28 August 1976. For a general overview of the Law of 14 July 1976, *see*, Van Bael & Bellis, *Business Law Guide to Belgium*, CCH Europe, Oxfordshire, 1993, 545 et seq.
[2]   *Belgian Official Journal*, 26 July 1977.
[3]   For a full discussion on the Law of 14 July 1976, Flamme, MA, Matheï, Ph & Flamme, Ph, *Praktische Commentaar bij de reglementering van de overheidsopdrachten*, Nationale Confederatie van het Bouwbedrijf, Brussels, 1986, 109 et seq.

The fixed price principle relates to the fact that the contractor has to perform all the work necessary for the completion of the project for a fixed price agreed upon between the contractor and the awarding authority (Article 1, para 1).[1]

Regarding the fact that the contract has to be awarded on the basis of competition, the Law of 14 July 1976 distinguishes three main categories of contract award procedures which fall within its scope: *(a) Allocation (aanbesteding/adjudication)*: where the contract is awarded to the lowest tender; *(b) Tender (offerteaanvraag/appel d'offres)*: where the contract is awarded to the best tender; *(c) Negotiated procedure (onderhandse opdrachten/gré à gré)*: where free negotiations are aimed at. The criteria which determine the lowest tender are specified in the Law of 14 July 1976 itself and in the Royal Decree of 22 April 1977.

The award to the best tender allows the awarding authority more freedom when deciding to whom the contract should be given. This tender procedure is based on the fact that the most advantageous bid can be selected and does not automatically lead to an award.[2]

Free negotiations are possible in a number of limited cases where the public authorities may freely engage in all negotiations which they deem useful and can award the contract to the contractor or supplier of their choice. Consequently, Article 17 of the Law of 14 July 1976 lists 15 circumstances in which contracts may be awarded on the basis of free negotiations.

Regulatory developments resulting from the EU Public Procurement Regime: the Law of 24 December 1993

As a consequence of the implementation of the various EC Directives governing the European Public Procurement Regime, Belgium implemented the public procurement law of 24 December 1993 regarding the award of public contracts and certain works, supplies, and services contracts (hereinafter referred to as 'the Law of 24 December 1993').[3] The Law of 24 December 1993 specifically stipulates in its Articles 68 and 69 that it will be implemented by way of Royal Decrees. Several Royal Decrees have already been published in the *Belgian Official Journal, Belgisch Staatsblad/Moniteur Belge* but some of them are still forthcoming. The Law of 24 December 1993 has only partly come into force.[4]

The aim of the Law of 24 December 1993 is to provide a coherent and transparent public procurement regime. It is meant to comply with the recent EU Directives regulating the European public procurement regime. In

---

[1] For a further explanation, see Van Bael & Bellis op cit, 551.
[2] Van Bael & Bellis, op cit, 554.
[3] *Belgian Official Journal*, 22 January 1994; title IV of Book I and Book II of the Law of 24 December 1993 have recently been respectively amended by a Royal Decree of 10 January 1996, *Belgian Official Journal*, 26 January 1996, p 1636; and a Royal Decree of 18 June 1996, *Belgian Official Journal*, 25 June 1996, p 17.476. These Royal Decrees enlarge the principles encompassed in title IV of Book I and Book II to services.
[4] The entry into force of Book I of the Law of 24 December 1993 and of its implementing Royal Decrees is expected by 1 January 1997. The date of entry into force will be determined in a Royal Decree which is due to be published in the beginning of October 1996. Book II of the Law of 24 December 1993, which deals with the utilities sector, is, however, already applicable.

particular the regulation of the utilities sector at EU level made the renewal of the Belgian regime necessary.[1]

The Law of 24 December 1993 consists of the following main parts:

Book I: public contracts;

Book II: the opening up to competition within the Community of certain works, supplies and services contracts in the water, energy, transport and telecommunications sector; and

Book III: final provisions.

The first part of Book I (Book I, Title II–III) covers the so-called 'classic' public contracts. The second part of Book I (Book I, Title IV) regulates public contracts awarded by public authorities or public undertakings operating in the utilities sector. As opposed to the aforementioned Title, Book II regulates public tenders issued by entities which operate in the utilities sector on the basis of special or exclusive rights granted by a competent authority of a Member State. The monetary value of these tenders has to be equal to or greater than the amounts determined by Royal Decree.

Scope – ratione personae

According to Article 4, para 1 of the Law of 24 December 1993, most of the provisions of the said law apply to the federal government, communities, regions, provinces and municipalities, and associations formed by one or more of the said entities. Furthermore, Article 4, para 2 lists ten categories of public entities to which the Law of 24 December 1993 equally applies.

Scope – ratione materiae

As mentioned before, the Law of 24 December 1993 has a wide range and covers public tenders related to works, supplies and services.

The award procedures, provided in the Law of 24 December 1993, are quite similar to those of the Law of 14 July 1976 but impose additional requirements of publicity, even when a restricted procedure is chosen.

REMEDIES ENSURING COMPLIANCE WITH THE EU PUBLIC PROCUREMENT REGIME

The enactment of Directives co-ordinating the procedures for the award of public contracts rapidly proved insufficient to provide the European Community with a market in which businesses could freely compete. In the absence of any concrete and effective relief, many awarding entities did not hesitate to act in defiance of the said Directives. To put an end to the abuses of the awarding authorities, the Council completed the legislative structure with the adoption of two Directives.

The first Directive is Council Directive 89/665/EEC of 21 December 1989 on the co-ordination of the laws, regulation and administrative provisions

---

[1]   D'Hooghe, D, 'De wet vasn 24 December 1993 betreffende de overheidsopdrachten', *R.W.* 1994–95, 689 et seq.

relating to the application of review procedures to the award of public supply and public works contracts (hereinafter referred to as 'the Remedies Directive'). The second Directive is Council Directive 92/13/EEC of 25 February 1992 co-ordinating the laws, regulations and administrative provisions relating to the application of Community rules on the procurement procedures of entities operating in the water, energy, transport and telecommunications sectors (hereinafter referred to as the 'Utilities Remedies Directive').

These Directives impose on the Member States an obligation to introduce a minimum set of relief procedures against the unlawful award of a public tender. The Remedies Directive does so for the public contracts including services contracts.[1] The Utilities Remedies Directive provides for remedies for the award of public tenders which are issued by certain entities operating in the water, energy, transport and telecommunications sector. This Directive contains some specific remedies which the Remedies Directive does not contain.

The Remedies Directive 89/665/EEC

Although the Remedies Directive had to be implemented in Belgian law by 21 December 1991, Belgium did not issue any specific regulation aiming at the implementation of the Remedies Directive. Indeed, the competent government officials were of the opinion that the existing legal procedures complied with the requirements imposed by the Remedies Directive and provided for specific provisions when required by Community law.[2]

In the following sections we will analyse the types of relief available under Belgian law. After a general introduction, we will describe the procedures before the Council of State, the civil courts and the European Commission respectively.

General introduction

Legal disputes with regard to public procurement matters can be brought either before the administrative or before the civil courts. The question of which court is competent to deal with a specific public procurement dispute must be solved on the basis of Articles 144 and 145 of the Constitution. According to Article 144 of the Constitution, disputes with regard to civil rights are exclusively within the jurisdiction of the civil courts. Article 145 of the Constitution provides that disputes with regard to political rights fall also within the jurisdiction of the civil courts, save for the exceptions established by law.

On the basis of these constitutional provisions, the Supreme Court has held that, when by law a party is awarded a subjective right, the disputes which can arise with regard to the recognition of such right do not fall within the jurisdiction of the administrative courts, except if expressly provided by law.[3] This means that the civil courts are competent to safeguard a subjective

---

[1] Article 41 of the Council Directive 92/50/EEC of 18 June 1992 relating to the Co-ordination of procedures for the award of public service contracts (*OJ* (1992), L 209/1) extends the scope of application of the Remedies Directive to service contracts.

[2] See eg Article 137 of the Royal Decree of 8 January 1996 which requires the co-operation of the Belgian awarding authorities with the European Commission in cases where the latter would make use of the corrective mechanism.

[3] Supreme Court, 27 November 1952, *Pas*, 1953, I, 189.

right, which can either be a civil or a political right, and the administrative courts are competent to safeguard an objective right. According to the Supreme Court a subjective right is a right which is conditioned by the existence of a precise legal obligation directly imposed upon third parties by a rule of objective law as well as of a personal interest on the part of the party which is claiming the performance of this obligation.[1] In order to assess whether a claim relates to the recognition of a subjective right, the courts will use as the criterion the 'true' subject of the claim. Nevertheless, as will be set forth below, often the same claim can be brought before both the administrative and the civil courts, depending on the manner in which it is formulated, namely as the pursuance of a subjective or an objective right.

According to the above principles a considerable number of disputes regarding public procurement will be dealt with by the civil courts, even if they very often relate to the conduct of public entities. Indeed, the relationships between public and private entities which arise in public procurement matters often create subjective rights. Moreover, a large part of these subjective rights which private parties can invoke against public entities are considered in Belgium as civil rights and are thus within the jurisdiction of the civil courts.

The administrative court which is competent to deal with public procurement matters is the Council of State. The Council of State has the power to suspend and/or annul a decision of public entities regarding public procurement.

The civil courts which are competent to deal with disputes regarding public procurement are either the Court of First Instance or the Commercial Courts. In view of the urgency of these matters, disputes concerning public procurement will often be brought before the President of either of these courts acting in summary proceedings.

Remedies before the Council of State

Annulment
Article 2, para 1(b) of the Remedies Directive provides that:

> 'Member States shall ensure that the measures taken concerning the review procedures ... include provision for the power to ... *either set aside or ensure the setting aside of decisions taken unlawfully*, including the removal of discriminatory technical, economic or financial specifications in the invitation to tender, the contract documents or in any other document relating to the contract award procedure' (emphasis added).

The annulment procedure before the Council of State[2] complies with this requirement. Indeed, the Council of State is competent to annul unilateral, discretionary acts of administrative public authorities which infringe an objective rule of law. The aggrieved party who seeks recourse to the Council of State has to show a personal, direct, actual and legitimate interest.

Recourse can be sought against enforceable unilateral administrative decisions of the appropriate authorities. This means that the aggrieved party can file a claim against any unilateral enforceable decision, as long as such decision has an effect on the final award decision. Unilateral decisions in the context of a public procurement procedure are mostly of a composite

---

[1]   Supreme Court, 10 March 1994, *TBH*, 1995, 15; *TRV*, 1995, 176.
[2]   Art 14 of the Co-ordinated Laws of the Council of State of 12 January 1973, *Belgian Official Journal*, 21 March 1973.

nature. This means that there is a string of successive administrative acts of which the last one is decisive and the previous ones have a preliminary character with regard to that last one.[1] Therefore, remedies are only available against preliminary decisions which had an influence on the final award decision provided these are the cause of any deficiency in that final award decision. A distinction should be made between such preliminary decisions which are subject to challenge, and purely preparatory measures, which are not legally binding and not subject to an action for annulment.[2]

In summary, the Council of State has competence over the award procedure, which includes the initial tender until the decision to award the contract itself, this being the final administrative act.[3] Examples of decisions which can be reviewed by the Council of State include but are not limited to: decisions affecting the choice of procedure (public, restricted or negotiated); decisions regarding the choice of candidates; in the event an award is not granted, decisions to recommence the procedure or to start a different one; and, finally, decisions in awarding the contract itself.[4] Once the public entity has chosen a candidate, the award decision will be notified. From the moment of notification, a contract is deemed to be concluded between the chosen contractor, supplier or service provider and the awarding authority.[5] As soon as the contract is concluded, the Council of State is no longer competent since it can only review unilateral administrative acts. Hence, the suspension or annulment of such a contract belongs to the exclusive jurisdiction of the civil courts.

The annulment by the Council of State has a retroactive effect but has no influence on the contract between the contracting authority and a contractor. However, as will be further explained below, the advantage of such an annulment decision is that it facilitates a settlement with the contracting authority or the filing of a claim for damages with the civil court.[6]

Interlocutory procedure
Article 2, para 1(a) of the Remedies Directive provides that the Member States should ensure the possibility of obtaining

> '...at the earliest opportunity and by way of interlocutory procedures, interim measures with the aim of correcting the alleged infringement or preventing further damage to the interests concerned, including measures to suspend or to ensure the suspension of the procedure for the award of a public contract or the implementation of any decision taken by the contracting authority...'.

The Belgian interlocutory procedure also complies with this requirement. Indeed, the Law of 19 July 1991[7] introduced the administrative interlocutory procedure. Accordingly, the Council of State can take all useful measures, by way of provisional, but immediate, decisions. This interlocutory procedure makes it possible to avoid the undesired consequences of seemingly unlawful public acts.

---

[1] Stevens, J, 'Rechtscontrole van de overheidsopdrachten', *TBP*, 1994, 303–321.
[2] Council of State, 25 June 1954, *Oliver*, no 3512.
[3] Council of State, 11 February 1964, *De Moor*, no 10.434.
[4] Mast, A. & Dujardin, J, *Overzicht van het Belgisch Administratief Recht*, Story-Scientia, Brussels, 1994, 165.
[5] Article 36 of the Royal Decree of 22 April 1977.
[6] Stevens, loc cit, 327.
[7] *Belgian Official Journal*, 12 October 1991.

Suspension   There are two types of suspension procedures before the Council of State: an ordinary suspension procedure and a provisional one which is only applicable in case of extreme urgent necessity.

The ordinary suspension procedure

Conditions   According to Article 17, para 2 of the Co-ordinated Laws of the Council of State,[1] only acts or decrees (in this case, public decisions taken in an award procedure) which qualify for annulment, can be suspended. According to that provision, a suspension of the execution of an award can only be granted if: (i) the grounds which are raised against that decision are serious; and (ii) if the immediate execution of the act or decree would cause a serious prejudice which is difficult to remedy.

A suspension is only possible if those two conditions are satisfied. In addition, the aggrieved party must file an application for annulment within 60 days from the notification of the contested decision. In the absence of such an application in due time, the suspension will be repealed by the President of the Chamber of the Council of State which granted the suspension.

The first condition for suspension relating to the seriousness of the grounds does not create great difficulties. When the grounds seem *prima facie* well-founded, they can be considered to be of a sufficiently serious nature.

In contrast, the second condition relating to the existence of a prejudice difficult to remedy has led to contradictory judgments. The problem lies in the divergent case law established by the Dutch- and French-language Chambers of the Council of State.

The French-language Chambers are rather reluctant to accept a prejudice which is difficult to remedy. They espouse the view that a refusal to award a public contract only constitutes a pecuniary loss which can be compensated by the award of damages and does not justify a suspension of administrative decisions.[2] Thus, the mere fact of not being granted the award is not sufficient. Consequently, in order to prove a serious prejudice which is difficult to remedy, special circumstances have to be adduced which cannot be compensated by damages. Although some circumstances have theoretically been accepted as sufficient to constitute such a prejudice (eg, the fact that an award refusal causes significant problems for the aggrieved party), no case has yet been reported where sufficient proof has actually been accepted.[3]

The Dutch-language Chambers seem to adopt a more realistic approach. They accept the existence of a prejudice which is difficult to remedy as soon as the aggrieved party could have reasonably expected to obtain the award. Therefore, grounds such as the financial importance of the market, the loss of references[4] and prestige on a national or international level are taken into account. Accordingly, the Dutch-language Chambers are ready to accept the existence of a serious prejudice difficult to remedy whenever an annulment without previous suspension cannot grant sufficient relief to the aggrieved party.

It would appear that the interpretation of the French-language Chambers is too strict and does not conform with Article 1, para 3 of the Remedies

---

[1]   *Belgian Official Journal*, 21 March 1973.
[2]   See Council of State, 27 October 1989, *UPEA*, no 33.304; Council of State, 16 November 1990, *PVBA Goffart Healthcrafts*, no 35.846.
[3]   Council of State, *SA Pagem*, no 38.383, 20 December 1991, *T Aann*, 1992, 234.
[4]   Council of State, 7 October 1993, *Van Hool*, no 44.399.

Directive. This provision in conjunction with Article 2, para 1(a), provides that the harm or likelihood of harm is sufficient to claim a suspension in an interlocutory procedure. Hence, the risk of definitely and irrevocably losing the opportunity to be awarded the contract should be sufficient to claim a prejudice that is difficult to remedy.

This is in conformity with the general theory of rehabilitation underlying Article 1382 of the Civil Code which provides that specific performance should have priority over other remedies. Regarding the award of public contracts, specific performance implies a new chance of obtaining the contract. However, at the time that an unlawfully rendered award decision is annulled, the contract has often already been concluded and performed and any chance of obtaining the contract is lost. In order to safeguard that chance, the suspension of the performance of the contract is necessary.

However, even if the two conditions set forth above are satisfied, the Council of State is not obliged to grant a suspension, since it enjoys a discretionary power in considering the public interest[1] and other relevant interests. This discretionary power seems also in line with Article 2, para 4 of the Remedies Directive, according to which

'...the body responsible may take into account the probable consequences of the measures for all interests likely to be harmed, as well as the public interest, and may decide not to grant such measures where their negative consequences could exceed their benefits.'

The influence of an underlying contract on the suspension   If the suspension of an award decision would be inadmissible each time the contract based on that decision has already been concluded, the suspension procedure would become meaningless. Indeed, public authorities usually notify the award decision immediately so that the underlying contract is automatically concluded. In initiating a suspension procedure, the aggrieved party hopes to obtain the contract after the suspension and the annulment has been granted. Therefore, the conclusion of the contract (through the notification of the award decision) should not preclude the suspension procedure from achieving its intended effect. This should certainly be the case when the performance of the contract has not yet taken place or when only minor works have been performed so far.[2] On the other hand, when the contract is (almost) completely performed, the effect of the suspension becomes meaningless. Specific performance is then no longer possible and only compensation by payment of damages can be obtained.

In summary, not every decision subject to annulment can be suspended and the impact of the suspension will depend on the stage of performance of the contract itself. However, the majority of legal authors are of the opinion that the existence of an underlying contract can no longer be an excuse to circumvent the rules applicable to public contracts.[3] Consequently, the existence of a contract cannot preclude the Council of State from suspending the award decision. However, we will see below that although the suspension of the unilateral administrative decisions (including an award decision of a public

---

[1]   Council of State, 2 April 1993, *Krier*, no 42.543.
[2]   Council of State, 13 October 1992, *Egta Contractors*, no 40.734.
[3]   Flamey, P, 'Hebben de beroepsprocedures inzake overheidsopdrachten nog zin', *TBP*, 1995, 240.

tender) is possible, the impact of a suspension on the contracts which are concluded on the basis of such decisions remains doubtful.

<u>The effects of a suspension</u>   Judgments suspending a public decision are binding upon the courts. This is important because the suspension of the award decision by the Council of State involves the suspension of the consent of one of the contracting parties, which is a validity requirement of the underlying contract. Since the contract is no longer valid, different effects may ensue depending on whether the issue is raised by the awarding public entity or by the aggrieved private entity. For its part, the public entity can, in order to limit the negative effects, refuse to continue to perform the contract, by claiming the nullity of the contract before the civil courts. In contrast, the aggrieved party can claim the suspension or nullity of the contract and argue that the resulting illegality infringes public policy (which is a prerequisite for a third party to ask the suspension or annulment of a contract concluded between two parties).[1] It is generally accepted that the principle of equality which must be observed when awarding public contracts concerns public policy.[2]

According to Article 17, para 4 of the Co-ordinated Laws of the Council of State, the Council of State should pass a judgment on the action for suspension within 45 days of the filing of the petition for suspension. If a suspension is granted, the Council of State should decide on the action for annulment within six months as from the judgment granting the suspension. During these six months, the suspended act cannot be executed. This implies that a suspended award decision which has not yet been notified, may or may not be notified. If a notification nonetheless takes place, the contract is not valid.

The provisional suspension procedure in case of extreme urgent necessity   The ordinary suspension procedure sometimes takes too long to be fully efficient and to avert a serious prejudice that is difficult to remedy. To overcome this problem, Article 17, para 1, section 3 of the Co-ordinated Laws of the Council of State provides for a provisional suspension procedure.

In addition to the two conditions of the ordinary suspension procedure, a third condition has to be fulfilled: the extreme urgent necessity. This can be regarded as a 'fast-track' suspension procedure allowing an aggrieved party to prevent the awarding authority from concluding the contract.

If a provisional suspension is granted by the President of the Chamber, it has to be confirmed within 45 days by the plenary Chamber, in which the President of the Chamber who granted the suspension does not take part.

Interim relief   According to Article 18 of the Co-ordinated Laws of the Council of State, the Council of State can order interim measures to safeguard the interests of the parties and anyone who has an interest in the case.

These interim measures can only be ordered when a suspension has been ordered simultaneously. However, contrary to the suspension procedure, interim measures can only be granted by unanimity of votes. Therefore, the Council of State seldom imposes interim measures. It should be noted that the interim measures rarely have an influence once the notification of the award decision has taken place. Indeed, the notification implies the conclusion

---

[1]   Council of State, 13 October 1992, *Egta Contractors*, no 40.734, *TBP*, 1993, 345.
[2]   Supreme Court, 19 November 1970, *T Aann*, 1971, 143, 150.

of the contract for which the Council of State has no competence. Accordingly, if the contract has already been concluded, the aggrieved party can only obtain relief with the Commercial Court or Court of First Instance. Those Courts have the exclusive competence to grant interim measures prohibiting the further execution of the contract.

This provision for interim measures is also in line with Article 2, para 1(a) of the Remedies Directive which provides that the Member States shall provide for:

'... interim measures with the aim of correcting the alleged infringement or preventing further damage to the interests concerned...'.

Penalty payment for delay in performance

Article 36, para 1 of the Co-ordinated Laws of the Council of State provides that the private party claiming the annulment can request that a penalty payment be imposed on the public entity for any delay in performance. This can only be done if the annulment decision obliges the public entity to issue a new public act or decision. In order to ensure the effectiveness of the review procedures before the Council of State, the imposition of such a penalty payment has become a necessity since more and more public entities do not comply with the judgments given by the Council of State.

According to the relevant case-law of the Council of State,[1] such a penalty payment is only possible when an award decision has not yet been notified or when the contract has been annulled or cancelled *ex nunc* by the civil courts. Only in such a case can an annulment decision oblige the public entity to render a new award decision.

Remedies before the civil courts

The action based on the torts liability of the public authority
Any third party who deems itself to be unlawfully rejected in an award procedure can claim damages based on the torts liability of the public entity, in accordance with Articles 1382 and 1383 of the Belgian Civil Code. Article 1382 imposes on every party causing damage to another party due to its own fault, the obligation to compensate such damage. Article 1383 of the Belgian Civil Code completes Article 1382 by providing that damage due to omission or negligence also engenders such liability.[2]

In order to obtain relief in public procurement procedures, an aggrieved tenderer must prove (i) the fault, negligence or omission of the public entity; (ii) the injury suffered and (iii) the causal link between the fault, negligence or omission and the injury.

Fault, negligence or omission The fault, negligence or omission of the public authority will most likely consist of the non-compliance with an order or prohibition, imposed by a legal or regulatory provision or by a general principle of law, such as the principle of equality.[3]

---

[1] Council of State, 29 June 1993, no 43.537; Council of State, 22 February 1994, no 46.174.
[2] Cornelis, L, *Beginselen van het Belgische buitencontractuele aansprakelijkheidsrecht*, Brussels, Maklu, 1989, 19.
[3] Stevens, J, loc cit, 303.

When no justification, such as an inevitable error, can be given or in case of a failure to observe a legal requirement which imposes a specific conduct or enunciates a prohibition, the illegality of the decision at issue will serve as conclusive evidence that the public entity made a mistake.[1]

Some public procurement rules require a specific conduct of the public entity such as for instance the prohibition to award a contract through the negotiated procedure, except in those cases expressly provided by law. Other rules leave more leeway to the public entities such as the determination of the most advantageous regular tender or the decision to terminate an award procedure. However, even in such cases where the public authority disposes of a large discretionary power, it has to comply with specific rules of proper administration.[2] For example, the authority must investigate the list of candidates in an objective, prompt and professional manner. Non-compliance with those rules will also be regarded as a fault, even if the public entity enjoys considerable freedom in taking its decision.[3]

Whether or not an annulment procedure was started before the Council of State against the illegal award decision does not influence the possibility for the civil courts to examine the torts liability of the public entity. However, a prior annulment procedure before the Council of State can bring about some advantages for an aggrieved tenderer. First of all, contrary to the procedure before the civil courts where parties have to adduce all relevant documents, a procedure before the Council of State is led by the judge himself. The inquisitorial character of the procedure before the Council of State reduces the burden of proof which rests on the aggrieved tenderer. Secondly, as supreme administrative court, the Council of State is generally regarded to be more competent in public matters. Finally, an annulment of the illegal public decision by the Council of State automatically shows the fault of the public entity and dispenses the plaintiff from adducing further evidence in a subsequent procedure before a civil court.[4] The judgments of the Council of State annulling a public decision can be invoked against any person and are binding upon the civil courts.

Conversely, the absence of a claim for annulment or a decision leading to the inadmissibility of the claim does not prevent the civil courts from examining the torts claim.[5] Even when a claim is found to be admissible but rejected on the merits, it is not binding upon the civil judge when assessing the liability of the public entity.[6]

Injury In public procurement procedures, a candidate does not have a subjective right to obtain the contract. Consequently, the injury cannot consist of the fact that the candidate would certainly have been awarded the contract, if the public entity had not taken the illegal public decision. However, the candidate is entitled to a fair treatment by the public authority based on the general principles of equality and competition. These principles are applicable in every award procedure. Accordingly, the candidate has the right

---

[1]   Gerard, Ph, 'La responsabilité des pouvoirs publics en matières de travaux publics: de l'Etat à la Région', Recyclages Facultés Universitaires Saint-Louis, 1989, 23.
[2]   Gerard, Ph, loc cit, 28.
[3]   D'Hooge, D, loc cit, 655.
[4]   Liège, 12 October 1989, *T Aann*, 1990, 319; Liège, 16 January 1986, *Ann Dr Liège*, 1986, 240, with observations by Lewalle, P.
[5]   Liège, 16 January 1986, *Ann Dr Liège*, 1986, 247, with observations by Lewalle, P.
[6]   D'Hooghe, D, *De gunning van overheidscontracten en overheidsopdrachten en het toezicht door de Raad van State en de gewone rechtsbanken*, Die Keure, 1993, 658.

not to be rejected in a discriminatory or any other unlawful manner. If the public entity commits an illegal and wrongful act, the chance of being awarded the contract can be lost. In such a case, the loss of a chance to obtain a certain advantage constitutes the injury and is a sufficient ground to claim damages.[1]

Causal link   The candidate who was not granted the contract owing to a fault of the public entity has to prove that, if the fault had not been committed, he would at least have had a chance to be appointed as contractor. A causal link between the fault of the public body and the damage suffered must thus be shown. This can be shown easily in cases where the candidate-contractor was the only legitimate subscriber and the public authority did not have an obvious ground to cancel the actual procurement procedure. In such a case, the aggrieved candidate can easily prove the loss of a contractual advantage and consequently claim damages.[2] However, it is clear that, where the public authority has only disregarded formal requirements, such as the requirement to give reasons, and did not treat any candidate on a preferential basis, the loss of an actual chance will be more difficult to prove and damages harder to obtain.

The award of damages   Although specific performance is preferred when seeking relief, it is hard to obtain this kind of relief in public procurement procedures. Specific performance aims at restoring the situation in such a manner as if the illegal act had not occurred. Accordingly, this would imply a second chance for the aggrieved candidate to be granted the contract in a new award procedure. However, such a result can only be obtained through an annulment decision by the Council of State. Indeed, the civil courts lack the competence to create a situation that is similar to the one created by an annulment decision of the Council of State.[3] A specific performance can thus not be ordered by a civil court. Nor can it be ordered in a case where the illegal award decision has already been notified and a contract has been concluded. Indeed, specific performance would require that the contract itself be annulled. However, the aggrieved candidate can claim damages which should compensate as adequately as possible the damage suffered by the candidate.

The allocation procedure   With respect to an irregular award of a public contract by allocation, Article 12 of the Law of 14 July 1976 expressly provides that, if the contracting entity does not award the contract to the candidate which submitted the lowest tender, it must pay an indemnity amounting to ten per cent of the value of that tender, net of VAT. The public entity is, however, not strictly bound by the lowest regular tender. The lowest regular tender may be disregarded on the basis of a reasoned decision by the Prime Minister (in the case of contracts awarded by the State or a legal entity governed by public law falling under the authority of a Minister), the competent Minister

---

[1]   Ronse, J, *Schade en schadeloosstelling*, Story-Scientia, Gent, 1984, 83; see also, Brussels, 12 November 1985, *Limb Rl*, 1985, 36.

[2]   See Luik, 2 March 1989, *T Aann*, 1991, 119. See also Court of First Instance Luik, 27 February 1987, *T Aann* 1991, 330; Brussels, 8 January 1974, *T Aann*, 1974, 92, with observations by Flamme, MA. Compare Court of First Instance Brussels, 28 June 1977, *T Aann*, 1978, 113; Court of First Instance Brussels, 15 November 1971, *T Aann*, 1972, 252, with observations by Massard, M.

[3]   See the opinion of the Advocate-General Ganshof van der Meersch under Supreme Court, 16 December 1965, *JT*, 1966, 313.

(in the case of contracts awarded by other legal entities governed by public law which are supervised by the Minister concerned) or the Governor of the Province (in the case of contracts awarded by provinces, municipalities and authorities dependent upon the provinces or municipalities) (Art 12(1) of the Law of 14 July 1976). The Council of State has adopted a restrictive view regarding the reasons which may be relied upon in this context. The reasons invoked must relate to such matters as the expertise and trustworthiness of the bidders or the quality of the materials used.[1]

The public entity awarding the contract may also disregard the lowest tender, if it adopts a reasoned decision to that effect and if the difference between the tender preferred by the public entity and the lowest regular tender does not exceed a specific percentage of the latter and remains below a specific amount. Both the percentage and the amount are specified in a Royal Decree. The percentage is currently fixed at ten per cent and the difference between the lowest tender and the preferred tender amounts to a maximum of 250,000 BF (Art 34(4) of the Royal Decree of 22 April 1977).

In allocation procedures, obtaining the ten per cent damages will be quite easy. Since the public entity awarding the contract has little or no discretionary power, the candidate offering the lowest tender will only have to prove that his tender is indeed the lowest. A previous annulment of the award decision by the Council of State will facilitate such proof.

The invitation to tender and negotiated procedures In contrast with the allocation procedure, the invitation to tender and the negotiated procedures do not provide for specific legal provisions concerning the amount of damages to be awarded. In the invitation to tender procedures, the public entity may select the most advantageous regular bidder. In the limited number of cases where contracts are awarded through negotiation, the public entity can award the contract to the contractor or supplier of its choice. In both procedures, the public entity has a considerably wider discretion than in an allocation procedure. It is therefore hard to prove that a public entity committed a fault in selecting a candidate. When the fault of the public entity is not clearly established, many aggrieved parties prefer to launch proceedings with the Council of State. As mentioned above, an annulment of the award decision by the Council of State conclusively shows the illegality of the decision and hence the fault of the public entity. Furthermore, the annulment decision is also binding on the civil courts.

However, due to the discretionary power of the public entities in these procedures, the Council of State annuls the award which selected a specific candidate but cannot issue an award decision on behalf of the public entity. Hence, the fact that the Council of State has annulled the award decision in favour of a certain candidate does not necessarily imply that the award should have been granted in favour of the candidate claiming the annulment. If the aggrieved party cannot prove that it should have been granted the award, damages will be difficult to obtain. Accordingly, the amount of damages to be paid under these procedures is fixed by the civil courts in a discretionary way. The economic value of the contract, including the expected profits, often serves as the basis for assessing such damages.[2]

In cases where no certainty exists as to whether the contract would have

[1] Council of State, 19 February 1991, no 36463, not yet reported.
[2] See Court of First Instance Brussels, 9 November 1971, *JT*, 1971, 192, with observations by Flamme, MA.

been granted to the aggrieved candidate by means of an invitation to tender or negotiated procedure, the civil court should make an estimation of the damages to be awarded in function of the actual chance of being granted the contract.[1] Consequently, the damages should be of such an amount as to cover the extent of this lost chance.[2] Moreover, the judge should also take into account the expenses incurred by a candidate, such as administrative and research expenses.[3] However, in cases where the tender could only have been awarded to the rejected candidate, the civil courts tend to apply the ten per cent rule.[4]

Compliance with the Remedies Directive   The Belgian regulatory and judicial framework with respect to the award of damages, as described above, can thus be considered to comply with Article 2, para 1(c) of the Remedies Directive which provides that:

'Member States shall ensure that the measures taken ... include provision for the powers to ... award damages to persons harmed by an infringement.'

Interim measures

Infringement of subjective rights of the aggrieved party determines the competence of the civil courts   Since disputes in public procurement matters often require a swift solution, the aggrieved party will in the majority of cases try to obtain interim relief. As indicated above, a party can file a petition with the Council of State in order to suspend the award decision. If a subjective right is infringed or if the underlying contract is concluded, that party may also try to obtain interim measures from the President of the Court acting in summary proceedings.

Article 584 of the Judicial Code provides that the President of the Court of First Instance or, in matters which relate to the specific competence of the Commercial Court, the President of the Commercial Court, has the power to impose interim measures in cases which he deems urgent. The law does not provide for a definition of the notion 'urgency'. According to the Supreme Court, a case is urgent when an immediate decision is desirable to avoid considerable damage or serious harm or when the ordinary judicial procedure is not able to solve the dispute in a timely fashion.[5]

Furthermore, Article 1039 of the Judicial Code stipulates that '*judgments in summary proceedings do not prejudice the case itself ...*'. This principle is linked to the fact that judgments in summary proceedings are provisionally enforceable (Article 584, section 2 and Article 1039 of the Judicial Code). The Supreme Court has confirmed that it is prohibited for the judge in summary proceedings to anticipate the decision in a definite and irrevocable manner with regard to the rights of the parties.[6] This implies that the relief ordered in summary proceedings cannot bind the court which will hear the case on the merits.

---

[1]   Devroey, M, 'De problemen van de procedure van offerte-aanvraag', *T Aann*, 1982, 304, 315.
[2]   Gerard, Ph, loc cit, 54.
[3]   Stevens, J, loc cit, 313.
[4]   See Court of Appeals Brussels, 26 June 1992, *T Aann*, 1993, 203.
[5]   Supreme Court, 21 May 1987, *Arr Cass* 1986–1987, 1287; *Pas*, I, 1987, 1160.
[6]   Supreme Court, 9 September 1985, *Arr Cass*, 1982–1983, p 51; Supreme Court, 14 June 1991, *TBH*, 1992, 261.

With regard to disputes in public procurement matters, it is important to note that the President acting in summary proceedings has the power to decide upon an infringement of a subjective right, even if such an infringement was committed by a public entity. Since the Supreme Court has held that the President acting in summary proceedings may assess the apparent rights of the parties,[1] the President is consequently allowed to review the alleged illegality of a decision of a public entity. Although it is the rule that such review in summary proceedings may only be a prima facie review, it appears that in public matters this review is rather thorough since possible interim measures can have serious consequences.

The variety of forms of relief which the President may grant by way of interim measures in public procurement matters is wide. Examples of interim measures which have been ordered in public procurement matters are the following: a prohibition to perform an agreement until the Council of State decides on the annulment of the award decision, a suspension of the provision of the specifications to the selected undertakers, a suspension to execute the award decision given after a public tender, a prohibition to commence the works or an order to stop them if they have already been started, etc.

The Council of State has the exclusive power to suspend an act or decree susceptible for annulment and to order interim measures, with the exception of those which relate to subjective rights. In contrast, the President of the Court acting in summary proceedings is competent to order interim measures to terminate an apparent infringement of subjective rights. Thus, as indicated above, the question of which court is competent will be determined on the basis of the nature of the right which is invoked by the aggrieved party. This implies that a decision can be challenged before the Council of State or the President of the Court acting in summary proceedings depending on the manner in which the claim is presented. However, this choice is limited by the fact that the President of the Court acting in summary proceedings can by no means suspend an administrative act.

Complementary nature of the interim measures issued by the Council of State   It should be pointed out that it is not only the kind of relief that can be obtained from the President acting in summary proceedings which differs from that which can be obtained from the Council of State. Also the injury that has to be shown is different. While in a suspension proceeding before the Council of State the aggrieved party must prove a serious prejudice which is difficult to remedy, in summary proceedings it is sufficient to demonstrate harm or a risk of being harmed with regard to a subjective right. This corresponds to the condition laid down in the Remedies Directive.

From a practical point of view the aggrieved party must be aware that the interim measures that can be requested either from the Council of State or from the President of the Court acting in summary proceedings are of a different nature and in some cases may be complementary.

For instance, if the agreement has already entered into force or if the works have already been started or are about to start, an aggrieved party can simultaneously or successively file a petition for suspension of the award decision with the Council of State and, if a subjective right has also been infringed, launch an action with the President of the Court acting in summary

---

[1]   Supreme Court, 29 September 1983, *Arr Cass*, 1983–84, 85, *RW*, 1984–85, 751, *Pas*, 1984, I, 84; Supreme Court, 21 March 1985; *Arr Cas*, 1984–85, 1008, *RW*, 1986–87, 89, *Pas* 1985, I, 908, *JT*, 1985, 697.

proceedings in order to obtain a court order prohibiting the works to be started or to be continued.

Thus, in view of the fact that the Council of State can only suspend the award decision, it may be necessary, in anticipation of the decision of the Council of State on the annulment of the award decision, to obtain simultaneously safeguarding measures from the President of the Court acting in summary proceedings. However, it appears that this complementary functioning of the Council of State and the President of the Court acting in summary proceedings which offers the tenderers a reasonable legal protection would be in jeopardy if the Belgian judges in summary proceedings were to continue, as they have done in the past, to refuse interim measures on the basis that the aggrieved party lacks the required interest because the Law of 14 July 1976 provides for compensation by way of payment of damages and not for any kind of specific performance. If this trend continues, it would appear that the legal protection afforded by Belgian public procurement law does not satisfy the requirement of Article 2, para 7 of the Remedies Directive and Article 2, para 8 of the Utilities Remedies Directive which require an 'effective enforcement' of the decisions taken by review bodies. The question remains whether the more recent case law which accepts that an aggrieved party can obtain specific performance but that for this purpose a balancing of interests must be made, will provide effective legal protection to the aggrieved party since it appears that the balancing of interests[1] mainly benefits the contracting entity.

Action for annulment of the contract
Belgian case law and legal literature have traditionally been reluctant to annul, at the request of a prejudiced third party, a contract infringing public procurement rules. An agreement was considered to be a matter of the parties and of the parties only. However, the legal literature as well as the courts seem to be changing their point of view on this matter.[2]

According to Belgian contract law, a third party can bring an action for annulment of a contract whenever this contract is in breach of rules of public policy. The key principles of equality, competition and equal access to public contracts that must be observed in public procurement procedures are generally accepted as belonging to public policy. Accordingly, any prejudiced third party should be able to question a violation of those principles. This was also recognised by the Council of State in its *CCN case* which will be discussed in more detail below.[3] However, a flaw in the consent of one of the parties to a public contract is considered to affect only that party's private interests and does not fall within the scope of public policy. Consequently, only the public entity itself and the chosen contractor or supplier could question an alleged lack of consent and accordingly claim the annulment of the contract.

However, the legal authors do not seem to agree on whether the suspension or annulment of an award decision of a public entity by the Council of State affects the consent given by that public entity. Some believe that an annulment of an award decision by the Council of State causes the consent, which is a necessary prerequisite to conclude a valid contract, to disappear.[4] This point

1   Brussels, 22 April 1993, *T Aann*, 1993, 239. See also, Liège, 7 October 1996, not yet reported.
2   See Flamey, P, loc cit, 239.
3   Council of State, *EGTA Contractors*, no 40.734, 13 October 1992, *TBP*, 1993, 345.
4   Pro: Stevens, J, loc cit, 317; Flamey, P, loc cit, 238; Remion, FM, 'Le Conseil d'Etat et les marchés de l'administration', *Ann Dr Liège*, 1960, 427–460.

of view is also found in the case law.[1] Even the Council of State shared this opinion in the *CCN* case in which it stated that

> '...the suspension of the consent of one contracting party, being a validity requirement of the contract, can incite the public authority not to perform the contract – in order to limit its own injury – and to claim the annulment of the contract before the civil judge'[2] (translated).

Some authors are even of the opinion that the President of the Court acting in summary proceedings can prohibit the continuation of the works on the basis of an annulment decision. They also share the opinion that the President of the Court acting in summary proceedings can oblige the public authority to claim the annulment of the contract before the civil courts, under forfeiture of a penalty payment in case of non-compliance.

Irrespective of the fact that legal literature and case law gradually acknowledge the possibility of annulling an existing contract at the request of a third party,[3] some authors, however, still defend the theory of the immunity of concluded contracts.[4] This was also the view of the Court of Appeals of Liège, which in a recent case decided in the *Van Hool* case that for the sake of legal certainty a contract should not be annulled, especially when damages can constitute an adequate relief.[5] The French-language Chambers of the Council of State seem to share that opinion. However, as suggested above, this case law may run counter to Community Law. Even the Court of Justice observed in the *Van Hool* case that according to the latest case law development, Belgian law did not preclude the annulment of a concluded contract.[6] Moreover, this case law development does not seem to be a deliberate choice of the Belgian legislator. Although Article 2, para 6 of the Remedies Directive and the Utilities Remedies Directive allow the Member States to restrict the consequences of unlawfully concluded contracts to damages only, Belgium has not taken up this possibility. Consequently, the theory of the immunity of contracts seems difficult to defend.

The acceptance of the immunity of contracts would involve the total undermining of the annulment and suspension powers of the Council of State and would reduce its decisions to a mere basis for subsequent damages claims. Accordingly, the interlocutory administrative procedure could only have an effect in the limited circumstances where an award decision has not yet been notified and a contract has not yet been concluded. This would mean that the remedy provisions in public procurement procedures, as required by the Remedies Directive and the Utilities Remedies Directive, would become totally inefficient, since the public entity could circumvent them by immediately notifying the award.

---

[1]   Namur, 27 April 1992, *JT*, p 497.

[2]   Council of State, 13 October 1992, *EGTA Contractors*, no 40.734, 13 October 1992, *T Aann*, 366.

[3]   See Council of State, 16 October 1990, *Van Goethem*, no 35.657, *RW*, 1990–1991, 813, Council of State, 28 June 1991, *Aralco*, no 37.387, *T Aann*, 1992, 30, Council of State, 1 October 1991, *AEG*, no 37.788, *T Aann*, 1992, 236, Council of State, 13 October 1992, no 40.734, *T Aann*, 1992, 366.

[4]   Flamme, MA, 'Le contentieux des commandes publiques et le sort des contrats irrégulièrement conclus. Comment concilier la competénce des juges nationaux et le contrôle des organes communautaires', comments on Court of First Instance Namem, 28 August 1994, *JT*, 1994, 694.

[5]   Liège, 7 October 1996, not yet reported.

[6]   Case C-87/94R: *Commission v Belgium* [1994] ECR I-1395, para 35.

Co-operation with the European Commission

Although the Belgian government is of the opinion that the current rules satisfy the requirement of the Remedies Directive, it proved nonetheless necessary to provide for specific provisions ensuring compliance with specific aspects of that Directive. This has been done in the Royal Decree of 8 January 1996 on the award of public works, supplies and services contracts and the concession of public contracts[1] (hereinafter referred to as the 'Royal Decree of 8 January 1996') which implements Titles II and III of Book I of the Law of 24 December 1993. According to Article 3 of the Remedies Directive, the European Commission may request information concerning public tenders from the Member States if it considers that a clear and manifest infringement of Community provisions in the field of procurement has been committed. The Royal Decree of 8 January 1996 provides in its Articles 137 to 139 for a mandatory co-operation of the Belgian administrative authorities with the European Commission in the event the European Commission calls for the corrective mechanism.[2] Generally speaking, the awarding entity has the obligation to co-operate with the national authorities which are competent to submit the documents and information requested by the European Commission. The awarding entity has among other matters, the obligation to provide the Prime Minister with all information and all documents deemed necessary to ensure an appropriate response if the European Commission so requests. This obligation has to be fulfilled within ten days after the receipt of the official notification by the Commission.

Article 138 ensures that the Prime Minister or the Minister for Economic Affairs can be informed about all the developments relating to the award of a public contract. The submission referred to in this provision will have to be accomplished in accordance with the rules which will be set out by the aforementioned authorities.

Similar provisions are provided for in the Royal Decree of 10 January 1996 relating to the public procurement of works, supplies and services contracts for entities operating in the water, energy, transport and telecommunication sectors which implements Title IV of Book I of the Law of 24 December 1993.[3]

The Utilities Remedies Directive 92/13/EEC

Council Directive 92/13/EEC of 25 February 1992 co-ordinating the laws, regulations and administrative provisions relating to the application of Community rules on the procurement procedures of entities operating in the water, energy, transport and telecommunications sectors[4] (hereinafter referred to as the 'Utilities Remedies Directive') regulates public tenders which are issued both by (i) public authorities or public undertakings operating in the utility sector and by (ii) entities which operate on the basis of special or exclusive rights granted by a competent authority of a Member State.[5] The

---

[1] *Belgian Official Journal*, 26 January 1996, p 1730.
[2] For a description of the corrective mechanism, see eg Trepte, PA, *Public Procurement in the EC*, CCH Europe, Oxfordshire, 1993, 230–231.
[3] *Belgian Official Journal*, 26 January 1996, 1686 et seq.
[4] *OJ*, (1992), L 767/14.
[5] Article 1, para 1(a) of the Utilities Remedies Directive Article 2, para 1(a) and (b) of the Council Directive 90/531/EEC (*OJ* (1990), L 297/1) and Article 2, para 1(a) and (b) of the Council Directive 93/38/EEC (*OJ*, (1993), L 199/84).

Law of 24 December 1993 makes a clear distinction between the tenders issued by these two types of contracting entities and provides for an individual set of rules for each of them.

Public tenders which relate to the utility sector and are issued by public entities or public undertakings are regulated by Title IV of Book I of the Law of 24 December 1993.[1] This Title has been implemented by the Royal Decree of 10 January 1996 relating to the public procurement of works, supplies and services in the water, energy, transport and telecommunications sectors[2] (hereinafter referred to as the 'Royal Decree of 10 January 1996'). However, neither Book I of the Law of 24 December 1993 nor the Royal Decree of 10 January 1996 have yet come into force.[3]

Public tenders in the utility sector issued by entities which operate on the basis of special or exclusive rights granted by a competent authority of a Member State are regulated by Book II of the Law of 24 December 1993.[4] This Title has been implemented by the Royal Decree of 18 June 1996 relating to the opening of certain works, supplies and services contracts to the competition in the framework of the European Community in the water, energy, transport and telecommunications sectors[5] (hereinafter referred to as the 'Royal Decree of 18 June 1996'). In contrast with the other parts of the Law of 24 December 1993, Book II of the Law of 24 December 1993 has already come into force.[6]

It should be noted from the outset that the Law of 24 December 1993 is silent about any remedy available for a party having an interest in obtaining a particular contract. The pertinent remedies will be found in the two aforementioned Royal Decrees and in the general principles of Belgian contract and tort law.

Relation between the Utilities Remedies Directive and the Remedies Directive

The Utilities Remedies Directive is very similar to the Remedies Directive. Indeed, both provide for a general framework of remedies which the Member States are required to provide to parties that have suffered injury or risk suffering such injury.

---

[1]   This Title of the Law of 24 December 1993 has recently been amended by a Royal Decree of 10 January 1996, *Belgian Official Journal*, 26 January 1996, 1636. This Royal Decree, which enlarges the principles encompassed in Title IV of Book I to services, is different from a second Royal Decree of the same date implementing Title IV of Book I of the Law of 24 December 1993.

[2]   *Belgian Official Journal*, 26 January 1996, 1686.

[3]   The entry into force of Title IV of Book I of the Public Procurement Act of 1993 and of the Royal Decree of 10 January 1996 is expected by 1 January 1997. The date of entry into force will be determined in another Royal Decree which is due to be published towards the end of 1996.

[4]   This Title of the Public Procurement Act of 1993 has recently been amended by a Royal Decree of 18 June 1996, published in the *Belgian Official Journal*, 25 June 1996, 17.476. This Royal Decree, which enlarges the principles encompassed in Book II to services, is different from a second Royal Decree of the same date implementing Book II of the Law of 24 October 1993.

[5]   *Belgian Official Journal*, 25 June 1996, 17.478: this Royal Decree repealed the Royal Decree of 26 July 1994 on the same subject-matter.

[6]   The Royal Decree of 26 July 1994 relating to the opening of certain works and supply contracts to the competition in the framework of the European Community in the water, energy, transport and telecommunications sectors stated that Book II and the Royal Decree itself entered into force on 1 September 1994.

However, unlike the Remedies Directive, the Utilities Remedies Directive also contains some specific procedures which can be regarded as alternative dispute resolutions. These procedures ensure a stricter compliance with the EU public procurement regime.

In the following sections, we will first briefly describe how the Utilities Remedies Directive organised a general framework of remedies before the national jurisdictions; thereafter, we will analyse how the Belgian legislator has implemented the Utilities Remedies Directive.

Remedies before the national jurisdictions

The Utilities Remedies Directive
Unlike the Remedies Directive, the Utilities Remedies Directive enables the Member States to establish effective relief before national jurisdictions in two different ways (Article 2):

- either by offering parties that are harmed or risk being harmed the possibility to combine interim measures with the possibility of setting aside unlawful decisions;
- in providing parties that are harmed or risk being harmed with procedures on the merits offering them measures other than those mentioned above. In particular, this will include the power to issue an order for payment of a particular sum, in cases where the infringement has not been corrected or prevented.

In both cases the Member States have to award damages to the persons injured by an infringement.

Implementation under Belgian law
In the absence of specific rules implementing this aspect of the Utilities Remedies Directive, it can be assumed that Belgium has combined the two options. Indeed, as is the case for the implementation of the Remedies Directive, all the remedies available under general principles of Belgian law are available to persons seeking relief against a contracting entity. Therefore, the possibility of (i) obtaining interim measures, (ii) decisions being set aside, (iii) obtaining penalty payments and (iv) obtaining damages also exists in the utility sector.

Competence of the courts for the tenders issued by entities enjoying special or exclusive rights pursuant to Article 47 of the Law of 24 December 1993
Article 1, para 3 of the Utilities Remedies Directive states that the Member States shall ensure that review procedures are available, 'under detailed rules' which the Member States may establish.

However, in many cases where the contracting entity enjoys special or exclusive rights pursuant to Article 47 of the Public Procurement Act of 1993, it is not clear which court is competent to hear a specific case. As mentioned above, according to Article 14 of the Co-ordinated Laws on the Council of State, the Council of State is competent for annulment procedures of specific acts of the administrative authorities. However, neither the legal authors nor case law offer clear guidance to determine which entity should be considered as an administrative authority.

Indeed, especially in the utilities sector, the Belgian State has in the last decades sought the collaboration of the private sector to accomplish the tasks which were traditionally entrusted to it. For this purpose, a lot of entities have been created in which public entities have equity participations, veto rights, blocking minority rights, etc. The question as to whether such entities are administrative authorities often has to be assessed on a case-by-case basis. This legal uncertainty may cause both the Council of State and the civil courts to declare themselves incompetent and leave the harmed persons without any remedy. Several legal authors have therefore called for a clearer definition of what is to be understood by the notion of administrative authorities.[1]

In order to clarify this matter, some initiatives to amend the Belgian Judicial Code have already been taken, yet without any concrete outcome. This possibility is still under discussion.[2]

Remedies outside the national jurisdictions

The specific procedures included in the Utilities Remedies Directive are the attestation system and the conciliation procedure. Furthermore, the Utilities Remedies Directive also provides for a corrective mechanism in which the European Commission plays a major role. The implementation of all these measures in Belgian law will be discussed in detail in the following sections. The corrective mechanism under the Utilities Remedies Directive will be discussed briefly since it has already been outlined under the implementation of the Remedies Directive.

The attestation system

Articles 113 to 116 of the Royal Decree of 10 January 1996 seek to implement the attestation system into Belgian law for public tenders issued by public entities or public undertakings operating in the utility sector. The same is done by Articles 23 to 26 of the Royal Decree of 18 June 1996 for the tenders issued by entities enjoying special or exclusive rights pursuant to Article 47 of the Law of 24 December 1993. In fact these provisions constitute a nearly literal transcription of the relevant provisions of the Utilities Remedies Directive.[3] In doing so, the Royal Decree of 10 January 1996 and the Royal Decree of 18 June 1996 failed to implement the Utilities Remedies Directive correctly. Indeed, in neglecting to determine concrete conditions which the attestors have to fulfil, the Belgian regulatory framework makes it impossible for the attestation system to be operative. The applicability of the attestation system will therefore be dependent upon Ministerial Decrees which can be enacted respectively pursuant to Article 125 of the Royal Decree of 10 January 1996 and Article 36 of the Royal Decree of 18 June 1996. However, such Ministerial Decrees are not yet envisaged by the competent authorities. It may therefore be feared that the attestation system will, at least in the near future, remain a dead letter under Belgian law. In the light of the above it may be feared that Belgium will be considered to have failed to implement the attestation system.[4]

---

[1] See, for example, Stevens, J, *loc cit*, 305.
[2] See eg, Articles 30 and 31 of the Draft Royal Decree which became the Royal Decree of 26 July 1994 (in the meantime repealed), which implemented Book II of the Law of 24 December 1993.
[3] Articles 3 to 7 of the Utilities Remedies Directive.
[4] This was also the opinion of the Council of State which gave an advice on the draft of the Royal Decree which became the Royal Decree of 26 July 1994 (in the meantime repealed), implementing Book II of the Law of 24 December 1993 (Opinion of 19 May 1994, L 23.200, P 31).

The conciliation procedure

Here again, the conciliation procedure provided for in the Royal Decree of 10 January 1996[1] and in the Royal Decree of 18 June 1996[2] is almost a true transcription of the relevant provisions of the Utilities Remedies Directive.[3] However, the situation is completely different from that existing under the attestation system. In this case, the European Commission has a leading role. The fact that the Royal Decree only copied the Utilities Remedies Directive does not imply negative consequences associated with the attestation system since this does not prevent the conciliation procedure from being operative.

However, the question still arises whether the conciliation procedure will be effective. Since the conciliation procedure is not compulsory, it may be feared that the contracting entities will be reluctant to co-operate in such a procedure. Indeed, many contracting entities could fear that in participating in a conciliation procedure they act in defiance of Article 1676 of the Belgian Judicial Code which prohibits public entities to conclude arbitration agreements. Yet, the conciliation procedure seems to differ on essential points from an ordinary arbitration procedure. The Royal Decrees and the Utilities Remedies Directive clearly specify that the legal actions taken pursuant to the conciliation procedure shall be without prejudice to the rights of the person requesting the conciliation procedure, of the contracting entity or of any other person. As the outcome of this procedure is not legally binding upon the parties participating in the procedure, the process seems to be clearly distinguishable from an arbitration procedure. Moreover, even if this procedure had to be considered as a form of arbitration, Article 1676 of the Belgian Judicial Code should arguably be disregarded as it conflicts with provisions of EU law.[4] Finally, it could be argued that a more recent and specific law overrules the preceding and general law.

In assessing whether to participate in a conciliation procedure, the parties concerned will have to consider if the participation in such a procedure is less cumbersome than filing a claim under the corrective mechanism or starting a procedure for failure to act in accordance with Articles 169 and 170 of the EC Treaty.

The corrective mechanism

When prior to a contract being concluded the European Commission considers that a clear and manifest infringement of the Community provisions in the field of procurement has been committed, it may start the corrective mechanism which is provided for in Article 8 of the Utilities Remedies Directive. This procedure is similar to that provided by Article 169 of the EC Treaty.

Article 117 of the Royal Decree of 10 January 1996 and Article 27 of the Royal Decree of 18 June 1996 implement the corrective mechanism into Belgian law for public tenders in the utility sector.

Like the Royal Decrees implementing the Remedies Directive, these two Royal Decrees only state that the contracting entities are obliged to co-operate with the authorities responsible for communicating a reply to the Commission.

---

[1] Articles 118 to 121 of the Royal Decree of 10 January 1996.
[2] Articles 28 to 30 of the Royal Decree of 18 June 1996.
[3] Articles 9 to 11 of the Utilities Remedies Directive.
[4] See Case 6/64: *Costa v ENEL* [1964] ECR 585 and Case 106/77: *Simmenthal* [1978] ECR 629.

PRACTICAL APPLICATION OF REMEDIES: THE *CCN* CASE AND THE *VAN HOOL* CASE

At the outset we have emphasised that Belgium considers its current rules governing the remedies available in public procurement matters to be in conformity with the EU public procurement regime which is currently in force.

Does this mean, however, that when purporting to satisfy European demands at the regulatory level, Belgium has actually put in place an adequate system of enforcement? As was already stated in the introduction, two recent Belgian cases concerning the enforcement of the public procurement regime seem to indicate that the Belgian system lacks the required cohesion to ensure an appropriate means of redress for the aggrieved contractor.

The *Centre de Communication Nord/Communicatiecentrum Noord ('CCN')* case

The tender in this case related to the construction of a building of 32,000m^2 and of additional parking places for 500 cars. The Brussels Capital Region (hereinafter the 'Region'), the awarding entity, granted the tender unlawfully to a contractor called Sofibru. EGTA, the contractor to whom the tender should have been granted, initiated proceedings with the Council of State after the notification of the decision to the contractor. As indicated before, this notification constitutes under Belgian law the conclusion of the contract between the awarding entity and the contractor.

The fundamental question in this case was whether the Council of State could set aside or suspend the decision of the awarding entity while contractual relations between the awarding entity and the contractor concerning the execution of the contract were already concluded. It should be repeated that the jurisdiction of the Council of State does not extend to the suspension or setting aside of contractual relations between private parties and the administrative authorities. The Council of State held that it had the potential to suspend or set aside the award decision and therefore suspended the award decision of the Region.[1]

Since the decision of the Council of State had no direct practical influence on the contract being implemented between Sofibru and the Region, EGTA brought an action before a civil court in order to obtain interim measures causing the works to cease. The Region and Sofibru argued that the contract concluded between them could not be challenged by EGTA since EGTA was only a third party and had therefore no locus standi. However, the Brussels Court of Appeal ruled that the principle of res inter alios acta could in the present situation not be invoked against EGTA.[2] Indeed, the Court was of the opinion that since the Council of State had suspended the award decision, the award decision was apparently tainted with an absolute nullity on which every interested third party could rely. However, as the Council of State had not yet set aside the award decision, the Court of Appeal declared that it was unable to set aside the contract between Sofibru and the Region. It therefore commissioned an expert to assess to what extent the works could be safely suspended. Surprisingly enough, following the review of the works by an expert, the Court of Appeal decided not to suspend the contract on the basis of

---

[1]   Council of State, 13 October 1992, *EGTA Contractors, T Aann*, 1992, 366; *TBP*, 1992, 345.
[2]   Brussels, 25 March 1993, *T Aann*, 1993, 232.

a balancing of interests.[1] It decided that the interests of the Region and of Sofibru could not be overlooked.

Only one month later, the Council of State set aside the suspended decision. The award decision being set aside, EGTA tried to obtain the setting aside of the contract between the Region and Sofibru before the civil courts. At first instance and on appeal the action was declared admissible but unfounded on the basis of a balancing of interests.

Following its failure to have the contract set aside, EGTA desperately tried to obtain an order from the Council of State imposing upon the Region, under the exposure of a forfeiture of a penalty payment, the issuing of a new tender for the rest of the works which still had to be carried out. However, the Council of State did not accede to this request since such a tender could not take effect as long as the civil courts had not set aside the contract based on the first award decision.[2]

The *Van Hool* case

This case concerned the award of a public contract for the supply of buses to Espace Mobile International (hereinafter referred to as 'EMI') by the Socit Regionale Wallone du Transport (the Walloon regional transport company, hereinafter referred as 'SRWT').

The invitation to tender issued by SRWT involved the supply over a period of three years of 307 public transport buses, for an estimated sum of 2,022,918,000 BF (excluding VAT).

The dispute concerns the preparatory acts prior to the award decision, in which SRWT's board of directors recommended in a memorandum dated 2 September 1993 to award contracts for 37 vehicles to Jonckheere and for 280 vehicles to Van Hool.

Subsequent to the aforementioned recommendation by SRWT's board of directors, EMI filed additional memoranda amplifying its observations which led to the award of 280 vehicles to EMI, instead of the original preferred contractor, Van Hool, on 6 October 1993.

On the same date, Van Hool filed a complaint with the Council of State in order to obtain a suspension of the award decision under the extreme urgent necessity procedure. The suspension was duly granted on 7 October 1993.[3]

Unfortunately for Van Hool, the suspension of 7 October 1993 had to be confirmed by the plenary Chambers of the Council of State within 45 days. The latter refused to confirm the order and dismissed the application for suspension and adoption of interim measures lodged by Van Hool.[4] On the same date, SRWT proceeded to notify the decision to EMI, awarding the order for the 280 vehicles to the latter.

Having received a complaint from Van Hool, the European Commission put Belgium on notice in November 1993 pursuant to its supervisory powers under Article 169 EC Treaty. Belgium was thereby requested to submit its observations for having breached, among others, the principle of equal treatment. After an unsatisfactory answer on behalf of the Belgian State, the

---

[1] Brussels, 22 April 1993, *T Aann*, 1993, 239.
[2] Council of State, 22 February 1994, *EGTA Contractors, T Aann*, 1994, 395.
[3] Council of State, 7 October 1993, *JJ*, 1993, 647.
[4] Council of State, 17 November 1993, *T Aann*, 1994, 24.

Commission filed an application for interim measures with the President of the European Court of Justice. In an order dated 22 April 1994, the European Court of Justice rejected the request to impose interim measures. This order was based on the fact that the Commission had failed to display the diligence required of a party relying on the urgency of interim measures. Moreover, balancing the interests between observing the public procurement rules and the immediate replacement of the bus fleet for safety requirements, the President was of the opinion that the balance tilted in favour of safety. Therefore the Court dismissed the application for interim measures.[1]

On the merits of the case, the European Court of Justice held in a judgment dated 25 April 1996, that Belgium's practices were in breach of the obligations imposed by Council Directive 90/531/EEC of 17 September 1990 on the procurement procedures of entities operating in the water, energy, transport and telecommunications sector.[2]

Regarding the civil proceedings, Van Hool filed a claim for suspension of the performance of the contract concluded between SRWT and EMI under forfeiture of penalty payments for the amount of 100,000,000 BF per day in case the imposed measure were disregarded. The Court of First Instance of Namur rendered a judgment pursuant to Article 19, para 2 of the Belgian Judicial Code.[3] This provision enables the civil court to impose interim measures if such imposition does not interfere with a decision on the merits of the case.[4] The Court of First Instance of Namur stated that interim measures can only be granted when a sufficient apparent right is available. The Court was of the opinion that it was impossible to award interim measures to an aggrieved party in a contractual claim, if during the procedures on merits, it would appear that the aggrieved party was not entitled to such measures. On the basis of those considerations, the Court of First Instance of Namur rejected Van Hool's claim.

It furthermore stated that the only remedy available was compensation for damages since Van Hool had no subjective right in the award of the public contracts. This is part of the discretionary competence of the public entity and only the latter has the power to decide whether or not to award a public contract. The Court of Appeal recently confirmed[5] the absence of a subjective right on behalf of Van Hool to claim the annulment of the contract between SRWT and EMI. Regarding the claim to suspend the contract pursuant to Article 19, para 2 of the Judicial Code, the Court of Appeal again confirmed the judgment of the Court of First Instance.

CONCLUSION

Belgium considers its current regulatory regime to be in conformity with the Remedies Directive and the Utilities Remedies Directive. A provision-by-provision analysis of this regime seems to support that assessment. However, a review of the complex litigation in the *CCN* and the *Van Hool* cases shows that the existing rules do not yield the result envisaged by the Remedies

---

[1]   President of the Court, 22 April 1994, *T Aann*, 1994, 296.
[2]   Case C-87/94, *Commission v Belgium*, 25 April 1996 (not yet reported).
[3]   The Court which is competent to hear the case pursuant to Article 19, para 2 of the Belgian Judicial Code is also competent to hear the case on the merits afterwards.
[4]   Court of First Instance Namur, 24 August 1994, *T Aann*, 1994, 407.
[5]   Liège, 7 October 1996, not yet reported.

Directive. For example, the fifth and sixth recitals of the Remedies Directive stipulate that:

'since procedures for the award of public contracts are of such short duration, competent review bodies must, among other things, be authorised to take interim measures aimed at suspending such a procedure or the implementation of any decisions which may be taken by the contracting authority; the short duration of the procedures means that the aforementioned infringements need to be dealt with urgently';

and that

'it is necessary to ensure that adequate procedures exist in all the Member States to permit the setting aside of decisions taken unlawfully and the compensation of persons harmed by any infringement';

The *CCN* and *Van Hool* cases have clearly shown that adequate relief is not easy to obtain. Although Belgian law does not exclude the possibility to suspend or set aside an award decision of a public entity or a subsequently concluded public contract, the current dominant case law seems reluctant to grant this type of relief.

As mentioned above, this situation is mainly due to the restrictive interpretation of the (French-language Chambers of the) Council of State concerning the requirement of a serious prejudice difficult to remedy and to a failure on the part of the civil courts to take the interests of the aggrieved party into account.

In order to comply with the spirit of the Remedies Directive and the Utilities Remedies Directive it seems that the Council of State should follow the interpretation of its Dutch-language Chambers and focus on the interests of the aggrieved parties. Likewise judgments of the sort pronounced by the Court of First Instance of Namur and the Court of Appeal of Liège according to which the aggrieved party cannot claim any subjective rights as to the award of a public contract seem in flagrant contradiction with the spirit of the Remedies Directive.

A further problem arises from the simultaneous jurisdiction of the administrative and civil courts. The co-operation between the aforementioned courts has proven to be defective in practice.

In conclusion, the problem is not so much whether the Remedies Directive and the Utilities Directive have been properly implemented in Belgian law, but much more how restrictively the courts will interpret the resulting regulatory framework.

CHAPTER 5

Remedies in Denmark

Mogens Flagstad and Christian Tang-Jespersen

INTRODUCTION

On 22 January 1972, the Treaty concerning the accession of the Kingdom of Denmark, Ireland and the United Kingdom of Great Britain and Northern Ireland to the European Economic Community was signed. The Accession Treaty came into force on 2 January 1973, and according to their own request the Faeroe Islands were not covered by it, whereas Greenland – being a part of the Kingdom of Denmark, and therefore also a member of the EEC – left the EEC in 1985 according to their own wishes.

The Danish Accession Act granted the main body of EC legislation direct effect in Danish law without any specific act of incorporation.

However, according to Article 189 of the EC Treaty a directive is only binding upon any Member State to which it is addressed as to the result to be achieved. As the choice of means and modalities of directive incorporation are left to the national authorities, a brief overview is given as to the means whereby a directive can be incorporated into Danish law, before the actual rules on public procurement are examined.

Generally speaking, it is the ordinary means of incorporation according to international law which apply to directives: either they can be redrafted or they can be incorporated by reference in Acts or Regulations.

Redrafting of directives can be the cause of both legal and practical problems, eg by erroneous redrafting or uncertainty when the rewording is construed. On the other hand it is a prerequisite for the use of incorporation by reference, that the wording of the directive in question fulfils the requirements of clarity applicable to the drafting of Danish acts.

In certain cases, when it has not been possible to incorporate a directive in its entirety, the Danish incorporation Act has directly restated certain words, sections or expressions from the directive.

Within certain fields directives have to be amended fairly often, and this would lay a large burden on the legislative bodies, should all directives be incorporated by legislation. Accordingly, it happens in Denmark, that the Act, by which a directive is incorporated, gives a Minister specific authority to implement rules concerning the incorporation of later directives on the same subject or just to implement amendments to the directive in question.

HISTORIC REVIEW

Denmark has a long tradition of rules concerning contract award procedures: In a regulation from 1621 concerning ecclesiastical income and real estate, the Danish King Christian IV ruled that any necessities of the church must be procured according to the 'best possible purchase'.

However, no real legislation was made before the Ministry of the Interior in 1888 established a Commission to examine the possibility of using tender procedures in conjunction with governmental building projects. The result was a report from 1889 which contained three main suggestions:

(1) A proposal for rules relating to public employees and the use of public or mandatory tender procedures for the performance of governmental building projects and the delivery of supplies related thereto.
(2) A proposal for standard terms related to agreements on and performance of governmental building projects by means of public or mandatory tender procedures.
(3) A proposal for standard terms related to the agreements on and delivery of supplies to governmental building projects by means of public or mandatory tender procedures.

The proposals did not become law. However, they did have an influence as the report formed the basis for the standard terms, which in 1899 were used for the establishment of governmental railroads and in 1890 for the construction of private railroads by the Ministry of Public Construction Works.

Although the Commission was only established in respect of government buildings, and the report mainly related to construction work, the rules for construction works influenced government procurements generally.

However, since then Danish legislation most recently *Licitationsloven* dating from 1966 [the Tender Procedure Act][1] in conjunction with the general Monopolies Act[2] has mainly related to construction works.

The Tender Procedure Act provides for two types of tender procedures, procurements which allow the inviting body to choose freely between submitted tenders or to reject them all, and mandatory invitations for tenders, where the inviting body must either accept the cheapest offer or reject all the offers.

Fines may be imposed for violation of the Tender Procedure Act and in severe cases it may lead to imprisonment. Claims concerning violations of the Act could previously be lodged with the local police department, and before charges are made, the case must be presented to *Monopoltilsynet* (now *Konkurrencerådet*) [the Competition Council].[3]

When the Tender Procedure Act was passed, the term 'invitation to tender' had the following meaning:

'An invitation simultaneously submitted to a definite or indefinite number of tenderers on identical terms to submit written, binding and concealed tenders within a specified time limit for a construction project or delivery, while the invitation indicates to each of such tenderers that others have been invited to submit tenders,

---

[1]   Act No 216 of June 8, 1966 relating to invitations for tenders.
[2]   Act No 102 of March 31, 1995 relating to supervision of monopolies and restrictions on competition.
[3]   In respect of *Monopoltilsynet* and *Konkurrencerådet* reference is made to section 3 relating to current Danish legislation.

and that all the tenders will be opened at a time and place specified in the invitation, where the tenderers usually are entitled to be present.'[1]

Although Danish national tender procedures are similar to contract award procedures under the EC public procurement regime contractors do not have a right to be present when tenders are opened nor do they have a right to receive information concerning the other tenders.

Accordingly, Danish tender procedures and the EC public procurement regime are not identical and they should not be confused.

Danish legislation has traditionally focused on contract award procedures in relation to public works contracts[2] and prior to the EC public procurement regime there was practically no regulation of contract award procedures in relation to other types of public contracts.

The Tender Procedure Act still applies in Denmark, but in case of a conflict with EC law, the EC rules will naturally prevail.

'Mestergris'[3] Supreme Court judgment

Generally speaking the problems relating to public procurement were not subject to public attention until the 'Mestergris' judgment of 1910.[4]

In conjunction with an invitation to submit tenders for the construction of a sanatorium on behalf of 'national foreningen til Tuberkulosens Bekaempelse' [The National TB Committee], which was performed under the rules applicable to public construction projects, it was by accident revealed that all 29 potential contractors had participated in a meeting two days before expiry of the time limit for submission of offers. At the meeting they all agreed to increase their respective tenders by DKK 17,000 (corresponding to 8% of the contract value), and the winning contractor should distribute this amount between the others.

The Supreme Court stated that the contract value had to be reduced by DKK 17,000 as the procurement had been distorted by the secret agreement, and by keeping the agreement secret, the suppliers had violated the law.

CURRENT DANISH LAW

According to current Danish legislation public procurements are subject to the EC directives on Public Works, Public Supply Contracts, Public Service Contracts, and Utilities (examined below), the Tender Procedure Act (examined above), *Udbudscirkulaeret* [the Government Rules on Tender Procedures] and Circular Orders related to the public procurement of construction works. The rules can briefly be described as follows:

---

1   Axel H. Pedersen *Licitation* (1955 Copenhagen,) G.E.C. Gads Forlag. According to Danish legislation, such rules – *cirkulaeret* – which are issued by one administrative body and directed to another administrative body, are binding upon the administrative body to which they are directed. As a rule Circular Orders are only binding upon a subordinate body, and they do not bind other authorities or individuals.
2   In particular the Danish Ministry of Housing issued the Circular Order of 1 July 1970 on procurement of construction works subsidised by the state.
3   UFR 1911.18H.
4   See p 86, n 2.

As stated above, the Tender Procedure Act still applies,[1] and the Act applies to both public and private entities. Although the Act was amended in 1989, the main principles have remained unchanged. Government Rules on Tender Procedures[2] require all government authorities to periodically invite tenders for the performance of certain operational tasks which can be performed by external suppliers. Contracts are awarded to tenders which offer the lowest possible price and the best performance.

The Tender Procedure Act contains no threshold values, and accordingly certain tasks, the value of which are under the thresholds specified in the EC directives, will only be covered by the Tender Procedure Act. The Governmental Rules on Tender Procedures contain rules on the proper procedure for publicity, specifications and selection in respect of tasks outside the EC directives.

Furthermore, the Circular Order on contract award procedures in respect of public construction works from the National Housing and Building Agency[3] should be noted, as it contains provisions on contract award procedures applicable to construction projects subsidised or made by the Government.

The Circular Order specifies the use of either public or limited tender procedures. Limited tender procedures require that the lowest bid must be accepted, whilst public tender procedures require that the contract must be awarded to the lowest possible tender, provided that the supplier with the lowest offer is not financially unsound.

The tender procedure must furthermore be unambiguous and structured in such a manner that the scope and contents of the tasks in question are clearly defined, and furthermore the rules of AB92[4] must be complied with.

AB92 specifies rules regarding construction works and deliveries related thereto. The essential aspects are rules relating to the division of work between the contractor(s) and the building owner during tender procedures and construction, rules relating to changed procedures and unexpected events, division of risk between the parties, the effects of delay and shortcomings, delivery of work, collateral and payment rules. Generally speaking, AB92 reflects common rules under Danish legislation relating to construction works.

Although the Danish Competition Act[5] is not directly related to the rules specified above, it is important to stress that the Competition Act applies to public authorities, in so far as they perform commercial activities.

Complaints in respect of national tender procedures can be made under the Danish Competition Act which seeks to prohibit restrictions and distortions of competition.

The Competition Act is administered by the Danish Competition Council [*Konkurrencerådet*] (previously 'Price Control Council' and 'Monopoly Council'), which consists of 14 members and a chairman. The chairman is appointed by Royal Resolution for an unlimited period, while the other members are appointed by the Minister of Industry for a period of four years each. The chairman and seven of the members must be independent of commercial interests, whereas the remaining seven members are appointed on recommendations from a wide range of business organisations.

[1]   Act No 216 of 8 June 1966 as amended by Act No 818 of 19 December 1989 which came into force on 1 January 1990.
[2]   Circular Order No 42 of 1 March 1994 by the Danish Ministry of Finance.
[3]   Circular Order No 50 of 14 April 1989.
[4]   Common Terms and Conditions Concerning Work and Delivery at Construction Projects from 1992, issued by the National Housing and Building Agency: *Almindelige Betingelser* 1992.
[5]   Competition Act No 114 of 10 March 1993 as amended by Regulation No 357 of 9 July 1995.

Implementation of Competition Council decisions and the administration of the legislation is performed by a secretariat operating under the direction of a manager, who has the authority to negotiate with undertakings. As the Competition Council makes its own decisions on the basis of written material – prepared by the parties or the secretariat – it must be emphasised that the undertakings and their representatives have no right to appear in person before the Competition Council. According to the Competition Act the Competition Council handles cases either on the basis of complaints or on its own initiative.

If public activities are performed by commercially independent undertakings, which are not otherwise covered by the rules applicable to public authorities, the Competition Council can directly order such undertakings to remove restrictions which are harmful to free competition.

In respect of public undertakings, including undertakings otherwise covered by the rules applicable to public authorities, the Competition Council can only submit an opinion to the public authority in charge of the activity, and then such authority must weigh the competition law interests against other public interests. The Competition Council cannot intervene directly against public authorities.

Judgment from the European Court of Justice in C-243/89: *Storebaelt* case[1]

Although the new directives in public procurement were not an element in the 'Great Belt' case, as they were not in force at the time, this case has had a great impact on the Danes' consciousness of the new EC rules on public procurement.

The company A/S Storebaeltsforbindelsen, which is wholly owned by the Danish state, wanted to build a road and railway connection across the Great Belt. In the OJ a notice was published concerning a restricted tender procedure concerning the construction of a bridge across the Western Channel of the Great Belt. The construction was part of a total project at an estimated value of DKK 29 bn and the specific construction had an estimated value of DKK 3 bn.

In the terms specified in the invitations to tender, the following was stated:

'The contractor must to the furthest extent possible use Danish materials, consumables, workforce, and equipment.'

Furthermore, the invitation to tender contained terms relating to the calculation of prices according to the contractors' obligations to develop the plan and complete the project, and carry the risks involved therein, while it was emphasised that:

'If a tender is submitted for the performance of an alternative project, including project responsibility placed with the contractor, the tender shall state a reduction price which applies, if the contracting authority decides to take over the responsibility for planning of the project.'

Five international consortia were invited to submit a tender, and after negotiations with the different tenderers, a contract was concluded with the 'European Storebaelt Group' ('ESG'). However the contract concluded with

---

[1] *Commission v Denmark* [1993] ECR I-3353.

ESG was on the basis of an alternative offer negotiated after the submission of its original tender.

Pursuant to Art 169 of the EC Treaty the Commission filed a claim against the Danish State for breach of its obligations under EC law, and in particular with reference to Arts 30 (free movement of goods), 48 (free movement of workers), and 59 (free movement of services) as well as Directive 71/305/EEC of the EC public procurement regime relating to public works contracts.

The Commission claimed that the negotiations with ESG led to the award of a contract containing provisions contrary to the invitation to tender, and were contrary to the principle of non-discrimination.

The Commission alleged that the contract awarded by Storebaelt to ESG differed materially from the specification in the invitation to tender; as a result the other contractors had not been able to compete on an equal footing.

The first complaint related to the above quoted section concerning Danish supplies:[1] the incompatibility of the section with Arts 30, 48 and 59 of the Treaty was not disputed by the Danish government, but the government claimed that whereas the section in question had been removed before a contract was signed with ESG, whereas the Danish government had acknowledged in writing that the section was incompatible with EC law and, furthermore, had acknowledged its responsibility towards the other tenderers, the government should be acquitted on this point.[2]

The Court of Justice stated that even if the problematic section was removed shortly before a contract was signed, the entire tender procedure had been performed on the basis of a section which was incompatible with EC legislation, and which had the ability to affect the composition of individual consortia as well as the content of offers.[3]

Furthermore, the Court of Justice stated that even though the Member State in question would not dispute the incompatibility with the Treaty and furthermore acknowledged its responsibility, including an obligation to pay compensation, the Commission could still request the Court of Justice to state the existence of incompatibility with the Treaty.[4] On these grounds the Court of Justice dismissed Denmark's claim for acquittal, and the Court of Justice accepted the Commission's claim on this point.

The second complaint concerned the negotiations on the basis of a proposal which was incompatible with the terms of the invitation to tender.

The first defence of the Danish government was that the principle on non-discrimination did not relate to the directive. The Court of Justice stated that although the directive contains no explicit reference to the principle of non-discrimination, this obligation is contained in the objectives of the directive, and accordingly Denmark's claim was rejected.

Concerning the negotiations undertaken by 'A/S Storebaeltsforbindelsen', the Court of Justice stated that according to the principle of non-discrimination all tenders must comply with the terms of the invitation to tender, as this will secure objective comparison between the submitted tenders.[5] As ESG's tender contained a price offer which did not cover obligations for preparation of a detailed project and assumption of full responsibility for preparation

[1]   C-243/89: *Commission v Denmark* [1993] 1 ECR 3353, paras 23–31.
[2]   Ibid, paras 24 and 28.
[3]   Ibid, para 26.
[4]   Ibid, para 30.
[5]   Ibid, paras 36 and 37.

and performance thereof, including the risk of changes in the anticipated volumes, the Court of Justice stated that ESG's offer on an alternative project was incompatible with the common terms of the invitation to tender.

As the common terms opened no possibility for reservations in the tenders, it was the opinion of the Court of Justice that the principle of equality prohibited A/S Storebaeltsforbindelsen from taking ESG's alternative tender into consideration.[1]

On these grounds the Court of Justice accepted the second complaint of the Commission. Thus, the Court of Justice finally stated that Denmark had committed a breach of its obligations according to EC law and, in particular, Arts 30, 40, and 59 of the EC Treaty and Directive 71/305/EEC.

THE INCORPORATED DIRECTIVES

The first directives on public supply and public works contracts were incorporated into Danish law by means of Circular Orders from the ministries in question. At a later stage the directives have been incorporated by legislation as the issued Circular Orders did not sufficiently take into consideration that the directives contained rights which the undertakings can invoke before the Courts.

As a rule Denmark chose not to redraft the directives, but usually to incorporate them by means of reference, and the texts of the directives have been attached as appendices to the Acts. In order to counterbalance the reduced 'user friendliness' of this method of implementation the relevant authorities have prepared guidelines of their own.

Accordingly, it can be stated that the Council Directives on public supply and works contracts,[2] the utilities sectors,[3] and public service contracts[4] have been implemented in Danish law.

POSSIBLE REMEDIES

There are two sets of possible sanctions in respect of public procurement.

The European Commission and the Member States have power under the EC Treaty to bring an action for infringement of the Regime against another

---

[1] Grounds No 41–43.

[2] Council Directive 71/305 concerning the co-ordination of procedures for the award of public work contracts and Directive 77/62 concerning co-ordinating procedures for the award of public supply contracts were implemented by Act No 366 of 1990 as amended by Act No 377 from 1992 and as published in Promulgation Order No 600–1992. Further reference is made to Regulation No 595 of 14 September, 1990 by the National Housing and Building Agency, as amended by Regulations No 498 of 25 June 1991 and No 297 of 5 May 1993. Directive 93/37 – being a codification of Directive No 71/305 with amendments – has been incorporated by virtue of Regulation No 201 of 27 March 1995. Regulation No 510 of 16 June 1994 by the Danish Ministry of Business and Industry. Section 1.1 of the regulation states: 'The contracting authority must comply with the provisions of Directive 93/36/EEC of 14 June, 1993 concerning the co-ordination of procedures for the award of public supply contracts.' The directive is attached to this regulation. Directive 93/36/EEC is a codification of Directive 77/62 with amendments.

[3] Directive 93/38/EEC on the excluded sectors, and by which the scope of Directive 90/531 is extended to cover services, is implemented by Regulation No 557 of 14 June 1994 by the Danish Ministry of Business and Industry and Regulation No 558 of 24 June 1994 by the National Housing and Business Agency.

[4] The Services Directive 92/50/EEC was implemented by Regulation No 415 of 22 June 1993 by the Danish Ministry of Business and Industry.

Member State. Contractors can either commence proceedings before national courts against the contracting authority or they can lodge a complaint with the national authorities established according to the directives on review procedures.[1]

It is interesting to examine who the interested parties are and who must comply with the directives. Generally speaking, anyone can notify possible violations to the Commission in order to have the case brought before the ECJ, while in respect of cases before national authorities the national procedural requirements concerning relevant legal interest must be complied with.

According to the case law of the ECJ, the public authorities covered by the regime are municipalities,[2] county councils[3] and semi-public authorities.[4] Furthermore it could be questioned whether concessionary undertakings are covered. However, according to the principle in Art 90 of the EC Treaty and the judgment in the *Foster* case,[5] this is probably so.

Thus all public authorities, as well as undertakings and organisations over which public authorities have a decisive influence, are covered by the regime.

Disappointed tenderers have the following possible means of redress:

(1) A complaint to the Commission in order to have the tender procedure declared invalid by the ECJ for which see introductory chapter on powers of the Commission.
(2) To file a claim for compensation before a national court in the case of a loss due to failure of or incorrect implementation of a directive in a Member State.
(3) To make use of the national complaints procedure specified in the directives on review procedures.
(4) To make use of the direct effect of the directives under a lawsuit in a Member State.

REVIEW PROCEDURE[6]

Due to the requirement of promptness in the review procedures, the directives on review procedures 89/665/EEC and 92/13/EEC have in Denmark been implemented by the establishment of a specific administrative body,

---

[1] Council directive of 21 December 1989 on co-ordination of the legislation, regulations, and administrative provisions relating to the application of review procedures to the award of public supply and public work contracts (Directive 89/665 as amended by Directive 92/50) and on entities operating in the water, energy, transport, and telecommunications sectors, Directive of February 25, 1992 (Directive 92/13).

[2] Case 103/88 *Fratelli Constanzo v Commune di Milano* [1989] ECR 1839.

[3] Case 194/88R *La Spezia: Commission v Italy* [1988] ECR 5647.

[4] Case 31/87 *Gebroeders Beentjes v Netherlands* [1988] ECR 4635.

[5] Case 188/89 *Foster v British Gas plc* [1990] ECR I-3313.

[6] A specific complaint procedure in respect of tenders exists through an *Udliciteringsråd* [Board for Tender Procedures] according to the Tender Procedure Act established by the Danish Ministry of Finance. Basically, the suppliers who find themselves incorrectly treated by a governmental authority can file a complaint with the Board for Tender Procedures which may – but does not have to – make a statement on the case. Should the suppliers find that the rules have been violated, it will notify the relevant ministry about the case, and the further procedure is left to the ministry. The Board for Tender Procedures cannot handle complaints related to the EC Directives on public procurement.

'*Klagenaevnet for Udbud*' [The Appeal Board for Public Procurement].[1] As this body will probably have a decisive influence on the way the directives in the future will be construed under Danish law, the position and current case law of the Danish Appeal Board for Public Procurement is examined here.

After an examination of the 1992 legislation, the Commission has stated that Denmark failed duly to incorporate the review directive, thus an amended Act[2] has recently been presented.

Structure

The Appeal Board consists of a chairman, a number of deputy chairmen, all of whom must be qualified judges, and a number of expert members who must possess a particular professional, technical or legal expertise.

Authority

The risk of developing more national review procedures and case law has been minimised, as the Appeal Board has been granted a very large field of authority – including complaints related to all directives on public procurement, to violations by a contracting authority of Art 7 of the EC Treaty, concerning non-discrimination, and Arts 30 and 59 on the free movement of goods and services and related to the competition rules in Art 85, 86, and 90.

It should be noted that the Appeal Board cannot, on its own initiative, examine whether the contracting authorities violate their obligations under the procurement directives: thus, a formal complaint must be filed, and when filing the complaint the complaining contractor must notify the authority in question of the alleged violation and that a complaint is filed with the Appeal Board.

Legal interest

According to the legislation, complaints can be filed by anyone with a legal interest and by the specific organisations[3] and public authorities that have been granted a general right of complaint.

It should be noted that a body under the Danish Competition Council named *Konkurrencesekretariatet* [The Secretariat of Competition] has been granted this right, and it is recommended that a potential complaint is discussed with the Secretariat before filing a complaint.

---

[1] Act No 344 of 6 June 1991, as amended by Act No 1006 of 19 December 1992 and Regulation No 72 of January 30, 1992 as amended by Act No 206 of March 29, 1995. The amendments were incorporated into Danish legislation by Directive 92/13.

[2] The amendment of the Act concerning the Appeal Board for Tender Procedures. Act No 206 of 29 March 1995.

[3] A large number of organisations are listed in the Executive Order No 26 of 1 January 1996. Those mentioned below are only examples: LO [the Danish Trade Union Congress], *Dansk Arbejdsgiverforening* [the Danish Employers Organisation], *Entreprenørforeningen* [the Danish Contractors Association], *Håndvaerksrådet* [the Danish Federation of Small and Medium Sized Enterprises], and *Dansk Industri* [Confederation of Danish Industries].

According to basic principles of Danish law, the term 'legal interest' covers anyone with a specific, essential, and current interest in the matter.

In each individual case the Appeal Board makes its own decision on the existence of a 'legal interest', and this decision can be reviewed by a Danish court.

Consideration of a case will usually be in writing, but the chairman of the Appeal Board may decide – if the circumstances so require – to permit oral representations.

The powers of the Appeal Board are: (1) to suspend a tender procedure or the implementation of illegal decisions; (2) to set aside illegal decisions; or (3) to order a contracting authority to remedy the tender procedure, which powers are in accordance with the directives.

According to Danish law it must be assumed that the plaintiff shall establish facts that make the existence of a violation probable, and make it probable that the interruption of the procedure is necessary in order to protect his legitimate interests. Furthermore, the Appeal Board must by itself evaluate all the interests involved in the case.

The circumstances which may give rise to a cancellation of a tender procedure were not specified in Act No 1006 of 19 December, 1992. However, as it will appear from the examination below of current case law from the Appeal Board, the power of cancellation has actually been used.

Furthermore, it must be noted that there was no sanction in the event that a contracting authority failed to comply with a decision by the Appeal Board, and accordingly decisions by the Appeal Board could not originally be enforced. This is contrary to the directives on review procedures, both of which contain provisions which require appropriate remedies for the enforcement of decisions by the national review authorities. Subsequently, the Commission noted in its critique that the Act concerning the Appeal Board contains no sanctions for non-compliance with decisions by the Appeal Board.

Furthermore, the Commission emphasised that the current provision concerning presentation of fines by the administration in some cases has the result that no means of interference are available, when the utilities directive is violated.

Thus, the Minister of Business and Industry has proposed an additional provision[1] to meet the criticisms of the Commission, which has not been adopted, specifying that penalties can be imposed for intentional or grossly negligent non-compliance with prohibitions or orders contained in decisions by the Appeal Board or a court of law.

The amended Act of 1995 implies that in the future the Appeal Board will have no authority to consider cases against contracting authorities who exploit a geographical area by performing investigations for, or extraction of, oil, gas, coal or other solid fuels. According to the Act, such cases must be considered by *Sø og Handelsretten* [the Maritime and Commercial Court of Copenhagen].[2]

Finally, the Commission stated that certain provisions of the review directive

---

[1] The amendment of the Act concerning the Appeal Board for Tender Procedures. Bill No L123 of January 1995.

[2] The Act on Appeal Board for Tender Procedures No 1006 of 19 December 1992 granted the Appeal Board powers to impose fines in respect of contracting authorities within the off-shore industry, ie contracting authorities who, according to specific or exclusive rights, can exploit a geographical area by performing investigations for, or extraction of, oil, gas, coal or other solid fuels.

have not been explicitly incorporated in the Act. These relate to claims for compensation, procedures for attestation of the contract award procedure by contracting authorities, and rules related to a conciliation procedure.

These issues are taken into account in the amended Act, except for the attestation procedure, as it was considered more appropriate to incorporate this in the Danish 'transformation regulation' related to the directive concerning the excluded sectors.

Conciliation procedures

Regarding the conciliation procedure,[1] specified in the utilities remedies, the amended Act of 1995 contains a specific conciliation procedure for infringements of the Regime by utilities.

The Act explicitly refers to the directive's provision concerning the conciliation procedure.

Decisions

The Appeal Board makes its decisions by a simple majority, and it must state the grounds upon which the decision is based, including the opinion of a possible minority group.

Decisions must be notified to the parties in writing, and within eight weeks they may appeal the decision to a court of law.

Up until now, the Appeal Board has made 26 decisions, of which several were decided in favour of the plaintiff.

Examination of the current caselaw from The Danish Appeal Board for Public Procurement

Four times a year the Competition Council issues the publication *Dokumentation* [Documentation] which contains examinations of decisions by the Competition Council, tender procedures, and international issues.

In Documentation 1994/4, the section relating to EC tender procedures contains a report on all decisions made by the Appeal Board for Public Procurement until the end of 1994. Hereinafter, all decisions by the Appeal Board for Public Procurement are to be published in this periodical. However, the decisions have been quoted anonymously until Documentation 1995/3 where it was decided that all future decisions were to be released in full.

Decision by the Appeal Board - 12 August 1992[2] -'Construction of a ferry'

A shipyard complained that, without performing a tender procedure according to the supply contracts Directive (77/62/EEC as amended by 88/295/EEC),

---

1   Art 9–11.
2   The Appeal Board for Tender Procedures has organised its decisions according to the decisions date, but when a decision is used as documentation it would be wise to state the headline given by the Appeal Board.

a local authority had contracted for the construction of a ferry to be used on a ferry service run by the local authority.

The Appeal Board stated that the supplies directive did not apply to public supply agreements made by undertakings performing transportation by land, sea or air. Furthermore, the Appeal Board stated that the utilities directive had not yet been incorporated into Danish law when the contract was signed, and accordingly the directive and its recitals could not be applied when deciding the case.

Finally, the Appeal Board rejected an argument that the contract was covered by the works directive.

Decision by the Appeal Board – 18 January 1994 – 'Tender procedure for medical supplies'

A public partnership performed a restricted tender procedure in respect of certain medical supplies while stating their names 'or equivalent'. The plaintiff, who, together with other suppliers, was invited to submit a tender, claimed that the use of trademarks in the tender procedure gave it the character of a technical specification, which would eliminate other suppliers.

A complaint was filed against the tender procedure, with a claim for suspension of the tender procedure until it was in compliance with the legislation.

After a hearing of the defendant, the Appeal Board found no grounds for a suspension.

The defendant claimed that use of the trademarks was made in order to bring an exact description, but this method had not ruled out any contractors.

Furthermore, it was claimed that the criteria for award of the contract complied with Community law and were legal, impartial, and objectively evaluated.

The Appeal Board decided that the proper procedure would have been to use the generic denomination of the products in question, but when the entire tender procedure was taken into consideration, this could not make it an unauthorised tender procedure. The criteria for award of the contract had not been applied in a subjective or discriminating manner, and as no grounds were found for requirements concerning an additional objectivity in the criteria, the criteria were found to comply with the supplies directive and the claim was rejected.

Decision by the Appeal Board – 20 January 1994 – 'Tender procedure for an autoclave'

After a restricted tender procedure the plaintiff was invited to submit a tender for delivery and erection of an autoclave in a governmental institution. However, the governmental authority in question chose a tender from a supplier other than the plaintiff. In a complaint to the Appeal Board, allegations were made concerning illegal discrimination, insufficient grounds for the decision and the use of criteria which were so comprehensive and general that the public supplies directive was in fact circumvented.

According to the report, the selected tender was more expensive than the complainant's but from a comprehensive evaluation it was considered to be the financially most advantageous tender.

On the information presented, including the contracting authority's written report, the Appeal Board had no grounds upon which it could contest the validity of the contracting authority's evaluation. It was not possible to establish that the defendant had used the procedure illegally in order to exclude or discriminate against the plaintiff when awarding the contract, and thus the complaint was rejected.

Decision by the Appeal Board – 17 June 1994 – 'Tender procedure for various accessories'

In order to enter into a two-year framework agreement, the plaintiff announced in the OJ an invitation to tender for various types of equipment. The basis of selection was chosen as the most economically advantageous tender but no order of priority was given to any of the individual criteria.

The plaintiff submitted a tender, but he was notified that the offered prices were unattractive and that a contract had been made with another supplier.

In the complaint it was claimed that the contract should have been awarded to the lowest tender since the selection criteria were not set in order.

The case was considered on the basis of written submissions. The Appeal Board briefly stated that it appeared from the invitation in the OJ to submit tenders that the criteria for award of the contract were not exclusively the lowest price, but induced certain criteria stated without priority. Thus the complaint was dismissed.

Decision by the Appeal Board – 3 November 1994 – 'Contract for removal of refuse'

The plaintiff was a partnership established in the 1980s. The partners were a number of municipalities.

In 1988 the plaintiff signed contracts with a number of private carriers for the removal of refuse within the municipalities. During the case it appeared that the defendant had arranged a contracts renewal meeting with the carriers, with whom he had previously signed contracts, and with one of these carriers the contract was not renewed, but in July 1993 his contract was transferred to one of the other carriers.

A carrier complained that the waste management company had acted contrary to the services directive by neglecting to use a tender procedure in respect of contracts for removal of waste within one of the municipalities. Furthermore, it was claimed that the plaintiff would have submitted a tender for the available contract, had tender procedures taken place.

The defendant acknowledged the services directive was applicable to the defendant, but he claimed that the contract was concluded before the services directive was required to be implemented on 1 July 1993.

The Appeal Board found that it was not shown that the contract had been concluded before 1 July 1993, when the services directive came into force, and therefore the authority was in breach of the Regime.

Using its powers for the first time the Appeal Board cancelled the contracts, stating:

'The defendant's decision concerning the signing of an agreement with 'the carrier under notice' concerning removal of refuse in the municipality during the period 1 January 1994 – 31 December 2001 and acknowledgement of the transfer of rights under such contract by 'the carrier under notice' to another carrier, is cancelled.

Following this decision the plaintiff filed a suit with a claim for indemnification and was awarded DKK 685,000 [above ECU 90,000].

The ruling has not yet been published.

Decision by the Appeal Board – 18 November 1994 – 'Tender procedure for optical aids'

A municipality issued in the OJ an invitation to submit tenders for two years' delivery of spectacle lenses, optical aids and contact lenses for the citizens of the municipality under Art 58 of *Bistandsloven* [the Danish Social Security Act].

A professional association objected to the invitation on a number of points, and the municipality amended it in a number of respects, including the quantity to be delivered.

Two tenders were put forward from an optometrist and from a professional association on behalf of a number of opticians. The tender from the professional association contained a number of reservations, including reservations relating to price and to a requirement in the invitation concerning regular forwarding of statements concerning turnover.

The municipality accepted the optometrist's tender. The professional association then filed a complaint against the municipality for award of the contract in violation of the public supply directive, and one of the reasons was that the stated volume was incorrect.

Furthermore, the plaintiff claimed that a price warranty was contrary to basic principles for tender procedures, as the contractor bears the risk of losing the contract if other suppliers undercut his prices during the term of the contract.

The defendant claimed that the stated volume was based on an estimate, and in any case the value of the procurement surpassed the thresholds related to tender procedure. Furthermore, the defendant found that taking all aspects into consideration, the financially most advantageous tender had been chosen, and thus the defendant had committed no violation of the public supply directive.

The Appeal Board did not accept that the statement of volume contained in the invitation was erroneous to such a degree that the tender procedure should be cancelled. This was partly owing to the volume being merely an estimate.

The Appeal Board could not decide upon the validity of the price warranty, as the rules related thereto were outside the authority of the Appeal Board.

As the Appeal Board found the accepted tender to be the lowest, and as no grounds were found to set aside the defendant's evaluation concerning the accepted tender as the financially most favourable, the Appeal Board could not disregard the tender procedure, and the complaint was dismissed.

Part decision of 8 March 1995 on suspensive effect (Projekt Filmhus I).

An architect brought a government institution's decision not to award him a consultancy job before the Appeal Board.

The plaintiff, who after a prequalification phase was invited to tender together with a number of other tenderers, requested that he be given a temporary injunction suspending the performance of the job until the Appeal Board had pronounced its final decision in the case.

The Appeal Board refused to suspend the award on the grounds that the project was urgent and a prima facie case of infringement had not been sufficiently made out.

The request for a suspensive effect was, therefore, rejected. It should be noted that at the final hearing the architect's claim was dismissed.[1]

Decision of 31 May 1995 – a question concerning an invitation of tenders for terminal rights, etc, in connection with ferry service

A shipyard brought an action against a ferry service company before the Appeal Board for having violated the public procurement directive, the utilities directive and the services directive by:

- having made an agreement about a bareboat charter without an EU invitation for tenders,
- having selected a shipping company without an EU invitation for tenders,
- because the two ports which the company serves had granted terminal rights without an EU invitation for tenders.

The ferry service company, against which a complaint had been filed, stated in this connection that the municipalities had no decisive influence on the ferry service company, and that there was free access to the ports, since anyone could establish a ferry service from the two ports.

Considering that the ferry service company in the complaint cannot be characterised as a person pertaining to public law according to the definition in the public procurement directive, it was not found that the Regime had been infringed.

The Appeal Board also said that it has no authority to order the plaintiff to pay costs of the defendant.

Decision of 8 June 1995 – consulting engineering – rejection of tender

A government institution was responsible for a restricted invitation for tenders, according to the services directive, for consulting engineering in connection with the reconstruction of a building.

The government institution received six tenders but rejected them all on the grounds that they did not comply with the invitation to tender. Thereafter the contract was awarded by negotiation – purportedly in accordance with a permitted derogation under the directive.

The Appeal Board found that the government institution had been entitled to reject the tenders and no relief was granted.

Decision of 22 June 1995 – invitation to tender an insurance service.

An oil company invited tenders for its insurance requirement in connection with the services directive. The invitation for tenders was effected through an insurance broker whose fee was to be paid by the tenderers.

The plaintiff, an insurance company, accepted the broker mandate, but refused to pay a fee. Another insurance company through which a provisional

---

[1]   Decision of 18 May 1995 (*Projekt Filmhus II*).

insurance had been effected for a transitional period and whose tender price was considerably lower, was awarded the contract.

The plaintiff claimed that the decision on the acceptance of the tender should be cancelled and claimed that in being connected with the hiring of the insurance broker the consulting and intermediary functions had been mingled in conflict with the Directive.

The Appeal Board found against the complainant and no relief was granted.

Decision of 23 June 1995 – threshold value of public procurement directive

This decision is interesting as it concerns the question whether the Danish Chamber of Commerce might be assumed to have a legal interest in the complaint and, therefore, be entitled to file a complaint in pursuance of section 4, sub-section (1), no 1 of the Appeal Board Act. It was held that the complaint was admissible and the Chamber of Commerce had a sufficient interest in the contract. Further the complaint was successful and the Appeal Board held that a series of contracts whose individual works did not exceed a Community threshold would have done if their total aggregate value had been taken as the correct measure, as they ought to have been. However, the only relief granted appears to have been a declaration.

Decision of 7 July 1995 – conclusion of a contract for installation and operation of town equipment

A firm filed a complaint about the municipality's conclusion of a contract with another firm for installation and operation of town equipment.

The plaintiff claimed unsuccessfully that the contract specifications had been drawn up in order deliberately to suit the successful tenderer.

Decision of 23 August 1995 – invitation of tenders for library furniture

A municipality invited tenders for supply of furniture to expand the municipality's central library. In this connection the head of the library contacted a firm which had previously supplied furniture to the library. This firm then co-operated with the library executives to draft the invitation for tenders. The firm in question then submitted a tender which was accepted, and one of the other tenderers then complained to the Appeal Board claiming that illegal discrimination had taken place.

In the circumstances the Appeal Board held that the defendant had the burden of proving that its extensive contacts with the successful tenderer did not render the procedure unfair.

On the facts it was held that the defendant had failed to discharge this burden and moreover that the description and technical specifications in the invitation for tenders constituted an infringement of Art 8, sub-article (6) of the Supplies Directive.[1] The decision to award the contract was set aside and the defendant was ordered to pay the plaintiff's legal costs.

Decision of 21 September 1995 – inspection of documents

In a pending case the defendant produced a number of appendices and maintained at the same time that some of the appendices in question – in

---

[1]   77/62 as amended and replaced by 93/36.

this connection information about the defendant's operational and financial conditions and about the defendant's know-how – were subject to general rules of secrecy and, therefore, could not be submitted to the plaintiff. The plaintiff claimed access to inspect these appendices.

The Appeal Board held that the plaintiff was a party to the case, and therefore ought to be entitled to all the relevant documents. However, after reviewing the appendices itself the Appeal Board only made a limited number available to the plaintiff.

Decision of 25 October 1995 – cancellation of a decision to invite tenders

A municipality issued a restricted invitation for tenders for a traffic control system pursuant to the utilities directive. Four firms were invited to tender, but only one submitted a tender, and at the same time one of the other firms filed a complaint against the municipality. The Appeal Board decided to suspend the contract and procedure.

The plaintiff asserted that:

(1) the terms of the invitation for tenders should have contained technical data and functional descriptions which were necessary in order to submit a tender;
(2) contrary to the rules the defendant had not at the plaintiff's request supplied further information about the tender material in due time.

The plaintiff was successful in all the allegations mentioned above, and so the Appeal Board cancelled the municipality's decision to implement the invitation for tenders concerned.

Decision of 23 January 1996 – emergency procedure

A municipality invited tenders for consultancy services in connection with the extension of a school after a restricted tender procedure pursuant to the services directive using the emergency procedures reducing the time for submission of tender.

The plaintiff claimed that the emergency procedure was not justified and illegal award criteria had been adopted. In addition the plaintiff applied part way through the hearing for the decision awarding the contract to be set aside.

The Appeal Board found that:

(1) the defendant was not entitled to invite tenders for the consultancy services using emergency procedures;
(2) the defendant had ignored the proper time limits;
(3) the defendant had used an illegal award criterion, and also that the invitation to tender was improperly drafted.

Notwithstanding, the Appeal Board held that the decision could not be cancelled.

The Appeal Board stated expressly in this connection that this was due to the fact that the plaintiff had not requested interim measures to suspend the decision and that the complaint was made more than four months after the decision was taken to use unlawful award procedures.

Decision of 23 January 1996 – tenderer's right to choose

A municipality invited EU tenders for collection of refuse and large refuse objects on the basis of the lowest tender.

The plaintiff claimed that the contract ought to have been awarded to it as it had submitted the lowest tender. In fact the contract was awarded to a contractor whose tender price was 1% greater than the plaintiff's. The Appeal Board found that on the facts the two tenders were indistinguishable on price and therefore it would not intervene.

Decision of 31 January 1996 – non-discrimination and prohibition of negotiation

The defendant invited EU tenders for recording forest preservation in Land Registries. The plaintiff was of opinion that the winning tenderer had been given an unfair opportunity to amplify its tender and thus violate the non-discrimination principle and prohibition against past-tender negotiations.

The Appeal Board was of opinion that the defendant had not participated in negotiations with the winning firm, but had only looked for a technical clarification of a tender, and that it was only a question of having a definition of the precise extent of the tender.

As the advertised award criteria were used stringently as the basis for the award and the standard prices were directly comparable, the complaint was not admitted.

Decision of 21 February 1996 – tender not received in due time

A contractor succeeded in recovering his costs after bringing an action in respect of a contracting authority's decision to consider a tender which was submitted after the deadline for submission of tenders but before the tenders were opened. It was held that the late tender should have been excluded.

Decision of 2 April 1996 – cancellation of invitation for tenders

A municipality had invited tenders for a ferry after a restricted tender procedure pursuant to the public procurement directive. Because of a number of errors committed by the municipality's technical advisers the municipality decided to cancel the invitation for tenders.

The plaintiff claimed that the municipality's cancellation of the invitation was invalid, and the contract should be awarded on the basis of the municipality's original invitation for tenders.

The Appeal Board stated at its own initiative – which the defendant then admitted – that the defendant had violated the public procurement regime by fixing the following criteria for award of the contract: '[The defendant] reserves the right to choose freely between tenders'. Without regard thereto the Appeal Board did not find that the defendant's cancellation of the invitation for tenders, and in this connection the decision to implement a new invitation for tenders, was in conflict with the public procurement directive as the implementation of the original invitation was encumbered with such considerable errors that the cancellation of the invitation was the only correct procedure.

Decision of 26 April 1996 – reservations in tender

Following a restricted procedure two contractors were invited to tender for a public works contract. Both submitted tenders subject to reservations. The contracting authority requested one of the tenderers to abandon its reservations before awarding it the contract. As a result the other tenderer brought a complaint which was upheld by the Appeal Board. The decision awarding the contract was set aside. However the Appeal Board also held the plaintiff tenderer's bid could not be considered by the authority since it too contained reservations.

Decision of 30 May 1996 – phrasing and use of the award criteria

The defendant invited tenders for a service concerning refuse collection after a restricted tender procedure pursuant to the services directive.[1] The plaintiff – who had submitted a tender for two of the services, but had not been awarded these – filed a complaint saying that the decisions were in conflict with the award criteria.

The Appeal Board found that the defendant had acted in conflict with the services directive by phrasing the award criteria vaguely.

Nevertheless, the Appeal Board found no reason to assume that the defendant had not made its decision in compliance with the established award criteria.

In defending its decision the authority claimed it had a right to attach importance to its previous experience with the plaintiff in connection with previous contractual relations – which the Appeal Board upheld, rejecting the complaint.

Decision of 4 June 1996 – ordering authority

The defendant placed an invitation for tenders in the Official Journal of advertising for aids for handicapped persons and then made a price agreement for a product which was not mentioned as a product range in the advertisement. On a complaint brought by a contractor the Appeal Board found that there was an award of a public contract, there was an obligation to invite tenders, and that the basis of the invitation was misleading.

Decision of 4 June 1996 – interpretation of draft of a European standard

A municipality invited tenders for public procurement of school desks and chairs after a restricted tender procedure. The tender material included a draft of a European standard for teaching purposes, and so these requirements had to be observed by the tenderer. The plaintiff maintained that the municipality had ignored EU's non-discrimination principle when awarding the contract.

[1] 92/50/EEC.

In the Appeal Board's opinion the municipality contract specifications did not comply with the European standard for school furniture and the municipality had ignored the non-discrimination principle.

The Appeal Board also stated that if the plaintiff had filed a claim for cancellation of the decision, this claim would probably have been admitted.

Decision of 13 June 1996 – rejection to accept adviser's tender
for prequalification

A municipality invited tenders for drawing up plans using restricted tender procedures pursuant to the services directive. The plaintiff, a firm of consulting engineers, had performed an environmental examination for the defendant in the field in question for which tenders were now invited. The defendant had then rejected the plaintiff's request to be prequalified on this basis.

Irrespective of the fact that, in the Appeal Board's opinion, contracting authorities have a wide discretion to evaluate whether its advisers can be excluded from submitting tenders on the basis that they would receive preferential treatment, the Appeal Board established that in connection with the environmental examination the adviser (plaintiff) had not taken possession of information which could justify a rejection, and so the defendant's rejection was not justified.

Suspensive effect of complaint

It follows from a notification of Act on The Appeal Board for Public Procurement[1] that a complaint will only have automatic suspensive effect to the extent laid down in legislation. At present, there is no Danish legislation which gives automatic suspensive effect to complaints.

However, the Appeal Board can decide to suspend contract award procedures in its discretion, weighing the seriousness of the alleged infringement against the consequences of suspension for all interests concerned, including the public interest. The Appeal Board has not yet given comprehensive guidance as to when it will exercise its discretion.

However, it has to be assumed ordinary principles of Danish law apply: The general rule is that there must be reasonable grounds to believe that an infringement has occurred.

So far as applying to set aside contract award procedures is concerned, it is apparent from the foregoing review that the Appeal Board will attach importance to this possibility whenever there has been an application for interim measures.

Cancellation of illegal decisions

As it is known, the Appeal Board can reject a case or, in reality, settle it in whole or in part, in this connection cancelling unlawful decisions, interrupting the tender procedure provisionally or directing the contracting authority to

---

[1]   Notification of Act on the Appeal Board for Public Procurement (invitation of tenders for building and construction works and public procurement in the EU) No 1166 of 20 December 1995 as well as in pursuance of its sections 4, 8 and 12, notification of the Appeal Board for Public Procurement, notification No 26 of 21 January 1996.

regularise invitations for tenders; cf section 5 of Notification of Act on the Appeal Board for Public Procurement Act No 1166 of 1995.

In cases where the authority has invited tenders, but where the invitation is defective, the Board may cancel illegal decisions or direct the contracting authority to regularise the invitation for tenders.

The advantages and disadvantages of a complaint

It was expected that the establishment of the Appeal Board would generate more cases than in fact was the case. This may imply that undertakings abstain from filing complaints, as they are afraid of blacklisting by contracting authorities.

Because of the plaintiff's obligation to notify the contracting authority about the complaint, it must be assumed that the companies, for tactical reasons, are reluctant to file complaints. The Appeal Board acknowledges the problem.

Notwithstanding, the Appeal Board knows of cases which have settled prior to reaching a hearing, and it is considered that the deterrent effect of the review procedure may explain the paucity of cases in Denmark.

As previously stated, certain trade associations have standing to make a complaint.[1] This implies that the aggrieved party can let its association file a complaint on its behalf, and thus to a certain extent maintain anonymity, helping to resolve the problem of 'biting the hand that feeds you'.

According to the principle of non-discrimination, similar organisations from other EC Member States must have an identical right of complaint, and thus it should always be considered whether a complaint can be filed by the applicable trade association in the plaintiff's own Member State.

Costs

The amended legislation of 1995 gives the Appeal Board the power to order costs against a contracting authority where an applicant has reasonable cause to bring an action.

Timing aspects

As the Appeal Board is composed of experts, and as it must be expected that the Appeal Board fairly quickly establishes an expertise within this comparatively complicated field of responsibility, it is probable that fairly flexible handling of cases can be expected.

After the Appeal Board's activities have become more visible – partly through the publication of a decision dated 3 October 1994, where the plaintiff's claim was accepted – an increase in the caseload is expected.

It is difficult to predict how long it takes to handle a case – it depends on the type of case, the submissions by the parties and the reaction time, but it seems that the Appeal Board handles its cases in less than 12 months. This should be seen in the light of alternative court action, where cases can easily take several years to resolve.

---

[1]   Cf p 93, n 2, above.

Address

Complaints should be sent in writing to the following address:

Klagenaevnet for Udbud
Sekretariatet
Kampmannsgade 1
DK – 1780 Copenhagen V
Danmark
Telephone no: (+45) 33 30 76 21
Facsimile no: (+45) 33 30 77 99

COMPENSATION

The Appeal Board cannot decide upon claims for payment of compensation, and thus such claims must be handled by a court.

Both of the remedies directives grant contractors the right to apply to set aside decisions taken unlawfully, to suspend the contract award procedures and to apply to have infringements corrected. No specific implementing provision has been introduced to provide for the award of damages to contractors harmed by infringements of the Regime. According to Danish law on damages in contract, the party who has suffered a loss can as a general rule, when liability is established, demand that his loss be calculated either on the basis of the 'interest in due performance' under a contract *or* as 'loss suffered'.

Applying Danish principles governing the recovery of damages for breach of contract, the principle of 'interest in due performance' would require that the plaintiff be placed in the same financial position as he would have been had the contract been awarded properly in accordance with regime. It is however a precondition for obtaining compensation in accordance with 'interest in due performance', that the contract which forms the basis for the claim would have been awarded to the applicant. Such a claim would typically be for loss of profits.

In contrast is the principle of 'loss suffered' by which loss is calculated as the amount which must be paid to place the plaintiff in the financial position he would have been in had the infringement not occurred. Typical claims would be the expenses incurred in connection with the preparation of tenders.

Under Danish law of tort, it is necessary that the infringement be characterised as negligent,[1] that a loss should have been suffered, and that a causal link between the negligent act and the loss can be established.[2]

Due to the requirement of causation, it was debatable whether Danish law properly implemented the requirement in the utilities remedies directive that contractors should recover the costs of submitting a tender if their chance of winning the contract has been adversely affected.[3]

However, since Art 2.7 of the utilities remedies directive has been

---

[1]　According to the traditional definition of negligence, a person has acted negligently if he fails to apply the caution and care which would be applied by a reasonable man in similar circumstances.

[2]　It is a requirement that the negligent act has caused damage in order to establish liability to pay damages – causality must be established.

[3]　Directive 92/13, Art 2.7.

implemented by the Danish amended legislation of 1995 §.13a,[1] liability for damages will be established if an undertaking can prove that there has been an infringement and that the undertaking in question would have had a real chance of winning the contract, and his chance has been adversely affected by the infringement.

DEBTS TO THE STATE

In order to facilitate the collection of debts to the state, the Act concerning limited access for debtors to submit tenders at public procurement[2] requires Danish authorities to demand from the potential contractors a statutory declaration concerning the extent of such contractors' unpaid payable debt to the authorities. 'Debt to the authorities' is defined as unpaid taxes, duties, and contributions to social security schemes.

If the unpaid debt due is more than DKK 100,000, the contracting authority cannot, as a rule, accept the tender, although it may otherwise meet all the conditions. It is questionable whether the Act violates EC legislation – eg it permits the contracting authorities to apply other criteria than specified in the procurement directives – but as no basic principles of EC law seem to be violated, the Act must be considered to be valid.

[1]   Amendment of the Act on Appeal Board for Tender Procedures Bill No L123 of January 1995.
[2]   Act No 1096 of 21 December 1994 – Ministry of Finance.

CHAPTER 6

Remedies in Finland

Laura Kalliomaa-Puha

INTRODUCTION

Finland already had some legislative codes dealing with public procurement prior to the EC regime – or to be exact, prior to EEA, the European Economic Area Treaty. Since the rules for the short period between EEA and the EU membership were almost the same, I am not going to discuss that era. The ideas of transparency and competition were familiar to the Finnish government purchasers, at least in theory. These ideas were part of the EFTA agreement ever since the foundation of the organisation[1] as well as other international organisations: Finland was already then party to the GATT Agreement on Governmental Procurement[2] not forgetting co-operation between the Nordic Countries[3] and in the United Nations.[4] There was also a decree on government procurement, *Asetus valtion hankinnoista*,[5] which stressed transparency, openness and competition, even though competition was in practice understood as competition between Finnish participants: Finnish origin was one of the decisive criteria. However, being a small country, Finland could not restrict itself to Finnish products alone, since there were simply not enough domestic products for all requirements, so public buyers were already then used to purchasing from abroad. Further, even prior to EU membership, the recession of the 1990s played its part in forcing authorities to take the cheapest offer.

The decrees on government procurement

The decree No 1070 on Government Procurement sets out the basic parameters in public procurement before the EC era. The decree provided for economically

---

[1] European Free Trade Association, Stockholm Convention, Art 14, sets out the principle of equal treatment to Member States. However, in 1967 an explanation was given in order to achieve this result more fully in: The Lisbon Ministerial Agreement, VII EFTA Bulletin 1967, No 2, pp 2–6. Finland became a full member only in 1986, but associate membership from 1961 has been considered the equivalent to full membership in most respects.

[2] Finland has been a member since 1980, SopS 84/1980, 1130/80.

[3] The Nordic Ministerial Council had plans for purchases by local administrations to be opened to the other Nordic countries, see *Nordiska Ministerrådets Utredning* 1990:63.

[4] The UN Commission on International Trade Law, UNCITRAL, has been working on a Model Law on Procurement. Also guidelines for the third world countries have been made, see Gösta Westring *International Procurement. A Training Manual.* UNCTAD/GATT, UNITAR, The World Bank and the International Band for Reconstruction and Development, 1985.

[5] No 1070/79, altered by No 827/87, see also the General Terms for Government Procurement, *Valtion yleiset hankintaehdot*, VYHE 1989.

advantageous purchases, competition, fair treatment of sellers, good quality of the products bought and Finnish origin. Therefore, if the Finnish origin clause is left out, the principles are very much the same as those of the EC directives.

Even though authorities could, according to the decree, pick, if possible, four or more tenderers, they had to consider tenders coming from outside the original tenderers providing the tender was made in due time. But since the authorities did not have any obligation to publicise the intention to award a contract, potential Finnish tenderers – let alone foreign ones – were hardly aware of the plans the officials might have. This shows again the importance of the advertising rules in achieving transparent procurement. The authorities had to judge bids according to reasonable criteria. They could pay attention to price, technical quality, form of payment and other terms such as trustworthiness of the seller, time of delivery, Finnish origin, warranty clauses and the expenses of care and attention.

These rules covered only supplies and services. However, there were rules for works on broadly similar principles, though in somewhat looser form.[1]

State purchases only

Public authorities can be divided into two categories in Finland. First, government officials, meaning all state authorities like ministries, central administration or county administration. Secondly, local administration, which is the responsibility of municipalities.[2] This division is important in Finland, since the municipalities have autonomy – the state officials have power to instruct the municipalities only if there is an Act giving the state such powers in a certain case. Thus any rules of a lower hierarchy, like decrees, cannot justify any interference. Since the rules of public procurement were made by decree, the rules in force before the EC directives covered only state officials. That went for both national and international rules. A large amount of public purchases both in quantity and in value was therefore left outside the rules and legal supervision. Some of the municipalities had instructions of their own, usually stating that purchases should be made economically and fairly. In the municipalities also political reasons probably had the strongest influence; if for example employment seemed to require it, construction work was given to the local contractor even though its offer was not the cheapest.

REMEDIES PRIOR TO THE EC REGIME

Absence of specific remedies

Specific remedies for public procurement are definitely new. Even though the EFTA rules offered some surveillance and an opportunity for complaint, they were hardly ever used. The GATT rules and the Finnish decree had no remedy provisions at all. However, in the absence of a legislative code,

---

[1] See the Decree on Bidding of Government Construction, *Asetus valtion rakennustöiden teettämisestä urakoitsijoilla* No 358/61 and decision of the Ministry of Transportation, which specifies the rules, No 185/83 and General Terms on Government Construction Contracts, *Rakennusurakan yleiset sopimusehdot*, YSE 1983 RT 16–10193.

[2] There are over 455 municipalities in Finland and 11 counties.

something could still have been done. Apart from cases which raised criminal issues, there were three different possibilities to seek for remedy.

Political consequences

In most cases the only liability that might arise was political. Especially in municipalities at least the biggest purchases were and are decided by democratically elected bodies, like city councils. There were no laws forcing local authorities to follow the ideals of transparency, competition or openness, but at least the most conspicuous cases probably did not take place because of political pressure – not all the construction work could possibly be given at any price to the nice nephew of the mayor.

Administrative appeal

There was, however, the possibility of making an administrative complaint or an administrative appeal providing the purchasing decision was made in a proper manner. If the complaint or appeal was successful, the decision could be overruled or even changed. To be capable of appeal, a decision had to contain a final and conclusive settlement of an individual case. Often procurement decisions did not; the formal decision was made at a very late stage or no official decision was made because the officials have authority to make smaller purchases on their own. Administrative appeal is not possible in respect of initial or tentative decisions made at the preparatory stage, nor of technical decisions concerning merely the implementation of a decision. Recommendations as well as decisions of a general nature, such as project plans or instructions concerning implementation, also fall outside the scope of appeal. But when a formal decision had been concluded, an appeal could be made by any person whose right or legally protected interest was directly infringed or affected by an administrative decision. This possibility concerned only municipalities and the state, so that publicly owned companies were not covered.

Firstly, an administrative complaint, *hallinto kantelu*, could be used. The appellate authority's jurisdiction is restricted to legal matters and it cannot rule on the decision's expediency. The appellate authority cannot set aside a wrong decision. But it can force a public entity to fulfil its official duties – that is to act according to Finnish law. Complaints can be used even when no formal decision has been made, contrary to appeals. That can be useful during the bidding process, since the formal decisions are only usually reached at the end of the process.

Administrative judicial appeal is the general form of instituting the appeal procedure. This is further divided into two separate forms of appeal. An administrative appeal, *hallintovalitus*, is usually made 'against' the state. It is hardly administration of justice, but administrative activity where the superior authority supervises its subordinates. Thus the superior authority can change the decision to improve it even in cases where the decision has not been illegal. This might be useful in cases where there have not been any formal mistakes in the procurement procedure, but one wants to argue that a bid was economically the most advantageous tender. There is also power to affirm or overrule a decision. Usually the enforcement of the decision is postponed until the administrative appeal has been resolved.

Decisions made by municipal authorities within the field of municipal self-government may be challenged by a municipal appeal, *kunnallisvalitus*. One cannot ask for consideration of expediency, but a breach of a legal rule must be alleged. Municipal appeal cannot change the decision of a municipality, but the decision can be overruled, affirmed or it could be sent back for re-evaluation. An appeal does not suspend the decision's enforcement automatically, but the appellate authority can prohibit or interrupt enforcement either on application or *ex officio*.

In the absence of a legislative code governing procurement procedures in municipalities, grounds for appeals might have been hard to find. It was easier when the state was involved, since it was subject to the Decree on Government Procurement. Now that problem has disappeared.[1]

Damages

It was possible to recover damages even before the EC era. To recover compensation, a claimant had to show that it would have won the competition with the best offer. This would be difficult in every case. Since it was usually the economically most advantageous offer which succeeded, it was not sufficient to show that the claimant's offer was the cheapest, and clearly it would be difficult to argue that its offer was the best.

According to *Vahingonkorvauslaki*[2] (Compensation Act), the starting point in the Finnish tort law system is that each party must take responsibility himself or herself for damages which he or she may have suffered. There must be some ground to require somebody else to pay for the damage, either showing that the damage was caused on purpose or by negligence. Damage is caused on purpose if it is intentional or at least thought of as a possible consequence of the action, or when the conduct is in reckless disregard of the interests of others in a situation where it was probable that the consequence might occur. Such a ground could be found when the government was buying – the Decree on Government Procurement set out the rules according to which each purchase should have been made. In the case of municipalities, in the absence of a legislative code such ground might have been harder to find. Yet, some of the municipalities' own instructions might have been enough or it could have been argued that unfair procurement was against the principles of good administration.

The Act also categorises damages and leaves out purely financial damages: according to the Act only personal injuries (*henkilövahingot*) and material damages (*esinevahingot*) can usually be compensated.[3] All other financial loss, which is not linked to personal injuries or damage to tangible objects, could not, therefore, be compensated – eg expenses involved in submitting a tender or the loss of anticipated profit could not come into consideration.

There was and continues to be, however, an exception to the Act. Even purely financial losses can be compensated if the damage has been caused by a criminal act, by a public authority or if there are other very strong

---

[1]   Administrative appeals are still available in respect of municipality procurements under the Kunnallishki Municipality Act 1976.
[2]   *Vahingonkorvauslaki* No 412/74.
[3]   Compensation Act, chapter 3, paragraphs 1 and 2 and chapter 5, paragraph 1.

arguments.[1] At first sight, the second possibility seems attractive: in public procurement cases possible damage has certainly been caused by a public authority, so there might be a chance to recover compensation in respect also of financial losses. However, the notion of 'public authority' in the Compensation Act is far from simple. Damages caused by public authority are considered to mean damages caused by an act or decision, made by a public authority according to those rules, which *limit personal freedom or other constitutional rights*. Whether or not procurement decisions are such decisions is unclear. It can be argued both ways: an unfair procurement procedure could be in breach of the principle of equality and it would limit one's economic possibilities, but would it limit personal freedom? This may occur in the decisions which directly affect the freedom or health of citizens or the right to dispose of one's property.[2]

It could also be argued that even though unfair procurement was not a criminal offence, it was against 'good practice' and therefore comparable to a criminal offence. 'Other very serious reasons' has been interpreted to include acts in breach of good practice, such as the professional ethics of the Bar or the ethics of journalism.[3] Traditionally the Finnish courts have been reluctant to widen the notion of damages and the amount of compensation has been modest.[4] Contractual damages are to some extent regulated by their own principles, especially when speaking of financial losses and the burden of proof.

Under decree No 1070/79 mentioned above, the Ministry of Trade and Industry was empowered to give more detailed instructions for government purchasing. It did this in decree No 1071/79, as amended in 1989, which set out the general terms which should be followed unless otherwise specifically agreed in writing in individual cases. There still exist such terms though they were somewhat altered in 1993 to comply with the EC directives.[5] The agreement must be made, if possible, in standard form, and it should contain a damages clause. This states that

'The Supplier is not entitled to obtain compensation from the Buyer in respect of any indirect expenses and damage due to a breach of the contract. The Supplier is entitled to obtain compensation for direct expenses and damage due to negligence on the part of the Buyer but not exceeding the price of the Goods involved by the breach.'[6]

---

1   Compensation Act 5:1.
2   See further about the notion of 'public authority' and the cases in Eero Routamo/Pauli Ståhlberg: *Suomen vahingonkorvausoikeus*, Lakimiesliiton kustannus, Helsinki 1995, pp 162–168.
3   See cases in Routamo/Ståhlberg, pp 211–212. See further about 'very special reasons', p 211 et seq.
4   There are various reasons for this, eg the idea that it was for the welfare state to take responsibility for providing basic security to every citizen. Therefore the level of compensation of personal injuries in Finland seems from an international perspective rather low. The welfare system was also operated through compulsory insurance, eg to cover working accidents or traffic accidents. See further Juha Pöyhönen *Contracts and Torts*, pp 59–86 in *An Introduction to Finnish Law*, edited by Juha Pöyhönen, Finnish Lawyers' Publishing, Helsinki 1993.
5   See *Julkisten hankintojen yleiset sopimusehdot*, General Terms of Public Procurement for Finland, of 22 December 1992 (JYSE 1994), decision of the Ministry of Trade and Industry No 1417, valid from 1 January 1994. The changing of the name from government purchasing to public purchasing, together with the addition of a paragraph on procurement of spare parts and maintenance, was about the only change.
6   General Terms of Public Procurement for Finland 1993, paragraph 17.

The clause, therefore, sets a limit on the amount of damages paid – the price of the goods bought – and restricts the buyer's responsibilities. With regard to the distinction between direct and indirect expenses, this follows the line taken by the Compensation Act No 412/74: no purely financial loss is covered. Contractual damages are also excluded.

Unfair contract terms?

Standard contracts and stipulations have provoked discussion in Finland lately. Standard form contracts are, in Finnish academic writings, defined as contracts in which one party, who is eg in a monopoly situation, or is an organisation which has unilaterally drawn up the contract and is the strongest party, can impose its will so that the other party, if it really wants to enter the contract, must adhere to the proposed clauses.[1] Legal practice has developed principles of interpretation concerning the validity of such clauses: for example individually negotiated terms are stronger than standard terms, in the event of breach; written terms are stronger than printed ones and standard stipulations must be interpreted against the party who drafted them. The Contracts Act of 1981 gives power to amend contract terms for reasons of equity. This would be possible also with public procurement contracts – the preparatory works state explicitly that contracts made by a public authority can also be made equitable, if the contracts made are similar to private contracts.[2] This could be said about purchasing agreements – they are covered as such by private law, even though in the process leading to the agreements, public authority or governmental powers, might have been used. Therefore the general terms of government procurement – as well as other possibly unfair terms of government purchase contracts – might sometimes be judged to be unreasonable and thus amended according to the Contracts Act, *Oikeustoimilaki*, section 36.[3]

REMEDIES POST IMPLEMENTATION OF THE REMEDIES DIRECTIVES

The Remedies Directives have been implemented in Finland by the Act on Public Procurement No 1505/92, which at the same time implements the whole of the public procurement regime: the supply, services, works and utilities directives. The Act is a framework law stating the main principles leaving the details to two different decrees – one for supplies, construction and services and one for utilities.[4] It is worthwhile noting that the law covers *all public procurement* – only the decrees speak about thresholds. Therefore even the smallest purchase decision can be challenged on grounds of openness, a public authority's duty to exploit the opportunities of competition, rejection of a

---

[1]   The definition by Juha Pöyhönen n 14 above, p 80.
[2]   The preparatory works of the Contracts Act, *Oikeustoimilaki*, HE 247/81, p 10.
[3]   See further as to the Standard Contracts: Thomas Wilhelmsson *Vakiosopimus*. Lakimiesliiton kustannus, Helsinki 1995. Note that the Contracts Act can be used to amend or even set aside all unfair contract terms, not just standard contracts.
[4]   *Asetus kynnysarvot ylittävistä tavara- ja palveluhankinnoista sekä rakennusurakoista* No 243/95 and *Asetus kynnysarvon ylittävistä vesi- ja energiahuollon, liikenteen ja teletoiminnan alalla toimivien yksiköiden hankinnoista* No 567/94 as amended by No 244/95.

candidate or tenderer or criteria for the award of contracts.[1] The third chapter of the Act deals with the remedies.

Before the EC regime, public procurement had a sole objective: how to make procurement most attractive, easiest and cheapest to the buyer, the public authority. The seller's rights were not an issue. This was changed by the new remedies rules. If a public authority does not follow the public procurement rules, the remedy can be found following three different routes. Damages must be sought in courts of first instance according to normal civil procedures. All other procurement matters – that is setting aside of any part of a wrong decision, prohibiting the public authority from following the wrong decision or ordering the public authority to amend its action and interim measures – are left to a special tribunal called the Competition Council, *kilpailuneuvosto*. This division of powers is also important with regard to timing: the Competition Council has jurisdiction for only as long as a contract has not been concluded. After that the only available remedy comes from the court of first instance – damages. Thirdly, the system of administrative appeals and complaints still exists, providing a parallel route to a remedy. In those rare cases where a formal decision has been made before the actual conclusion of contract, there is the possibility of challenging a decision by an appeal. Before a formal decision has taken place, a complaint could be used.

The situation is probably best shown by the following diagram:

INVITATION FOR   COMPLETING
TENDERS   THE CONTRACT

The powers of
Competition Council   →

setting aside or amending the decision,
prohibition from following wrong decisions, interim measures

The powers of first instance   →
→compensating damages

The powers of Administrative   →
Courts

* complaint   * administrative appeal
→ overruling/changing the decision

PROCEDURE

Competition Council

The Competition Council has jurisdiction to deal with competition matters and those public procurement cases which exceed the thresholds. It has seven part-time members and a secretary-general, who drafts and introduces the cases to the council. It is considered to be an administrative tribunal, but its process does not differ substantially from that of the ordinary court.

---

[1] See chapter 2 of the Act.

Anyone whose rights are infringed or endangered by public procurement procedure can institute the proceedings. The Act states plainly that 'an interested party' has standing, so standing seems to have been interpreted quite broadly. In practice this would mean that entrepreneurs who would have had a chance to win the contest had the procurement procedures been correctly followed, have standing.

An applicant is required to inform the public authority in writing of his intention to start proceedings before submitting the matter to the Competition Council. The form of this announcement has not been laid down. In the preparatory works of the Public Procurement Act it is considered that a regular letter or facsimile would be sufficient. But it must be kept in mind that the applicant must show in the final appeal that he has notified the public entity, so the notification must be made in a verifiable manner. Therefore using a regular letter might not be advisable. The action must be started before the conclusion of the actual contract – if the contracting entity has already made the procurement contract, only damages are available as remedy.[1]

The application must be submitted in writing. Besides the showing of the proper notification to the public authority, there are no other instructions on the form of the application, so a free-form statement of grounds is sufficient. Promptness should not be a problem. The Competition Council has been able to act quite quickly – there have been interlocutory decisions given in a day, though usually the whole process takes a couple of months.[2]

Courts of first instance

The questions of damages are settled in courts of first instance.[3] Proceedings are started by filing an application for a summons, in which the plaintiff must individualise his claims. The correct forum is usually the forum domicilii – that is the court of that locality where the defendant has his domicile. But in public procurement cases the forum which most often will come in question is determined by the Compensation Act, chapter 7, section 4:

'Action for damages *against a public authority* must be started in the court which has jurisdiction in the locality

(1)   where the action causing damage was done or
(2)   where the omitted action should have been done or
(3)   where the damage occurred.'

If the correct forum cannot be found accordingly, proceedings could be started in Helsinki City Court. However, when the *state* is the defendant, proceedings can also be started in the forum domicilii of the plaintiff. To conclude, when the state is the defendant most often the Helsinki City Court is the correct forum, since most of the administration is situated in Helsinki. In the case

---

[1]   In some cases also administrative appeals, see below.
[2]   See further as to the procedure in the Competition Council, Maija Laurila *Kilpailuasioiden käsittely viranomaisissa ja tuomioistuimissa*. Lakimiesliiton kustannus, Helsinki 1995. Publications of the Helsinki University Institute of International Economic Law No 18.
[3]   This was confirmed in *Naamanka v Pudasjärvi municipality*, Decision of the Competition Council, 26.1.1995, decision 11/359/95, p 10.

of municipalities, the correct forum is most likely to be the local court, which has its jurisdiction in the area of the municipality.[1]

Once the application for summons has been filed, the court will conduct the proceedings. The summons will be served on the defendant and he will be given a chance to answer the claims. If the defendant does not answer and the case seems clear, a default judgment can be given. Otherwise the process continues by preliminary proceedings, preparation, during which the parties can settle – the purpose of the preparation is to clarify the object of the trial and to gather material to be presented in the trial. If no settlement is reached, the case will go on to a main hearing. In this case it will usually take at least two months before the case will be decided – in large and difficult cases, several months.

Administrative complaints and appeals

As mentioned previously, public law also offers a way of forcing a public entity to follow the public procurement rules. Administrative laws allow various possibilities.[2]

Under well-established case law, any person whose right or legally protected interest is directly infringed or affected by an administrative decision is considered to have the right to lodge an administrative appeal against that decision. Gradually the doctrine concerning standing has been expanded to include those whose rights or interests are affected by a decision even though they do not occupy the position of a party. Thus standing has been extended to those who are indirectly but factually affected by a decision. Organisations and associations have generally been granted standing only as ordinary parties and when the appeal is directly connected with their statutory tasks. As for municipal appeals, a considerably broader approach is applied. Decisions by municipal authorities may be appealed both by the immediate parties concerned and by any member of the municipality, including associations having their domicile in the municipality. In procurement matters the appellant can be a party or at least could claim that the decision directly affects him. Thus standing would hardly become a problem.

With these complaints and appeals, chasing the correct appellate authority can be problematic. Since the appellate authority cannot usually move the case to the right authority *ex officio*, it is important to find out the correct forum. Ordinarily an administrative appeal must be lodged either with the superior authority or with the County Administrative Court. The final authority is thus the Supreme Administrative Court.[3]

The appeal procedure is instituted by a written appeal, which must state the claims and the grounds for them, and to which the decision being appealed

---

[1] The judicial districts are usually bigger than one municipality.

[2] The ones most often at issue are the Municipal Act (1976), Administrative Procedure Act (1982) and the Administrative Appeals Act (1950).

[3] On the basis of their spheres of authority, the courts of law in Finland are divided on the one hand into courts with jurisdiction in private civil and criminal cases, and on the other hand into administrative courts, which are mainly concerned with disputes with a public interest between public authority and private persons. The separate administrative court system in Finland is similar to that in several other European countries that subscribe to the so-called Continental legal system, such as France, Germany and Sweden. See further as to the legal procedure in Finland, Antti Jokela *Legal Procedure*, pp 243–294 – in *An Introduction to Finnish Law*, edited by Juha Pöyhönen, Finnish Lawyers' Publishing, Helsinki 1993.

must be attached. The appeal period is usually 30 days. There are some formal requirements for the appeal, although it is usually permitted to supplement appeal documents to correct deficiencies and omissions even after they have been filed. The grounds for appeal cannot, however, always be supplemented, so those should be stated carefully. This is particularly important in the case of a municipal appeal – there the appellate authority may only study the case on the grounds stated in the original appeal papers.

Normally all decisions made by public authorities can be complained of or appealed. However, the definition of public authority in administrative law does not coincide with that in the public procurement regime: for example publicly-owned enterprises, which might easily be covered by the public procurement rules, do not make decisions which are subject to administrative complaints or appeals. With all the other remedies now available, administrative appeal may not be the most attractive choice. The procedure in the County Administrative Courts is quite slow[1] – or at least slower than in the other tribunals – and there is not the expertise which the Competition Council has on public procurement matters. Yet, when the final contract has been made and one's chances are therefore lost in the Competition Council, the County Administrative Courts' powers to set aside the decision may be most valuable.

However, this possibility may not exist for much longer. In the preparatory works for the Public Procurement Act this parallel possibility was remarked upon but, for the time being, left there. If it becomes a problem, state the preparatory works, removing this possibility will be considered.[2, 3]

Appeals

One can submit all decisions to superior courts. The decisions of the Competition Council can be appealed by submitting an appeal to the Supreme Administrative Court in the way prescribed in the Administrative Appeals Act[4] (Public Procurement Act 12 §). Irrespective of the appeal, the decision of the Competition Council will be followed, unless otherwise prescribed by the Supreme Administrative Court. However, when the Council has taken interim action and ordered prohibitions or obligations under penalty of a fine, no separate appeal will be allowed for those decisions. Usually the administrative appeal cases follow the same route, finishing with the Supreme Administrative Court. The appellate authorities in the civil procedure are the Courts of Appeal and then the Supreme Court.

INTERIM RELIEF

When the public procurement rules have been infringed and the damage cannot be redressed by means of compensation after the contract has been made,

---

[1]   The average time in which cases were solved in the County Administrative Court of Uusimaa-County was 6.6 months last year. Even if the case was handled as urgent it would take about eight weeks.

[2]   *Hallituksen esitys* 154/1992, p 15.

[3]   See further as to administrative complaints and appeals Olli Mäenpää *Hallinto-oikeus.* Werner Söderström Osakeyhtiö, Juva 1991, pp 342 et seq, or in English, Olli Mäenpää *Administrative Law,* in *An Introduction to Finnish Law,* edited by Juha Pöyhönen, Finnish Lawyers' Publishing, Helsinki 1993, pp 297–343.

[4]   *Laki korkeimmasta hallinto-oikeudesta* 50/154.

the aggrieved tenderer may consider applying for interim relief. The Competition Council may:

(1) prohibit or suspend the implementation of the decision, or if no formal decision has been made, otherwise order that the procurement shall be temporarily suspended until the Competition Council has decided the matter.

The Council can also:

(2) restrain the contracting authority from applying a clause in a document or otherwise applying an incorrect procedure, or
(3) oblige the contracting entity to correct its infringement.

The council can back up its decision by threatening fines. Even construction works which are already under way could be stopped and held in suspension until the final decision, provided that works have been started before the conclusion of a contract, eg on the grounds of a letter of intent; or the question is of a subcontract.

In urgent cases the chairman himself of the Competition Council may order an interim measure.

Even though the Act itself is silent on the applicant's burden of proof, it is considered that the requirements of EC practice apply equally in Finland.[1] Therefore the applicant should show that:

(1) the rules on public procurement have been breached;
(2) the breach causes the applicant damage; and
(3) immediate action is necessary to avoid serious and irreparable damage.

The council must also take into consideration interests other than the applicant's alone as expressly stated in the Public Procurement Act, section 10:

'In deciding on an application for the measures referred to in paragraph 2, the Competition Council shall ensure that the negative consequences caused by the measures to the adversary or other parties' rights or the public interest do not exceed its benefits.'

In the above-mentioned example, that would mean balancing the costs of stopping the works at a construction site and the demands of the applicant. So this rule widens the court's discretion. The Council must also take public interest into consideration. What is meant by 'public interest', or any of requirements (1) to (3) above, cannot yet be said. However, the writer is strongly of the opinion that the Council will thoroughly study the rules developed in the EC practice and rely on them. The system is, after all, the EC system, and if this common goal is to be achieved, it requires common interpretation. The Competition Council has also in its previous practice extensively applied the concepts of the EC competition regime. The Council also states explicitly:

'The material of interpretation of the Public Procurement Act consists of not only the Finnish preparatory works but of the public procurement directives of the EC.'[2]

---

[1] For example the instruction book issued by the Ministry of Trade and Industry states this explicitly, Elise Pekkala/Merja Toikka (eds) *Julkiset hankinnat*. Kauppa- ja teollisuusministeriö, Valtion painatuskeskus Oy, Helsinki 1994, p 51 of chapter 8 (Ministry Guidelines).
[2] *Sirolan Liikenne Oy*, Decision of the Competition Council, 24.8.1995, decision 6/359/95.

Finally, the Ministry of Trade and Industry guidelines refer to the case law of the EC court.[1]

FINAL RELIEF

Powers of the Competition Council

First the Competition Council can set aside totally or in part the decision of the contracting authority. In practice this would mean mostly municipalities, because other entities seldom make formal decisions during the process, before the conclusion of the contract. The Council has jurisdiction only to set aside but not to change any decision.

Secondly, the Council can restrain the contracting entity from applying a clause in a document concerning the procurement or otherwise applying an incorrect procedure. In order to strengthen its decision, the Council can order the prohibition under penalty of a fine under the Threatening Fines Act.[2]

Thirdly, the Council can oblige the contracting entity to correct the infringement. This implements section 2, paragraph 1(c) of the Second Remedies Directive, but in Finland the rule also covers contracts covered by the First Remedies Directive. This would mean a 'positive' obligation requiring the entity to take action as contrasted with an obligation merely to refrain from doing something. This obligation may also be strengthened by the threat of fines.

What can an administrative appeal do?

Administrative means can also be considered as final relief – as mentioned previously, a procurement decision can be overruled, affirmed or changed also by administrative appeal.

Damages

As mentioned earlier, under the Compensation Act, only personal injuries and material damages could be compensated. Therefore it was necessary to make arrangements that purely economic losses would also be compensated. Instead of changing the Compensation Act, it was decided to include damages explicitly in the Public Procurement Act. The eighth section of the Public Procurement Act states:

> 'Anyone who, in the course of a procedure which is contrary to this Act or to the provisions or to regulations issued by virtue of this Act or the provisions of the Agreement on the European Economic Area, causes damage to a supplier, must pay compensation for this damage.'

This is interpreted to mean that the costs incurred in taking part in the tendering, eg drafting the tendering documents, could also be compensated.

---

[1]   *Ministry Guidelines*, p 51 of chapter 8.
[2]   *Uhkasakkolaki* 90/1113.

As regards the utilities sector, the presentation of evidence has been made easier than under the Compensation Act. The section continues:

'Where a claim for damages relates to the costs of the procurement procedure, it is sufficient for damages to be awarded that the candidate or the tenderer can prove an infringement referred to in section 1, and that without this infringement *he would have had a real chance of winning the contract*. This section shall apply to any procurement regulated by decree in compliance with the Agreement on the European Economic Area.'

The plaintiff must show that he would almost definitely have been number one in the competitive bidding. According to the preparatory works, this proof must therefore exceed mere probability of winning.[1] The last sentence together with the decrees on utilities and supplies, services and works confirm that the easier evidence requirements apply to the utilities sector.[2] In practice, the difference can be quite slight from the plaintiff's point of view. It may not be much easier to show that you had a real chance of winning than to show that you would have won; the facts you refer to are most likely the same. The most difficult decision is left to the judge pondering the difference.

In addition to the provisions of the Public Procurement Act, other rules of the Compensation Act apply. Thus in case of supplies, services and works, the rules previously in force still apply. As there is nothing said about the period of limitation, it is the general period of ten years.

Costs

In the courts of first instance, ordinarily the losing party is ordered to cover the winner's costs as well as his own. Only if the case has been so unclear that the losing party has had good reason to bring the claim, or only part of the plaintiff's claims have been accepted and others lost, will each party bear their own costs.[3]

There are no specific rules on costs in the Competition Council or the County Administrative Court. Here it seems that the principles in force in normal civil procedure could, at least to some extent, be applied in the Competition Council as well as in the County Administrative Courts. There have not been many cases in the Council to date, but costs have been awarded in some cases.[4] Since the awarding of costs is in the court's discretion, the arguments presented by Mr Bedford elsewhere in this book on the award of costs in all cases could well succeed in Finnish Courts.

REMEDIES UNDER THE UTILITIES DIRECTIVES

As mentioned earlier, in Finland both the Remedies Directives were implemented by the same Act, the Public Procurement Act, and most of the

---

[1] Preparatory works, 154/1992, p 14.
[2] Decree No 567/94 as amended by No 244/95 states in section 27 that section 8 of the Public Procurement Act is applied in the utilities sector.
[3] See the rules on costs, Procedural Code, *Oikeudenkäymiskaari*, chapter 21.
[4] See eg the case *Sirolan Liikenne*, 24.8.1995, decision 6/359/95. Also Maija Laurila is of the opinion that a contractor may be able to recover costs on an application to the Competition Council. See p 114.

governing rules for different procurement procedures have not been used. The remedies are almost the same whether the procurement takes place in the supplies, works, services or utilities sector. However, less evidence is required in a case concerning damages in the utilities sector. With regard to the attestation system and conciliation, these have not been implemented in Finland, but may be invoked in the same way as other EC law can be in Finland.

CHANGES TO THE PUBLIC PROCUREMENT ACT

Already after four years of practice, the Public Procurement Act has been found in need of change. At present there is a committee working on it and its report is due before the end of 1996. Two of the main considerations are the amount of damages and improving prospects in the Competition Council. Since the complaint in the Council can only be made before the conclusion of a contract, the possibility to complain does not actually exist in some cases: when the contract is signed immediately after the announcement of the results of the competitive bidding, by the time one knows what to complain of, one's chances in the Competition Council are gone. At least in this respect, the plans for changing the Act are well founded.

USEFUL ADDRESSES

The Competition Council
PB 230
SF-00171 Helsinki
tel. + 358 + 9 + 1601
fax + 358 + 9 + 160 3666
The Helsinki City Court
Pasilanraitio 11
PB 25
SF-00241 Helsinki
tel. + 358 + 9 + 1571
fax + 358 + 9 + 157 2717
The County Administrative Court of Uusimaa (Southern Finland)
Ratapihantie 9
PB 120
SF-00521 Helsinki
tel. + 358 + 9 + 173 531
fax + 358 + 9 + 1735 3479

CHAPTER 7

Remedies in France

Hubert Amiel

The revival in 1985 of the process of opening up public contracts at the European level by the Commission at Brussels is the source of true Community law in the making in the French legal system. As a result of European Council directives, the legislature and the Government have adopted several instruments profoundly modifying the 'Code of Public Contracts'. These instruments aim to instil transparency and consistency into administrative procedures by submitting the making of certain contracts to rules in relation to advertising and competition.

To ensure the correct application of the provisions by the national administrative and jurisdictional authorities, the Council of the Communities has issued two directives known as '*directives recours*' (ie directives which provide a possibility of a claim) that allow a business which considers itself irregularly ejected from a public service contract to make a claim before a judge or an independent administrative authority, swiftly and effectively.

On the one hand, it is a question of directive number 89/665 of 21 December 1989 co-ordinating with the administrative and regulatory legislation relating to the application of claims procedures for the making of supply and works contracts. This directive concerns the standard sectors.

On the other hand, it is a question of directive 92/13 of 25 February 1992 co-ordinating with the administrative and regulatory legislation relating to Community rules on the procedures for making contracts with the utilities in the water, energy, transport and telecommunications sectors. This directive regulates claims under the agreements concluded in the industries which rely on networks – the so-called excluded sectors.

These directives require the Member States to introduce swift means for seeking redress in relation to breaches of the EU Public Procurement Regime – including interim procedures designed to correct breaches of Community law or breaches of national law enforcing Community law, in relation to the conclusion of public contracts, and final measures quashing illegal decisions and to award damages and interest to persons injured by the breach.

The French Parliament by the laws of 4 January 1992, 29 January 1993 and 23 December 1993 has implemented these directives by provisions forming the 'Code of Administrative Tribunals and Administrative Courts of Appeal'. These regulations set out a summary procedure, permitting the president of the administrative tribunal, before the conclusion of the contract, to order the party who has failed to comply with its advertising or competition obligations, to comply. In the field of public contracts or of public service agreements, this judge can even order the suppression of clauses or conditions appearing in the contract which misinterpret these obligations. This procedure is now called a 'pre-contractual reference'.

On the other hand, no particular legislative measure has addressed the declaring void of irregular clauses in certain contracts agreed in the excluded sectors, neither has the subject of damages or interest been addressed on the grounds that French administrative law already provides a means of resort allowing these demands to be satisfied.

The pre-contractual reference was then necessary to complete the means of redress, which the Commission wanted to be effective and swift, to punish the breaches of Community law, or national laws enforcing the same rights. Furthermore it seems that this new procedure before the administrative judge distinguishes itself fundamentally from traditional procedures falling within the competence of the administrative courts.

If it is not possible to enjoin the making of an irregular contract, the standard procedures of the administrative courts can open up the possibility for a business, which has been the victim of the EU regime, to demand that the contract be declared void after the event and eventually to obtain damages and interest. These procedures have a remedial character. On the other hand the pre-contractual injunction permits the judge to be asked, before the conclusion of the contract, to take injunctive measures, to suspend or even declare void, in the case of breach of the advertising or tendering rules. It has a preventive character which assures its effectiveness.

But the standard procedure has a much wider application since it permits every breach of the law to be remedied either in relation to the conclusion of a public contract or to an agreement for the delegation of a public service, whilst the pre-contractual injunction only punishes, even before the signing of the contract or agreement, irregularities which affect advertising or tendering. That is to say that these procedures respond to different ends and constitute a package destined to ensure respect for rules governing administrative contracts in conformity with the expressed objectives of the two European Council directives.

THE PREVENTIVE PROCEDURE OR THE PRE-CONTRACTUAL INJUNCTION

In order to gauge the specific character of the pre-contractual injunction, it is appropriate to underline that this action distinguishes itself plainly from the common law injunction which exists in French law in the state and administrative courts. The injunction at common law is an urgent procedure which allows the president of a jurisdiction to take conserving measures intended to prevent a situation of law or fact becoming irreversible. It is a swift and drastic procedure which, because of this, is subject to strict conditions. It is necessary in general to demonstrate that the request does not conflict with any serious issue which would take it out of the competence of the judge of the facts. It is for this reason that it is customarily said that the injunction is an urgent interlocutory procedure in relation to what is immediately apparent.

These conditions notwithstanding, and to accelerate procedures in order to respond to the demands of the Community directives 89/665/EEC and 92/13/EEC, the legislature has opened up the injunction to litigants who do not satisfy all of these criteria. Even if urgency has not been shown, the judge can take final measures and resolve difficulties of substance. Article 50 of law number 93-122 of 29 January 1993 which has become article L.22 of the Code of Administrative Tribunals and of Administrative Courts of Appeal confers on the presidents of administrative tribunals considerable powers allowing them to stop in injunction proceedings the irregular conclusion of public contracts or of agreements to delegate public service in all sectors. In the excluded sectors, for certain categories of contract, article 4 of law number 93.1416 of 23 December 1993 which has become article L.23 of the Code of Administrative Tribunals of Administrative Courts of Appeal gives injunctive powers to this same judge. In the two cases, it is a question of preventing lapses in relation to the publicity or competition rules before the conclusion of the public contract in the case, or the taking of any decision in the contract award procedure.

To balance the importance of the powers of the judges in this area and as a result of the consequences which can follow a judgment, the legislature has subjected the implementation of these procedures to strict conditions in conformity with Council directives.

The implementation of the pre-contractual injunction

So as not to change the nature of the finality of the reference procedure, but without moving away from the stipulations contained in the Community directives, the legislature has set the pre-contractual reference proceedings in a rigorous procedural framework which necessarily limits their use. These conditions relate at the same time to the substance and to the procedural rules.

The conditions of substance

The injunction procedure is open to entrepreneurs, suppliers, contractors of public services, as much as to certain administrative authorities in the case of a violation of an advertisement or tendering rule, when awarding a public contract or delegating a public service.

Failure to comply with the advertising or competition rules

A pre-contractual reference application can only be made in respect of an infringement of the advertising or competition rules concerning public contracts or agreements in relation to the delegation of a public service. No other claim founded on the violation of another rule or envisaging another type of administrative contract can be entertained under this procedure. The plaintiff must utilise the standard administrative law procedures in such circumstances.

Thus if an applicant claims that a comparison between himself and the successful tenderer would show that he ought to have been awarded the contract, he must bring his action before the judge of the substantive issues, that is to say the administrative tribunal dealing with the matter according to common law procedures.[1] This apparent strictness is at the same time sensibly mitigated by jurisprudence.

---

[1] Administrative Tribunal of Strasbourg, 25 February 1994: Société Westhinghouse.

It is appropriate in the first place to underline that Council directives only punish violations of Community law, or national laws enforcing Community laws, under national law. The French legislature has extended the obligations of contracting authorities to take on board all the publicity and competition rules whether their origin is Community law or exclusively national law.

It should be added in the second place that the emerging jurisprudence seems to give a wide interpretation to notions of advertising and tendering. Thus the President of the Administrative Tribunal of Paris decided that nothing should be done which would fail to recognise the principle of equal access to contractors for public contracts.[1] The judge at the injunction proceedings applies the general principles drawn from administrative jurisprudence under which, even when a public body has a free choice with whom it should contract, it has to follow contract award procedures and ensure equality of treatment among the businesses tendering.[2]

It will be the task of the Supreme Court to state precisely the limits of the interlocutory judge's competence and to determine the conditions which ought to be satisfied to respond to the requirements of publicity and competition imposed by Community law and French national law.

Agreements capable of being referred to the president of the administrative tribunal for his consideration

Equally it must be stressed that the procedures instituted by articles 22 and 23 of the Code of Administrative Tribunals and Administrative Court of Appeal do not concern all administrative contracts. A pre-contractual reference is only available in respect of a public contract within the meaning of the EU Public Procurement Regime, namely a public supply, works or services contract or a works or supply contract under the utilities regime.

Article 22 applies to public contracts, that is to say contracts in relation to works, supplies or services requisitioned by a public authority or by a private person acting on behalf of a public authority. The classification of these agreements arises from the method of remuneration of the entrepreneur, the supplier or the provider of the service depending on whether he collects a sum from the public authority or from his principal in settlement of his involvement or whether he is remunerated by the award of a concession.

Article 22 covers agreements for the performance of a public service. This category of agreement has a very precise meaning in French law. It concerns agreements authorised by public authorities intending to entrust the management of a public service, more often industrial or commercial but sometimes administrative (as in the exploitation of motorways), to a person of good standing, whether private, semi-public or public. These agreements, which take the form of a concession of a public service, leave a very large discretionary power to the public authority in choosing the concessionaire. Nevertheless, the requirements of advertising and competition must be respected in whichever sector they apply.[3] It is necessary finally to include in this category contracts which French law classifies in the group of concessions

---

[1]   Administrative Tribunal of Paris, 2 November 1994: Eiffage – SPIE Batigole – Fougerrolles – SPIE Sitra. Actualités juridiques, Droit Administratif 1995, p 147.

[2]   Conseil d'Etat, 22 April 1983: Auffret, Report of Lebon, p 160.

[3]   Administrative Tribunal of Rouen, 13 August 1993: Société Socetxho for the standard sectors: the Administrative Tribunal of Lyon, 8 September 1993: *Society for Urban and Rural Management v Prefect of La Boire* for the excluded sectors.

for public works and which belong in certain respects to the delegation of a public service when 'the remuneration of the entrepreneur consists all or in part in the right to perform the work'.

In the judgment given by the Administrative Tribunal of Paris on 2 November 1994, concerning the stadium destined to stage the football World Cup in 1998, an agreement to delegate a public service was held to be subject to article 38 of the law of 29 January 1993. Such an agreement is concluded between the state and the enterprise charged with building and exploiting the works.

Article L.23 of the Code of Administrative Tribunals applies to the excluded sector. The award of supply and works contracts are subject to publicity and competition requirements where the value is equal or superior to thresholds fixed by ministerial decree, and where they are concluded between a supplier or entrepreneur in the sectors of water, energy, transport and tele-communications and private law groups formed in relation to public bodies, private legal organisations created to satisfy needs in the general interest, the industrial and public service industries of the state and the societies of the French mixed economy. Finally by article 48 of the law of 29 January 1993, certain service contracts in the excluded sectors become subject to advertising and competition rules and thus contractors can seek a pre-contractual reference for infringements of these rules.

With the benefit of these observations, it could be said that the French legislature has gone beyond Community demands in applying the procedure for a pre-contractual injunction to a number of contracts which were not envisaged by the directives of 1989 and 1992.

The conditions of the procedure

The pre-contractual reference provided for by articles L.22 and L.23 obeys non-derogatory rules of procedure of which the aim is to respond to the specific requirements demanded by Community directives. These procedural rules concern the admissibility of a claim and the development of an action before the administrative tribunal.

Conditions of admissibility

The action is not admissible unless three conditions are satisfied.

The first condition relates to the applicant's right to sue. In every case envisaged by articles L.22 and L.23, the persons capable of acting are those who have an interest in the conclusion of the contract and those who are likely to be injured by an infringement of the rules. It is not necessary for the applicant to be an enterprise which might have had a serious chance of obtaining the contract, nor even to have participated in the tendering process. Complaint can be made to the Prefect in the district where the contract is concluded. Further by the fourth indented line of article 22 and article R.241-23 the Prefect may act as intermediary with the Commission when the corrective mechanism is invoked and a clear and manifest violation of obligations which have their origin in Community law is invoked. The state will be represented sometimes by the Minister for contracts relating to the public establishments of the state, sometimes by the Prefect for contracts concluded by a public authority, in conformity with the requirements of decree number 92-964 of

7 September 1992. These requirements equally concern contracts concluded by a private body acting on behalf of the state, a local authority or a public body, which is not of an industrial or commercial nature.

The second condition is provided by article R.241-21 of the Code of Administrative Tribunals which obliges the applicant, before making a referral to the judge, to give notice of his complaint to 'the body bound by the obligations of publicity and competition'. This formality, authorised by the directives, has as its aim the friendly settlement of conflict before any recourse to litigation. This is why it is obligatory under pain of the application being held inadmissible. The administrative authority allows a delay of 10 days for the matter to be settled; once this period has passed or the complaint is rejected, the president of the administrative tribunal can then be seised of the matter.

Finally, the third procedural condition relates to the moment when the judge is seised of the matter. Article 22 provides that the president of the administrative tribunal can be seised of the matter before the conclusion of the contract. Article 23 provides for its part that the judge can only give judgment before the conclusion of the contract when certain conditions defined in the article apply.

These formulae which are sensibly different but have a similar meaning merit being interpreted. A literal reading of the text would show that the judge can be seised of the matter before the conclusion of the contract but that nothing will prevent the applicant from raising the matter after this phase. Such an interpretation is not acceptable to the extent that the aim of the pre-contractual reference is to prevent the signature on an irregular contract. One can deduce from that that the moment the contract has been signed, the interested parties should renounce this procedure and take recourse to the common law in administrative matters, either to declare the contract void or to obtain reparation for prejudice suffered.

From the moment when the president of the administrative tribunal is properly seised of the issue, he has to decide on the form of the injunction. The form of words from articles 22 and 23 has a precise meaning. It means that the president of the tribunal must observe the rules governing the procedure of the reference hearing and in particular, the relative demands for urgency at the time of preparation of the file. Moreover, the law gives him a time limit of 20 days to come to his decision.

On the other hand, unlike under the procedure for a reference at common law, the president of the administrative tribunal is not limited by the constraints which restrict the powers of the interlocutory judge in the administrative courts. He can in particular deal with the merits of the claims and take some final measures.

It is for this reason that the Council of State, in a judgment of the full court on 10 June 1994,[1] has reinforced the public and contradictory character of the procedure of the administrative reference in relation to the pre-contractual reference procedures. The president of the tribunal is obliged to make the parties support their written observations by presenting their cases in the course of a public hearing. This measure is inspired by the desire to respect article 6 of the European Convention of European Rights and Fundamental Freedoms which requires openness in judicial proceedings.

---

[1]   Community of Cabourg.

It is explained equally by the consequences attached to the decision of the *juge des référés* (the judge dealing with references in the administrative courts) as they are defined by article R.241-24 of the Code of the Administrative Tribunals. It is appropriate indeed to underline that the judgment of the president of the tribunal is incapable of appeal, it becomes law immediately and it cannot be contested except on grounds of procedural error or illegality in the *Cours de Cassation*. This urgent procedure is remarkable because unlike the results of the interlocutory judgment a pre-contractual reference is final.

The effects of the pre-contractual reference

Articles L.22 and L.23 declare that the president of the administrative tribunal, or the judge whom he nominates, should decide the form of the reference. In effect if the procedure followed is that of a reference one can only consider it as a true reference if one examines on the one hand, the powers of the judge and on the other hand, the authority attached to the judgment that he gives.

The powers of the pre-contractual juge du référés (ie judge of reference)

The measures which the president of the tribunal is able to take in the framework of the pre-contractual reference proceedings

The president's powers very much exceed those of the *juge des référés* and even those that the administrative judge recognises that he has the right to take in the framework of a trial of issues of substance. They are of three types: the judge has the power of injunction, of stay of execution and of annulment.

The French administrative judge has always refused to accept that he has the power to address injunctions directly to administrative authorities. This reserve justifies itself by the desire of the judge not to conduct himself as an administrator and to respect the principle of the separation of powers. It should also be added that this renunciation also has as its origin the judge's fear of seeing his decisions ignored by an administration reticent to obey.

Community law has not been sensitive to these arguments. The French legislature has therefore expressly provided that the president of the administrative tribunal can order a person responsible for an infringement of publicity obligations or competition requirements to conform to these obligations. In other words the president of the administrative tribunal has the power to compel a public authority to obey what he considers to be the correct conduct in law with regard to the imperatives relating to publicity and competition. The president can in this regard decide how a publicity or competition rule should be understood and, at any stage of the action, he may forbid the public authority from engaging in a new procedure if he thinks that the publicity or competition rules have been disregarded.

The power of injunction provided by articles L.22 and L.23 of the Code of Administrative Tribunals applies in the standard sectors and the excluded sectors and to all public contracts and agreements for the delegation of a public service.

Although by articles 7–2 of Law No 92–1282 of 11 December 1992 the French Government has expressly reserved its freedom under the Utilities Remedies Directive to impose penalty payments in relation to certain defined utilities in lieu of granting the president powers of injunction, stay or annulment.

Article L.22 equally permits the president of the administrative tribunal to suspend the conclusion of a contract or the implementation of all the decisions taken in relation to its award. This procedure allows the conclusion of the contract to be suspended until the contracting authority responsible for the breach conforms with its obligations. It also constitutes an innovation insofar as in administrative French law, the *juge des référés* cannot prevent the performance of an administrative decision, even in a case of urgency.

In this way, in relation to all the public contracts, save in the utilities sector, the president of the administrative tribunal can suspend not only the completion of the contract but also the performance of all the decisions that affect even indirectly the validity of the contract whether in terms of positive decisions or simple abstentions.[1]

These conserving measures have not been extended across the board. The legislature in the vote on the law of 23 December 1993 considered that the financial and economic stakes would be too high and that save in the circumstances of a pre-contractual reference, the *juge des référés* ought not to be given a blanket power to suspend.

It is also for this reason that contracts made by private or semi-public persons in the excluded sectors cannot be the object of definitive measures to annul them.

It may be observed that the powers of annulment attributed to the president of the tribunal, as opposed to the powers to stay, are those of a judge of substance and not of a *juge des référés*. In effect the decision to annul or the suppression of a clause or contractual condition has a definitive character which it is not possible to review except by certain modes of challenge, the case in point being an appeal to the *Cours de Cassation*. Whereas, in French law, an interlocutory stage only has a provisional character and can always be overturned by the trial judge, the formula utilised by the legislature does not allow any ambiguity regarding the extent of the powers of the judge. The introduction of the pre-contractual reference, giving as it does the president of the tribunal the power to take decisions after an investigation of the merits of a claim, removes the risk, which might otherwise exist, if a trial judge were to take a final decision which conflicted with an earlier interlocutory decision to suspend the conclusion of a contract.

The choice of measures

In the domain of contracts and agreements and conventions envisaged by article L.22, the plaintiff can formulate three types of claim before the pre-contractual judge. He can ask for an injunction, a stay or an annulment. There is no doubt whatever that the plaintiff can ask for the three remedies simultaneously, and that the president can choose the remedy which appears to him the most opportune to ensure respect for the publicity or competition

---

[1]   Administrative Tribunal of Caen, 9 September 1992: Sociétés Sols; Administrative Tribunal of Grenoble, 11 January 1994: Sociétés Routière Chambard; Administrative Tribunal of Besancon, 14 April 1994: – Chamber of Commerce Bigoni – SMBTP Livera.

rules. Nevertheless the question arises whether a judge may grant an annulment when only a stay is sought.

According to the author it seems improbable that the judge may choose the measure which seems opportune without regard to the prayer formulated in the pleadings. In effect, the judge is bound by the limit of the request of the plaintiff and cannot, without deciding beyond what was sought, order a more severe measure than was requested in the claim. On the contrary, if the pleadings seek the annulment of the contract the judge can reduce the remedy to a simple injunction or stay, measures which are less severe than annulment because of their suspensive nature. In other words, the judge could always decide upon a stay when annulment is requested. On the other hand he cannot decide on a final measure when the plaintiff has only asked for a conserving measure.[1] Therefore in practice the plaintiff always has an interest in asking the president of a tribunal for the full gamut of remedies to allow the judge the choice which seems to him the most appropriate to ensure respect for the obligations which are imposed on the contracting authority in relation to publicity and competition.

The execution of the decision

Finally, we shall examine whether French law ensures that the president of the administrative tribunal's decisions are capable of being adequately enforced. On this point, two fundamental principles are opposed and their contradiction has without doubt influenced the French legislature.

On the one hand, French administrative law requires that judgments cannot be enforced against public authorities. Certainly this rule has undergone some notable exceptions with the obligation provided by the law of 16 July 1980 and reinforced by the law of 8 February 1995. It is thought that public persons ought to perform immediately decisions of the courts.

On the other hand, directive 89/665 imposes a duty on Member States to ensure that decisions taken by review bodies 'must be executed in an efficacious manner'. Directive 92/13 is more explicit in that it provides that review bodies may be given the power to impose penalty payments on default which do not comply with the excluded sector regime.

Caught between these two contradictory imperatives, the French legislature has instituted different means of enforcing judgment in the standard and excluded sectors.

(a) In the event that a contracting authority fails to comply with an order under article L.22, a contractor can have recourse to a damages claim, whereas a state representative may refer the case to an administrative tribunal pursuant to the referral procedure for the annulment of the contract.

(b) The requirements of article L.23 which apply in relation to the excluded sectors are potentially more coercive in that the president of the tribunal may choose in certain defined excluded sector contracts to impose a fine (interim or final) designed to ensure the observance of his decision in accordance with the directive of 25 February 1992.

But the pronouncement of these coercive measures is always at the discretion of the judge. Furthermore, an interlocutory fine can only be imposed after

---

[1] Administrative Tribunal of Lille, 12 December 1994: ARB AER Rianta Bewley Ltd, Administrative Law 1995, 169.

the expiration of a time limit fixed by the judge. These measures are not automatic and where circumstances dictate they may be refused.

If the decision has not been implemented within the time period, the judge can always enforce the fine taking account of the behaviour of the person to whom the order has been directed and the difficulties that have been encountered in enforcing it.

Furthermore article L.23, in conformity with directive 92/13/EEC article 2(4), provides expressly that the judge can take into consideration the probable consequences of an interim fine on the interests of all concerned, notably the public interest, and decide not to impose it if its negative consequences could exceed its advantages.

Finally the fines will not be imposed if it is established that the failure to comply or the delay in compliance was in whole or in part due to a foreign cause.

On the subject of interim or final fines, the judge always decides on the form of the order but his decision is capable of appeal before the Administrative Court of Appeal. It will be noticed that the legislature has provided, in relation to fines, a double jurisdiction taking account of the consequences that could attach to this type of measure and the powers of judgment conferred on the president of the administrative tribunal. They are then placed under the control of the Administrative Court of Appeal in conformity with R.132 of the Code of Administrative Tribunals.

In this way Community law has permitted the insertion into French law a preventive procedure which opportunely complements the avenues of traditional law in relation to administrative contracts.

THE PROCEDURES OF *DROIT COMMUN*

The Remedies Directives did not give rise to the adoption of special laws by the French Parliament in areas where there already existed routes of challenge allowing the administrative judge to annul unlawful decisions and to award damages and interest to persons affected by infringements. Certainly the routes are not as swift as the directives demand but it doubtless appeared inopportune for the legislature to impose a time limit for giving judgment.

The ordinary procedures of contentious business before the French administrative courts allow them to review every irregularity committed by the signatories to a public contract or an agreement for the delegation of a public service, and not merely breaches in the obligations of publicity and competition. In consequence, these procedures have a much greater application than the pre-contractual referral. But the review will normally take place after the conclusion of the contract, and probably whilst it is in the course of being performed. These procedures are of two types. The judge can, under very strict conditions, annul an irregular contract. If this annulment reveals itself to be ineffective or impossible he can then award an indemnity as recompense for the prejudice experienced by the business as a result of the breach. It can be observed then that these procedures bring about sanctions in the form either of an annulment or of an award of damages and interest.

The application to annul

The directive 89/665/EEC imposed on the Member States the duty to provide bodies with the power to annul unlawful decisions. This obligation is satisfied by article L.22 of the Code of Administrative Tribunals and Courts of Administrative Appeal. By contrast it has been suggested that since, in relation to certain specified contracts awarded in the excluded sector, article L.23 does not confer a power of annulment, it therefore fails to comply with the Utilities Remedies Directive. However, such is to ignore that the Member States are free to limit the powers of a review in the excluded sector to the imposition of penalty payments in lieu of power of annulment: article 2(1)(c) 92/13/EEC. In consequence, one can conclude that the obligations tending to result in a claim for annulment have been assured in France.

Three procedures allow for the legality of all administrative contracts, notably public contracts or delegations of a public service to be tested before the administrative judge, and if successful, to obtain their annulment. These procedures are sometimes difficult in practice and can be ineffective.

However, it is a necessary preliminary in order to obtain an award of damages to establish that there has been an infringement of the public procurement regime by applying to the administrative tribunal to set aside or annul the infringement.

Setting aside irregular contracts

Where a contract has been concluded in breach of the regime, the contract itself can only be set aside on the application of the contracting authority or the successful contractor. Needless to say such a right of action is useless to an unsuccessful contractor seeking to found a damages claim on an infringement of the regime.[1]

Excess of powers

An excluded contractor may seek to annul any decision in the contract award procedure which can be characterised under French administrative law as a unilateral act. Under French administrative law an application to quash a unilateral act may be brought on the grounds that the public body has exceeded its powers by infringing the regime. Thus every step in the award procedure to which the excluded contractor has not given his consent is a unilateral act on the part of the public body.

The theory of detachable acts

The conclusion of an administrative contract, in particular important contracts like public contracts or agreements for the delegation of a public service, gives rise to the elaboration and the signature of a purely contractual document. More often than not the document is preceded, accompanied or followed

---

[1]   Council of State, 20 January 1978: Syndicat National de L'Enseignement Technique Agricole Public. Actualités juridiques, Droit Administratif 1979, p 37.

by unilateral decisions which, without being integrated with the contract strictly so-called, are all the same indispensable to its validity. They are called detachable acts.

For instance contracts made by local authorities are signed by the executive which must be duly authorised by the authority to act on its behalf. In the same way, after signature of the contract, an approval is sometimes necessary. These authorisations or approvals are characterised as unilateral acts capable of being made the object of a claim for excess of power before the administrative jurisdiction.[1] Thus if an authority or approval has not been properly constituted an application can be made to the administrator to condemn the act for excess of power. However, the effectiveness of this procedure can be doubtful, even if the consequences of setting aside the detachable act are taken to a logical conclusion with the result that the contract itself be condemned.

In the first place, certain contracts are without detachable acts and therefore they cannot be attached indirectly by a third party. Secondly, the annulment of the detachable deed intervenes necessarily after the conclusion of the contract and even sometimes after its complete execution. Thus even if successful, the annulment will not have the practical effect of enabling a disappointed tenderer to retender for the contract.

Finally, where the public body agrees to indemnify the plaintiff following the annulment of a detachable act, it may be permitted to proceed with the contract itself. Although this practice can be criticised for enabling public bodies to escape the consequences of their unlawful activities, it has been upheld in the Council of State.[2] Thus whilst the administrative judge must tease out the consequences flowing from the annulment of the detachable act, the contract itself is not necessarily to be regarded as null and void. However, whether the force of this established jurisprudence will continue in effect is now open to question following the enactment of article L.8.2 of the Code of Administrative Tribunals and Administrative Courts of Appeal under the law of 8 February 1995. Whereas the administrative tribunal has always had power to cancel a detachable act by article L.8.2 it seemingly has the power of injunction as well to order this public body to take the steps necessarily implied by the annulment within a time limit.

Although it is still too soon to say precisely how this power of injunction may be used in the future it may open the possibility to excluded contractors to apply to suspend the performance of concluded contracts.

Referral from the Prefect

Formerly the Prefect had responsibility for ensuring the legality of local government action. In his capacity as guardian of the law he effectively had the power to annul illegal administrative acts. Now as a result of the law of 2 March 1982, the Prefect's power over local government extends to the referral of illegal administrative acts to the administrative judge for examination.

To ensure respect for this principle, the law provides that the principal acts emanating from local authorities or their public establishments must be referred to the representatives of the state, who have a time limit of two

---

[1]   Council of State, 4 August 1905: Martin.
[2]   Council of State, 1 October 1993: Societé le Yacht Club International de Bormes les Mimosas. Legal Administrative Law News, p 810.

months to take the matter to the administrative tribunal with the aim of pursuing the remedy of annulment.

Thus the Prefect may refer public contracts to an administrative judge for examination and possible annulment.[1]

The procedure is considered inadequate by the majority of commentators to the extent that the Prefects, for political or practical reasons, hesitate to refer actions for the examination of the judge, however tainted with flagrant illegality they are. Furthermore in the area of public contracts or delegation of public services this facility is too rarely utilised.

Moreover, this course can only be exercised by the Prefect. Nevertheless article 4 of the law of 2 March 1992 gives the right to citizens to ask the Prefect representing the state to set the procedure in motion against every agreement concluded in irregular circumstances, whether it is a question of a lack of advertisement or prior competition between the businesses.

To increase the effectiveness of this measure the law of 22 July 1982 has expressly provided that the Prefect can join to his action for annulment a request to stay execution. This would be granted if the matter is serious and of the sort to lead to the annulment of the decision.

This procedure, unfortunately too little utilised, permits the suspension of an irregular contract within a very short timescale on the initiative of the Prefect acting either spontaneously or at the request of a private person.

The availability of an indemnity/remedy in damages

A contractor who would have been likely to obtain a public contract incontestably suffers a prejudice in the case of an infringement of the regime which it has proved impossible to annul. It falls to the administrative judge to repair the damage suffered by the contractor by ordering the public body to indemnify the costs of tender or to pay damages for the loss of the contract. If the annulment is not granted or if it comes too late, a tenderer, excluded unlawfully from contract award procedures, may request the award of an indemnity from the judge. The existence of the power of the administrative judge to order damages against a public body explains the absence of specific French regulation to implement the requirement in the Remedies Directives that the Member States provide review bodies with the power to award damages.

The public power will only be liable under certain conditions and the indemnity is only accorded in the circumstances and subject to the limits defined by the jurisprudence. In the event that liability is not seriously contested there exist the means under which R.129 of the Code of Administrative Tribunals to obtain by means of a reference payment on account of an eventual award of indemnity.

The conditions under which a public body can be made responsible for damages

The responsibility of public power is only engaged if the plaintiff provides evidence of an infringement and the loss of a serious chance of obtaining

---

[1] Council of State, Section, 26 July 1991: Community of Sainte Marie. Record of Lebon, p 302.

the contract. In terms of procedure, a contractor must request an indemnity from the public body prior to commencing an action at a very early stage.

A contractor unlawfully excluded from a contract award procedure in spite of being a third party to the contract, can find in the illegality an opportunity to engage the responsibility of the parties who have concluded it. However it should be noted that under French administrative law a remedy in damages may be dependent on the annulment of or a declaration that the contested decision is unlawful. There is express provision in the Remedies Directive which permits the Member State to require a plaintiff to apply to set aside an unlawful decision in order to claim damages.[1]

The plaintiff has to provide evidence of the fault to be imputed to the public authority. Such is the case where a contract has been completed despite the fact that the rules of competition have been infringed. This irregularity constitutes a fault and is of the kind to engage the responsibility of the administration in relation to third parties.[2]

It is important nevertheless to state that not every illegality is liable to constitute the foundation of administrative responsibility. There are also illegalities which are too informal and remain in principle without any influence on the situation of excluded contractors and which are capable of regularisation.

Finally, a contractor who considers himself unlawfully excluded must establish a culpable illegality as the source of the loss of the contract which he should have had serious chances of obtaining. In default of this link between cause and effect he will not be able to obtain satisfaction.[3] In effect in order to claim an indemnity the plaintiff has to demonstrate that he has a serious chance of obtaining the contract, albeit without having to prove that the contract would have been awarded to him.

The loss of a serious chance

Even if the proof of culpable illegality is presented by the plaintiff he will not be indemnified unless he shows that he had a serious chance of obtaining the contract or the delegation of the public service.[4]

The Remedies Directive 89/665/EEC provides only for the principle of indemnity, leaving it to the Member States to work out freely when an award should be made.

On the other hand, the Utilities Remedies Directive 92/13/EEC provides that expenses incurred in the preparation of an offer or the participation in a tendering procedure should be recoverable on proof by the plaintiff that he had a real chance of winning the contract, a chance which, following a violation of Community law, has been adversely affected.

These conditions, which only concern excluded sector contracts and claims for reimbursement of expenses of preparing a tender, are not contradicted by the rules of administrative responsibility in French law where they apply to all contracts for indemnity.

The judge alone is responsible for assessing a contractor's loss of a chance. He will take into consideration the elements of real expense relative to the

[1] Article 2(5) Directive 89/665/EEC.
[2] Council of State, Section, 28 March 1980: Centre Hospitalier de Seclin. Report of Lebon, p 787.
[3] Council of State, 19 April 1985: Commune de Vitrolles. Droit Administratif, No 291.
[4] Council of State, Section, 13 May 1970: Monit C/Commune de Ranspach. Report of Lebon, p 332.

situation of the contractor, to the state of advancement of the negotiations or the evaluating procedures, or the chances of other contractors and in general all the elements which will enable him to make a decision.

Importantly, the judge will take into account the moment when the illegality was committed. If the contract was at a final stage, to the extent that the business was at the point of obtaining it, the judge will think that the loss of a chance was certain and will hold the administration responsible. Thus the stage that the contract award procedures had reached at the time of the infringement is critical.

The repair of prejudice

From the point when fault is established, when the loss of a serious chance to obtain the contract is demonstrated and there exists a causal link between the infringement and the failure to win the contract, the plaintiff will be able to claim damages and interest covering the entire prejudice which he has suffered. The indemnity will be calculated in accordance with the amount of expenses he was exposed to in order to participate in the different phases of the contract awards procedure.[1] Meanwhile, the indemnity can be reduced, even suppressed, by the judge, if he forms the view that the plaintiff has not taken all the necessary measures to mitigate his loss.

The evaluation of prejudice

The fundamental rule is that reparation ought to cover the entire amount of prejudice. But this rule is applied flexibly by the French administrative judge who takes into particular consideration the state of advancement of the agreement at the moment when the candidate lost his chance.

In all cases, the candidate irregularly excluded who had a serious chance of obtaining the contract will obtain, with justification, the repayment of all his expenses of preparing his tender at the time of the tendering.

That is to say that on this point French law has anticipated the demands of Community law and a contractor can readily obtain an indemnity for such damage as contemplated by article 2(7) of directive 92/13/EEC.

However, a contractor can equally claim damages in respect of his loss of profit on the basis that he would have won a contract or that he lost a serious chance of winning it. But the rules of valuation are more delicate to apply because they are based on uncertain elements.

In principle the evaluation is made by the administrative judge on the basis of the submissions made by the plaintiff. Notably he takes into consideration the average profitability of the capital which the plaintiff had to invest into the operation. Naturally it is the plaintiff's duty to prove the amount which he was intending to invest and the profitability generated by this type of investment in the sector concerned.

Thus the evaluation often gives way to great practical difficulties taking into account the opposing arguments that will be produced in front of a judge. This is why the jurisdiction will often have a tendency to designate an expert or a group of experts to determine the amount which has not been won.

[1]   Council of State, 10 January 1986: Société des Travaux du Midi. JCP 86, No 20698.

Naturally reparation does not mean accumulating two indemnities. It is not permissible for an excluded contractor to benefit from a double indemnity corresponding at the same time to a refund of his expenses in making his tender and his loss of profit. It falls to the judge to determine judicially the amount of the indemnity in accordance with one of the two criteria and in accordance with the state of advancement of the negotiations.

Conditions under which the indemnity may be reduced

It is evident that no indemnity will be granted or that an indemnity will be reduced, if the public authority can refute the existence of administrative responsibility on the grounds of novus actus interveniens or force majeure.

But in relation to the unlawful exclusion of a candidate from a public contract or a delegation of a public service, the jurisprudence of the Council of State has revealed a specific principle which leads to a reduction of the amount of damages and interest in relation to the prejudice suffered.

Without demanding that the plaintiff proves that the contract would have been awarded to him if the breach had not been committed, the judge fashions an indemnity based on the probability of the plaintiff winning the contract. He notably takes into account the state of advancement of the procedure. If the contractor was unlawfully excluded at the beginning of the procedure, he may claim only a discounted benefit.[1] On the other hand, if the contractor is excluded at the end of the procedure at the time when there was a very serious chance of obtaining the contract, a sum equal to the total amount which would have been received had the contract been won would be recoverable.

---

[1]   Council of State, 26 March 1980: Centre Hospitalier de Seclin. In this case, an enterprise kept out at the beginning of the procedure only obtained a payment of 50% of the benefit which it could legitimately draw from the activity during the duration of the performance of the contract.

CHAPTER 8

Remedies in Germany

Thomas Schabel

FORMER LEGAL SITUATION

General view

Before the EC or rather EU directives were applicable, the German law of public procurement markets essentially consisted of two so-called *Verdingungsordnungen* (regulations), the regulation for works ('VOB') and the regulation for services except works ('VOL'). *Verdingung* is a historical expression for long-term employment contracts in craft and agriculture, showing the feudal source of public procurement markets. Thus, there is no relation to the current opinion in Germany which regards public supply and public works contracts as of equal importance.

Both VOB and VOL regulate not only in part A the procedure leading to the contract, but in part B also the general contractual terms of the subsequent contract. The following text deals exclusively with part A of the regulations.

Since the award of public contracts has been an instrument of economic policy – this is the EU's opinion as well – the regulations were related to specific economic political objectives. In particular, in post-war Germany, these were the furtherance of the middle class, the borderlands, and institutions for badly handicapped people.

Both regulations are formulated continuously by a so-called *Verdingungsausschuß* (committee), one committee for works and one for other activities. These committees are conferences held by representatives of public contracting entities, economic associations, and other experts. As a result of these regular conferences, the most recent and effective drafts of VOB and VOL are promulgated in the *Bundesanzeiger* (Federal register).

The regulations are not binding for public contracting entities under statute, but by reason of administrative directives. These obligatory directives are based upon the federal and state budget law principles of economy and economical use of public funds.

The inclusion of the whole procurement law into the *Haushaltsgrundsätzegesetz* (Law of Budget Principles) – explained in detail in the text below – is continuing this disputed tradition of the economy.

VOB's binding effect was not disputed for all public contracting entities including local authorities. By contrast, VOL was binding merely for federal and state authorities, whereas local authorities successfully avoided its application to their awards of public contracts. Behind that lay the purpose of preferring the local tenderer and enforcing the local economic policy by means of public supply and service contracts.

Insofar as public institutions furthered building projects of non-state entities like universities, hospitals, or cultural institutions with public means, the application of VOB and, in part, VOL has been established in the respective *Zuwendungsbescheid.*

Public works contracts

The former edition of VOB, part A was largely comprehensive for the award of public works contracts. The application of VOB was either based upon budget law or stated in the *Zuwendungsbescheid.* Therefore, VOB does not regulate specific entities, rather it connotes a duty in respect of good administration.

First, it describes the scope of subject application by defining works in contrast to other activities. It applies strictly to the work of building. Fixtures and fittings required for the specific purpose of a building are not ranked with works. Such things are put into a 'finished cover', eg for a hospital or a telephone exchange institution. In such a case all parts of a building project up to the first telecommunication equipment belong to works, but not, for instance, medical technology or even technical devices for energy. This distinction resembles the basic principles of §§ 638 and 93ff *Bürgerliches Gesetzbuch* (Civil Code) and, thus, shows a congruence with the private law.

The core of VOB, part A is the procedure for award of contracts which roughly is divided into three basic types: public advertisement, restricted advertisement, and free hand award. Consistent with the principles of competition, VOB, part A itself sets up the priority of public advertisement over both other procedures which are merely allowed in certain prescribed, exceptional cases.

The public authorities' obligation properly to describe the subject matter of the contract is set out in detail. In particular, the required performance is to be described in a manner allowing all tenderers equally to understand, calculate, and offer the performance.

Furthermore, VOB regulates the essential content of award documents and gives a framework for subsequent terms of contracts. Likewise, it prescribes what kind of information shall be given in the award notice. The actual procedure of submission is relatively strictly regulated. Certain time limits have to be complied with and the contents tender are regulated. Regarding VOB, part A, tenders have to be submitted by a certain time and are opened in presence of the tenderers. Price negotiations are prohibited, tenders are taken to mean what they say, and only the doubtful contents of a tender may be clarified by consultation with tenderers.

This prohibition of negotiations is regarded in some circles as a burden on the whole award procedure, since it is alien to the practice of a free economy. However, this criticism overlooks the fact that tenderers are forced from the beginning to calculate as tightly as possible in order to win the contract, if a contest is conducted in strict compliance with the regulations. Thus, tenderers are not able to take into consideration in their tender any possible negotiations. They have just 'one shot'.

Moreover, the valuation of tenders by several steps is prescribed exactly. The award has to be given to the most acceptable tender taking into consideration all technical, economic, and functional aspects. All candidates and not only the successful tenderer have to be informed. The award follows private law principles. The cancellation of an advertisement is also subject to strict requirements.

Public supply contracts

VOL, part A regulated the award of public supply contracts in an almost identical way to works and VOB, part A. Only one distinction need be mentioned: tenderers cannot require to be present when tenders are opened. § 1 VOL, part A deals not only with supply contracts, but also with contracts for services. From the latter are excluded professional services such as architectural or engineering services.

As mentioned in the beginning, VOL, part A did not acquire the significance for services that VOB, part A did for works, since it was only applicable to federal and state authorities. For instance, local authorities are bound merely by the general principle of competitive award, but are free in the form of award.

Public contracts for services

The German award procedure traditionally divides services into those typically provided by tradepeople and professional services like architecture or engineering. The former may be advertised in free contest, whereas for the latter group there is a state statute of fees which excludes price comparison.

Trade services

Only federal and state contracting entities were obliged by VOL, part A to advertise trade services. This refers, for instance, to computer, security, cleaning, maintenance, repair and other services, but not, for instance, to insurance or banking services to which the full rigour of the EU services regime[1] applies.

Professional services

Public contracts for professional services are mainly in the fields of civil engineering: architects, engineers, project leaders, controllers, and other professional groups. For the selection of the supplier, there are no regulations. 'Principles and directives' which mainly regulated architecture contests, existed only for contests in the fields of area planning, town building, and civil engineering. These 'GRW 1977' are applicable to the contests of federal public authorities and, in accordance with several resolutions of state governments, of state public authorities. However, the question whether to carry out a contest at all lay in the sole discretion of the public authority itself.

The GRW 1977 prescribe mainly two different procedures, the open and the restricted procedures. In the open procedure, any architect active predominantly in the 'area of admission' may submit a tender. By contrast, in the restricted procedure, only previously selected persons are invited to participate. There are fundamental and programmatic contests which serve as general clarification of a task, determination of the design basis, or finding of basic solutions.

Further, idea contests may be carried out in order to bring a multitude of ideas for the solution of the task. However, most common are realisation

[1] Directive 92/50/EEC Annex 1a.

contests with a strongly defined program and definite requirements for performance. Such realisation contests produce the planning foundation for realisation of a project.

Moreover, the GRW 1977 have specific provisions for composition and proceedings of the jury, participation of the chamber of architecture, preparation for the contest, and procedure. Likewise, the level of the prices is prescribed by provisions for calculation. As a rule, the contract to realise a project must be awarded to the lowest tenderer.

Contracts of utility entities

First of all, the contracting entities in the water, energy, transport and telecommunication sector are to be distinguished by their legal form: in Germany, water, energy, transport and telecommunication undertakings mainly belong to public entities or regional authorities like local authorities which have established so-called *Eigenbetriebe* (owned enterprises). Like their owners – federal, state or local authorities – these entities or owned enterprises were bound by VOB, part A and VOL, part A.

This is different from water, energy, transport and telecommunication entities organised in a private form, eg as a public company or private limited company. Regardless of ownership by any public body such as a federation, state, or local authority, there were no regulations for these privately organised entities.

Remedies

The former remedies for candidates and tenderers in the award procedure were influenced by the prevailing opinion that the law of public procurement procedure belongs to private law. Accordingly, supplier and contracting entity were treated equally in contrast to the position in public law. Since fiscal activity was regarded as belonging to private law, the principle of freedom of contract was applicable to contract formation and, in particular, selection of supplier. Thus, in the general opinion, interventions in an unfinished procedure in favour of a tenderer were not allowed. There is only one case known where the tenderer obtained a preliminary injunction restraining the contracting entity from awarding the contract to the preferred firm. Yet, the preliminary injunction was annulled by the *Oberlandesgericht* (Court of Appeals) the next day. So far, there is no other decision known.

In order to give an affected tenderer a possibility of complaint, several states founded so-called 'VOB-offices at the middle administration level'. They have no power of decision and can only advise and mediate in disputes.

For that reason, aggrieved contractors have only sought to make claims for damages in respect of unlawful contract award procedures. A candidate or tenderer could claim damages if he proved harm caused by a violation of a rule of procedure. In the common case, his loss, induced by relying on a statement made, consisted of the expenses of making the tender. A tenderer could claim damages for loss of profit if he could prove that he would have been awarded the contract in a correct procedure. However, because of the discretionary power of the contracting entity in evaluating the most acceptable tender, this happened only rarely. The jurisprudence has increased in the last few years and is explained only briefly in some case groups:

- Damages claims were induced by a statement in an advertisement that all tenderers were equal. But certain firms were excluded implicitly from participation by the specification of a certain, rare product or if contracting entities awarded the contract to a contractor who previously had been commissioned to design the contractual specifications.
- The omission of vital price or performance indices in the contractual specifications might breach the duty of disclosure and found a damages claim.
- Similarly the acceptance of a late tender might give rise to a damages claim.
- Most court decisions dealt with examination, valuation, and selection of tenders. In particular, there were discussions about offences against the duty to examine and correct, the duty to disclose a recognised calculation mistake, or the prohibition of price negotiations. Even though courts concluded regularly that VOB, part A did not have as its purpose the protection of tenderers, in case of formal violations a damages claim might be sustained.
- The unlawful cancellation of an advertisement could induce a damages claim.

German case law serves as a guide to the interpretation of VOB, part A and will be valid in future.

IMPLEMENTATION OF THE EU DIRECTIVES INTO GERMAN LAW

In general, the implementation of the EU Directives into the German procurement law was done with the purpose of preserving the former structures and adapting to new conditions only if necessary.

This way caused several, and for outsiders almost incomprehensible, complications. The first drafts of the Directives for co-ordination of works and supplies were relatively easy to integrate into VOB, part A and VOL, part A. Essentially, they prescribed procedures corresponding with the former procedures when the threshold value is reached. The open, restricted and negotiated procedures correspond to public advertisement, restricted advertisement and free hand award. Only the provisions for publication and the several time-limits were integrated into the regulations by adding so-called 'A-paragraphs'. At first contracting entities operating in sectors were excluded. However, after inclusion of these entities, extension of the procurement law to professional service contracts, and establishment of legal protection for candidates and tenderers, complicated sub-divisions and repeated rules were becoming necessary.

The discussions about the right way of implementing the EC Directive into the German procurement law started at the same time as the EC Council was preparing the Directive on remedies. The Directive followed an explicit German desire and merely gave permission to establish so-called 'court-like institutions'. Therefore, the Directive was not following the Italian or French way, by subjecting award decisions to review by administrative courts.

Nevertheless, there were two different ways discussed in Germany: the 'budget law solution' and the 'procurement law solution'. Regarding the second solution, there would have been enacted, as in Austria, a uniform procurement law regulating the several procedures and legal protection. However, the 'budget law solution' was chosen and, in Autumn 1993, was inserted into the *Haushaltsgrundsätzegesetz* (Law of Budget Principles) by adding three additional sections. In February 1994, the 'award regulation' and the 'regulation of review' were enacted on this basis.

The Law of Budget Principles ('HGrG') is a 'modern' federal law which in 1969 set economic aims for both the federation and the states. The instruments of this law were efficient in the following approximately two decades. In the first section, § 57a HGrG, the affected public entities and other publicly, financially or legally governed entities are enumerated. § 57b HGrG regulates the review of award decisions by the award review authorities and their competences. Finally, in § 57c HGrG, the review of the decision of the award review authority by award supervision committees is regulated.

§ 57a HGrG authorises the federal government to issue regulations for 'notice, award procedure, selection and examination of the firms and the tenders, conclusion of the contract, and other questions of award and contest procedure'.

The '*Vergabeverordnung*' (Award Regulation), issued on this basis on 22 February 1994, refers public works contracts to VOB, part A and public supply contracts to VOL, part A. Services have not been regulated yet, but this is expected shortly. Therefore, there is a three-tier structure:

* 57a Haushaltsgrundsätzegesetz (Law of Budget Principles) 26 November 26 1993
Vergabeverordnung (Award Regulation), 22 February 1994
VOB, part A (works); *VOL, part A* (supplies)

Before the individual scope of the provisions are described, the following tables show, first, the structure given by the EC and, secondly, the German norms filling out the EC structure.

On the one hand, the EC Directives subdivide the subject of contracts into works, supplies, and services. On the other hand, the directives subdivide the entities into public sector authorities and entities operating in the water, energy, transport and telecommunication sectors (utilities). Therefore, the following scheme arises:

works	*supplies*	*services*
public sector authorities:		
Dir. 93/37/EEC	Dir. 93/36/EEC	Dir. 92/50/EEC
utilities: Directive 93/38/EEC		

In Germany, this scheme might also be drawn, but with two distinctions. First, services are divided by trade and professional subjects. Further, entities in the water, energy, transport and telecommunication sectors are partly in public hands, and partly in private. Hence follow several subdivisions complicating the structure significantly:

works	*supplies*	*services*	
public sector authorities:			
VOB/A title 2	VOL/A title 2	trade: VOL/A title 2	prof.: VOF*
utilities ruled by public entities:			
VOB/A title 3	VOL/A title 3	trade: VOL/A title 3	prof.: VOF*
utilities ruled by private entities:			
VOB/A title 4	VOL/A title 4	trade: VOL/A title 4	prof.: VOF*

Public works contracts

Procurement law for civil engineering was regulated so far uniformly in VOB, part A. This regulation had proved a success and was mainly retained after implementation of the EU Directive for co-ordination of works. Yet, the problem of regulating different facts was arising: awards of public entities below the value of the threshold, award procedures according to the Directive for co-ordination of works, awards of public entities, and awards of privately organised entities.

The solution was found by forming the VOB, part A specifically for each field of these contracts and creating four separate award regulations. However, for reasons of tradition, the traditional provisions were brought into the regulations for public, classical and sector, entities. Thus, these VOB titles now consist of 31 traditional and 13 EC-caused sections. On the other hand, the traditional measures continue in a separate part which is title 1. Title 4 for private sector entities consists of 13 sections.

For public entities VOB, part A, title 2 is to apply. As mentioned above, this regulation not only regulates award procedures according to EC law beyond the threshold value, but also award procedures according to traditional law below the threshold value. This parallelism is overcome by inserting at certain parts so-called 'A-sections' regulating the same facts as the traditional sections with the same number. Accordingly, the section order is determined by the traditional sections, the so-called 'basic sections'.

Thus, § 1a regulates the obligation to apply the A-sections whereas § 1 merely defines works. § 3a regulates the different types of procedure according to EC law, § 3 according to traditional law. However, this parallelism has been extended by inserting references to the basic sections into the A-sections. By that, a complicated box system arises. For instance, in the procedure of § 17a (preinformation, notice, dispatch of award documents), the application of the provisions of the Directive for co-ordination of works[1] is required as well as application of 17, number 1, section 2 and § 17, number 2, section 2. The reference from the EC law regulated in the A-sections to the traditional basis sections can be found relatively hidden in § 1(a), number 1, section 1, sentence 1:

> 'The provisions of the A-sections are to apply *in addition to the basic sections* for works beyond a total estimated value of the building project ... of not less than 5 million ECU.' (emphasis added)

The A-sections correspond mainly to the provisions of the Directive for co-ordination of works. § 1a regulates the calculation of the threshold values, also in part lots, and the other scope of application according to the Directive for co-ordination of works.[1] According to VOB, part A, section 2 services which serve for manufacture, but consist mainly of supplies and assemblage, are to be advertised if the value exceeds the threshold value of 200 000 ECU.

§ 3a regulates the types of award procedure, open, restricted and negotiated procedure, and establishes with reference to § 3, number 2 the priority of open procedure. The exceptional cases for restricted or negotiated procedures with or without public award notice are regulated in 3a as well.

§§ 8a, 9a, and 10a contain the provisions of the Directive about participants in the contest, performance description, and award documents. However, the order of technical specifications prescribed by the Directive is not regulated in an A-section, but in basic section § 9 'description of performance'. Also referred to there is Annex TS 1 which reproduces the wording of the respective Annex of the Directive.

§ 17a regulates, as mentioned, preinformation, notice, and dispatch of award documents corresponding to the Directive's provisions and refers to the pattern of this Directive for the notice in the open, restricted, and negotiated procedure.

Time limits for candidature and tender are regulated, in accordance with the Directive, in § 18a. The prohibition against considering award criteria not mentioned in the notice or in the award documents is regulated in § 25a, 'tender valuation'. Art 30, section 4 of the Directive[1] for tenders which appear to be abnormally low in relation to the service to be provided has been taken into § 25, number 3, section 2, but not into the corresponding A-section.

On the basis of the Directive the cancellation of the advertisement and the procedure annulment have been regulated in § 26a with reference to § 26. Likewise, § 27a refers to § 27 for the treatment of unconsidered tenderers. § 28a regulates the award notice as prescribed by the Directive, § 30a the report to the EC Commission.

Finally, § 32a describes the rudimentary award procedure for building concessions and the award to building concessionaires.

---

[1]   Works Directive 71/305 as amended and consolidated in Works Directive 93/37.

Public supply contracts

As mentioned at the beginning, the general acceptance of VOB, part A by public entities was significantly higher than the acceptance of VOL, part A which regulated the award of public supply contracts for services except works. Only among federal and state contracting entities did it gain acceptance, but not among other public entities such as local authorities.

In particular the contractual terms of VOL, part B, obligatory to agree upon according to VOL, part A, were criticised for imprecision and impracticability.

Through the implementation of the Directive for co-ordination of supplies[1] into the German procurement law, VOL, part A has the same rank as VOB. The problems of VOL's application are now partly included in EC law. Further, VOL, part A, title 2 regulates the award procedure in a way nearly identical to VOB, part A, title 2[2].

Thus, as in VOB, part A, there are four different titles. The first title regulates only awards below the value of the thresholds. The second title implements the provisions of the Directive for co-ordination of supplies for 'classical' public entities. The public entities operating in the water, energy, transport and telecommunication sector are subject to the third title of VOL, part A, whereas the fourth title is only applicable for privately-organised sector entities.

It is now necessary, in VOL, part A, title 2, to distinguish between the provisions implementing the EC Directive, the A-sections, and the traditional provisions, the basic sections.

The reference to the basic sections can be found in § 1a, number 1, section 1:

> 'In an award procedure of supply contracts with a total estimated value of not less than 200 000 ECU ... are to apply, *in addition, the A-sections marked sections of the VOL/A. As far as the provisions are not inconsistent with the A-sections, the other provisions are not affected by the application.*' (emphasis added)

In this way, there has been expressed, similarly to VOB, the principle that not only the thirteen A-sections, but also the other, traditional basic sections are to apply. By that, the law of award procedure for public supply contracts becomes complicated and without any hesitation, can be said to lack transparency.

The scope of application of the implementation provisions of the Directive is described, according to the Directive, comprehensively in § 1a. Likewise in VOB, part A, the types of procedure are prescribed as open, restricted and negotiated procedures. The priority of the open procedure and the exceptional cases of restricted and negotiated procedures are determined by means of reference to the basic sections.

§ 7a sets up the criteria that may be required from the participants in the contest. They also are orientated on the Directive for co-ordination of supplies[1] and section 4 refers to § 7, number 5 where reasons for exclusion are laid down.

§ 8a regulates award documents and fixing of technical specifications. By contrast to VOB, part A, title 2, which regulates this in Annex TS, this is regulated directly in § 8a which sets the order of the applicable provisions starting with the European provisions.

Notice and invitation to tender are regulated in § 17a according to the Directive. For the open, restricted and negotiated procedures certain patterns

---

[1] Supplies Directive 77/62 as amended, and consolidated in Supplies Directive 93/36.
[2] See discussion under heading 'public works contracts' above, p 142 et seq.

are prescribed in Annexes A to C. However, there is missing a reference to the basic section § 17 which contains significantly more requirements for a notice. The time-limits for receipt of a tender and request to participate are mentioned in § 18a. Within the restricted procedure, the time-limit may be reduced in a matter of great urgency to fifteen days which resembles the speed procedure.

The particular duty to examine tenders, which appears to be abnormally slight in relation to the services to be provided, is set out in § 25a. § 27a prescribes notice of the award in the *Official Journal of the European Communities* according to the pattern in Annex E to VOL, part A within 48 days after award.

Finally, § 30a regulates the obligation to inform and report to the EC Commission, and § 31a prescribes that the contracting entity has to determine the review authority already in the notice.

Public contracts for services

As shown above, in Germany there was traditionally a distinction between 'trade' and professional services. This different treatment continues in the implementation of the Directive for co-ordination of services[1] which does not make such a distinction. According to the Directive, it is necessary to distinguish merely between two groups of services (Annex Ia and Ib). The latter are subject, up to now, only to the duty to report to the EC Commission and are not yet required to advertise under the procedure of the Directive.

However, the point of time for implementation of both the trade and the professional services provisions was passed long ago on 1 July 1993. This can be explained only by the fact that it is desirable to carry out the implementation for trade and professional services uniformly at the same time, but that there are particular difficulties for professional services.

Trade services

The VOL as 'Verdingungsordnung for performances' was the award regulation under which trade services were to be treated at least by the federal and state authorities. Therefore, the implementation of this part does not cause much difficulty. Merely the scope of application has to be changed, which refers at present with all the other A-sections only to 'supply contracts'. As far as plans for amendment are concerned, it can be said it is very likely that essentially the provisions for supply contracts will be applicable to contracts for trade services.

Professional services

The EC procurement law for services, introduced after the Directives for co-ordination of works and supplies, is concerned with the professional area, in particular services by architects and engineers, structures not accustomed to price contest.

In Germany, public entities as well as private entities are bound, regarding remuneration of architecture and engineering services, by a fee regulation, the HOAI, which regulates the remuneration. Accordingly, for a certain

---

[1]   Services Directive 92/50.

building project there is only a certain fee which is to be calculated in advance according to specific parameters like building costs, grade of difficulty, and extent of performance. The regulation is mandatory law for prices and most public entities act in accordance with these provisions. There is no statistical material about the HOAI enforcement by private entities.

The consequence of such tight price provisions is that public entities are not allowed to carry out price contests in the award procedure for architecture and engineering contracts and, therefore, the tenders may not be compared by the level of remuneration.

Through the formulation of Art 36, section 1 of the Directive for services:[1]

'Without prejudice to national laws, regulations or administrative provisions on the remuneration of certain services, the criteria on which the contracting authority shall base the award of contracts ...', (emphasis added)

the prohibition against comparing tenders by the level of remuneration is not affected. Thus, the Directive does not proscribe a price contest and, by that, accepts the national prohibition of these for professional services.

Thus, with the implementation of the Directive arose the problem of what kind of criteria might be applied for architecture and engineering performances.

The Directive makes, in Art 36, section 1a, merely a general statement:

'... various criteria relating to the contract: quality, technical merit, aesthetic and functional characteristics, technical assistance and after-sales services, delivery date, delivery period or period of completion, price...'

These criteria are to apply in Germany since without the EC Directive the price cannot be taken into account for the award of architecture and engineering contracts.

The institutions responsible for implementation of the Directive held very early the point of view that architecture and engineering services are not suitable for either the open or restricted procedure because of their artistic and intellectual nature. According to Art 11, section 2c of the Directive there is an exceptional case when

'... the nature of the services to be procured, in particular in the case of intellectual services and services falling within category 6 of Annex Ia, is such that contract specifications cannot be established with sufficient precision to permit the award of the contract by selecting the best tender according to the rules governing open or restricted procedure.'

Art 13 of the Directive for services regards, supposedly at the request of Germany, contests as the first stage in the award procedure and, therefore, regulates those principles continuously (*kursorisch*). Indeed, design contests for architects are advertised in Germany for larger building projects. These design contests are a chance for young architects to get a contract and to become known. A lot of famous architects started their career this way, so that design contests are an essential part of building in Germany. Since the Directive has made design contests the first stage of the award procedure for architects and engineers, design contests ought to be regulated as well in the proposed regulation for professional services in Germany. Even though a structure to this end has been devised, a regulation for professional services has not yet been issued.

---

[1] Services Directive 92/50.

The regulation will for the most part copy the other regulations except that the award procedure is going to be merely the negotiated procedure with prior publication of a contract notice. If a design contest is carried out and was advertised in the *Official Journal of the European Communities*, there is no further notice necessary. Technical specifications can be referred to Annex TS which has the same contents as the Directive for co-ordination of services.[1]

The contracting entity may select without restriction any party he likes to negotiate with out of all candidates. Of course, this selection procedure is extremely problematic.

A list of designs can give reliable information about qualification of the candidates only by a close examination of it. For that reason, procedures carried out in anticipation of a decree of the VOF according to the Directive have been criticised again and again, since the selection of candidates is arbitrary. The impact of strictly objective procedures is that contracts are only given to successful and large firms, which prevents innovation and reduces the chances of young architects.

There is another problem with architecture contests: depending on the size of the building project, architects were admitted from smaller or bigger areas to participate in the contests, either from several states or from the whole of Germany. Such a limitation of admission necessarily results in an exclusion of EC foreign candidates. However, Art 13, section 4 of the Directive[1] prohibits the limitation of participation by reference to the territory or a part of a territory of a Member State. Therefore, there is a suspicion that the number of participants in architecture contests will increase immensely and public entities shrink from architecture contests because of the extremely high expense of examination.

As soon as the parties for negotiation are selected by the contracting entities out of the candidates, the problem arises of a genuine comparison of their performances. Thus, the draft of the regulation for professional services, 'specific provisions for the award of architecture and engineering services', says that proposals, excluding remuneration, can be invited from selected candidates.

Since these provisions are strongly disputed and contain legal risks the VOF has not yet been issued.

Contracts awarded in the excluded sectors

Public entities operating in the water, energy, transport and telecommunication sector were, according to German procurement law, subject to the application of VOB, part A and, if owned by the federation or the state, the VOL, part A. By contrast, private entities did not need to have regard to provisions in this area of contracts.

The distinction of a contracting entity by its legal form is not known to the EC Directive.[2] Thus, there arose problems with the implementation of the Directive since the distinction was sought to be upheld. The problem was solved by giving both different entities their own regulations. Public entities are to apply VOB, part A, title 2 and supplies VOL, part A, title 3 in which the so-called 'B-sections' implement the EC law. For private entities VOB, part A, title 4 and VOL, part A, title 4, being shorter and more liberal provisions, are applicable.

In order to clarify the discussion here, title 4 of VOB and VOL are first

[1]   Services Directive 92/50.
[2]   Utilities Directive 90/531 as amended by 93/38.

discussed since they serve exclusively to implement the Directive and have no reference to public sector entities.

Contracts of private utilities entities

Title 4 of VOB, part A and of VOL, part A, affect merely privately-owned sector entities. Both titles consist of thirteen sections marked as 'SKR' in order to distinguish them from titles 1 to 3 of VOB and VOL.

First, § 1 SKR VOB, part A, title 4 defines works and the scope of application of title 4 in the same manner as § 1a VOB, part A, title 2. The only exception, according to the Directive on Excluded Sector Entities,[1] is the exclusion of works contracts by third parties such as contracts of building contractors, hire-purchases or leasing agreements. Therefore § 1 SKR VOB, part A, title 4 does not contain the rule of § 1a (2) VOB, part A which says that a works contract arises if the performance consists mainly of supplies, and works activities are merely incidental performances, provided that the threshold value of not less than ECU 200,000, net of sales tax, is exceeded.

§ 2 SKR VOB, part A, title 4 prohibits discrimination and protects the confidentiality of the tenderers' award documents.

§ 3 SKR VOB, part A, title 4 regulates the award procedure as open, restricted and negotiated procedure without setting an order of application. According to the Directive, a contracting entity is free to choose one of these procedures provided that he made an invitation to a contest. § 3 SKR VOB, part A, title 4 regulates, similarly to § 3a VOB, part A, title 2, the exceptions from the obligation to invite to a contest.

The special form of a 'framework agreement' is regulated in § 4 SKR VOB part A, title 4. § 5 SKR VOB, part A, title 4 sets up the criteria for the selection of the candidates in restricted and negotiated procedures. § 5 (5)ff SKR VOB, part A, title 4 establish the 'prequalification system', named as the 'review system', which is new for Germany. The global description has been taken from the Directive.

§ 6 SKR VOB, part A, title 4 determines the application of technical specifications in the performance description, § 7 SKR VOB, part A, title 4 prescribes which contents the award documents shall include.

Further, § 8 SKR VOB, part A, title 4 regulates different forms of invitation to a contest in open, restricted and negotiated procedures, the review system, and the 'regular advertisement' as allowed by the Directive as a special form of procedure. This includes a reference to the respective formula which is added to title 4 and resembles the Directive.

The regulatory notice, according to the Directive, serves as both pre-information and invitation 'beforehand' to a contest for intended projects, so that a later invitation need not be repeated for the specific contract. This regulatory notice is prescribed in detail in § 8(2) SKR, sec 3 VOB, part A, title 4.

§ 9 SKR VOB, part A, title 4 deals with the time-periods for candidature and tender according to the Directive. Deviating from the Directives for co-ordination of works and services, the time-period for the tender in the restricted and negotiated procedure may be set by agreement at, usually, three weeks, and at least ten days from the date of dispatch of the invitation.

§ 10 SKR VOB, part A, title 4 regulates tender valuation and prescribes the review of tenders which appear to be abnormally low in relation to the performance to be provided. § 11, 12 SKR VOB, part A, title 4 regulates

---

[1] Utilities Directive 90/531 as amended by 93/38.

the notice of award, the duty to preserve documents, and the duty to report to the EC Commission in order to make control possible.

By § 13 SKR VOB, part A, title 4 the award review authority has to be named in the notice and in the award documents.

Finally, VOL, part A, title 4 regulates the award by privately organised entities in the water, energy, transport and telecommunication sector in a similar manner. Since the award regulation with provisions as to the scope of application of the SKR-sections was issued after the new draft of VOL 1993, § 1 SKR VOB, part A, title 4 contains a comprehensive enumeration of the entities to which it applies.

The other provisions of VOL, part A, title 4 correspond largely with VOB, part A, title 4.

There has not yet been carried out an implementation of the Directive for co-ordination of services in the area of excluded sector contracts.[1] It is observed only that an effort was made by the energy industry not to distinguish between trade and professional services and to insert both into VOL, part A.

Contracts of public utilities entities

As mentioned earlier, in the area of water, energy, transport, and tele-communication there are entities belonging traditionally to the federal or state administration or other public authorities such as local authorities. For those there shall be applied, on the one hand, the liberal provisions of the Directive on sector entities, on the other hand, the traditional provisions of the procurement law for public entities. Both have been linked to each other in VOB, part A, title 3 and VOL, part A, title 3 which causes several contradictions.

Consequently, as in VOB, part A, title 2 and VOL, part A, title 2, not only the award provisions resulting from the Directive, but also the traditional basic sections, are to apply. The application of the basic sections cannot be doubted since their validity is regulated in the respective § 1b and also in § 1a of VOB, part A, title 2 and VOL, part A, title 2. On the other hand, the Directive provides explicitly for the freedom of the contracting entity to choose from the open, restricted and negotiated procedures. However, this is contradictory to the rule in § 3, section 2 VOB, part A, title 3 and § 3 (2) VOL, part A, title 3 which provides for the priority of open advertisements and allows restricted advertisements and free hand awards only in certain, exceptional cases. This question has not been solved yet. According to § 57 HGRG, provisions implementing EC law enjoy priority over the traditional provisions. Thus, at least for non-state public, contracting entities, such as 'owned enterprises' of public authorities, freedom to choose the procedure has to be upheld.

By means of the regulatory notice, it is possible to publish, for certain contracts, with the invitation to a contest a declaration of intention, limited to one year. Because of that publication the contract need not be advertised in the *Official Journal of the European Communities*, but may be awarded freely to one of the interested parties, § 17b (2), section 3, VOB part A, title 3 or § 17b (2), section 3 VOL, part A, title s. Likewise, according to § 17b (1), section 1c; (3); § 8b (5)ff VOB, part A, title 3 or § 17b (1), section 1c, (3); § 8b (5)ff VOL, part A, title 3 or Art 30 Directive on Excluded Sector Entities,[1] in a prequalification system, published in the *Official Journal of*

---

[1]   Utilities Directive 90/531 as amended by 93/38.

the European Communities, later contracts may be awarded without any further public notice. However, the principle of priority of the open procedure is not compatible with these possibilities of choice.

The remaining specialities of the SKR-sections correspond with the B-sections.

Remedies

The first two Directives, the Directives for works and for supplies, could be integrated relatively easily into the German procurement law. Likewise, the Directive for sector entities could be integrated mainly by adoption of these implementation rules. By contrast, the legal protection of the EC rights necessary to obtain enforcement of the co-ordination directives has been completely strange to the German procurement law. As mentioned above, attempts to uphold the former structures had already been made before the Directive on remedies. These attempts had the result that tenderers may enjoy entire legal protection by the courts, but also that the creation of 'court-like institutions' was made possible. Owing to the several conflicts of interests and the difficulty in finding a juridically respectable solution it took almost three years to issue the implementation provisions.

First, the following table shows which provisions of the Directive on remedies were implemented into the German law, where gaps remained, and where additional provisions were created.

acc. to *EC Directive on remedies 89/665*	acc. to § *57a,b,c HGrG* and 'Nachprüfungsverordnung' (*regulation of review*)
Art 1, sec 3: review being initiated by s.b. interested in a specific contract	§ *57b, sec 3:* award review authority becomes active by request of an offended tenderer or if indications of a violation are given
Art 2, sec 1, a: preliminary injunction to	
– remove legal violation	no implementation
– avoid further harm for the affected interests	no implementation
– set out the procedure or cause to set out	§ *57b, sec 4,4:* preliminary injunction to set out the award procedure;
no mention	§ *2, sec 1 NpV:* order to the award authority not to continue the procedure and not to award the contract
– other decisions	no implementation

Art 2, sec 1,b:	*§ 57b, sec 4, 2:*
– to annul unlawful decisions	obligation of the award authority to annul unlawful decisions or to decide according to law;
no mention	*§ 57b, sec 4, 3:*
	substitute decisions for public entities
to strike out discriminating technical, economic, or financial specifications in the award documents	no implementation
Art 2, sec 1,c:	*§ 57b, sec 6:*
damages for victim of the violation	private law rules of damages are not affected
Art 2, sec. 2:	*§ 57b, sec 1:*
competences of section 1 can be distributed to different bodies	review of the award procedure in the first instance by the award review authority
no mention	*§ 57c, sec 1 and 5:*
	review of the whole award procedure by award supervision committees in the second instance only regarding legal questions
Art 2, sec 4:	*§ 57b, sec 4, 5 to 7:*
preliminary activities can be required to balance public and tenderer interests	setting out possible only after balancing all interests
Art 2, sec 6:	*§ 57b, sec 4, 8:*
impacts of the authorities acc. to Art 2, sec 2 for the contract, closed after award, conforms to national law	after the award only determination of unlawfulness or lawfulness of the award procedure and
	§ 2, sec 2 NpV:
	setting out the procedure possible until award of the contract
Art 2, sec 8:	*§ 2, sec 3, 1 NpV:*
decision of non-court body has to be in written form	decision of the award review authority has to be in written form
no mention	*§ 57b, sec 5:*
	right of the award review authority to get detailed information from public entities of the review

By § 57b and § 57c HGrG, in combination with the regulation of review, an out-of-court procedure has been created which is working in two different jurisdictions of which the second and last one is named 'court-like' jurisdiction.

A tenderer, feeling aggrieved, may file a complaint with the award review authority which can review the whole award procedure. For that, the authority is furnished with all essential rights of the Directive on remedies. Thus, it may set out the award procedure, annul unlawful decisions, and has a right to information from public entities. However, after award of a contract the authority may only determine the legality or illegality of the decision, but may not set out the procedure.

An aggrieved tenderer may file a complaint with the award supervision committee within four weeks. The committee has the right to review the decision of the award review authority regarding matters of law. As stated by the federal award supervision committee itself in their first decision, the scope of review includes, similarly to an appeal to the *Bundesgerichtshof* (German Supreme Court) the power to review the legality of the investigation of the facts.

According to the Directive on remedies, a right to damages shall be provided for a tenderer harmed by violations by the award authority.

§ 57b, section 6 HGrG, the existing rules for damages apply which, in the opinion of the author, are to be taken from private law and correspond with the former jurisdiction as described above.

By contrast, a damages claim by a public entity against a tenderer who obtained unlawfully an annulment or delay of the procedure, as regulated in § 945 ZPO (Civil Procedure Statute) for preliminary injunctions, has not been created.

The federation and the states are still establishing the necessary jurisdiction such as award review and supervision authorities. The 'VOB-offices' can be used in part as the award review body. The VOB-offices are middle administrative authorities (for the states: district government). They have no authority to intervene or supervise, but will mediate and give advice to contracting authorities and tenderers.

The award supervision committees are not personally, but functionally independent from the other federal and state administrations. In particular, the members are not subject to direction by the administrations. These posts are filled by lawyers and, further, consist of representatives of contracting entities and suppliers. According to the jurisdiction of the European Court of Justice, Directives are directly applicable and bestow personal rights on citizens when a Member State does not implement the Directive in the prescribed period of time. Remarkably, by contrast to Italy (Costanzo), there has not been such a procedure in the three years in which the Directive has not been implemented. It is very likely that German participants in the procedure held back on the use of their rights under the Directive on remedies and the other Directives. Furthermore, foreign tenderers did not participate to an extent leading to possible procedures initiated by them.

This is now changing slowly after the creation of the two new jurisdictions. In particular, the award review authorities are used relatively often, whereas the award supervision committees were barely used. For instance, until May 1995 only two cases were brought to the supervision committee. The structure of the award review and supervision authorities with their relatively reduced rights raises increasing problems, arousing controversy. However, it can be ascertained that the majority of writers dealing with procurement law are accepting the new structures.

Discussions began with the question about the legal source: in part, it is questioned whether or not the Law of Budget Principles (HGrG) is the right place to insert the procedure of review, and if reference is made to the correct constitutional provision. HGrG is only allowed to set general parameters for the conduct of the federation and the states within the frame of Art 20 *Grundgesetz* (Basic Law), but has no real power to intervene in procedures. Moreover, it is doubtful if the conduct of private entities, in particular in the water, energy, transport and telecommunication sectors, is subject to such a provision.

Some authors regard the guarantees of the Directive on remedies and the provisions of the co-ordination Directives as subjective rights of the tenderer which are not protected sufficiently by the review procedure now created. It is argued that the remedy guarantee of Art 19, sec 4 *Grundgesetz* allegedly prescribes in such a case a more effective and, especially, judicial protection.

Moreover, the legal relations between the award review authorities and the public entities which are not part of state administration are not yet clarified at all. The authorities have, according to the wording of the regulation of review, significant rights to intervene in the award procedure of these entities, eg setting out the procedure, making orders not to award the contract, or specifying information rights. These non-state entities are, in particular, local or other independent authorities such as research institutions or local unions. According to administrative law, these interventions of an award review authority into the procedure of non-state entities are regarded as administrative acts. In general, administrative acts as, for instance, legal supervision over local authorities can be brought to administrative courts. Thus, local authorities and other non-state authorities may go to administrative courts and seek legal protection in the form of preliminary injunctions. Of course, the same is to be said with regard to privately-organised sector entities.

An aggrieved, public or private, non-state entity cannot file a complaint against decisions of the award authority with the award supervision committee, which can be seen as another mistake of the award procedure. According to § 57c, sec 6, 2 HGrG, this legal protection consists merely in a party asserting a violation of the award provisions.

By that provision, tenderers whose interests are affected by the decision of the award review authority are excluded from the right to complain. For instance, a tenderer with the best prospect of getting the contract cannot file a complaint against the successful activity of another tenderer in getting the contract with a less favourable tender. However, this mistake of the regulation of review has been corrected by a decision of the award supervision committee. The right to complain was given to a tenderer, even though he had not filed a complaint with the award review authority and was only affected indirectly by their decision.

Affected non-state entities have no right to complain to the award supervision committee either. They will turn to the administrative courts when they are not satisfied with a decision of the award review authority.

Furthermore, the legal quality of committee decisions towards both tenderers and non-state entities is not yet clear. Such decisions might have far-reaching consequences, including after conclusion of the procedure, for tenderers and non-state entities regarding possible damages claims. Thus, such a decision has to be characterised as an administrative act which may be the subject matter in administrative courts. There the dispute could be pursued whether or not the two-tier review procedure is followed by the third jurisdiction of the administrative courts.

Finally, it is not clear if decisions of the award review authority or the supervision committee are procedural requirements for a damages claim by the aggrieved tenderer. It is conceivable that a court requires tenderers to use the procedure of the award review authority and the supervision committee before filing a complaint with the courts. Consequently, a court could in fact deny their competence for the damages claim and dismiss the suit. However, there is no known jurisprudence about that.

The award supervision committee makes a decision on its own if it finds there is a violation of an EC directive. Yet, if such a violation is questionable the committee is obliged, according to Art 177 EC Treaty, to refer the legal question to the European Court of Justice.

Another problem arises from the work of the award review authority and the supervision committee. It is doubtful if the standard of review is exclusively in the A-sections, B-sections, and SKR-sections of VOB, part A and VOL, part A which are the provisions implementing the EC law into the German law. On the other hand, insofar as awards are subject to titles 2 and 3 of the regulations they might be reviewed under the basic sections.

According to § 57a HGrG, the newly established procurement law serves explicitly for implementation of the EC directives:

'For the fulfilment of the obligation of the EC Directives ... the federal government regulates the award by public entities...'

Indeed, titles 2 and 3 of the regulations in the respective A and B sections, as shown above, contain comprehensive references to the basic sections. However, surprisingly the provisions of the basic sections are not applicable for advertisements for the whole EC area. Therefore, the basic sections cannot apply the standard of review for the review procedure since this application is not covered by the authorisation provisions.

FINAL CONSIDERATIONS

An indication of the quality of the implementation of the EU award regulations in Germany might be seen in the suit at the European Court of Justice, brought by the EU Commission against the Federal Republic of Germany after continuous disputes (Az. C – 433/93; ABl.EG Nr. C 338/11, 15 December 1993), which was decided on 11 August 1995 [1995] ECR I-2303.

Even though the judgment concerns the former drafts of VOB/A and VOL/A, and the standard of review is the drafts of BKR and LKR in force before 1993, the pleaded arguments are very much alike and applicable to the present legal situation as well.

In the opinion of the Court, VOB/A and VOL/A are not rules of law. They are not statutes or, at least, regulations and their existence is not guaranteed, since they might be changed by the competent *Verdingungsausschuß* (Committee) without legislation. With reference to former decisions of the Court, it is said that there is no legal security for tenderers. The Award Regulation's reference to § 57 HGrG (which was known when the suit was brought in November 1993) does not alter the fact that VOB/A and VOL/A are not binding on the parties.

The Court criticises also the fact that there is no possibility for affected tenderers to enforce the award procedure judicially. The aims of the EU directives (publication, transparency, equal market access and prohibition of discrimination) have not been realised effectively by VOB/A and VOL/A. There are no subjective rights for the tenderers in cases where public entities violate the award procedure. The award procedure is not transparent, and negative decisions based upon VOL/A need not be reasoned.

For that reason, the German regulations for implementation of the EU directives must be regarded, for the present, as temporary. Accordingly, there is no great encouragement for companies from other European states which consider an application for public contracts in Germany in cases where they notice unfair treatment by public entities in the award procedure.

Indeed, for the implementation of the directives, award review authorities and award supervision committees were set up in the Federal Republic and most of the states (*Länder*) of Germany. These have started their activities and issued several decisions, some published, which have promoted discussion about procurement law.

On the other hand, the relationship to civil and administrative courts is, as shown above, not clarified yet. Thus, in the known case *General Electric v VEAG*,[1] the American tenderer, who felt passed over, went directly to the *Landgericht* (Trial Court) in Berlin to prevent the award by a preliminary injunction. Even though the suit was not successful, it was, at least, held admissible by the court. Likewise, in the appeal the *Kammergericht* (Court of Chamber) considered the case admissible.

Consequently, as a safe route in a similar case, it should be recommended to a foreign tenderer to seek legal protection both with the award supervision committee and the civil courts.

As present, there cannot be given any schematic recommendation to foreign tenders. Perhaps the necessary clarification will be brought through another breach of contract suit of the Commission against Germany regarding deficient implementation of the EU directives. The deficient implementation by Germany has been the subject of several discussions in Brussels and Bonn. Otherwise, the judicature will have to repair again the mistakes of the legislature.

---

[1] NVwZ 1996, 413.

CHAPTER 9

Remedies in Greece

Vassiliki Papaioannou

The Directive 89/665 on remedy procedures relating to public works and supplies contracts was introduced into Greek law at the same time as Directives 71/304, 78/305, 78/669 and 89/440 by Presidential Decree 23/93.[1] However, the decree merely mentions in its title Directive 89/665 but does not take up at all the rules enacted in the field of remedies but only those relating to the prerogative of control of the Commission of the European Communities on an infringement of the rules of European Community law.

Thus, the opportunity tenderers could have to seek cancellation of illegal decisions, payment of damages or the adoption of interim measures either to remedy the alleged violation or to prevent other attacks on the interests concerned must be reviewed from a national law point of view and according to the rights provided in that field of national law.

In the absence of a statutory instrument designed to systematise legal procedures with respect to public contracts, the analysis remains complicated, based on the principles derived from legal rules and case-law from the Council of State, Administrative Courts and Civil Courts.

It is necessary, before addressing the issue of remedies, to understand rules that govern the drawing up of public contracts and corresponding procedures. This is all the more important as remedies, under Greek law, depend upon the stage of the tendering process, a number of claims before an administrative jurisdiction being possible during the call for tender period.

Drawing up of public contracts procedure

Rules governing public contracts differ depending on whether they apply to public works, supplies or services contracts.

Works contracts

The most sophisticated legal system applies to the drawing up of public works contracts; rules have been enacted well before corresponding Community directives were adopted. Indeed from the end of the nineteenth century, Greece has developed a legal system applicable to public works. Indeed, according

---

[1] The presidential decree mentions in its title Directive 78/669 at the same time as the other directives which have to be transposed although it has been abolished by Article 1 of Directive 89/440.

to Constantin Markakis, 'On 23 March 1894 was published the first decree on public works, which was a version of the French'.[1]

> 'More specifically, in the field of public works, the drawing up of a public works contract following a call for tenders seems to become for the time a general rule thanks to the specific provision of Art 1, para 1 of law 5367/1932 according to which all contracts relating to the execution of public works or supply of machines, equipment or goods relating to the performance of public works are awarded after a public call for tenders.'[2]

At present, public works are governed by law 1418/1984, amended by law 2229/94 and by corresponding decrees 09/86 and 472/85 taken to implement it.

Pursuant to article 96, paragraph 7 of law 1892/90, amending article 2, paragraph 1 of law 1418/84 on public works, the latter applies to all the works ordered by 'public bodies'.

Pursuant to article 51 of law 1892/90, these public bodies are:

(a) all the public services belonging to the Greek Government, and being represented by it,
(b) any public legal entity,
(c) any agency or company, either public or concessionaire, as well as any private legal entity granted a public character or having a public interest,
(d) banks totally or partly belonging to Government,
(e) any subsidiary of legal entities mentioned under (b) and (c) save firms of local communities.

The above-mentioned law provides for the possibility of extending by means of presidential decree the enforcement of law on public works to works ordered

• by agricultural co-operatives
• by private companies in which the Government participates or that are subsidised by it
• by public-orientated foundations not belonging to the public sector but whose purpose is closely related to the public interest.

In some other cases and in order to take into account different characteristics of some entities or some works, the law also provides for the possibility of excluding certain works from the scope of the law on public works by means of presidential decrees or ministerial orders.

The rules on settlement of contracts and the procedure of call for tenders provided by law 1418/84 apply to all public works, that is to say all the works performed by the above-mentioned bodies.

Pursuant to that law, a public works contract may be awarded only after a call for tenders based on an open or restricted procedure. This rule has been laid down, as has already been indicated, well before the promulgation of the works Directive. The legislative decree 321/1969 article 86 is included

---

[1] Paper given at the 4th Congress of the administrative judges in Athens on 7–9 November 1994.
[2] Markakis, Constantin. *On the taxation of toll camels – an attempt to understand the romantic age of public works in Greece* (not yet published).

in law 1418/84 which allows mutual agreement only in certain limited cases set out as follows:

(a) works requiring specific knowledge,
(b) works the cost of which do not exceed 150,000 drachmas,
(c) works that are performed in extremely urgent cases,
(d) if the previous call for tenders has failed, but only if 'the terms of the contract that has been drawn up do not differ significantly from those of the previous call for tenders, unless they are more favourable to the Government'.

Thus, even if the works and supplies Directives were not adopted by Greek law until 1993, Greek law had already adopted more restrictive rules in that field than those laid down by European law.

Indeed, law 1418/84 governing the contracts on public works makes the call for tender compulsory not only for public contracts in the strict sense but likewise for concessions of public works to which the same rules apply.

Generally speaking, as soon as a contract involves the building of a public work (ie classic public contract, concession of works or services) it is governed by the law on public works.[1] Like Belgium and Italy, Greece requires that bidders appear on professional lists called 'technical companies books'. Participation of foreign companies that are not registered on those national books (MEEP and MEK) is allowed by an order of the Minister of Public Works if they offer similar qualifications.

Bidders belonging to countries in which such books are kept are required to provide a certificate of registration that shows on which grounds the registration has been authorised. This certificate of registration constitutes a presumption that the bidder can perform works similar to those mentioned in the book.

Presidential decree 23/93 introducing the works Directive into Greek law adds that the bidders belonging to a country in which such professional books are not required cannot bid for the building of works more important than those they have already built in their country or in other countries of the Community.

The call for tenders under the open procedure is the most common and all companies meeting the required conditions can bid.

The restricted procedure is used in case of important works; at first, all companies which think they meet the required conditions can join in the pre-qualification stage; only the companies selected at this stage will be invited to bid by the Authority. It must be noted here that the works Directive (71/305 amended by Directive 89/440) has been adopted as such by Greek law, without any modification or adjustment, in that Presidential Decree 23/93 contains exactly the same rules as the Directive.

The call for tenders process is divided into two stages. The first is the submission of bids to the Call for Tenders Commission and the second the evaluation of those bids by the Awarding Commission.

Article 4 of Presidential Decree 609/85 provides that tenders are called 'on the basis of the relevant tender notice'; this legislative provision entitles

---

[1] This rule has been confirmed by law 2050/91 which recalled that concerning a concession contract, public works will be executed in accordance with the public works legislation whereas the contract of services supplied by the concessionaire in the framework of the contract will be governed by the principle of free consent.

the Contracting Authority to determine the requirements of the call for tenders. According to established case law of the Greek Council of State, the tender notice is statutory and is mandatory for bidders as well as the Contracting Authority. The consequence is that it is impossible for a bidder to withdraw once he has made a tender, which implies a tacit acceptance.

The law also provides that the awarding of the contract is done 'on the basis of the corresponding study'. But instead of carrying out the study, the Contracting Authority often calls for tenders in the framework of a system of Studies and Building of works' where both a technical tender (the study) and a financial tender are required.

The required documents as well as the financial and technical tenders are submitted by bidders in three sealed envelopes. As regards building studies, the Awarding Commission will examine and evaluate the technical tender. It is only when the technical tender is deemed to meet the required standards that the Commission will open and consider the financial tender.

The lowest bid is not the only criterion; the Commission must take into account 'all elements relating to the capacity and credibility of the applicant as well as the completion of works within a given time period'. It must be careful when rejecting the lowest bid on the grounds that it does not meet the other requirements; in this case, its decision must be justified because if it is not, the rejected applicant is entitled to request the cancellation of the call for tenders, citing the insufficient justification of the Commission's report.

In the field of restricted procedure, the pre-qualification Commission consisting of a maximum of seven members draws up the list of the pre-qualifying companies, and the process is afterwards identical to the one described below.

Supplies contracts

Public supplies contracts are governed by law 1977/88 as amended by law 2000/91. This legislation applies to supplies ordered by:

- the Greek Government
- local communities
- public legal entities
- public concessionaires companies and agencies including:
  - state-owned banks, whether owned in their entirety or by majority holdings
  - government-owned private legal entities
  - companies linked to such legal entities
  - consortia comprising one or several of the above-mentioned legal entities.

Contracts drawn up by such entities must use the open or restricted call for tender procedure.

Mutual agreement is possible only in the following cases:

- in the case of irregular tenders, if all bidders are invited for negotiation and if initial requirements of the call for tenders are not significantly changed
- in the case where no bid at all or no relevant bid has been submitted in response to an open or restricted procedure, insofar as the initial

requirements for the contract are not significantly modified and provided that a report is transmitted to the Commission

- when the products in question are manufactured solely for research, experiment, study or development purposes
- when due to their technical or artistic qualities or for reasons relating to the protection of exclusive rights, the manufacture or supply of products can only be fulfilled by a specified supplier
- if absolutely necessary, when a real emergency is due to events unforeseen by the Contracting Authorities, which is not consistent with time scales required by open, restricted or negotiated procedures
- for supplementary deliveries made by the first supplier with a view to the partial renewal of supplies or existing installations
- when the price of the goods does not exceed 200,000 ECU.

Public contracts for services

Directive 92/50 on public contracts for services has not yet been introduced into Greek law despite the fact that it should have been, by presidential decree, by July 1993.

At the present time, only one circular letter has been published, on 27 August 1993, in relation to the transposition of this Directive. However, it is not binding or enforceable. Thus, at present, no Greek legislation makes mandatory the call for tenders in the field of public contracts for services.

However, taking into account the case law of the European Court of Justice on the direct effect of directives and the requirement for Greece to include this Directive in its domestic law before July 1993, it is highly likely that public contracts will henceforth be governed by procedures provided for in the relevant directive, that is to say by means of call for tenders or competitions.

Excluded areas

Directive 90/531 on the award of contracts in the excluded areas must be introduced into Greek law before 1 January 1998. Thus Directive 92/13 on remedies for infringements relating to contracts reached in the excluded areas cannot be applied in Greece before that date. However, domestic provisions do not make any distinction between the various areas of works or supplies. Existing legislation applies to all of them.

REMEDIES

The European Commission took French and Belgian laws as a model to ensure that its Directive 89/665 brought about a minimum matching of national remedy systems so that decisions made by Contracting Authorities in the Member States can at all stages of the procedure be subject to an efficient and quick remedy in case of infringement either of Community law in the field of public contracts or national rules transposing this law.

Under the Directive, there are three powers that Member States are required to confer for remedial proceedings of a judicial or administrative nature:

(a) to order as quickly as possible, by means of emergency interim proceedings, if necessary, measures aimed at either correcting the alleged violation or preventing other harm to the interests concerned, including suspension of the award procedure or suspension of the irregular decision,
(b) to cancel the illegal decision and discriminatory specifications appearing in the contract documents,
(c) to grant damages.

The Directive leaves it to Member States to define the procedure with respect to instituting proceedings to set aside a decision and to claim damages as well as appropriate remedial proceedings, while at the same time indicating that even these courts may have a judicial or administrative function. They are also entitled to decide on interim measures pending the outcome of an enquiry concerning the public interest.

It has already been noted that Greece did not transpose Directive 89/665, limiting itself to a mention of it in the title of the presidential decree on the application of Community directives applying to public contracts. Apart from that mention, no legislation has been enacted to organise a legal system of remedies and to give to the appropriate jurisdictions the powers provided for by the Directive in the field of interim measures, cancellation of illegal decisions and damages.

Indeed, we can say as a general rule that if domestic law is already in accordance with a directive, there is no necessity to take positive steps to include it: 'The transposition of a directive does not necessarily require a legislative action'.[1]

Although Greece, like other Latin countries, has a rather elaborate system of administrative remedies at all stages of proceedings, it is true that the system of judicial guarantees offered by Greek law is not efficient enough and does not comply with the requirements of the Directive, more particularly concerning the possibility of interim measures and the speed of proceedings.

In the absence of an instrument incorporating the remedies Directive, the analysis of the administrative or judiciary remedies should be done on the basis of the legislation on public contracts and the case law of the Greek Civil and Administrative Courts.

Administrative remedies

Greek law allows and organises the lodging of a complaint at almost all the stages of procedure. The lodging of complaints is governed by article 20 of P.D. 609/85 which states that

'complaints can be lodged only by companies which participate in the call for tenders or have been excluded from it at any stage of the procedure. Complaints can only be lodged at the stages of pre-qualification, submission and checking of tenders and for reasons that appear during the corresponding stage ... The decision is made by the superior authority.'

With regard to complaints at the pre-qualification stage, the time period for submission is five days from the day of the prequalification statement.

---

[1] Court of Justice, 23 May 1985, quoted by Flamme, Maurice 'Le point sur le contentieux', Revue du Marché unique européen 3/93.

With regard to complaints at the stage of submission of tenders, they must be laid before the President of the relevant Commission in a two day time-period from the notification of the Commission's decision.

It is to be noted that if the Call for Tenders Commission considers that the tenders do not meet the formal requirements, it returns to the applicant the sealed letters including his financial and technical tender without opening them.

If the bidder lodges a complaint within two days from the dismissal of his complaint for reasons of form, such as lack of documents, he has to annex the missing documents (such as police record or certificate indicating that the company is sound, etc). The tenders remain unopened until the announcement of the decision made as a result of the complaint.

The present legislation does not provide for the submission of a complaint at the time of the opening of financial tenders. This constitutes an important gap 'which should be filled by courts by means of an extensive interpretation and enforcement of the general provisions governing remedies against administrative decisions'.[1]

Judicial remedies

Cancellation of illegal acts

The call for tenders comprises several successive steps, each one depending on the previous one and the last one incorporating all the previous acts so that they lose their independence.

The last step concerns the decision to approve or to reject the result of the call for tenders. According to the procedure, the Awarding Commission puts forward a number of bids, the acceptance of which by the relevant Contracting Authority will tie the parties in a binding contract.

Like other Latin countries, Greece has adopted the theory of detachable acts; acts are considered as detachable if they occurred before the conclusion of the contract and have as their objective that conclusion, for example the call for tenders notice, the acceptance of the result of the call for tenders, etc.

Concerning public contracts, Greek law makes a distinction between:

(a) acts before concluding a contract but aiming at its conclusion, such as the call for tender notice, the tendering process, etc,
(b) acts concerning interpretation, implementation or cancellation of the contract such as termination for breach, fixing of unit prices and so on.

Only acts of the first type are deemed detachable and can be subject to a request for their cancellation before the Council of State. The second category acts create administrative disputes within the competence of Administrative Courts. Moreover, third parties are entitled to request the cancellation of detachable acts, even after the conclusion of the contract.

The administrative act the cancellation of which is requested must be enforceable, which means it must entail a mandatory act or a default

---

[1] Tzika-Hatzopoulou, Alice, *Building of Public Works* (4th edn.), Athens – Edition Papasotiriou (1994).

without any other proceedings or judicial decision.[1] Each party having an interest in bringing an action can petition to cancel an illegal decision before the Council of State in accordance with general provisions relating to the cancellation of administrative acts.

The interest in bringing an action can be exercised by any natural or legal person whose rights have been infringed in a real or legal situation which is protected by law. In particular, under decree 18/1989, article 47, concerning a petition to cancel a decision, the interest in bringing an action is justified when the contentious act has caused a material or moral prejudice to the petitioner and when he suffered this prejudice when he was in a well defined position recognised by rules of law (Council of State 4037/1979, 86/1988).

The interest in bringing an action has to exist concurrently:

(a) at the time of the promulgation of the contentious act,
(b) when the demand for cancellation is brought, ie when the petition has been lodged,
(c) when the case is pleaded (Council of State 2319/1984, 2865/1987, 2973/1989).[2]

Under established case law, the interest in bringing an action must be personal, direct and present, 'an interest in bringing an action which is to come or occasional or inaccurate, hoped or passed makes unacceptable the petition for cancellation.' (Council of State, 3564/1977, 2398/1980, 2449/1980).[3]

We can note immediately the difference between the interest in bringing an action as required by Greek law with respect to cancellation of a decision and the definition given by the Directive under the terms of which an interested person is 'any person having or having had an interest in obtaining a definite works or supplies public contract, and who has been or was in danger of being injured by an alleged violation.'

In Greek law, conditions for introducing proceedings to cancel a decision are more severe than those provided for in the Directive since in reality, under Greek law, only an existing prejudice can justify a demand for cancellation. In addition, we may note that generally speaking, the acceptance of this request will be examined in accordance with the legislation prevailing at the time of the promulgation of the contentious administrative act or at the time of the contentious default (decree 18/1989, article 77, paragraph 5). Moreover, the existence of an interest in bringing an action as well as all the conditions for acceptance are automatically reviewed by the Council of State (decision 2856/85).

Reverting to the various detachable acts comprising a call for tenders, we must indicate that according to the case law of the Council of State, any

---

[1] The above-mentioned rule is illustrated in a judgment of the Council of State (no 3306/91) where the relief sought was the cancellation (a) of a decision of the awarding Commission accepting a bidder's petition brought before an administrative tribunal and validating its financial proposal, (b) of a subsequent decision of the Awarding Commission rejecting another petition brought by the same bidder, and (c) of a decision approving the awarding of the works to the said bidder. The Council of State said that only the last decision was enforceable 'having completed the call for tenders procedure after having incorporated the two last decisions'.

[2] Decisions quoted by Spiliotopoulos, E, *Public Law* (5th edn). Athens – Komotini, Sakoulas Editions (1991).

[3] Spiliotopoulos, E, op cit.

company that has participated in the call for tenders without challenging the legality of the terms of the call for tenders notice is not entitled afterwards to request the cancellation of this notice as it is considered to have tacitly recognised its legality. Indeed Greek law recognises the principle that tacit or express acceptance of an administrative act precludes the participating party from challenging its validity (State Council 432/1983, 3547/1987, 2836/1987, 3306/1991).

Under established case law, the call for tenders notice is a statutory act which binds bidders as well as the Contracting Authority (Athens Administrative Court of Appeal 2555/1987). On the other hand, the injured bidder can request the cancellation of subsequent administrative acts, including the approval of the choice of the Awarding Commission by the Minister or its refusal by the Administration.

Furthermore, the Directive authorises the Review Bodies to remove the technical, economic or discriminatory details included in the call for tenders documents, in the specifications or in any other document relating to the procedure of drawing up the relevant contract. But in Greek law, when we are faced with detachable administrative acts, their cancellation is possible according to the process described above. However, if details are included in the specifications which are not enforceable, a request to annul is not permitted, only a claim for compensation from the plaintiff on the basis of the precontractual liability of the Contracting Authority (see heading 'Indemnification', below) is admissible.

More often, the circumstances surrounding the call for tenders that the Council of State cancels, either for illegality or for insufficiency of reasoning, are either the Minister's approval of the bidder as proposed by the Awarding Commission or the refusal of the authority to approve the choice of the Commission. When the cancellation is pronounced for insufficiency of reasoning, the Contracting Authority has to take the same decision again but on a better reasoning.[1]

The cancellation of the decision of the Awarding Commission, of the acceptance by the Minister or its refusal by the relevant Minister can also be pronounced for illegality. This is the case when supplies offered by the bidder do not correspond to the call for tenders standards (Council of State 1325/1976) or when the awarding decision is made by an incompetent Authority (by the Chief District Officer instead of the Director of technical services of a district when the works have been ordered by the 'prefecture', Council of State 3175/1987).

The request to annul the decision must be made within a 60-day period plus 30 extra days if the applicants live abroad as of the date of the publishing or notification of the act. This request can be lodged only against enforceable

---

[1] I will quote for example a decision of fundamental importance of the Council of State, no 2468/1982, with respect to a case in which one of the bidders had requested the cancellation of a Ministerial decision approving the choice by the Awarding Commission of the company Control Data Greece Inc for the supply of computers to the Greek Customs, as well as the decision of the Awarding Commission.

The Finance Minister's decision to accept Control Data Greece Inc was initially set aside by the Council of State for inadequate reasoning, the Awarding Commission having chosen the second lowest bid, because of the quality of its products but without relevant grounds; following this cancellation, the Awarding Commission has suggested the same bidder again and the Minister has once more accepted this choice. The Council of State having once more deemed that this new decision was also insufficiently reasoned, the matter was referred again to the Awarding Commission 'for further evaluation with respect to reasoning'.

acts arising from Administrative Authorities or public legal entities (decree 18/1989, article 45).

In reality, even after the cancellation of the contentious act, the petitioner will be granted only damages since the proceedings before the Council of State extend over one to three years and no interim measures are provided for.

Indemnification

Pursuant to the Directive, any person having or having had an interest in signing a specific public contract for supplies or works and who is or may be injured by an alleged violation is entitled to claim damages.

In Greek law, the civil liability of the Government is ruled by sections 105 and 106 of the introductory law to the Civil Code which provides that indemnification can be claimed when an illegal act or a default is made by a Government body or public legal entities in the execution of their duties save if the act or the default has been imposed by public interests.[1]

Anybody having suffered damage can claim for indemnification before the Administrative Court in accordance with law no 1406.83, section 1, paragraph 2. The judgment issued by the Administrative Court is subject to appeal but even the decision given by the Administrative Court of Appeal is not enforceable against the Government, which executes only decisions issued by the Council of State. Given the length of proceedings before those three jurisdictions ie two to four years, the payment of the indemnity occurs very often nine to ten years after.

Claim for indemnification independent from the other remedies (such as a request to annul) can be brought in an autonomous way. When considering the case, Administrative Courts can review the legality of the administrative act or the default subject of course to a res judicata decision issued by the Council of State after a request to annul. Thus the annulment of the illegal act is not a pre-requisite to a claim for indemnification.

Damages may be awarded to:

(a)   the bidder having suffered from a pre-contractual fault from a Government body
(b)   the bidder illegally excluded from the call for tenders for content and form reasons
(c)   the provisional successful bidder who has not been in a position to conclude the contract because of the cancellation of the call for tenders or because of the lack of approval of the awarding statement by the Contracting Authority.

Pre-contractual liability

With respect to public contracts, Greek law distinguishes between the pre-contractual liability of the Contracting Authority and the contractual liability.

Doctrine and case law deem that provisions of the Civil Code relating to the role and the importance of the parties' consent when concluding the contract

---

[1]   Pavlopoulos, P, *Civil Liability of the State.* Athens – Komotini Editions Sakoulas (1989).

must also apply to public contracts since these contracts derive from the consent of two contracting parties.

On the other hand, it is deemed that the public contract differs from the private contract at the stage of its implementation, when the public contractor's prerogatives appear. These upset the balance between both contractors and give the contract its public character.

On the basis of this reasoning, the rules governing precontractual liability apply to the call for tenders and more generally speaking to the stage before the conclusion of the contract by virtue of sections 197 and 198 of the Civil Code, whereas liability concerning the implementation or the termination of the contract is governed by section 7, paragraph 2 of law 1418/1984 on public works. We will see hereafter that the indemnity granted on the basis of the pre-contractual liability of the Contracting Authority includes real prejudice and loss of profit whereas in the field of contractual liability, the defendant is only ordered to compensate for the real prejudice.

In the case of public contracts, concluded after a call for tenders, publishing the call for tenders notice is an invitation to enter into negotiations and thus opens the pre-contractual stage.[1] Bids constitute proposals for the conclusion of the relevant contract. Finally, the tendering process leading to the conclusion of the contract is the acceptance of the bid and therefore of the proposal.

Therefore, all the stages of the procedure, from the publishing of the call for tenders notice to the conclusion of the contract, are governed by sections 197 and 198 of the Civil Code on the precontractual liability.

Given this liability, the Contracting Authority has an obligation to inform, defined by case-law as the obligation 'to give the contractor information and clarifications on the the content of the contract including those that may affect the contractor's decision' (Athens Administrative Court of Appeal decision no 247/1947, 1837/1987, 922/1988, Komotini Administrative Court of Appeal, decision no 45/1988).

So it has been held that the defendant is liable for mistakes or omissions in the call for tenders documents (Athens Administrative Court of Appeal, decision 2892/1987) and that the successful tenderer having to perform works under less favourable conditions than those which would have been agreed by contract if he had been aware, when concluding the contract, of everything, can claim compensation. The most usual case is an under-estimate of the cost of the works resulting from inaccurate information provided by the Government services.

According to established case law concerning such cases, compensation for the prejudice must cover the difference between the income resulting from the implementation of the contract and the income which the contractor would have earned had the contract been concluded without error on the part of the contracting authority. In accordance with section 298, paragraph 2 of the Greek Civil Code, the patrimony situation which would have prevailed if no mistake had been made is assessed 'in the light of normal conditions or specific circumstances including preparatory steps' taken by the claimant.

The prejudice can be proved by any means including witnesses (decision no 16898/1979 of Athens High Court).

---

[1] Georgiadis, A and Pavlopoulos, P, 'The liability from negotiations in the frame of public contracts', Nomico Vima 1987, Volume 35, pp 701–706.

Cancellation of the call for tenders or non approval of the awarding statement

In this second category of claims for compensation, a tenderer, although making a lower bid, failed to conclude a contract with the Government services, either because of the cancellation of the call for tenders or because of the non-approval by the Contracting Authority of the choice of the Awarding Commission.

Two judgments of fundamental importance given by the High Court of Athens and by the Administrative Court of Appeal of Crete are a good example.[1]

In the first case, the applicant, who had made the lowest bid, was temporarily awarded the contract of public works but the Minister of Public Works subsequently cancelled the call for tenders on the grounds that there was no real competition; his decision set aside by the Council of State for illegal reasoning whereas in the meantime, works were subject to a new call for tenders and awarded to another bidder.

By a second Order, the Minister of Public Works cancelled a new call for tenders but this second Order was again cancelled by the Council of State. The High Court granted the applicant an indemnification equal to the loss of profit generated by the illegal behaviour of the Authority on the basis of the profit that the applicant could have expected 'given normal developments, particular circumstances and including preparatory measures it had taken'.

In the second of the two cases, the relevant Contracting Authority had not approved the choice of the joint venture by the Awarding Commission in its statement and decided on a new call for tenders following which another bidder was accepted.

Upon the request of the claimant, the Council of State set aside the decision and the claimant claimed for compensation on the grounds of the non-approval of the statement of the Awarding Commision which excluded it from concluding the contract even though it was the lowest bidder.

The Court acceded to its claim pursuant to section 105 of the introductory law to the Civil Code and rejected the implementation of section 8 paragraph 4 of statutory order 724/79 providing that 'if the call for tenders is cancelled or is not approved for any reason, no bidder can claim for compensation'. It found that even if no compensation can be claimed in case of cancellation or non-approval of the call for tenders for a legal reason, this is not true when the reason is illegal. The indemnity granted included the expenses for final studies, loss of profit and moral prejudice.

Disqualification of a bidder during the call for tenders

The disqualification of a bidder during the call for tenders makes it difficult for him to claim subsequently, in his demand for compensation, that he would have been awarded the contract. In such a case, a claim for compensation is based on the illegality of the exclusion and the prejudice consists in the impossibility of being awarded the contract.

If the claimant has been disqualified after the evaluation of bids (thus for a reason of content and not of form), he must establish that without this illegal disqualification, he would have been in a position to conclude the

---

[1]   Quoted by Moukiou, Chryssoula, 'Commentaries of the decision no 114/94 of the Administrative Tribunal of Patras', Public Works Case Law, Part 2, 901/13.

contract, ie he has to establish a link of causation between the Government Services' fault and his disqualification. On the other hand, if the bid was disqualified before being open, ie for a reason of form, the claimant cannot maintain that the contract would have been awarded to him since his bid was not even known[1] to allow this to happen; in that case, the claimant must establish a link of causation between the Government Services' fault and the impossibility for him to have his bid examined by the Awarding Commission.

In both cases, it is difficult to establish a link of causation between the fault and the potential damage and the Greek Administrative Judge is reluctant to acknowledge the existence of such a link of causation or to acknowledge a prejudice which he considers not proven (Decision no 114/94 of Patras Administrative Court).

The demand for compensation is very often dismissed while the illegality of the disqualification is acknowledged by the Court. However, the claimant should at least be indemnified for his losses and for his real prejudice resulting from expenses incurred for the preparation of the bid.

Interim measures

Greek law does not provide for interim protective measures protecting the disqualified bidder which would aim at suspending the contracting procedure and enable the bidder illegally disqualified to join in again.

However, Directive 89/665 imposes on Member States an obligation to take without delay and through emergency proceedings interim measures to remedy the alleged violation or prevent other damages, including measures designed to suspend the challenged public works contracting procedure or the implementation of any decision made by the Contracting Authority. It has already been said that this Directive has not been introduced into Greek law but it does have a direct effect even in the absence of corresponding rules in the domestic law.

As has already been noted, the position of the Council of State's Commission for suspensive measures (Epitropi Anastolon) is different since this Commission finds that 'the Commission for suspensive measures examines whether the suspension of the implementation of the challenged act is appropriate but is not bound by Article 2 of Directive 89/665 of the European Communities and is not obliged to decide such a suspension.'[2]

Legislation on the operation and prerogatives of the Council of State (Presidential Decree 18/1989) requires that the act the suspension of which is requested leads to direct, hardly irremediable or remediable damages. If the damages are financial, which is the most common case in the field of public contracts, according to established case law, these damages are said to be remediable and there is therefore no reason for suspending the act.

Furthermore, the suspension of a decision can be requested only in the course of a demand to annul before the Council of State; Administrative Tribunals and Courts are competent only with respect to compensation claims following an illegal administrative act and do not have, in such a case, the power to order interim measures.

---

[1] Judgment quoted by Chryssoula Moukiou, op cit.
[2] Decision no 736/94 of the Commission for suspensive measures quoted by Chryssoula Moukiou, op cit.

In addition to this, a suspension of the proceedings or the implementation of the challenged act cannot be ordered by the Council of State (Epitropi Anastolon) if the public interest so required. If it is ordered, the suspension of implementation is mandatory for the Government Services, which are not entitled to promulgate another administrative act to replace the first one or 'to counteract the suspensive effect' (Council of State, decision 2044/88).[1]

Given the difficulty of obtaining interim measures and the length of proceedings for cancelling an administrative act before the Council of State, the bidder injured by a violation will be entitled only to an indemnity.

Conclusion

It is true that remedies provided for by Greek law do not meet the requirements of the Directive. Interim measures are almost impossible to take.

Moreover, although Greek legislation provides for remedies with respect to the cancellation of illegal administrative acts and indemnification, illegal specifications cannot be set aside because they are not enforceable.

Rules relating to the existence of a legal interest in bringing an action are particularly restrictive, notwithstanding that the Directive gives standing to any person who risks being harmed by an infringement of the Regime.

Moreover, proceedings are neither fast nor efficient; very often, works are performed before a decision is made on the validity of the call for tenders.

It is true that Greece must take the necessary steps to ensure that decisions made by the Contracting Authority can be subject to efficient remedies, including the possibility of interim measures designed to suspend contracting procedures in cases of reported violation.

The judicial power of Administrative Courts should then be extended in order to enable them to order, as civil courts do, interim measures including the power to suspend, for a short time, proceedings or the implementation of the contentious act, pending the decision of the Council of State on a request for its cancellation. It is obvious that the length of the proceedings of cancellation should also be reduced.

Moreover, any illegal administrative act should be able to be cancelled in the field of public contracts, including those concluded by private entities for which only civil courts have jurisdiction whereas they have no power to set aside any administrative act.

Therefore, all disputes relating to public contracts should be submitted to administrative courts, whether concluded by public or private persons.

Finally, administrative proceedings should be accelerated since we must keep in mind that even in the field of compensation, before the Administrative Court, the Administrative Court of Appeal and the Council of State, the injured party must at present wait for about ten years before being entitled to receive its indemnity.

[1]   Spiliotopoulos, E, op cit.

CHAPTER 10

Remedies in Ireland

Adrian Hardiman and Yvonne Murphy

REMEDIES PRIOR TO THE EC REGIME

Prior to the implementation in Ireland of the Remedies Directives of 1989 and 1992, the Public Procurement Directives were implemented in Ireland by administrative action. There was no legislation or statutory instrument: the method of implementation was to issue circulars to contracting authorities giving instructions on how Community obligations should be met.

In 1988 the Joint Parliamentary Committee on the secondary legislation of the European Communities issued a report in relation to *public works and public supply contracts*. In this, the system of implementation by circular was criticised:

'...The Joint Committee would doubt the correctness of this procedure insofar as setting down rules for dealing with tenders is legislative in character. In addition, circulars are less accessible to the public and interested parties. It is, therefore, desirable that rules be set out in regulations under the European Communities Act 1972. However, if the proposed compliance directive is adopted, the Committee is of the opinion that its implementation will require the enactment of legislation either primary or secondary.'

The system of administrative circulars was considered by the High Court of Ireland in *Browne v An Bord Pleanala (The Planning Board)*.[1]

Considering the implementation of the Environmental Impact Assessment Directive by administrative circular Mr Justice Barron held:

'...Such a circular does not have the force of law and for this reason cannot have incorporated any of the provisions of the directive into our domestic law.'

At the time the Joint Committee produced its report, it was apparently intended that the new Council Directives would also be implemented by administrative circular: its report and the *Browne* case appear to have influenced the decision to proceed by secondary legislation.

Irish official attitudes to the Public Procurement Directives, 71/305 and

---

[1] [1989] ILRM 865.

77/62, as amended, were enthusiastic. Summarising the position as of 1988, the Parliamentary Joint Committee quoted above stated:

> 'Ireland already operates more open tendering procedures for a greater proportion of its contracts than most other member states and the Department of Industry and Commerce considers that the balance of opportunities created by the new Public Supply Directive is in Ireland's favour relative to our European partners. The Construction Industry Federation is in favour of the Commission's proposals relating to public works and in light of the experience of its members considers that a Directive to ensure compliance with those proposals is essential.'

A principal feature of the system of implementation by administrative circular was that the contents of the circulars did not become generally known. This makes it difficult to assess the degree of application of the Public Procurement Directives. There are two features which suggest a somewhat unsatisfactory situation: there appear to have been very few occasions when tenders were advertised in the Official Journal, and the usual practice in relation to public works contracts was to require compliance of materials with Irish standards. This latter practice was subsequently found by the ECJ to contravene Article 30 of the EEC Treaty.[1]

Prior to the implementation of the Remedies Directives, there were very significant difficulties in seeking legal redress for contraventions of the Public Procurement Directives. There were no specific remedies available. Anyone seeking a judicial review of a decision to award a contract, or fixing the terms of a contract, would first have had to demonstrate that the Public Procurement Directives were of direct effect in Ireland.

However, such a person would have available to him the right to apply to the High Court for judicial review of such a decision, under a procedure based on the submission of sworn written evidence with a right to cross-examine in the event of conflict on fact.

The judicial review procedure does not appear actually to have been used by any person claiming that the Public Procurement Directives had been breached. It has been settled in Irish law that judicial review is available only in respect of actions of a public character and the awarding of a contract by a public body was, as in Great Britain, regarded as a matter of private law. However, the procedure extended to the granting of declarations and this remedy would appear to have been available.

Both injunctive relief and damages are available under the judicial review system (see Order 84 of the Irish Rules of the Superior Courts) and an absence of authority makes it difficult to speculate as to what the measure of damages would have been. The absence of a clear entitlement to general damages is probably a significant factor in explaining the lack of Irish litigation on the topic.

In practice, however, the scope of the remedy of judicial review for Public Procurement Directives enforcement would have been limited by the Irish courts' inability under this procedure to review a particular decision in detail. An applicant would have had to demonstrate that a particular decision was

---

[1]   *Commission v Ireland*: 45/87 [1989] 1 CMLR 225.

clearly and unambiguously wrong, and not merely contrary to the decision which the court itself would have made.[1]

Conclusion

Prior to the implementation of the Remedies Directives, the position of a person offended by an Irish authority's decision on the basis of alleged contravention of the Public Procurement Directives was at best a doubtful one. This fact probably explains the absence of specific Irish authority on the point.

THE IMPLEMENTATION OF THE REMEDIES DIRECTIVES

The implementation of European laws and acts in Ireland is governed, in general, by the European Communities Act 1972 as amended. Section 2 of the Act provided that:

'... From the 1st day of January 1973, the Treaties governing the European Communities and the existing and future acts adopted by the institutions of those Communities, and by the bodies competent under the said Treaties, shall be binding on the state and shall be part of the domestic law thereof under the conditions laid down in those Treaties.'

Section 3 of the Act provides that:

'A Minister of State may make regulations for enabling Section 2 of this Act to a full effect.'

The implementation in Ireland of the Remedies Directives was achieved in this way. Statutory Instrument 104 of 1993 gave effect to Directive 92/13/EEC, creating remedies in relation to entities operating in the water, energy, transport and telecommunications sectors. SI 309 of 1994 gave effect to Council Directive 89/665 EEC, providing remedies in relation to the award of public supply and public works contracts.

Pursuant to these instruments, the review procedures referred to in the Directives '... shall be carried out and exercised by the High Court'.

The necessity, in Ireland, to have these functions exercised by a court had been anticipated in the Joint Committee Report referred to above when the 1989 Directive was still being formulated.

'... If the proposed Directive to co-ordinate national measures is implemented it would appear in the light of the provisions of the Constitution that the function of setting aside decisions and indemnifying tenderers would have to be allocated to a court in this country.'

The EC Directives on public procurement, to which the review procedures now apply, are set out in Table I.

---

[1] See *Keegan v Stardust Victims' Compensation Tribunal* [1986] IR 642.

Table I. EC Directives on Public Procurement				
Subject of Directive	*EEC No*	*Applies to*	Transposed* into Irish Law	*Date of Instrument*
Works	93/37	Public Authorities (excluding Utilities)	SI 293 of 1994	16.9.94
Supplies	77/62 80/767 88/295 93/36	Public Authorities (excluding Utilities)	SI 37 of 1994	17.2.92
Works and Supplies Remedies	89/665	Public Authorities (excluding Utilities)	SI 139 of 1994	16.9.94
Services	92/50	Public Authorities (excluding Utilities)	SI 173 of 1993	29.6.93
Utilities Remedies	92/13	Utilities	SI 104 of 1993	21.4.93
Supplies, Works and Services (Utilities)	93/38	Utilities	SI 51 of 1995	28.2.95

* As of April 1996

Application of Remedies Directives

Unlike its UK counterpart, the approach in Ireland has been simply to adapt the terms of the two Remedies Directives into Irish law by the means of two simple statutory instruments. Apart from those two instruments, no separate body of regulations exists. Council Directive 89/665/EEC is introduced into Irish law by means of European (Review Procedures for the Award of Public Works and Public Supplies Contracts) (No 2) Regulations 1994 (SI 309 of 1994). The Utilities Remedies Directive 92/13/EEC is introduced into Irish law by means of European Communities (Review Procedures for the Award of Contracts by Entities Operating in the Water, Energy, Transport and Telecommunications Sectors) Regulations, 1993 (SI 104 of 1993).

Compliance with the Rules on Supplies, Works, and Public Services

SI 309 of 1994 (European Communities (Review Procedures for the Award of Public Works and Supplies Contracts) (No 2) Regulations) provides:

'The review procedures referred to in the Council Directive and the powers provided for in Article 2(1)(a) to (c) of the Council Directive shall be carried out and exercised by the High Court' (reg 4(1)).

'When considering whether or not to order interim measures the High Court may take into account the probable consequences referred to in Article 2(4) of the Council Directive and may decide not to grant such measures where their negative consequences could exceed their benefits' (reg 4(2)).

There is an obligation placed on the person seeking a review of a contract falling within the scope of Directives 93/36, 93/37, and 92/50, to notify the contracting authority of the alleged infringement and of his intention to seek a review (reg 5). If an infringing contract is subsequently concluded, it is provided that:

'...the High Court may in the exercise of its powers under Article 2(1) of the Council Directive—

(a) declare such contract, or any provision of such contract, to be void, or
(b) declare that the contract may have effect only subject to such variation as the Court shall think fit, including any variation required to protect the interests of a party to the contract who was not responsible for the infringement of the law concerned, or
(c) make such other order concerning the validity of the contract or any provision of it as the Court shall think fit'.

In addition the High Court may award damages to any person harmed by an infringement.

Compliance with the Utilities Directive

SI 104 of 1993 (European Communities (Review Procedures for the Award of Contracts by Entities in the Water, Energy, Transport and Telecommunications Sectors) Regulations) provides that the High Court may review procedures for the award of contracts in this area and that the procedures and powers provided for in Article 2(1) (a), (b) and (d) of Council Directive 92/13/EEC shall be exercised by the court (reg 4(1)). The obligation to notify the contracting entity of the alleged infringement and of the intention to seek review also applies (reg 5) as does the power of the High Court to award damages (reg 6).

The public interest requirement which the High Court must consider is spelt out in these regulations. Regulation 2 of the instrument provides that

'When considering whether or not to order interim measures, the High Court may take into account the probable consequences of the measures for all interests likely to be harmed, as well as the public interest and may decide not to grant such measures where their negative consequences could exceed their benefits.'

Scope of review

It is immediately apparent from the terms of the Remedies Directives that the scope of review which the High Court can carry out is very much broader than that available under the pre-existing procedures. There are no 'detailed rules' (Article 1.3 of each Directive) governing the review established in Ireland, but it is clear that the review provided for is a full one, allowing the court to investigate any decision relating to a contract 'on the grounds that such decisions have infringed Community law in the field of public procurement or national rules implementing that law'.

Both Irish instruments implementing the Remedies Directives provide that an application for review may be brought 'in a summary manner'. In Ireland this involves procedure by affidavit with a right to cross-examine the persons making affidavits (Order 40 of the Irish Rules of the Superior Courts). The standard of proof, as in all matters other than criminal trials, is the balance of probabilities.[1]

The Irish statutory instruments confer on the High Court the power to undertake the review procedures provided in the respective Council Directives and to exercise the powers referred to in Article 2 of each Directive. No specific provision is made for procedure other than the reference to disposal 'in a summary manner'. Both instruments speak of the review procedure being initiated by 'application', which is also the term used in the Irish Court Rules to describe the initiating step in an application for judicial review. It may be anticipated that more detailed procedural regulations will be made by rules or by rule of court. No provision is made for the time within which such application is to be made. The thrust of the Directives, however, gives primacy to 'interim measures with the aim of correcting the alleged infringement' which are to be taken 'at the earliest opportunity'. By analogy with judicial review time limits, it may be anticipated that the rules of court will provide a relatively short time for the institutional review application, probably three or six months.

Criteria of review: interim and interlocutory measures

These measures are closely analogous to the existing powers of the court to grant injunctions. The jurisdiction of the High Court in this regard was originally conferred by the Judicature (Ireland) Act of 1887 and is now governed by Order 50 Rule 6 of the Rules of the Superior Courts. The court may grant an injunction by an interlocutory order 'in all cases in which it appears to the court to be just or convenient to do so'.

Granting or withholding of interlocutory injunctions is governed by well-established principles. The test which the applicant for injunctive relief has to demonstrate to the court is that there is a serious question to be tried. The Irish courts have followed the House of Lords in *American Cyanamid Co v Ethicon Ltd*,[2] in which it was decided that it was sufficient for the plaintiff to establish that there was a serious question to be argued. It was not necessary for him to show that he had a prima facie case or that he would probably succeed at the ultimate trial. The leading Irish case is *Campus Oil Ltd v Minister for Industry and Energy (No 2)*.[3] Here the plaintiffs were a number of

---

[1]   *Banco Ambrosiano v Ansbacher & Co Ltd* [1987] ILRM 669.
[2]   [1975] AC 396.
[3]   [1983] IR 88.

independent oil producers who were obliged by regulation to purchase their supplies from the state-owned oil refinery at Whitegate. The Company issued proceedings claiming that the requirement was contrary to the Treaty of Rome and threatened to withhold compliance with the mandatory requirement. The State sought an injunction to compel them to comply until the issue could be decided. Applying the *American Cyanamid* test Keane, J granted an interloctury injunction.

If the court is satisfied that there is a serious question to be tried it has next to consider whether the balance of convenience favours the granting or the withholding of the injunction.

Keane J in his book *Equity and the Law of Trusts in the Republic of Ireland*[1] sets out the factors which should be taken into account, the first being whether there is any real necessity to grant an injunction at all, if damages assessed at the trial will prove an adequate remedy. The second test is whether the undertaking as to damages which the plaintiff is normally required to give will adequately compensate the defendant for the damage caused to him by the granting of the injunction if he is eventually successful. If neither of those considerations proves decisive he suggests that the court, as a counsel of prudence, will seek to preserve the status quo pending the trial of the action. In addition, where the damage likely to be suffered by either side as a result of the granting or withholding of the relief is not determinative, the court may take into account the comparative strength of the parties' respective cases.

Time limits

It is possible within the Irish system to have an interlocutory application heard within a matter of days provided the matter is tried on affidavit. If pleadings and discovery are not required, it is possible to proceed to a full hearing at an early date. Sometimes the hearing of the motion is treated as the trial of the action. Frequently a defendant will give an undertaking pending the trial of the action that he will refrain from doing the act sought to be restrained and in those circumstances an injunction would not be required.

The Rules provide that a deponent of an affidavit can be cross-examined on that affidavit. This power has been used with increasing frequency. Because cases in the Public Procurement area are likely to be significant in monetary terms, it is likely that parties will opt for this approach. If there is a dispute on the facts then the parties will either have to agree the issues to be tried and can opt for oral hearing on those issues, or the court can order that full pleadings be exchanged between them which inevitably is time-consuming.

The High Court as stated above is obliged to take into account the probable consequences of the measures for all interests likely to be harmed as well as the public interest. The implementation of that particular requirement will no doubt give rise to some interesting litigation in the future. *Commission v Ireland*[2] related to the call for tenders for work on a water supply scheme in the north eastern town of Dundalk. The tendering authority had sought to put a clause into the invitation for tender providing that the pipes to be used were to be certified as complying with an Irish standard. Ultimately the court found that Ireland had failed to fulfil its obligations under Article 30 EEC and Article 10 of the Council Directive 71/305. At the interlocutory

---

[1] Butterworths (1988), p 228.
[2] 45/87R: [1987] ECR 783, 1369.

stage, the Commission contended that contractors excluded from the tendering process would suffer irreparable damage unless the contract was suspended. This was not accepted by the court. Because the contract was for the augmentation of the Dundalk drinking water supply it was held that existing health and safety concerns could be aggravated if the contract was delayed. As a consequence the Irish government's argument that damages would be an adequate remedy was accepted.

Relevance of ECJ Decisions to the court's discretion

The ECJ's rules of procedure in relation to interim relief incorporate provisions similar in principle to those applied by the Irish courts. An applicant for such relief is required to state the circumstances giving rise to urgency and the factual and legal grounds establishing a prima facie case. In order to establish urgency, the applicant must show that an interim measure is necessary to avoid 'serious and irreparable' damage to the applicant. This mirrors the Irish court's concern to avoid the granting of interim or interlocutory relief if, in the end, the applicant can be fully compensated by an award of damages.

The uncertainty as to the precise scope of an award of damages (see below) and the fact that an applicant will in many cases have difficulty in demonstrating that he would have been awarded a particular contract but for an infringement, will lead to a situation in which interim interlocutory relief will probably be granted more easily than in other cases.

Another significant difference in the regime established by the Irish Statutory Instruments is the importance given to 'public interest considerations'. This is expressed in each case by permitting the court to take into account 'the probable consequences of the measures for all interests likely to be harmed, as well as the public interest' and to 'decide not to grant such measures where their negative consequences could exceed their benefits'.

There is little doubt that the Irish courts would follow the approach of the ECJ in such cases as *Lottomatica*,[1] *Dundalk*[2] and *Van Hool*.[3] In *Dundalk* the Irish government had contended that contractors excluded or disadvantaged by a requirement that certain equipment be used in a public water project might have an alternative remedy in damages. This contention must be based on an acceptance that compliance with a Public Procurement Directive is a duty owed to contractors, capable of giving rise to a right to damages. On the issue of interim relief, its refusal in that case on the grounds of health and safety concerns, militating against the delay which would be caused by such relief, suggests a criterion for the implementation of the 'public interest' criterion. It is less certain that the attitude of the ECJ in *La Spezia*[4] would find favour in Ireland. In that case interim relief was granted, interfering with the completion of an incinerator on the ground inter alia that the public body constructing it was itself responsible for bringing about the situation in which it was urgently required. The Irish courts would, it is thought, attach more significance to the actual necessity for the project in question, particularly if there was a health or safety requirement for it.

In the case where that sort of criterion was not present, such as *Lottomatica*,

---

[1]   C-272/91R: [1995] 2 CMLR 504.
[2]   45/87R: [1987] ECR 783, 1369.
[3]   C-87/94R: [1994] ECR I-1395.
[4]   194/88R: [1988] ECR 4559.

general administrative and economic arguments favouring rapid completion of a contractual procedure were held insufficient to resist interim relief, and this approach would be very influential in Ireland.

Damages

The availability of damages as a remedy to an offended party, and the likely extent of such damages is a matter important in itself and also has a very direct bearing on the likelihood of interim interlocutory relief being granted. There is no direct guidance on the criteria to be applied in the assessment of damages for the simple reason that the Statutory Instruments of 1993 and 1994 provide contractors with a new cause of action. As noted above, the Irish government itself canvassed the availability of damages for infringement of EEC Rules in the *Dundalk* case of 1988.

Both Irish instruments provide that damages may be awarded

(a)   where a contract has been concluded subsequent to its award, and
(b)   to a person *harmed* by an infringement.

Directive 92/13 provides (Article 2.7) in relation to damages for the costs of preparing a bid or participating in an award procedure that the person making the claim should only be required to prove an infringement and 'that he would have had a real chance of winning the contract and that, as a consequence of that infringement, that chance was adversely affected'. This provision may be of considerable guidance in the approach of the Irish courts to the question of damages.

The most obvious heads of damages are the costs of preparing a tender and lost profits, on the assumption that he would have won the contract.

The onus of proof will lie on the contractor and it is obviously very difficult to demonstrate, on the balance of probabilities, that any one tender would have been successful but for the infringement.

Where the claim is simply for the cost of preparing a bid or participating in an award procedure (at least in cases within Directive 92/13), the applicant has to show not only that he would have had 'a real chance' but for the infringement but that this chance was 'adversely affected'. This should not be an insuperable difficulty in any case.

In relation to a loss of profits claim, a contractor who can demonstrate a 'real chance' which is 'adversely affected' by an infringement, should be able to recover damages in respect of the loss of his chance, even though he is unable to demonstrate that he would, as a matter of probability, actually have been awarded the contract. In both tort and contract cases, damages are recoverable for the loss of a chance.[1] The quantification of damages under this heading proceeds on the basis of a finding in relation to the chances of success. This approach has been adopted by the Irish courts in relation to assessment of damages for other uncertain events, such as the possibility or probability that an injured person will, as a result of his injury, develop some disability or illness in the future which will affect his earning capacity. In such circumstances it has been held that the damages to be awarded 'should

[1]   See *Chaplin v Hicks* [1911] 2 KB 786, CA.

be commensurate with, and proportionate to, the degree of that possibility or probability as the case may be'.[1]

Moreover, the decision of the Supreme Court in that case was further qualified in a manner favourable to the plaintiff. The court held:

> '...If the degree of probability is so high ... that it remains only possible that the condition will not occur (a court) would be justified in acting on the assumption that it will occur, and should measure damages accordingly. On the other hand, if the possibility that no such event will occur is so great that it is only barely possible that it would occur, damages should nevertheless be awarded, but should be proportionate to that degree of risk, small though it may be.'

This approach clearly opens the possibility for a substantial award in respect of the loss of a 'real chance', even in claims for loss of profits. Furthermore, under Irish law relating to the award of exemplary or punitive damages, if the authority's conduct in infringing the procurement directives were 'arbitrary, oppressive or unconstitutional' or 'calculated to make a profit ... which may well exceed the compensation payable to the plaintiff', an award under this heading might be available. The nature of the subject matter here – disregard of illegal provision by public authority – renders such an award a real possibility.[2]

Effect of availability of damages on interlocutory applications

If, as suggested above, an aggrieved contractor will only rarely be able to demonstrate a probability that but for an infringement he would have been awarded a contract, this lessens very significantly the possibility of damages being an adequate remedy. Accordingly, at an interim or interlocutory stage, the case for interlocutory relief is considerably strengthened if the infringement is clearly shown, or shown to be very probable, and the prospect of damages appears to be a limited to loss of a chance.

On the other hand, if the contractor's claim is limited to costs of preparing a tender or participating in the awards procedure, the likely availability of full compensation would militate against the granting of relief, at least where that would be of an intrusive or inconvenient character.

It is likely that the form of interim or interlocutory relief will be guided, where possible, by the desirability of preserving the status quo until a final decision on the review is made. In most cases this will take the form of suspending the procedures for the awarding of the contract and subsequently correcting them to make them accord with the Public Procurement Directives.

---

[1]   See *Dunlop v Kenny* (29 July 1969, unreported), Supreme Court.
[2]   See *Kennedy v Ireland* [1988] ILRM 472.

CHAPTER 11

Remedies in the Netherlands

Karin I de Jong

SYNOPSIS OF THE DUTCH RULES FOR PUBLIC TENDERING

In this paragraph, the Dutch rules in the area of public tendering will be defined. It will quickly be evident that these rules are very much disassociated. The very first stipulation about public tendering can be found in a Royal Decree dated 1815 (see below). Thereafter, the rules for public tendering were incorporated in all sorts of general and specific laws, decrees, and regulations etc. It was ultimately to assimilate the EC directives in the area of public tendering, and to achieve clarity, that the framework of EEC regulations came into existence (see below). This paragraph deals both with those rules regarding government procurements which fall within the EC public procurements regime, and also the rules with regard to government procurements that will not fall under the EC public procurement regime.

The first rules in the area of tendering

The Royal Decree of 11 November 1815

Public tendering through the State Authorities[1] became mandatory by a Decree dated 11 November 1815. Article 1 of this Royal Decree goes on to say:

> 'Commencing on this date, all contracts of works and supplies on behalf of this country, costing more than five hundred guilders, must be conducted by public tendering.'

The Accounting Act of 1927

In the Accounting Act of 1927, we come upon legal rules for public tendering. This law contains rules for the placing of assignments for works implementation, and for the delivery of goods, and is only valid for the State Authorities. Article 33 of this Act stipulates:

> '1. All works to be undertaken outside one's own control, and deliveries, in either case having a potentially higher expenditure than £2.500, –, will be by public tender.

---

[1] State Authorities are the ministries and departments of Government.

2.   Notwithstanding this, justifiable deviations to this rule may be permitted by Ourselves through a decision of which a copy must be sent to the office of the Accountant General, both for similar cases, and also for each particular case.'[1]

This Article became ineffective, in practice, due to the frequently secret Royal Decrees under its para 2.[2]

The Accounting Act of 1976

In the Accounting Act of 1976 – which superseded the Accounting Act of 1927 – it is stipulated that by administrative measure, rules concerning the public tendering for works shall be made. These rules were laid down in the Tendering for Works Decree of 1973, in anticipation of the Accounting Act of 1976 coming into force (see below). Just like the Accounting Act of 1927, the new Accounting Act does not provide rules for assignments concerning provision of services. What is striking is that the new Accounting Act has no rules concerning supply of goods. The government had its hands free, until the EEC Directive of 1976[3] took effect concerning the supply of goods.

Rules concerning the supply of products

The Government Assignments Act for supply of products, and the Government Tenders Decree

The Directive on supplies of 1976 is incorporated in the Government Assignments Act for supply of products.[4] This Act was not only valid for the State Authorities, but also for joint-authorities such as provinces, municipalities, and water-boards. The Directive was, with Directive 93/36/EEC, completely revised in 1993. This revised Directive is implemented in Dutch legislation by means of the Government Tenders Decree.[5] The Government Assignments Act for supply of products is consequently annulled as of 13 June 1994.

---

[1]   This law did stipulate that public tendering must take place, but not how to continue further.

[2]   See: Note of Clarification by the Tendering for Works Decree, 6 April 1973, State Gazette 1973, 202, and Memorandum Clarification on Article 43 of the Accounting Act of 1976 (session 1973–74, 13077, page 31).

[3]   Council Directive 77/62/EEC of 21 December 1976, concerning the co-ordination of the procedure for the placing of public assignments for delivery, EC Publication Bulletin 1977 L 13/1.

[4]   Law of 13 June 1979, State Gazette 1979, 334, implementing regulations for the placing of government assignments for the delivery of products.

[5]   Decree of 4 June 1993, State Gazette 1993, 305, implementing regulations concerning the procedures for placing government assignments for the delivery of products, the execution of works and the performance of services.

Rules regarding the tendering for works through the State Authorities

The Tendering for Works Decree of 1973, and the Uniform
Tendering Regulations

The Tendering for Works Decree of 1973[1] was established in anticipation
of the new Accounting Act of 1976[2] coming into force, and under the influence
of the liberalisation Directive[3] and (especially) the co-ordination Directive.[4]
This Decree contains rules for the placing of assignments for execution of
works, and only applies for the State Authorities.

In Article 6 of the Decree, there is a distinction made between works for
which the estimated costs are 5 million ECUs or more (and therefore falling
under the EC public procurement regime), and those for which the estimated
costs are less than 5 million ECUs. The point of departure of this Decree
is that, for the former works a public tender or a tender with previous selection
must be held.[5] Such tenders should conform with the stipulations of the Uniform
Tendering Rule 1986,[6] which rule is a consequence of this Decree.

As a reflection of the Uniform Tendering Rule of 1986, a tendering rule
has been especially established for European tendering for works; the Uniform
Tendering Rule for EC tendering 1991.[7] This UAR-EC 1991 is a practical
outcome of the Directive for works. With the drawing up of this regulation,
the co-ordination Directive of 1989[8] is implemented in Dutch legislation.

Rules regarding tendering for works by the lower governing bodies

Tenders for works that do not fall within the EC procurement regime

Concerning the putting out to tender of works not falling under the EC public
procurement regime by lower public bodies such as provinces, municipalities
and water-boards, there are, at this time, no legal regulations for observance
by lower public bodies of rules for tendering.

The old Provincial Act[9] spoke, in its Article 107, about the authority of

---

[1] Decree of 6 April 1973, State Gazette 1973, 202, implementing regulations for the execution
of works.
[2] Especially Article 43 thereof.
[3] Council Directive 71/304/EEC of 26 July 1971, concerning discontinuation of restriction
on government assignments through the mediation of agents and affiliates, EC Publication
Bulletin 1971 L 185/1.
[4] Council Directive 71/305/EEC of 26 July 1971, concerning the co-ordination of procedures
for placing of government assignments for the execution of works, EC Publication Bulletin
1971 L 185/5.
[5] Article 2, para 2 Tendering for Works Decree of 1973.
[6] Decree of 2 June 1986, State Gazette 1986, 118. The Uniform Tendering Rule 1986 has been,
as a result of Article 5, clause 1 of the Tendering for Works Decree 1973, declared applicable
on all tendering done by the State Authorities.
[7] Decree of 15 November 1991, State Gazette 1991, 228. As a result of Article 5, clause 2
of the Tendering for Works Decree 1973, the State Authorities must declare the Uniform
Tendering Rule for EC tendering 1991 applicable on tendering within the scope of the European
Directive on Works.
[8] Council Directive 89/440/EEC of 18 July 1989, EC Publication Bulletin 1989 L 210/1, whereby
Directive 71/305/EEC was changed in important respects, and emphasised.
[9] Law of 25 January 1962, State Gazette 1962, 15.

the Provincial Executive Committee to fix the plans and conditions of tendering from and through the provinces' tasks of works. However, the law contained nothing about the tendering practices for provinces to follow. The latter prescribed rules have not been included in the new Provincial Act,[1] which came into force from 1 January 1994. This does not mean that all provinces have complete freedom in their choice of tendering methods, this freedom now being limited by general principles of good management.[2] These principles must equally be taken into account both by lower public bodies, and by the State Authorities.[3]

The old Municipal Act[4] contained, as well as an enactment of Article 107 Provincial Act, a prescription of the tendering practices for municipalities to follow when placing assignments to carry out works. Article 176, para 2 of the old Municipal Act stipulated that municipalities went out to tender publicly, unless there was specific reason in the interest of the municipality for private tender. This stipulation, with its practically unlimited possibility of evasion, led municipal authorities to prefer private tender, and even unofficial allocation was able to thrive. The new Municipal Act,[5] which came into force from 1 January 1994, similarly lacks any stipulation of tendering methods to be enacted by municipalities.

For tendering by water-boards, the regulations drafted by the provinces contain rules applicable to them. Therefore there are no uniform national rules for tendering practices for water-boards planning assignments of work.

In practice, the lower governing bodies tend to apply the Uniform Tendering Rule 1986, although this is not compulsory.

Tenders for works falling under the EC public procurement regime

In relation to tenders for works falling under the EC public procurement regime by lower governing bodies, the co-ordination Directive (71/305 as amended and consolidated in 93/37) has been implemented via the Law for Tendering for Works for Lower Public Bodies.[6] The way this implementation occurred was very simple: the relevant statutory bodies were simply compelled by the tender for works to apply the rules of the co-ordination Directive 'such as are detailed, or as shall be changed'. This Directive does not lend itself to direct application.[7] In practice, it is shown that the lower governing bodies opt to make the UAR-EC 1991 applicable, voluntarily.

---

[1]   Law of 10 September 1992, State Gazette 1992, 550.
[2]   About this, for example, see M.A.M.C van den Berg 'Samenwerkingvormen in de Bouw' (Forms of co-operative working in the construction sector), dissertation at Tilburg 1990, 337. See also the President of the Middelburg Court, 8 November 1990, Journal for Building Law 1991, p 408.
[3]   The government is not allowed to exercise authority based on civil rights, such as the right to tender, contrary to the principles of sound administration. Violation can constitute an unlawful act. The aggrieved party may start proceedings based upon an unlawful act as mentioned in Article 6:162 of the Civil Code.
[4]   Law of 29 June 1851, State Gazette 1851, 85.
[5]   Law of 19 February 1992, State Gazette 1992, 96.
[6]   Law of 23 November 1977, State Gazette 1977, 669, keeping regulations for placing of government assignments for the execution of works under the management of provinces, municipalities, and water-boards.
[7]   For the objections to such a direct implementation, see E.H. Pijnacker Hordijk in Journal for Building Law 1992, p 100, and P. Glazener in Advocatenblad 1990, pp 614 and 615.

The Framework Regulations EC-tendering rules

Meanwhile, incorporation of the EC public procurement regime took place in Dutch law, in rules in a different, less fragmented and more coherent manner. For this purpose, the Framework Regulations EC-tendering rules came into effect, effective as of 21 April 1993.[1] This Framework Act has two purposes: it aims as much to achieve one legal cadre for the implementation of existing and future rules within the scope of tenders, so as to enable such implementation in the national legal order to be accomplished within a short time.

On the basis of the Framework Act, two decisions have been taken (administrative orders) which implement the separate Directives: the Government Tenders Decree,[2] and the Public Utility Tenders Decree.[3]

In accordance with Article 4 of the Framework Act, the existing statutory laws concerning government tendering, recognising Article 34, clause 2 of the Accounting Act, and, consequently the statutory Tendering for Works Decree, the Government Assignments Act for supply of products, and the Law for Tendering for Works for Lower Public Bodies, based on the Act, have been withdrawn.

The implementation of the separate Directives in the Government Tenders Decree[4] and the Public Utility Tenders Decree[5] has been achieved in a simple manner: the named tendering services in the works, deliveries and services Directives, and that for public utilities, have been ordered to apply the Directives' prescribed procedures.[6]

THE AUTHORITIES IN THE NETHERLANDS WHICH ARE COVERED BY THE EC PUBLIC PROCUREMENT REGIME

The Directives on works, deliveries and services

The Directives on works, deliveries and services (93/37, 93/36 and 93/38) define the public bodies to which they apply (Article 1, para b). These bodies are called 'tendering services'. In the Netherlands, the following tendering services come under the directive:

• the State; ministries, government departments
• provinces
• municipalities
• local community rules
• public law establishments. These are establishments which:

---

[1] Law of 31 March 1993 to execute EEC measures concerning the placing of assignments for the delivery of products, the execution of works, and the performance of services, State Gazette 1993, 212.

[2] Resolution of 4 June 1993, State Gazette 305.

[3] Decree of 6 April 1993, State Gazette 1993, 214, keeping regulations concerning the procedures for placing of government assignments in the sectors of water and energy supply, transport and telecommunication.

[4] See Articles 4, 9 and 13 of the Government Tenders Decree, Resolution of 4 June 1993, State Gazette 305.

[5] See Articles 2 and 6 of the Public Utility Tenders Decree, Decree of 6 April 1993, State Gazette 1993.

[6] For the criticism (in my view justified) of this means of implementation, see for example A.G.T. van Wassenaar in Journal for Building Law 1993, p 589.

- have legal identity, *and*
- are established for the specific purpose of serving the common interest and without a commercial character,
- that are more than 50% financed by a tendering service, *or*
- of which control is subject to the supervision of a tendering service, or
- of which the regulatory organs (Management, Board of Directors, Supervisory Board) are, for more than half their number, appointed by a tendering service.

All government bodies, government services, or public law establishments which fall within the above categories – irrespective of their legal form – come within the active scope of the Directive on works, deliveries and services.

For example: several regional and local authorities set up an organisation to process household waste in an area. This organisation will take on the form of a limited liability company. In spite of the fact that the relevant limited liability company is not recognised in Dutch law as a public body, it corresponds with the different elements of a conceptual public corporation. Thus the limited liability company can be considered as a tendering service as far as the Directives are concerned.

It is not always so easy to determine if the organisation will fall within the scope of the Directives. This is especially so in the definition of the so-called public organisation.

Foundations, for example, that are more than 50% financed by the government shall be recognised as tendering services in the sense of the Directives. A foundation has, indeed, legal entity, has not been founded principally for commercial purposes, and, in this case, has been principally financed by the government.

In Appendix 1 of the 'works' Directive (Directive 93/37/EEC), a list of public organisations is incorporated. This list is not exhaustive; establishments not so named, but which correspond to the Directive's given definitions of a public organisation, must therefore also apply the Directives to their assignments.

The utility-sector Directive

The utility-sector Directive (93/38) not only has a bearing on government assignments, but also on assignments that have been placed through certain private companies. The utilities are also termed 'tendering services' in the utility-sector Directive. Thus, the definition of tendering service in the utility-sector Directive is broader than the definition of tendering service in the Directives for works, deliveries and services.

The Directive names several different types of tendering service:

(a) *the government*: the State (ministries, civil services), local councils, provinces, district water-boards, etc (Article 1, para 1);
(b) *public bodies*: these are organisations or companies (irrespective of their legal form!):
   - which have legal entity, *and*
   - are established with the purpose of fulfilling a general purpose, and are more than 50% financed by government, *or*

- of which over half the numbers of the regulatory bodies are named by the government, *or*
- of which the government controls the regulatory bodies (Article 1, para 1);

(c) *public companies*: these are companies over which the government has a dominant influence. Such influence should be assumed:

  - in the event that government (or a public body) has the majority of subscribed capital in the ownership of this company, *or*
  - has the majority of voting rights through the share-capital of the company, *or*
  - has appointed more than half of the members of the regulatory bodies of the company (Article 1, para 2);

(d) *companies or organisations* that (irrespective of their legal form) conduct their business on the basis of government-granted permit or exclusive remit (Article 2, para 1).

The important distinction that tendering services have in common is that they have a central role (called 'relevant activity' in the Directive) as a main task. These relevant activities are described in Article 2, para 2.

Relevant activities in the sense of this Directive are:

(a) the provision or exploitation of a network that is going to be used for public services in the area of production, transportation or distribution of:
  (1) drinking water (for example, the drinking water supply companies);
  (2) electricity (for example, the electricity production or distribution companies);
  (3) gas (for example, the Gasunie); and
  (4) heating (for example, companies for municipal heating services);

(b) the exploitation of a geographical area with the aim of exploring or exploiting its fossil fuels (for example, an oil company that extracts oil or gas in a certain area at sea or on the mainland);

(c) the exploitation of a geographical area with the aim of providing an airport, sea harbour, inland port, or other arrival facilities of transport by air, sea, or inland waters (for example, the Airport at Schiphol, or a municipal port concern);

(d) the exploitation of a public transport service concerning transportation by train, bus, trolleybus etc (for example, the Dutch Railways, municipal transport services, regional transport);

(e) the provision or exploitation of public telecommunications networks, or the provision of one or more telecommunication services to the public (for example PTT Telecom).

Consequently, to make the public utility Directive applicable, there should always be a tendering service with the relevant activity to conduct the business. For example, in the case that the Ministry for Internal Affairs leases some copying machines, this order will not fall under the public utility Directive because the Ministry of Internal Affairs – however it may be construed as a tendering service – does not conduct a relevant activity under the public utility Directive. Naturally, this order does fall within the scope of Directives for government procurements in the public sector, namely the Directive concerning government procurement of products. In the case, however, that the same copying machines were leased by the Schiphol Airport company, then this procurement would fall under the Directive concerning public utility, because the company practises both as a tendering service and as a relevant activity.

To get as complete as possible a summary of the tendering services in the Netherlands, reference should be made to Appendices I to X inclusive of the utility Directive (Directive 93/38/EEC).

THE REMEDIES DIRECTIVE 89/665/EEC

Directive 89/665 tries to ensure that the procuring bodies in the Member States live up to the existing Directives on government assignments. The aim of this Directive is that the Member States should create ways and means by which quick and effective legal action can be taken if an entrepreneur claims that the rules for tenders have been violated. This Directive is based on the idea of decentralisation, in the sense that the interested parties can take legal action. Particularly at the stage at which violations of the tender regulations can still be annulled, without too much damage, it is very important for concerned parties to have quick and effective access to legal action to protect their rights. In the preamble of the remedies Directive, the most important text has been emphasised, concerning the possibility of a provisional ruling (eg to suspend tender procedure) in urgent legal actions. The requirements that the remedies Directive[1] place on national legal procedures have, in the Netherlands, not led to legal measures. The Dutch State takes the position that its legal system already adequately suffices for this purpose.

THE REMEDIES DIRECTIVE 92/13/EEC

The remedies Directive 92/13/EEC[2] intends the same result as the earlier remedies Directive 89/665/EEC, but with regard to tender services operating in the sectors of water and energy supply, transport and telecommunications. The Directives are, for a large part, identical although Directive 92/13 is novel in the addition of verification action. This has the effect that a tendering service can have its tendering procedures checked, so that a verification attestation is obtained, wherein it is stated that its tendering procedures are being executed in a correct manner. The tendering service may, in subsequent announcements of tender actions, mention that it has such an attestation.

In common with Directive 89/665, Directive 92/13 has not been transposed into Dutch law, leaving the precise application of Articles 2, 6 and 9 open to question. The Dutch government runs the risk of being convicted by the European Court of Justice in a procedure started by the Commission under

---

[1] Council Directive 89/665/EEC of 21 December 1989, on the co-ordination of the laws, regulations and administrative provisions relating to the application of review procedures to the award of public supply and public works contracts, EC Publication Bulletin 1989 L 395, 33, as amended by Council Directive 92/50/EEC.

[2] Council Directive 92/13/EEC of 25 February 1992, on the co-ordination of the legal and administrative stipulations concerning application of the Community's regulation on procedure for placing assignments by services operating in the sectors water and energy supply, transport and telecommunication, EC Publication Bulletin 1992 L 76/14.

Article 169 of the EC Treaty, for failure to implement the mandatory provisions of this Directive. Also it is conceivable that an interested party in a procedure may claim damages caused by an unlawful act[1] from the Dutch government.

THE REVIEW BODIES AND THE REVIEW PROCEDURES

Two kinds of urgent legal action must be defined: the summary proceedings for the President of the District Court, and the urgent arbitration by the Board of Arbiters for Construction Firms.

The summary proceedings for the President of the District Court

In the Netherlands, one can conduct a summary proceeding before the President of the District Court in all cases in which an immediate ruling is required.[2] There are 19 District Courts in the Netherlands. The summary proceeding is based on a written summons after which an oral hearing follows.

Article 126 of the Code of Civil Procedure states that the defendant must be summoned before the judge of the district of his residence. In the case of a defendant being a company, partnership, etc, the President of the District Court is authorised in the place where the company, partnership etc, is established. The High Court has concurrent jurisdiction to try summary proceedings.[3]

A summary proceeding is a short, informal legal action of a totally different character to the ordinary law suit. The most important characteristic is that the decision of the President is a legal decision in anticipation, or a provisional order. A summary proceeding is not intended to achieve a definitive legal settlement. In this respect, Article 292 of the Code of Civil Procedure is of importance. This Article holds that the judge ruling over the main case is not restricted by the provisional decisions of the President. Parties are furthermore not obliged to begin proceedings after a summary procedure.

The legal arrangement of a summary proceeding is embodied in Articles 289 to 297 inclusive of the Code of Civil Procedure.

In most cases, a summary proceeding begins with the plaintiff's procureur[4] presenting a transcript of the summons to the President, with a request for a date and time to process to hearing.[5] The defendant is then summoned, as soon as possible, to appear on the date and time appointed by the President. The duration within which a summary proceeding may be pending varies from a day to several weeks – depending on the urgency of the case, and

---

[1] On the grounds of Article 6:162 of the Civil Code.
[2] The President of the District Court has the authority to pass judgment by means of a provisional measure in a summary proceeding on the grounds of Article 289 of the Code of Civil Procedure.
[3] There are thus, according to the normal regulations (Article 126 of the Code of Civil Procedure) and this special regulation, two different Presidents authorised, with the choice left to the plaintiff: judgment of the Supreme Court of 23 November 1917, NJ 1918, 6; W 10202 (Oudehoven/Brass).
[4] Lawyer who is allowed to submit records.
[5] Parties can also collectively and voluntarily come before the President for a summary proceeding (Article 290, para 2 of the Code of Civil Procedure). A subpoena is then not necessary.

the diary of the President of the Court. The defendant can appear in person, or be represented by a procureur. The plaintiff must be represented by a procureur.

The whole proceeding takes place in one session. The allegations and counter-allegations are explained, the President can interrogate, and witnesses can give evidence at the same session. The President has a lot of freedom at the hearing. A hearing of witnesses, an expert opinion, a judicial examination and many other activities can take place.

The President is at liberty to assess the evidential value of a proof. He can be satisfied with summary evidence.[1] The legal provisions on proof, as embodied in Articles 176 to 232 inclusive of the Code of Civil Procedure, are not applicable in a summary proceeding.[2]

The urgent arbitration by the Board of Arbiters for Construction Firms

In the event that an interested party requires an urgent legal case against a tender service, it will usually end up before the President of a District Court. This is not the case in a tender for works, when the Uniform Tendering Rule is applicable.

It has already been explained that two tendering regulations exist: the Uniform Tendering Rule EC 1991 that concerns tenders for works above 5 million ECUs, and the Uniform Tendering Rule 1986 that concerns tenders for work of a lower value.[3] A State Authority that procures a structure to be built, is compelled to use the appropriate Uniform Tendering Rule. In other cases, the relevant Uniform Tendering Rule can be applied voluntarily.

As well as the Uniform Tendering Rule EC 1991 and that of 1986, there is an arbitration stipulation that authorises the Board of Arbiters for Construction Firms, in Utrecht, to settle tendering disputes.[4] On the basis of Article 1020 of the Code of Civil Procedure, parties can, by agreement, subject disputes arising out of the result of an agreement or from the agreement itself, to arbitration.

For the validation of an agreement to go to arbitration, it is sufficient in principle that, by enactment of the main agreement, there is reference in writing to general conditions providing for arbitration – which are accepted by parties either explicitly or tacitly.[5] In cases where, in the tender service, a Uniform Tender Regulation has been declared applicable, and which the building contractor has explicitly or tacitly accepted, the Board of Arbiters for Building Companies is consequently authorised for possible tendering disputes.[6]

---

[1] See also the decision of the Supreme Court, 29 June 1928, NJ 1928, 1639, W 11887.
[2] Decisions of the Supreme Court, 29 January 1943, NJ 1943, 198; 5 December 1952, NJ 1953, 767; 19 December 1958, NJ 1959, 127; 16 February 1962, NJ 1962, 142.
[3] See p 187.
[4] Article 67 of Uniform Tendering Rule for EC tendering 1991, and Article 41 of Uniform Tendering Rule 1986.
[5] Article 1021 of the Code of Civil Procedure.
[6] Article 67 of the Uniform Tendering Rule EC-1991 and Article 41 of the Uniform Tendering Rule 1986 make clear that the arbitration stipulation is applicable to all parties involved with the tender. It is accepted that this means also a party that made a bid. Therefore, the Board of Arbiters is also competent in disputes where an assignment has not been allocated yet and disputes where a party has not been awarded an assignment.

Legally, arbitration is governed by Articles 1020 to 1076 inclusive of the Code of Civil Procedure.

The Board of Arbiters for Building Companies was established on 1 January 1907. The Board of Arbiters were granted powers to settle tender disputes by virtue of the Uniform Tendering Rule of 1986, dated 1 November 1986. Because both the UAR-EC 1991 and the UAR 1986 granted powers to the Board of Arbiters to settle tender disputes, the Board of Arbiters is now authorised to settle disputes both within and outside the scope of the EC tendering Directive.

The Board has about sixty technical arbiters as ordinary members. These arbiters are experts in tendering, and in the implementation of construction work, and are familiar with other aspects of this field. There are also about ten associate members, all lawyers. The ordinary members settle ninety-five per cent, or more, of disputes. In legally complex cases, and in judicial appeals, associate members are involved. The technical arbiters in any dispute are assisted by a juridically-educated secretary, who has an advisory role. In practice, a tendering dispute will be settled by three arbiters, one of whom is a lawyer.

Disputes within the meaning of the Uniform Tender Rules can, through the Board of Arbiters, be recognised as urgent – in which case urgent arbitration will ensue.[1] A tendering dispute will usually be treated as urgent, and lead to an urgent arbitration by the Board of Arbiters.

Furthermore, the judgment in an urgent dispute is final and binding. It is not deemed provisional as in the case of a judgment of the President of a District Court in a summary proceeding.

Each disputant has the right to put a written submission to the Tribunal. The Tribunal can allow a second submission.[2] In an urgent case, a written submission only occurs when the Tribunal finds this necessary.

In any event, parties in an urgent dispute get the chance to make an oral presentation.[3] There is no compulsory representation. Parties can appear in person, to conduct their own cases, or they can be represented by a lawyer or another person. A party representing himself can be assisted by another person.[4]

Article 18, clause 1 of the Statutes stipulates that the Tribunal operates honourably and fairly,[5] and decides by majority voting. Honour and fairness are not circumscribed by written or unwritten rules and regulations, with

---

[1] Permission must be obtained from the chairman of the Board of Arbiters to treat the dispute as urgent; it is his decision whether one or three arbiters are nominated. The disputes mentioned in the Uniform Tender Regulations are, however, always treated as an urgent matter by single request, which must be done in writing along with the notice to make the dispute pending; then the permission of the chairman is considered to be granted (Article 20, para 5 of the Statutes of the Board of Arbiters).

[2] See Articles 14, para 1, and 16 paras 1 and 2 of the Statutes of the Board of Arbiters.

[3] See Article 20, paras 8 and 9 of the Statutes of the Board of Arbiters.

[4] See Article 1038 of the Code of Civil Procedure, and Article 14, para 3 of the Statutes of the Board of Arbiters.

[5] Article 41 of Uniform Tendering Rule 1986, and Article 67 of Uniform Tendering Rule EC-1991 stipulate that the dispute '... is to be settled conforming to the Statutes of the Board of Arbiters for Construction Firms ...'. Article 18 of these Statutes stipulates that the Arbitration Board will decide honourably and fairly, unless parties have otherwise agreed.

the exception of those legal norms applying to public order and good morals.[1]
As from 1 September 1995 the second clause of Article 18, deviating from
clause 1, provides that disputes over tenders for works that fall within the
province of rules in anticipation of the prevailing Directive from the European
Communities covering the co-ordination of procedure for placing government
contracts for works, are subject to the rules of law.

An arbitral judgment is not immediately enforceable as is a juridical one.
It only becomes enforceable when the President of the Court authorises
execution of the judgment.[2]

Besides arbitration, it is still possible to go to the President of the District
Court to adjudicate a summary proceeding.[3]

In Articles 1 and 2 of the remedies Directive 89/665/EEC, several stipulations
are given with which the composition of the appeal tribunals and the procedures
by these bodies must comply. In the literature, a difference of opinion exists
as to whether the Board of Arbiters complies with these conditions.[4] This
difference of opinion relates to the question of whether the Board of Arbiters
has power to refer preliminary questions to the European Court of Justice.

Possible actions at law

Action taken at law against a tender service can be based on an unlawful
act.[5] Not complying with the regulation is unlawful in relation to passed-
over contractors/suppliers in whose interest the regulations are made. So is
failure[6] to comply with a rule in cases where the Uniform Tendering Rule
has been declared applicable. In that case, the tenderer has by its own action
committed the tender to proceed under the aegis of the Uniform Tendering
Rule. If it cannot then comply with the rules of the Uniform Tendering Rule,
it can be made liable for failure to do so.

---

[1]   Also, judges must judge honourably and fairly in disputes presented to them, and must honour
   fundamental regulations as 'pacta sunt servanda'. They must not supplement facts, and
   agreements of parties must not be replaced by laws and obligations on their extensions, other
   than those that flow from the agreement.

[2]   Article 1063 of the Code of Civil Procedure stipulates that the President of the District Court
   can only refuse the enforcement of an arbitral judgment if the judgment is, or has been,
   passed contrary to public order or good morals or, contrary to Article 1055 of the Code,
   has been declared provisionally enforceable or, contrary to Article 1056 of the Code, a penalty
   was imposed. When a penalty was imposed, the refusal will only concern the penalty. Article
   1056 stipulates that if a civil judge can impose a penalty, so can the Board of Arbiters.
   When there is no appeal possible of the judgment of the Board of Arbiters, or, when appeal
   is possible and the judgment has been declared provisionally enforceable, permission to enforce
   the judgment will be granted within a few days.

[3]   Articles 1022, para 2, and 1074, para 2 of the Code of Civil Procedure. On the grounds
   of Article 1051, parties can, however, agree that the Arbitration Board, or its President,
   can pass judgment in a summary proceeding. This authority must be explicitly granted. The
   arbitral summary proceeding is directed to achieve a provisional measure, or a legal provision
   in anticipation. Execution of this judgment is only possible after the President of the District
   Court has granted permission to enforce it.

[4]   In point of confirmation, G.W.A. van der Meent, Journal for Arbitration 91/4, pp 123 et
   seq., and E.H. Pijnacker Hordijk in Journal for Building Law 1992, p 100. In refutation,
   E.M.A van der Riet in Journal for Building Law 1992, p 112, P. Sanders in Journal for
   Arbitration 91/6, p 202, and P. Glazener, Advocatenblad 1990, pp 613 et seq.

[5]   On the grounds of Article 6:162 of the Civil Code.

[6]   On the grounds of Article 6:74 of the Civil Code.

Before the assignment is granted

In cases where the contract has not been awarded, a contractor/supplier can have a claim on the grounds that the tendering body:

- although obliged to do so has not made its intention to seek tenders public,
- has turned down a request to tender, or
- is of a mind to grant the assignment to another contractor/supplier.

The following actions at law are conceivable in a summary proceeding, or in an urgent arbitration by the Board of Arbiters for Construction Works:

- changes in the tendering procedure, so that they are in accordance with the tender laws,
- being admitted to the tendering procedure,
- an injunction relating to the contemplated call for tenders, or an injunction to award to the plaintiff, together with a suspension of the tendering procedure until the alleged violation of the tender law is dealt with.

To guard against the eventuality that the tendering service might not fulfil the decision of the judge/arbiter, the tendering service can be made liable to a penalty. The judge/arbiter can, on the grounds of Article 611(a) of the Code of Civil Procedure and on the demand of the plaintiff, determine that the tendering service shall be liable for each day that the decision remains unfulfilled.[1] The judge/arbiter must fix the amount of the penalty, but not set it higher than the plaintiff's claim.

The intention to go to tender is not publicly made known

When the procuring body – although obliged to do so – has not made its intention to go out to tender known, then a contractor/supplier can claim to be admitted in a summary procedure. The arbitration-clause incorporated in the Uniform Tender Rules is, in this case, not applicable, since no announcement has been made referring to the Uniform Tender Rules. The Board of Arbiters is in this case without jurisdiction. The problem in this case is, of course, that, without an announcement, a contractor/supplier is not in general informed, in time, of the invitation to tender.

A request to tender is turned down

In a case where a request to tender is turned down, a contractor/supplier that still wants to tender must be able to demonstrate either satisfactory compliance with the participation criteria, or acceptability if the right participation criteria were enforced.

---

[1] There are no general principles which clarify on what grounds a decision to enforce a penalty is decided. Often a claimed penalty is refused. See the decision of the President of the District Court Zwolle 27 July 1994, KG 1994, 315 and the decision of the President of the District Court Zutphen 5 August 1994, KG 1994, 316. In both cases the imposition of a penalty was refused because State Authorities tend to comply with judgments.

The procuring body has the intention to award the contract to another contractor/supplier

In this situation the contractor/supplier must prove that he has offered the most economical and most advantageous tender, or, if the procuring body has operated other criteria, that the contract would have been awarded to him if the right criteria had been applied.[1]

After the contract has been awarded

In theory it is conceivable that the President in a summary proceeding, or the Board of Arbiters for Construction Firms in an urgent arbitration, will suspend an already concluded contract. There are no examples of this known in practice. The following claims are possible in a basic procedure against a tender service:

• termination of the concluded agreement, and re-allocation of the contract to the tenderer following the tender rules,
• damages because the contract has been unjustifiably awarded to another.

Termination

From existing case law at this time, the first possibility is only conceivable in extreme cases. The unsuccessful contractor/supplier can claim the allocated award, and the other contractor/supplier accepts that his concluded agreement is terminated. A similar claim can be envisaged in the event that the contract is unjustifiably awarded to another contractor/supplier who was, or should have been, aware of it. Then, not only the procuring body, but also the contractor/supplier has acted unjustly towards the unsuccessful contractor/supplier.[2]

---

[1] An example of a case in which such a legal action was successfully achieved can be found in a decision of the Board of Arbiters for Construction Firms dated 26 May 1987 – see Journal for Building Law 1987, p 623. In this case, an action was undertaken by a construction consortium that had the lowest bid, but this was rejected on the grounds that, according to the Dutch state, the consortium did not have enough relevant experience. The consortium brought an action for an injunction against the State from assigning the work to another firm. The Board of Arbiters for Construction Firms held that the State's demands for experience criteria were ambiguous and, to the advantage of the consortium, arrived at the conclusion that it met the criteria, granting the action.

[2] In this context are of importance the judgment-in-appeal of the Supreme Court in the case *Pos/v.d. Bosch* of 17 November 1967, NJ 1968, 42; J. Spier, Agreements with the government, dissertation at Leiden 1981, p 93; the rulings of the Board of Arbiters for Construction Firms 13704 and 13713, Journal for Building Law 1989, p 552; and the ruling of the Board of Arbiters for Construction Firms of 15 July 1992, Journal for Building Law 1993, p 157. In the last judgment, the Board of Arbiters came to the conclusion that the procuring body (a municipality) had acted wrongfully to the contractor/supplier who made the lowest bid (the plaintiff) by unjustifiably awarding the assignment to another contractor/supplier after asking him, before the tendering procedure had ended, for an alternative bid outside the procedure and consequently regarding the bid as the best bid, made in accordance with the Uniform Tendering Rule EC 1986. The Board of Arbiters came to the conclusion that not only the procuring bodies but also the contractors/suppliers should follow the tendering rules. The Board of Arbiters therefore concluded that not only the procuring body but also the contractor/supplier had acted contrary to the Uniform Tendering Rule EC 1986 and

Damages

In general, when an award has been re-allocated, a replaced contractor/supplier only has available an action for damages. When the tender invitation is not announced, although the procurement body is obliged to do this, then the passed-over contractor/supplier has to show that on notification of the tender he would have bid, and that the contract should have been allocated to him. When the tender invitation was announced, but the assignment was wrongly let to another, the contractor/supplier will have to prove that he would have been awarded the contract if the rules of the Uniform Tendering Rule had been followed.[1]

A passed-over contractor/supplier can ask the procurement body for an explanation of the reason why he has not been awarded an assignment. This explanation can be used in evidence in a procedure seeking to prove that he would have been awarded the assignment if the tender action had been announced or if the rules of the Uniform Tendering Rule had been followed.

Furthermore, the passed-over contractor/supplier must prove his damage. Mostly the damages will consist of general costs and lost profits. Proof might be established by presenting the court with an audit report which has to show the return on investments made by the passed-over contractor/supplier in former years.

THE DURATION OF PROCEEDINGS

The time a proceeding may take varies between procedures and according to the type of procedure. Generally it can be said that a summary proceeding by the President of the District Court, and an urgent case by the Board of Arbiters for Construction Firms, takes from a few days to a few weeks.

---

consequently unjustly towards the unsuccessful contractor/supplier. The plaintiff demanded termination by the municipality of the contract and a new tendering procedure. This was rejected by the Board of Arbiters on grounds of the excessive damage that decision would lead to, while a new tendering procedure would not automatically lead to the granting of the contract to the plaintiff because the municipality was then not free to allocate the assignment nor to allocate the assignment to someone else. The damage of the plaintiff consisted solely of the costs made by the plaintiff in making a bid. The Board of Arbiters concluded that the limited interest of the plaintiff did not justify the termination of the contract, also because the contractor/supplier had already made considerable investments. Both the municipality and the contractor/supplier were ordered to pay equal parts of the costs of the procedure.

[1] An example of a case can be found in which compensation is granted on those grounds, in the judgment of the Court in Maastricht, 24 December 1987 – Journal for Building Law 1988, p 389. In this case, a municipality named Meersen had made the intention to go to tender known according to UAR 1971. In the intention it was stipulated that in the fulfilment of the contract, concrete-substance X had to be used. The plaintiff, Kunicon, entered the tender with two bids, one bid with the prescribed substance X and one with an alternative for substance X. The bid with the alternative was the lowest. After the lowest bid of the plaintiff was passed over, the plaintiff went to court and demanded compensation on grounds of unlawful act because the stipulation of the use of specific building materials is contrary to Article 10, clause 2 of the co-ordination Directive and the alternative was in accordance with all technical and other conditions. Consequently the assignment should have been allocated to the plaintiff on grounds of Article 29, clause 1 of the co-ordination Directive (93/38), the plaintiff being the contractor/supplier with the lowest bid. The plaintiff demanded 10% of the bid as damages for coverage of general costs and lost profits. The Court awarded the plaintiff his claim and the municipality was ordered to pay the costs of the procedure, being the party found to be at fault.

A basic procedure by the District Court, or a normal procedure by the Board of Arbiters for Construction Firms may on the other hand occupy a few months or several years. There are possible ways of shortening a basic procedure at the District Court. The plaintiff party can request the Court to expedite the summons.[1] Moreover, the plaintiff party can request the Court to dispense with replies and rejoinders.[2]

THE EFFECTIVENESS OF THE IMPLEMENTATION MEASURES

It is important that those inviting tenders, and interested contractors/suppliers, know the applicable tender regulations. They are then aware of the possibilities and risks in case a tender action does not follow these rules. Tenderers must be aware of possible losses, not only in the case where compensation must be paid, but also through the possible delays and extra costs of the tender action itself.[3]

Contractors/suppliers are decreasingly hesitant to take legal action over a tender, as awareness of their legal remedies has grown. The markets for government assignments are more competitive, and, thanks to the EC tenders Directives are clearer, so frequently action taken at an early stage is successful. For that matter, the threat of a complaint, or a claim for compensation, can be very effective in competition for an order. Nevertheless, overlooked contractors/suppliers do not make enough use of the possibilities to take proceedings against infringements of the legislation for implementation of Directives. A much-heard explanation for this is that contractors/suppliers are unwilling to go to law, having future assignments in mind.

---

[1]   See Article 7 of the Code of Civil Procedure.
[2]   See Article 145 of the Code of Civil Procedure.
[3]   Also, both Civil Judges and the Board of Arbiters will order the party found to be at fault to pay the costs of the procedure.

CHAPTER 12

Remedies in Spain[1]

José Mª Jiménez Laiglesia

INTRODUCTION TO SPANISH LAW ON PUBLIC PROCUREMENT

Public procurement of the Administration in Spain is regulated by specific administrative laws. The *Ley de Contratos del Estado* ('LCE') adopted in 1965 consolidated for the first time in Spain the law affecting administrative contracts. The LCE was followed by its developing legislation, the *Reglamento General de Contratación del Estado* ('RGCE') adopted in 1975.[2] This basic legal framework has been followed by the adoption of other legal acts affecting this matter. However, these two texts were, at the time of the accession of Spain to the European Community, the basic legal framework dealing with public procurement in Spain and were applicable to all administrative contracts in Spain.

The adaptation of the LCE and the RGCE to the EC Directives at that time applicable on public procurement took place at the time of Spain's accession to the EC in 1986.[3] However, since 1987 the European Commission has considered that the legal framework of Spanish procurement laws does not correctly implement the EC Directives, and this resulted in the Commission bringing an action against Spain before the European Court of Justice under Article 169 of the Treaty. In the case *Commission v Spain*, the European Court of Justice declared that several provisions of the LCE and the RGCE

---

[1] The following abbreviations are used throughout the text and footnotes in this chapter:
   ATS: Order of the Supreme Court
   ATC: Order of the Constitutional Court
   STS: Judgment of the Supreme Court
   STC: Judgment of the Constitutional Court
   LCE: Law of State Contracts
   RGCE: General Regulation of State Contracts
   LRJAP: Legal Regime of Public Administration and Administrative Procedure
   LJCA: Law of Administrative Contentious Proceedings
   LCAP: Public Administration Contract Law
   LPJDF: Law for Juridical Protection of Fundamental Rights
[2] Ley de Contratos del Estado approved by Decree 923 of 8 April 1965 and reformed by Ley 5/1973. Reglamento General de Contratación del Estado approved by Decree 3354/1967 and reformed by Decree 3410/1975.
[3] Royal Decree 931/1986 2 May and Law 33/1987 tried to bring into Spanish law the requirements of Community legislation at that time in force.

were not in compliance with EC Directives at that time applicable, specifically regarding works and supplies contracts.[1]

This case confirmed the need to reform the legal rules of public procurement in Spain which, in any case, was at that time in process. This has finally resulted in the adoption of the *Ley de Contratos de la Administración Pública* ('LCAP') which has brought an overall reform of public procurement laws in Spain.[2]

The current applicable laws, however, have not reformed the regulation of remedies available in Spain for infringement of public procurement law by the administrative authorities. The obligations imposed on Spain arising from Directive 89/665 (the 'Remedies Directive')[3] are within the field of the general administrative and judicial procedures for the review of administrative acts rather than in the provisions of the LCE, the RGCE or the reforming LCAP. In effect, it was considered that the Remedies Directive did not require to be transposed into Spanish law. An affirmation of this kind exists for instance in the Preamble of the LCAP.

The LCAP contains a detailed regulation of the works, supplies and public services contracts concluded by the Administration. However, these basic provisions also apply to other types of contracts (for instance transport, deposit, etc) if those contracts have a direct connection with the exercise of a public service or in cases where there is an objective need to protect the public interest as regards those contracts. It can also happen that specific provisions or laws designate that a particular contract enjoys an administrative nature. In these cases, the LCAP is always the basic rule which applies to these contracts.

The determination of the nature of a particular contract concluded by the Administration is relevant as regards the application of the provisions of the LCAP, but also in relation to the jurisdiction which enforces the provisions of the contract. As we will see later, all matters related to administrative contracts are subject to the procedures for ordinary administrative recourse (*recurso ordinario*) and to a special jurisdiction which is competent for administrative matters, the *jurisdicción contencioso-administrativa*.

Therefore, the distinction between 'administrative contracts' and 'private contracts concluded by the Administration', which are subject to civil law, seems to be essential to understand the legal regime of the contract and the procedure available to the party contracting with the Administration, wishing to initiate proceedings in order to obtain redress. However, the distinction has lost much of its former significance since under the LCAP an administrative contract has an extended meaning. Thus, the LCAP states that works,

---

[1]   Case C-71/92 *Commission v Spain* [1993] ECR I-5923, regarding public procurement contracts in the field of works and supplies. Provisions of Spanish law declared incompatible with the EC Directives affected essentially direct adjudication of contracts, rules regarding participation in award procedures, selection criteria and technical rules. See also Case C-328/92 *Commission v Spain* [1984] ECR I-1569, which declared incompatible with EC public procurement rules the Spanish rules regulating direct adjudication of supplies of pharmaceutical products to Social Security Institutions. Another case dealing with the compatibility of Spanish public procurement laws with EC law in specific cases is Case C-24/91 *Commission v Spain* [1992] ECR I-1989, referring to derogations from common rules established in Directive 71/305 for reasons of urgency in the context of the award of a public works contract.

[2]   Ley 13/1995, de 18 de Mayo, de Contratos de las Administraciones Públicas, State Official Bulletin (BOE) no 119, 19 May 1995.

[3]   Council Directive 89/665 of 21 December 1989 on the co-ordination of the laws, regulations and administrative provisions relating to the application of review procedures to the award of public supply and public works contracts; OJ 1992 L 395.

supplies and services contracts concluded by the Administration are considered administrative contracts.[1]

Furthermore, irrespective of the nature of the contract, all acts which the Administration has to undertake in order to prepare and award a contract are considered 'severable administrative acts' from the actual execution and enforcement of a contract.[2]

These considerations arise from the application of fundamental rules that affect administrative action. In this sense, the activities and procedures of the Administration are subject to the principle of legality, protecting private citizens from arbitrary decisions and any misuse of power. This general principle, which affects all the activities of the Administration, implies that whenever the Administration is party to a contract, it has to follow specific procedures, in our case contained in the LCAP, for the preparation and award of the contract.

In this sense under Spanish administrative law there exists a succession of administrative acts before the final award of a contract, which are subject to administrative laws and which can be challenged individually before the administrative courts. The consequences of the annulment of these severable acts will be examined below but it is important to remember that the validity of these different acts can be challenged and examined with autonomy from the contract itself.

The specific provisions of the LCAP adopted in order to implement the EC Directives on public procurement are applicable to all Spanish Administrations as basic law under Article 149.1.18 of the Spanish Constitution, although in some areas there might exist complementary legislation adopted by the different Autonomous Communities according to the LCAP and within their competences. In principle, then, and as regards the general applicability of the LCAP, all Spanish Public Administrations are subject to its provisions. Thus, the LCAP is applicable to the Spanish Central Administration, the Administration of the Autonomous Communities (17 in total) and local authorities. The different institutions of the Social Security services and contracts concluded by the Autonomous organs created by the different Administrations (Central, Autonomous and local) are also under the provisions of the LCAP.

As we have already said, the LCAP contains common rules for works, supplies, services and other administrative contracts. These rules refer to the capacity, solvency and classification of contractors, award procedures, publication of offers, execution of contracts etc. A detailed examination of the law and its compatibility with EC law is outside the scope of this chapter.[3] We shall study the remedies available to parties against administrative acts of the Spanish contracting authorities which infringe the provisions of EC

---

[1] Administrative contracts are those contracts whose direct object is the execution of works, the management of public services and the provision of supplies, consultancy and assistance. Contracts with a different object are also administrative whenever they are directly related to the specific aim of the contracting authority, when the contract directly satisfies a public goal or when a particular Law declares such a character (Article 5 LCAP and Article 4 of the LCE).

[2] Article 9.2 LCAP and Article 4.3 A of the LCE. See in general 'Contratos Administrativos y Contratos Privados de la Administración', Solas Rafecas, Tecnos 1990.

[3] See 'El Derecho Comunitario de la Contratación Pública', Santías Viada, Santamaría de Paredes and López Blanco, Escuela de Hacienda Pública, 1991 for an introduction to the implementation of EC law in this field in Spain. See also Dictamen 214/92 21.5.1992 and Dictamen 1270/93 2.12.1993 of the Council of State which dealt in detail with the compatibility of Spanish law, at that time in force, with EC public procurement law.

Directives and their implementing provisions in Spain. In this sense, it should be remembered that EC Directives, because of their declared aim of guaranteeing unrestricted competition between bidders in order to promote market integration, deal essentially with the award of contracts and all the preparatory measures rather than with the actual execution of the contracts.[1]

REVIEW OF ACTS OF THE ADMINISTRATION

Introduction

The Remedies Directives oblige Member States to set up non-discriminatory, rapid and effective review procedures of acts of the contracting authorities that infringe EC public procurement Directives or the national provisions that implement that law. The Directive demands that decisions of the review bodies should be reasoned and subject to judicial review.

As already said, in Spain there are no special review procedures or bodies set up specifically as a result of the Remedies Directive. Indeed, the option was never discussed of setting up a specific body to review acts affecting contracts under the public procurement Directives. It was considered that the Remedies Directive requirements were met in the general administrative review procedures.

Therefore, the procedures for challenging administrative acts capable of infringing public procurement law are contained in the general administrative laws applicable for the review of all administrative action. These are the *Ley 30/92 de Regimen Juridico de las Administraciones Públicas y del Procedimiento Administrativo Común* (the 'LRJAP') which deals, inter alia, with administrative review, and the *Ley Reguladora de la Jurisdicción Contencioso-Administrativo* (hereinafter the 'LJCA') which deals with judicial review of administrative acts.[2]

These stages, administrative review ('recurso ordinario') and judicial review ('recurso contencioso-administrativo') are interconnected. Access to the administrative courts with general jurisdiction on administrative matters is generally dependent on the prior exhaustion of the administrative review. This feature of the Spanish system, which in effect allows the Administration to be a party and the 'judge' at the same time, resulted in unnecessary delay in the exercise of the right to access to judicial review of administrative acts. The idea was to give the Administration the possibility to reconsider its decision and avoid the cost of a judicial procedure. However, in practice, it meant delays and sometimes, for parties which were not careful with the time-limits for introducing administrative recourses, the loss of the right to judicial review.

The LRJAP has tried to reform this area of the law by seeking to limit the cases when the administrative complaint is a necessary condition prior to judicial review and by improving the possibility of obtaining the suspension of the challenged act. However, the system is not that efficient and, in general, the obligation of prior exhaustion of the administrative process of recourses conflicts with the need for an effective judicial protection. We shall see that,

---

[1]   See for instance Opinion 214/92 of the Council of the State which adopts this distinction.
[2]   Ley 30/92, de 26 de Noviembre, de Régimen Jurídico de las Administraciones Públicas y del Procedimiento Administrativo Común (LRJAP) BOE no 285 27 November 1992. Ley Reguladora de la Jurisdicción Contencioso-Administrativa de 27 de Diciembre de 1956 (LJCA) BOE no 363 28 December 1956.

with regard to the protection of certain fundamental rights, this feature has been substituted for direct access to the Courts.

Access to administrative and judicial review of administrative acts

The awarding authority of a particular contract is competent to decide on the administrative complaints regarding the interpretation, modification, termination and effects of administrative contracts. The awarding authority can also review administrative acts prior to the awarding of the contract. The decision of the awarding authority ends the administrative stage and opens up the possibility of having access to judicial review of the act. The awarding authority is competent also to decide on interim measures (suspension of the act) and even damages, measures which we will examine later.

Notwithstanding this, Article 61.1 of the LCAP states that a judicial review is open against all administrative acts that put an end to the administrative stage. This reflects the aim of the general reform of administrative law in Spain: to give as wide and as quick access as possible to a judicial court. Acts which put an end to the administrative stage are listed in Article 109 of the LRJAP. One case which might be important in the field of procurement law is the case of administrative acts adopted by administrative bodies which do not have superior bodies (ie Ministries in the Central Administration). Therefore, administrative acts in the context of the award of a contract adopted by a body with no superior might be challenged directly before the 'jurisdicción contencioso-administrativa' without first having to exhaust the administrative stage.

Aside from exceptional administrative review procedures which we will examine later, a party lodging an administrative complaint must respect the time-limits laid down by law. The party must lodge the recourse within one month from the notification of the administrative act or its publication.[1] Third parties with an interest will be invited to present submissions.

The Administration must adopt a resolution on the matter within three months from the lodging of the complaint. The Administration can simply be silent: in this case, so-called 'administrative silence' is equivalent to a refusal, thereby opening judicial review for the affected party. If there is a negative express resolution of the Administration, the affected party must lodge the 'recurso contencioso-administrativo' within two months from its notification in order to have access to the judicial review of the act.[2] In cases of negative administrative silence, the affected party enjoys an extended time-limit: one year from the day the administrative recourse was lodged. Thus, the attitude of the Administration determines the time-limits for having access to judicial review.

In cases where there is no obligation to lodge an administrative complaint first, the affected party must lodge the 'recurso contencioso-administrativo' for judicial review of the act within two months from the notification of the act or its publication.

---

[1] Article 114 LRJAP. It should be recalled that all interested parties whose offers have not been accepted can demand a reasoned explanation from the Administration: in 15 days from such a request, which will normally be lodged at the time of the notification or publication of the result of the award, the Administration must give the reasons for rejection and the grounds for the adjudication of the contract (Article 94.4 LCAP).

[2] Article 58 of the LJCA.

Spanish administrative law does not impose strict formal requirements for lodging an administrative complaint. The complaint must be directed against an act identified and based on the grounds provided for in the law. Formal legal representation is not needed for the administrative stage although it is advisable.

In order to present an administrative complaint, the party must hold a legitimate and individual interest. This has been extensively interpreted by the jurisprudence so access to review procedures will not normally be an obstacle.

A third party with interests that can be eventually affected by the resolution of the administrative recourse will be considered an interested party in the proceedings. The law also provides for collective actions for organisations or associations with legitimate collective interests affected by the administrative act.

At any time during the review procedure, the party can present whatever allegations are deemed adequate for the case, allegations that must be taken into account by the Administration when deciding on the complaint. During the administrative review there may be a period for presentation of evidence (normally between 10 and 30 days, although it can be extended). Any means of evidence normally accepted in civil procedure can be proposed.

The LRJAP also provides for an exceptional procedure for reviewing administrative acts. Article 102 of the LRJAP deals with the *recurso de revisión*. In this exceptional review procedure, the Administration at its own initiative or following the request of any interested party may set aside any act which falls under any of the grounds of absolute nullity contained in Article 62 of the LRJAP after consultation with the Council of State. The importance of this 'recurso de revisión' lies in the fact that it is not dependent on time-limits or conditioned to the presentation of a previous action. Therefore even if time-limits for the ordinary action have expired, the party may initiate, invoking grounds of absolute nullity, this 'recurso de revisión'. The decision of the Administration in this special procedure is also subject to review by the administrative courts.

As regards general access to judicial review, the party must show a direct interest in the issue.[1] However, the wording of this provision has been very widely interpreted and a mere legitimate interest will suffice. If the party holds a subjective right which has been affected by the administrative act, it may ask for the restitution of this right: this allows the party not only to seek annulment of the act, but also to ask for restitution of the right or eventually a compensation for the infringement committed by the Administration. In order to demand compensation from the Administration at the judicial stage, it is necessary to have been a party in the previous administrative stage.

In general, the ordinary rules of evidence accepted in law are applicable in the judicial review of administrative acts (witnesses, experts, public and private documents etc). It is important to remember that the presumption of validity of an administrative act does not mean that the onus of proof lies with the party seeking its annulment. Therefore the general rule of the onus of proof applies: whoever (including the Administration) alleges that an obligation exists must prove it (Article 1.214 of the Civil Code).[2]

In general, any obstacle for challenging administrative acts must be strictly

---

[1]   Article 28 of the LJCA.
[2]   See in general 'Derecho Procesal Administrativo' Gimeno Sendra and others. Ed. Tirant lo Blanch Valencia 1993.

interpreted and applied in accordance with the right to obtain effective judicial protection and the right to a due process provided for in Article 24 of the Spanish Constitution.[1]

INVALIDITY OF ADMINISTRATIVE ACTS

In Spanish administrative law, the rule is that administrative acts which infringe the law are considered to be voidable. Absolute nullity is reserved for specific cases provided for in the law.[2] The LCAP confirms this position; the principle is that infringements of the law will be declared voidable (Article 64 LCAP).

The differences between voidable and void acts are essentially three: void acts can be attacked at any time, so a party seeking the nullity of an administrative act is not dependent on time-limits. It is important to bear in mind that without prejudice to the usual administrative recourse and judicial review, there is a specific review procedure, which we have already examined, for these types of act that can be initiated without being subject to time-limits; furthermore void acts cannot be cured nor validated; void acts are ex tunc, that is they are considered to be void since they were adopted.[3]

Grounds of absolute nullity are expressly contained in Article 62.1 of the LRJAP. They are those acts that injure the essential content of fundamental and constitutionally protected rights (Art 14-29 of the Spanish Constitution), acts which have been adopted by a manifestly incompetent organ, acts whose content is impossible, acts which infringe criminal laws or are adopted as a consequence of a crime and those that are adopted without any respect for established legal procedures. In addition, the public procurement laws in Spain introduce two more grounds for claiming absolute nullity: that the contract was awarded to an undertaking which is affected by any of the prohibitions or incompatibilities of the law as regards its economic, technical and financial capacity and the absence of a budgetary credit allotted to the contract under the Budget laws (Article 63 LCAP).[4]

Voidable acts are the general rule when considering infringements of the law by administrative acts. These acts cannot be challenged after the time-limits already described above have elapsed. In general, voidable acts are those that infringe the legal order.[5] Formal defects of an administrative act only make the act voidable when the act lacks an indispensable formal requirement (for instance the act is not reasoned) or prevents the party from exercising its rights. Non-compliance by the contracting authority with mere formal requirements does not give cause for invalidity of the act. As specifically regards public procurement laws, and prior to the adoption of the LCAP, Article 44 of the RGCE stated that other acts in this field might be declared voidable apart from the grounds contained in the general administrative rules. In particular acts which have substantial defects, from which it might be

---

[1] See for instance STC 160/85.

[2] See for instance STS 15 June 1990. This principle is based on the requirements of the public interest in the activity carried out by the Administration.

[3] See in general 'Régimen Jurídico de las Administraciones Públicas y Procedimiento Administrativo Común' Jesús González Perez and Francisco González Navarro. Ed. Civitas 1994.

[4] Despite the contract considered null whenever the contractor lacks the capacity or solvency required, Article 22 LCAP allows the contracting authority to keep the same contractor under the same obligations for the necessary time in order not to affect the public interest.

[5] Article 63 of the LRJAP.

reasonably possible to deduce that without their presence the contracting authority would not have awarded the contract or would have awarded it to a different undertaking, are also voidable. In principle there is no reason not to consider this cause of invalidity of the acts still applicable as it will normally involve an infringement of the law.

The declaration of invalidity of an administrative contract has to be preceded by a favourable opinion of the Council of State (Article 65 LCAP). As regards consequences of the invalidity of the acts, Article 66 of LCAP states that the declaration of invalidity of any administrative act preparatory to the contract or the award itself has as a consequence the invalidity of the contract itself which will be terminated. Both parties must return to each other what was received by virtue of the contract or, if that is not possible, its value. The successful bidder not responsible for the wrongdoing of the Administration can claim compensation for the damage suffered based on costs incurred and loss of expected benefits. We will examine later what consequences, in terms of rights to obtain compensation for the injured party, might result on the declaration of invalidity of the act.

It follows from this that the declaration of invalidity of a particular administrative act prior to the award of the contract impedes the award of the contract until the wrongdoing is remedied. However, this is not the usual situation taking into account the length of the proceedings necessary to confirm such invalidity. Normally, unless suspension of the award procedure is obtained, the contract will already be awarded when such a declaration of invalidity is made. Without prejudice to an eventual compensation, this system for setting aside contracts already concluded does not seem to result in any material advantage for the party bringing the case, which in any case will have to participate in the whole award procedure again; rather it seems more important for the party to obtain interim relief. This is further aggravated because, in the name of the public interest, the law provides that if the declaration of invalidity of a contract causes serious disturbance to the public interest, the same declaration can provide for the continuance of the contract until urgent measures are adopted in order to avoid harm to such public interest. This gives the Administration potential discretion despite judicial control of the real existence of the alleged public interest.

INTERIM RELIEF

Administrative acts have an executive character in Spain. In other words, they enjoy a legal presumption of validity and, subject to their notification or publication, they produce effects from their adoption.[1] This principle implies that the mere lodging of an administrative complaint or judicial action against an administrative act will not produce the suspension of the effects of the act automatically or any other interim measure that might be appropriate.[2]

However, effective judicial protection demands that interim relief should be available for parties intervening in administrative or judicial proceedings against the Administration. The length of the process might cause irreparable damage to the parties, a harm which might not be restored by a final favourable decision. In fact a decision of the administrative courts on a case can take

[1]   See Article 57 of the LRJAP. Public interest demands that the activity of the Administration should be continuous and regular (STS 24 October 1986).
[2]   Article 111 LRJAP and Article 122 of the LJCA.

a considerable time in Spain and, as we will see, it is not easy to obtain compensation for damages committed by infringing acts of the Administration.

Although we will concentrate our analysis on the possibility of asking for the suspension of the effects of the administrative act, which is the most important and usual interim measure in Spanish administrative law, it is important to remember that effective judicial protection requires that other interim measures should be available for parties. Suspension is an effective interim measure against acts that produce a material change in the situation; however it is of no material use, for instance, against acts that simply deny a right.[1] However, Courts are normally reluctant to impose positive action on the Administration for fear that it might affect the final decision on the case and cause harm to the public interest.

Simultaneously with the lodging of the administrative complaint, the party can ask for the suspension of the effects of the act which is challenged. Article 111 of the LRJAP states that the administrative authority competent to decide on the complaint can grant the suspension after a reasoned evaluation between the damage that the suspension might have for the public interest or the interest of third parties that might be affected by the decision, and the damage that the implementation of the act might cause to the party lodging the complaint.

The competent authority can grant the suspension for any of the following two reasons: when the execution of the act causes damage which is difficult or impossible to remedy or when the action is based on any of the grounds of absolute nullity.

When the party has requested the suspension of the act and the Administration has not responded to such a request within 30 days, the act is considered to be suspended.[2] This provision, which clearly improves the past situation, obliges the Administration fairly quickly to state the reasons why it considers that the act should not be suspended. Consequently it opens the door to judicial review of a denial.

Article 122 of the LJCA regulates this matter at the judicial level. The wording of this provision is fairly restrictive and traditionally the suspension of administrative acts has been considered an exceptional measure. This provision states that the filing of a 'recurso contencioso-administrativo' does not prevent the Administration from executing the administrative act, unless the Court decides otherwise because the execution will cause damage difficult or impossible to repair ('periculum in mora').

Only the Court can declare the suspension of the act but only after formal request by the interested party. The procedure is interlocutory, dependent on the main application, and can be initiated by the interested party at any time of the procedure, even on appeal. The Court is also competent to decide on the maintenance of the suspension granted by the Administration in the previous 'recurso ordinario', modify the interim measure during the procedure or even declare its termination if the circumstances so dictate. This responds to the interlocutory character of the suspension of the execution of the act.

The LJCA only mentions damage difficult or impossible to repair, as the criterion for granting the suspension of the act. However, the Courts, although with some hesitation, have introduced another criterion: the examination of

---

[1]   See ATS 16 February 1978 and 'Derecho Procesal Administrativo' pp 671 op cit supra, note 14. See, in general, García de Enterrís, 'La batalla por las medidas cautelares. Derecho Comunitario Europeo y proceso contencioso-administrativo español' Ed. Civitas 1992.

[2]   Article 111.4 LRJAP.

the 'fumus boni iuris', that is the initial examination of the merits of the points of law alleged by the interested party. The Courts will make at that stage a prior analysis of the probability that the administrative act will be considered illegal by the final judgment. This is similar to the suspension granted at the administrative stage when the party alleges grounds of absolute nullity of the act.[1]

As regards the analysis of which damage will be considered irreparable or difficult to remedy in order to grant the suspension of the execution of the act, the Courts had interpreted it as depending on the possibility of economic compensation. In other words, if the damage alleged by the interested party can be economically evaluated, interim relief will not be granted.[2] Moreover, it is not enough merely to allege the damage caused by the execution of the act. The interested party must at least provide the Court with some elements that allow it reasonably to conclude that damage will be produced if the suspension is not granted.[3]

However, this restrictive interpretation, based on the public interest which demands the continuity of the administrative action, has been modified by other jurisprudence relying on the wording appearing in the Preamble of the LJCA which states that interim relief should not be excluded merely because the damage arising from the execution of the act can be evaluated.

In this sense, public interest must be weighed against the interest of the party seeking the suspension of the act. Jurisprudence seems to evolve in the sense that the Court will make a balance of the different interests which are at stake in the particular case. As such, then, the public interest is present throughout the process of granting interim relief. If the public interest might be affected by the suspension of the act (for instance the suspension of the execution of a contract) the Court might decide to request guarantees from the party seeking the suspension that, if requested, are a necessary condition for the suspension being granted. Although this is a matter for each specific case, the right to effective judicial protection requires that the public interest alleged by the Administration should be specific and real, not something abstract and general.

In general then, the criteria for granting interim relief at the stage of judicial review are similar to the criteria adopted by the European Court of Justice.[4] Spanish Courts confronted by requests for interim relief based on the infringements of public procurement law are increasingly accustomed to the examination of the material arguments which establish a prima facie case and the urgency of the relief in order to avoid irreparable damage being done, taking into account at the same time the balance of interests at stake.

As regards public procurement, and to quote some examples, Courts have suspended an administrative act which did not recognise in the plaintiff the capacity to contract with the Administration, based on the impossibility of determining the damage done to the plaintiff as a result of not being able to participate in the award procedures,[5] or have suspended the effects of a unilateral termination of a contract by the Administration when public interest

---

[1] See STS 23 April 1991, STS 27 November 1991.
[2] ATS 27 January 1987 with the corollary that because the Administration can never be declared insolvent, damages of purely economic nature are not irreparable and therefore interim relief should not be granted.
[3] STS 3 March 1994.
[4] See cases C-272/91R *Lottomatica* [1995] 2 CMLR 504, and C-87/94R *Van Hool* [1994] ECR I-1395.
[5] ATS 16 December 1991.

was not affected.[1] On the other hand, suspensions of award procedures are rare; the public interest cannot tolerate delay, for instance, in necessary supplies or the construction of important public infrastructures.[2]

The request for suspension will be forwarded to any other interested party and the Administration in order to present their submissions. If the suspension has caused damage, the prejudiced party can ask for compensation. The onus of proof is on the party alleging the damage caused by the suspension of the act.

Finally, Law 62/78 of *Protección Jurisdiccional de los Derechos Fundamentales* ('LPJDF') provides effective and rapid procedures and time-limits for the protection of certain fundamental rights provided for in the Spanish Constitution.[3] The LPJDF provides for a special administrative review procedure established for the protection of special important rights; Articles 14 to 29 and 30.2 of the Spanish Constitution. Among the rights protected by the LPJDF, non-discrimination and equality before the law might be relevant for cases in the field of public procurement. Whenever an act of the Administration, including here also a factual situation, not necessarily a formal administrative act of the administrative authority,[4] affects one of those rights, the affected party may initiate directly a judicial action against the act without first having to exhaust the administrative stage. The Court is obliged to grant interim relief, that is to suspend the effects of the act, unless the Administration shows that the relief will cause a serious prejudice to the general interest.[5]

DAMAGES

Article 106 of the Spanish Constitution establishes the right of individuals to obtain compensation from injuries caused as a result of the activity of the Administration.

As regards infringements of public procurement laws, the general liability regime of the Administration is applicable. Thus, there is no specific rule or liability regime provided for in this area. We will analyse here non-contractual liability of the Administration by acts committed during the award procedures infringing the public procurement rules, not contractual liability derived from the execution of the contracts. As we mentioned earlier, this latter issue is contemplated in the LCAP as a consequence of the termination of the contracts, and damages in this case include recovery of expenses and loss of profit (Article 114 LCAP).

An administrative complaint or an action before the administrative jurisdiction may include a claim for damages caused by the unlawful act of the Administration. The substantive rules concerning liability of the Administration are contained in Articles 139 to 144 of the LRJAP. The procedural rules applicable are established by the Royal Decree 429/93 which

---

[1] ATS 9 July 1988. It is important to consider that once the contract is awarded the Administration has certain prerogatives: in particular, the Administration can interpret the contracts, resolve existing doubts, modify them under specific public interest requirements and terminate them. These prerogatives are subject to special requirements and are of course open to judicial review (Article 60 LCAP).
[2] ATS 2 January 1992.
[3] Ley 62/78, de 26 de Diciembre, de Protección Jurisdiccional de los Derechos Fundamentales de la Persona BOE no 3, 3 January 1979.
[4] STS 28 November 1990.
[5] ATC 786/86.

contains the applicable administrative procedures as regards liability of the Administration and in the LJCA for claims before the administrative jurisdiction.

Compensation for damages may be requested at either the administrative or the judicial stage albeit without necessarily having to do it in both stages. Therefore, it is not necessary to request compensation at the administrative level in order to be able to request the same at the judicial stage.

The declaration of invalidity of an act, both in the administrative and judicial review, does not necessarily imply the right to obtain compensation for the injured party. The liability system existing in Spain is based on the objective liability of the Administration. Therefore, the traditional system of non-contractual liability, which is based on negligence or fault, does not apply in relation to liability of the Administration.

A plaintiff requesting compensation will have to show, firstly, the real existence of damage which can be economically evaluated; secondly, that the damage was caused by the action of the Administration; and thirdly, that a direct link of cause and effect exists between the action of the Administration and the damage suffered.[1] In addition to these conditions, the damage should not have been caused as a result of force majeure and the claim has to comply with the established procedural requirements.

The damage has to be real, that is effective and economically evaluated. The onus of proof lies with the plaintiff. Hypothetical, eventual, future or conditional damages will not be compensated. The aim of the compensation is to put the plaintiff in the position he would have been in had there been no infringement.

In general, recovery of expenses incurred for participating in the award procedures does not create major problems. It will depend on the infringement committed and the actual proof of costs incurred.

However, in order to have a right to compensation for lost profits, the plaintiff will have to prove that he would have been awarded the contract had not the Administration breached the rules on public procurement. It seems, then, that the law does not provide for compensation for the loss of profit unless the plaintiff proves that he would have been awarded the contract. This is very difficult in cases where the contract award criteria are based on a number of factors, and not necessarily the lowest price, even if those factors are listed in the offer. Loss of a chance to obtain the award of the contract is not considered real and effective damage.

Compensation is therefore very difficult to obtain for parties which have not been allowed to participate in an award procedure or which have not been awarded the contract by virtue of an unlawful act of the Administration unless it is rigorously proved that they would have obtained the award of the contract.

This position explains the crucial need to obtain interim relief before the award of the contract (suspension of the award procedure and correction of the infringements) in order for the injured party to be restored to its rights.

In general, there is a time-limit of one year to claim compensation from the date that the act which caused the damage was adopted.[2] If the claim is presented after a declaration of invalidity of the act that caused the damage, the year begins from the day the declaration is firm.

---

[1] Article 139 LRJAP. Among many others, see SLTS 2 February 1980 and STS 3 January 1990.
[2] Article 142.4 of LRJAP and Article 4 of Royal Decree 429/93.

Although rare, the Administration can initiate on its own motion the procedure for the compensation of damages. Royal Decree 429/93 establishes the procedure to obtain compensation before the Administration, providing for a specific procedure to be followed by the claimant.

The infringement of the public procurement rules by the Administration can also trigger personal liability of the administrative staff responsible for the infringement if there existed, at least, serious negligence on their part.

Articles 28.2 and 42 of the LJCA recognise the possibility of claiming damages before the administrative jurisdiction. The law states that the plaintiff has to show that an individual legal situation has been affected in order to claim damages. An individual legal situation does not necessarily mean that the plaintiff must hold a subjective right individually infringed by the act of the Administration in order to obtain compensation. Generally, the same interest demanded from the plaintiff in order to seek the annulment of an act will be recognised for the claim of damages. The law treats the possibility of obtaining damages as an alternative remedy; that is, damages will be granted only when there is no other way of restoring the plaintiff to his right. This will normally be the case, taking into account that usually the contract will already have been awarded by the time that the act has been declared invalid.

REMEDIES DIRECTIVE IN THE EXCLUDED SECTORS

Directive 92/13 co-ordinates national provisions relating to the application of Community rules on the procurement procedures of entities operating in the water, energy, transport and telecommunication sectors. Spain had until 30 June 1995 to implement this Directive into national law. There is however a delay in the implementation of this Directive. It should be recalled that, oddly enough, Spain had until 1 January 1996 to implement the measures needed to put into effect Directive 90/531 and has until 1 July 1997 to put into effect Directive 93/38, both of them dealing with the co-ordination of procurement procedures in these economic sectors for works, supplies and services contracts.

It is as yet unclear how this implementation is going to be carried out. In general, the above described regime does not deal with this issue, taking into account that contracts concluded by these entities (listed in Directive 93/38) will be subject to civil law, not administrative law, owing to the legal nature of the contracting entities.[1]

This situation implies that there are obstacles to the implementation of the Remedies Directive in these sectors: for instance, civil courts cannot suspend the effects of a contract or take into account public interest adequately. Moreover, obligations contained in the Directive regarding the steps prior to the perfection of the contract and its execution do not seem to fall within the competence of a civil court. On the other hand, a general administrative review of the award of these contracts by the administrative jurisdiction might involve the establishment of a prior administrative complaint before the competent organ, which in turn will imply the re-establishment of control of the Administration over the procurement activities of private undertakings albeit with special or exclusive rights.

---

[1] This is recognised by the Commission in its 1990 proposal COM (90) 297 final. The Preamble of the LCAP states that this Law does not implement Directive 90/531 because of the nature of the entities affected.

In principle, the substantive rules affecting both the procurement activities of the majority of these entities and the remedies for the enforcement of these rules might have to be regulated by a specific implementing instrument because of the difficulties involved with the current system. However, nothing impedes the application of the general principles regarding the need to guarantee effective and rapid remedies in this case; some of these entities, despite their private nature, have 'delegated powers' from the administration and, therefore, their procurement action should be controlled under the same principles.

In any case, and despite the uncertainty of the future implementation of the different Directives, the LCAP provides that companies belonging to the 'public sector' (which is not defined), in which the Administration or public entities hold directly or indirectly the majority of the capital, will apply the principles of publicity and competitive tendering in their procurement activities, although not when the application of these principles is considered incompatible with the nature of the procurement.

CONCLUSIONS

If we examine the requirements for the enforcement of remedies for breaches of public procurement rules contained in the Remedies Directive, it appears that Spanish law, as it stands, complies with the minimum demanded. In general, access to review of the acts of the Administration is reasonably wide, interim relief is available and a system of compensation for damages caused by the infringements of the public procurement rules is open to injured parties.

Although the reform could have gone further, review of administrative acts in this field has also benefited from the reform of administrative laws. The new administrative laws have relaxed the requirement of exhaustion of prior administrative procedures in order to have access to the administrative jurisdiction and have also introduced a more effective system for obtaining suspension of the act in the administrative procedure which puts more pressure on the Administration. We can also observe that, despite the executive character of administrative acts and the natural reserve of what is, after all, a case-by-case approach, administrative courts are more prepared now than in the past to grant interim relief whenever public interest is not seriously affected.

However, if we examine whether the Spanish regime provides an 'effective and rapid' system of remedies and an incentive to affected parties to demand compliance from the Administration of the public procurement rules, it is evident that it needs certain improvements. It is true that these deficiencies, and in particular the length of the proceedings which might render the exercise of the rights conferred by the Directive illusory, are not specific to public procurement, but are a general problem with administrative courts, not even a particular problem of Spain. However, we should remember that it is precisely in this field where private parties need to be actively encouraged to attack illegal acts of the Administration. This is the reason why some commentators have proposed the need to establish specific procedures for the resolution of cases in the procurement sector, for instance through the creation of ad hoc organs with powers to decide on these matters, a possibility contemplated in Article 107.2 LRJAP.[1]

Furthermore, the current legal situation as regards the consequences of

---

[1] See J.M. Gimeno Feliu 'El control de la contratación pública' Ed. Civitas 1995.

the invalidity of a contract and the availability of damages to injured parties is not satisfactory. In the first place, the consequences of the declaration of invalidity, termination and liquidation of the contract do not provide a real incentive for interested parties to bring claims against the Administration. Owing to the length of the proceedings, the contract will normally have been awarded before the declaration of invalidity is adopted, leaving damages as an only means of redress. However, this situation is aggravated because of the difficulty of obtaining compensation. As we have seen, for parties seeking compensation, the need to show the link between the infringing act of the Administration and the damage suffered will continue to be a difficult task so long as loss of a chance to obtain an award of a contract is regarded as not being real damage under the Spanish system.

In general, Spanish courts are increasingly aware of the nature of EC law and the obligations derived from it, in particular the need to take into account EC legislation when deciding on a case. Hopefully this will bring a positive attitude towards parties seeking redress against acts of the Administration that infringe those rules, in order to provide for more effective and rapid remedies.

CHAPTER 13

Remedies in the United Kingdom

Becket Bedford

INTRODUCTION

Prior to the adoption of the EC public procurement regime, the award of public contracts was not open to challenge in the UK. Even after the regime came into force contractors had no clear means of redress against public bodies before the implementation of the Remedies Directives.

Unlike some other Member States, the UK, with the exception of the Local Government Act 1988 concerning the award of certain local government contracts, had not developed a distinct body of law of its own to govern the award of public contracts. As a result, unsuccessful tenderers for public contracts or contractors aggrieved by the procedures leading to the award of public contracts had no remedy.

It is an irony of Community law that the public procurement Directives[1] designed to open national markets to foreign competition, and particularly the Remedies Directives,[2] have given UK contractors domestic remedies against their own public bodies in their own Courts.

REMEDIES PRIOR TO THE EC REGIME

In the absence of a legislative code setting out the procedures to be adopted by public bodies when letting public contracts, a contractor had no basis either in private or public law to challenge the tendering process or the award of the contract itself.

Private law: non-contractual duties

Public bodies did not owe contractors general non-contractual duties under the common law either (1) to publicise their intention to award a contract; (2) to consider the bids of all or any interested parties; or (3) to judge bids according to reasonable criteria.

---

[1]   93/36/EEC; 93/37/EEC; 93/38/EEC, OJ No L199, 9.8.93; 92/50/EEC, OJ No L209, 24.7.92.
[2]   89/665/EEC, OJ No L395, 21.12.89; 92/13/EEC, OJ No L76, 23.3.92.

Private law: contractual duties

Public bodies could not be made liable for breach of any contractual duty if they chose to exclude tenderers from the bids procedure or if they chose to favour certain tenderers over others. For contractual duties could arise only at the stage when a contract was concluded. Of necessity, the procedures leading to the award of a contract preceded the conclusion of the contract itself and so, during the bids process, a public body owed no contractual duty to those excluded from the tendering process or those taking part.

Public law

The courts had long had a public law jurisdiction, now known as judicial review, by which the decisions of public bodies were susceptible to challenge, provided always that the decision complained of was a public law one.

Since the decision by a public body to enter into a contract was regarded as falling entirely within the province of private law, the procedures leading to the award of public contracts were similarly characterised as matters of private law.[1] However, the position would have been different, if a statutory code obliged public authorities to have due regard to the interests of contractors.[2]

REMEDIES PRIOR TO THE REMEDIES DIRECTIVE

Prior to the implementation of the Remedies Directive in the UK in 1991, contractors aggrieved by breaches of the EC public procurement regime lacked any form of dedicated redress. However, by virtue of the Community law doctrine of direct effect the courts were bound to protect the rights of individuals conferred by the EC public procurement regime.[3] Notwithstanding, legal uncertainty remained over the form that such protection should take. Unless a breach of the regime entitled a contractor to a remedy in private law, he had no general right to damages.

Damages

The courts were ready to award private law remedies against individuals or companies who breached Community law.[4] However, in the case of *Bourgoin*,[5] it was held that a breach of Community law by a public authority did not give rise to private law remedies, but only to a remedy in public law, namely judicial review. As a result a contractor who suffered loss arising out of the breach of the EC public procurement regime would have no claim for damages unless, exceptionally, it could be shown that a public authority had not merely breached the regime, but had in addition abused its powers.

The case of *Bourgoin* concerned a central government authority, but the

---

[1] *R v Lord Chancellor, ex p Hibbit & Saunders (a firm)* [1993] COD 326.
[2] *Ibid* at 328.
[3] *Beentjes* case 31/87 [1988] ECR 4635; *Fratelli* case 103/88 [1989] ECR 1839.
[4] *Garden Cottage Foods Ltd v Milk Marketing Board* [1984] AC130, HL.
[5] *Bourgoin SA v Ministry of Agriculture, Fisheries and Food* [1986] QB 716, CA.

ruling applied equally to all public authorities, including local government. However, by the Local Government Act 1988, the UK passed its own domestic legislation to regulate the procedures leading to the award of certain local government contracts, introducing what is known as 'compulsory competitive tendering'. The Act gave contractors a right to damages[1] in judicial review proceedings, limited to the recovery of expenditure reasonably incurred for the purpose of submitting a tender. The Act did not entitle a contractor to damages in respect of the profits he could have expected if he had won the tender.

Given the domestic law entitlement to limited damages against local authorities under the 1988 Act by virtue of Community law, in particular the cases of *Comet*[2] and *Rewe*,[3] the Courts would have been obliged to give contractors like protection against breaches of the EC public procurement regime by local authorities.

The absence of a general right to damages explains in part the failure of contractors both domestic and foreign to invoke the EC public procurement regime in the UK prior to the Remedies Directive. Equally, judicial review did not lend itself to the task of providing contractors with a simple and effective remedy for breach of the regime.

Judicial review

A contractor could apply for judicial review of the acts or decisions of a public authority taken during the course of the procedures leading to the award of a public contract. On an application for judicial review the Courts had power to set aside any decision found to be in breach of the regime or make an order requiring a public authority to comply with the regime. However, the Courts had no power to order a public authority to award a contract to the applicant and nor would the courts set aside a public contract once it had been concluded. In the case of *R v Lord Chancellor, ex p Hibbit & Saunders (a firm)*,[4] which concerned an application for judicial review of the award of a public contract to which the regime did not apply, it was stated that assuming the court had the power to set aside the decision to award a contract, once the contract had been concluded it could not be interfered with. In order for judicial review to be effective it was essential for the court to be asked to make a determination before the conclusion of the contract.

To take the most flagrant example of breach, if a contractor only learned about the award of a contract by a central government department after its conclusion, without its ever being advertised in the Official Journal, judicial review would be futile in the absence of a right to general damages. Even if the contract had been awarded by a local authority, the contractor would have no remedy in damages since he would not have incurred any expense in tendering.

In an urgent case where it appeared that a contract was likely to be concluded before it could be determined whether the regime had been breached, effective protection of a contractor's Community rights required the courts to make

---

[1] S 19(8) Local Government Act 1988.
[2] *Comet v Produktschap* case 45/76, [1976] ECR 2043.
[3] *Rewe v Landwirtschaftskammer* case 33/76 [1976] ECR 1989.
[4] [1993] COD 326.

an order restraining the public authority from awarding the contract before a full investigation of the merits of the case. A contractor could apply to the court for an interim order to prevent the award by a local authority of a public contract pending the outcome of a full hearing of an application for judicial review. However, there was considerable uncertainty over whether the court could make an interim order against central government, namely the Crown. The matter was not resolved in the affirmative until the decision of the House of Lords in the case of *R v Secretary of State for Transport, ex p Factortame Ltd (No 2)*[1] when it was held that an interlocutory injunction could be awarded against the Crown in order to protect the rights of individuals conferred by Community law.

Two further difficulties militated against the use of judicial review as an effective remedy for breach of the regime. In the first instance the test of whether the regime had been breached appeared to be heavily stacked in favour of the public authority. Finally, even if a contractor succeeded in showing that the regime had been breached, the decision whether to set aside the unlawful action was in the discretion of the court and the contractor could not insist on it as a matter of right.

The test for breach in judicial review

On an application for judicial review, any challenge to the exercise of discretion by a public authority during the procedures leading to the award of a contract, for example in the decision to use negotiated procedures or over the adjudication of the most economically advantageous tender, would be required to satisfy the court not merely that the decision was wrong, but that it was so wrong as to be perverse.

Where for instance a disappointed contractor complained that his tender more closely matched the contract award criteria than the successful contractor's tender, he could not ask the court to compare the tenders and judge for itself which was the most economically advantageous. In judicial review, the court is not entitled to substitute its decision for that of the public body. All that the court could do would be to examine the reasons of the contracting authority for awarding the contract to the successful contractor and determine whether the award was so unreasonable that no similar contracting authority could have come to the decision in question.

The exercise of discretion by the court

Even if a decision taken during the procedures leading to the award of a public contract were found to have breached the regime, it was not a foregone conclusion that the decision would be set aside. On an application for judicial review, the court always retains a discretion whether to grant the relief sought.

Thus, the courts would have to engage in a balancing exercise of the various interests: for example the interest of the applicant and the prospects of his winning the contract if it were re-let or if he were permitted to participate in the tendering procedure; the interests of the other tenderers or of the successful contractor; and the public interest in the performance of the contract.

[1]　[1991] 1 AC 603.

Conclusion

Given the limited circumstances in which judicial review could have provided a remedy at all; the lack of a general right to damages; the doubtful availability of interim measures against the Crown; the hurdles to be surmounted in persuading a court that a public authority had failed properly to exercise its discretion under the regime; and finally the discretionary nature of judicial review itself, it is small wonder that contractors did not seek to challenge the widespread failure of public authorities to comply with the EC public procurement regime prior to the implementation of the Remedies Directive.

REMEDIES POST IMPLEMENTATION OF THE REMEDIES DIRECTIVES[1]

The Remedies Directive has been implemented in the UK by Regulations 29, 31 and 32 of, respectively, the Public Supply Contracts Regulations 1995, the Public Works Contracts Regulations 1991 and the Public Services Contracts Regulations 1993.[2]

The Regulations do not create special tribunals composed of experts plus a member of the Judiciary to administer contractors' claims nor do they make a failure to comply with the Regime a criminal offence. Instead the Regulations empower contractors to bring actions against public bodies for breach of statutory duty, for damages and/or orders quashing the unlawful decisions of public bodies and for interim relief.

Compliance with the Regulations is a duty owed to contractors

The duty imposed on public bodies to comply with the regime is a duty owed respectively to suppliers, contractors and service providers (hereinafter collectively referred to as 'contractors').[3]

For the purposes of the Regulations a contractor is defined as a person who sought or who seeks or who would have wished to be the person to whom a public supply contract is awarded, and who is a national of and established in a Member State.[4]

Public or private law remedies

By the insertion into the Regulations of a procedural device, namely a requirement that proceedings shall be brought in the High Court,[5] the Regulations make clear that a contractor's remedies are private and not public law remedies.

Further confirmation, if it were needed, that the nature of a contractors'

---

[1] Council Directive 89/665/EEC on the co-ordination of the laws, regulations and administrative provisions relating to the application of review procedures to the award of public supply and public works contracts OJ No 395, 12.12.1989, p 33, as amended by Council Directive 92/50/EEC.

[2] SI 1995/201, SI 1991/2680, SI 1993/3228 respectively. SI 1995/201 replaced SI 1991/2679 on 21 January 1995.

[3] Reg 29(1) SI 1995/201, Reg 31(1) SI 1991/2680, Reg 32(1) SI 1993/3228.

[4] Reg 4 SI 1995/201, SI 1991/2680, SI 1993/3228.

[5] Reg 29(3) SI 1995/201, Reg 31(4) SI 1991/2680, Reg 32(3) SI 1993/3228.

remedies has changed from public to private law, since the implementation of the Directive, can be found in the express provision contained in the Regulations, that the Crown Proceedings Act 1947 shall not prevent contractors from seeking injunctions against the Crown.[1] Thus, it is submitted that contractors do not have the option nor are they obliged to seek a remedy in judicial review.

Nature of interim relief under the Regulations

Under the Regulations a court may grant a contractor interim relief and thereby suspend the procedure leading to the award of a contract and prevent a public body from concluding a contract once a decision has been taken to award it.[2] However once a public contract has been concluded the court has no power to set it aside.[3] To obtain interim relief in respect of a breach of the Regulations a contractor must apply for what is known as an interlocutory injunction. The court's power to award an interlocutory injunction is discretionary.

Nature of final relief under the Regulations

Where the Court is satisfied that a decision or action taken by a public body is in breach of the regime, it may set aside the decision or action, amend any document and/or award damages to a supplier who has suffered loss or damage.[4] It should be noted that the power of the Court to grant final relief is discretionary.

Procedure

A contractor is required to inform the public body of the nature of the breach complained of and his intention to bring proceedings before commencing an action. Furthermore an action must be commenced promptly and in any event within three months from the date of breach, although the court has a discretion to extend the period if there is good reason for doing so.[5]

Whereas civil proceedings in the High Court are generally commenced by writ, by virtue of the Rules of the Supreme Court 1965 Order 5, rule 3, where proceedings are required to be brought by any Act in the High Court they must be begun by originating summons. As stated[6] a contractor must bring proceedings in the High Court, therefore he must begin his action by originating summons.

Where the primary object of an application under the Regulations will be

---

[1]   If the Regulations were intended to give contractors public law remedies, the provision in the Regulations disapplying the Crown Proceedings Act 1947 would have been rendered superfluous after the case of *Re M v Home Office* [1994] 1 AC 377, in which the House of Lords ruled that the Crown Proceedings Act 1947 had no application in public law proceedings.

[2]   Regs 29(5)(a) SI 1995/201; 31(6)(a) SI 1991/2680; and 32(5)(a) SI 1993/3228.

[3]   Regs 29(6) SI 1995/201; 31(7) SI 1991/2680; and 32(6) SI 1993/3228.

[4]   Regs 29(5)(b) SI 1995/201; 31(6)(b) SI 1991/2680; and 32(5)(b) SI 1993/3228.

[5]   Reg 4 SI 1995/201 and SI 1993/3228; Reg 5 SI 1991/2680.

[6]   See p 221, note 5.

to force a defaulting public body to consider the tender of an excluded contractor so that he will not be deprived of the opportunity to win the contract, time will be of the essence, for once a public contract has been concluded, a contractor's only remedy will be for damages.[1] To this end, Article 1 of the Remedies Directive requires Member States to ensure that decisions taken by public bodies may be reviewed as rapidly as possible.

Originating summons procedure will undoubtedly produce some time-saving when compared to an action begun by writ. It dispenses with the need for pleadings and it allows the court to dispose of a case without hearing oral evidence. Instead of calling oral testimony at trial, the parties can rely on written evidence in the form of affidavits. Originating summons procedure thus shortens both the time it takes to get to trial and the length of the hearing itself.

However, the time-saving is unlikely to be sufficient to allow a contractor to obtain final relief before a contract is concluded. At least one month must expire after the issue of the summons before a date can be fixed for the first hearing of an application, and in practice the first hearing is unlikely to dispose of the case.[2]

Thus, in view of the likelihood that the public body complained of will have concluded any contract before the application comes on for final hearing, a contractor will lose the opportunity to tender altogether, unless, in addition to making an application by way of originating summons, he applies for interim relief and/or an expedited hearing.

Where, on the other hand, the failure of a public body to comply with the Regulations is irreparable save for the award of damages, in a case where the contract has been concluded and therefore can no longer be set aside, it could be argued with some force that it would be more appropriate to begin the action by writ as opposed to originating summons.

Interim relief

If a contractor has been unlawfully excluded from the procedures leading to the award of a contract, he can apply to the High Court for interim relief. The Regulations[3] provide that the Court may:

> 'by interim order suspend the procedure leading to the award of the contract in relation to which the breach of [the Regulations] is alleged, or suspend the implementation of any decision or action taken by the [public body] in the course of following such procedure;'

The Regulations do not offer any further guidance to the court on the matters to be taken into account on an application for interim relief. As a result, guidance must be obtained from the Remedies Directive and the principles which apply to the grant of interim relief in civil proceedings generally.

Article 2(1)(4) of the Remedies Directive sets out the conditions which may apply to the grant or refusal of interim measures as follows:

[1]   A contractor has no automatic right to damages where he has been deprived of the opportunity to tender. A contractor may seek damages if he has suffered loss as the result of a breach of duty owed to him by a public body under the Regulations.
[2]   Rules of Supreme Court, 1965, Ord 28 rr 1–4.
[3]   Reg 29(5)(a) SI 1995/201.

'... when considering whether to order interim measures the body responsible may take into account the probable consequences of the measures for all interests likely to be harmed, as well as the public interest and may decide not to grant such measures where their negative consequences exceed their benefits. A decision not to grant interim measures shall not prejudice any other claim of the person seeking these measures.'

By virtue of sections 37(1) and (2) of the Supreme Court Act 1981, the court has a wide and unfettered discretion to grant interim relief in civil proceedings where it appears just and convenient to do so. Interim relief takes the form of an interlocutory injunction and the court exercises jurisdiction to grant interlocutory injunctions under Rules of the Supreme Court 1965 Order 29. In the case of *American Cyanamid Co v Ethicon Ltd*[1] the House of Lords laid down general rules governing the exercise of the court's discretion in what is known as the balance of convenience test.

To apply for an interlocutory injunction, an applicant must establish first that there is a serious issue to be tried. In the context of a public procurement case the applicant must show that his is a case to which the Regulations apply and point to a breach of the Regulations which would entitle him to final relief if his case were proved at trial. An applicant is not required to show on the evidence that he has a strong case or even that it will in all probability succeed. However, the applicant will be required to show that he has a real prospect of success and that he is not simply wasting the court's time. If the court is satisfied that there is a serious issue to be tried it will proceed to the balance of convenience test which has been described as a two-stage process.[2]

Stage 1 of the balance of convenience test

At the first stage a contractor must show that an award of damages at a final hearing would not adequately compensate him for breach of the Regulations. If he does not, the court will refuse interim relief without further consideration of the balance of convenience test. If it is shown that damages would not adequately compensate the contractor, the contractor must go on to satisfy the court he has the financial resources adequately to compensate the public body for any losses caused by the interim suspension of the contract awards procedure, should it transpire at the final hearing that there has been no breach of the Regulations.

Where the contractor can give an adequate financial undertaking, the court should grant interim relief without passing on to the second stage of the balance of convenience test.

If the contractor cannot give a financial undertaking to the Court because the contractor has no resources, the court should proceed to the second stage of the balance of convenience test,[3] but it has been said that an interlocutory injunction will normally be refused.[4] Where on the other hand it is found

---

[1]   [1975] AC 396.
[2]   *Factortame (No 2)* [1991] 1 AC 603, HL.
[3]   Lord Diplock, *American Cyanamid v Ethicon Ltd* [1975] AC 396.
[4]   *Morning Star Co-operative Society v Express Newspapers Ltd* [1979] FSR 113.

that a contractor's financial undertaking is inadequate because it could not compensate for harm which may be caused to the public interest, the court must proceed to the second stage of the balance of convenience test.

When damages will not be an adequate remedy for a contractor

The classic case in which damages will not be an adequate remedy is where a claim for damages is not available at all: *Garden Cottage Foods Ltd v Milk Marketing Board*;[1] *R v Secretary of State for Transport, ex p Factortame Ltd (No 2)*.[2] The availability of a remedy in damages led the House of Lords Select Committee on the European Communities to conclude that the courts will in practice only rarely grant an injunction in a public procurement case.[3]

Damages will not be an adequate remedy where the harm which would be suffered is irreparable. In such a case it is usually contended that the applicant will be put out of business unless the injunction is granted, for it is said that nothing can compensate a man for the utter loss of his business'.[4]

In the cases of *Cutsforth v Mansfield Inns*[5] and *Holleran v Daniel Thwaites plc*[6] the court found that damages for breach of EC competition law would prove inadequate because the applicants would be driven out of business. A further justification for holding that damages cannot compensate for complete loss of livelihood may be that the amount of damages is 'wholly uncertain'[7] or there are 'insuperable difficulties of estimation'.[8]

In any event, damages may not be an adequate remedy where they would be very difficult to assess.[9] It is, therefore, surprising that the House of Lords Select Committee on the EC concluded that damages would usually be an adequate remedy for a contractor when the evidence before it suggested that damages would be extremely difficult to assess.[10]

The difficulty arises because of the need to decide whether the contractor would have won the contract if the Regulations had not been breached.[11] If a party has not been able to put a tender together at all it is submitted that a court would have no basis on which to determine whether it would have succeeded. Although the mere fact that damages may be difficult to assess does not mean that the court will not attempt to assess them,[12] the question on an application for an interlocutory injunction is not whether an assessment is possible, but whether it would do justice to the applicant.

---

[1] [1984] AC 130, HL.
[2] [1991] 1 AC 603, HL.
[3] The Committee comprised several distinguished members of the judiciary and was chaired by Lord Goff who gave the leading judgment in the case of *Factortame (No 2)*; para 65, 12th Report of HL Select Committee on the EC, 'Compliance with the Public Procurement Directives', 19 April 1988.
[4] Per Kay LJ, *J Lyons & Sons v Wilkins* [1896] 1 Ch 811 at 827.
[5] [1986] 1 CMLR 1.
[6] [1989] 2 CMLR 917.
[7] Per Wilberforce L *Garden Cottage Foods Ltd v Milk Marketing Board* [1984] AC 130 at 154 E–F.
[8] Per Diplock L, ibid at 143 A–B.
[9] *Alfred Dunhill Ltd v Sunoptic SA* [1979] FSR 337 at 365, CA; *Merchant Adventurers Ltd v M Grew & Co* [1972] Ch 242.
[10] 12th Report of HL Select Committee on the EC, 'Compliance with the Public Procurement Directives', 19 April 1988.
[11] See discussion on damages, below.
[12] Per Vaughan Williams LJ, *Chaplin v Hicks* [1911] 2 KB 786 at 792.

What must a contractor's undertaking in damages cover

A contractor who applies for an interlocutory injunction must give the public body an undertaking that it will pay damages to compensate for any harm which may result if at trial it should prove that there has been no breach of the Regulations. If an undertaking in damages would not be adequate to compensate the public body, the court must go on to consider the second stage of the balance of convenience test.

Thus a contractor must be prepared to meet the costs occasioned by any delay caused by suspending contract procedures or the cost of abandoning the whole procedure and having to begin again. By delaying the award of a contract, the public body may have to pay more than was originally intended to take account of price increases occasioned by the delay.

However, the obligation to give an undertaking in damages ought not to extend to loss or damage suffered by a third party contractor even where the contract has been awarded so long as it has not yet been concluded. Since the purpose of the injunction will be to prevent the conclusion of any contract, no contractual liability will attach to the public body for failing to do so. It should be remembered that where a contract has already been concluded, a contractor's sole remedy will be in damages and the court will have no jurisdiction to force the public body to cancel the contract and re-let it. It has been held that if an applicant does not have the financial strength to give an adequate undertaking in respect of the foreseeable losses which might arise, then usually an interlocutory injunction will not be granted.[1]

It is, however, submitted that notwithstanding a potential applicant's inability to give an adequate remedy in damages, the court must still proceed to the second stage of the test and seek to weigh the nature of the parties' uncompensatable disadvantages before deciding whether to grant an injunction or not. Thus the mere fact that a contractor does not have large resources will not prevent it from obtaining an injunction. In fact the contractor's lack of means may be the very factor which justifies the grant of an injunction.[2]

In addition to the straightforward financial expenses which a public body may be bound to incur if a contract awards procedure is abandoned or delayed, the question of damage to the public interest may also arise. It is quite conceivable that in the majority of cases the issue of public interest will not be a matter of concern and many examples can be given for instance where the contract aims to replace a fleet of ageing vehicles which are necessary for the performance of public duties. If the existing fleet is still operating then the public interest can continue to be served until the issue of whether the Regulations has been complied with has been resolved. However, there may be extreme circumstances where life and death issues arise, for instance concerning the supply of life-saving drugs in which case, regardless of the contractor's size, damages may not compensate for the harm which may be caused to the public interest.

---

[1]   *Morning Star Co-operative Society v Express Newspapers Ltd* [1979] FSR 113.
[2]   See the discussion of adequacy of a contractor's remedy in damages, supra. It should be noted that a public body can use financial strength as a criterion for excluding contractors from awards procedures.

Stage 2 of the balance of convenience test

If there is doubt as to the adequacy of the respective remedies in damages available to either party, or to both, the court must consider where the balance of convenience lies by weighing the respective uncompensatable disadvantages one against the other.[1]

The principal dilemma about the grant of interlocutory injunctions is that there is by definition a risk that the court may make a wrong decision, in the sense of granting an injunction to a party who fails to establish his right at the trial (or would fail if there was a trial) or alternatively in failing to grant an injunction to a party who succeeds (or would succeed) at trial. A fundamental principle is therefore that the court should take whichever course appears to carry the lower risk of injustice if it should turn out to have been wrong.[2]

Lord Diplock suggested that it is 'a counsel of prudence to take such measures as are calculated to preserve the status quo'. The status quo in a contract awards procedure might mean the situation existing immediately prior to the exclusion of the contractor where until the act complained of he was a party to the tender process; on the other hand where the contract has been awarded the status quo might prevent interference with the decision at an interlocutory stage. It is submitted that the earlier in the procedure that the injunction is applied for, the more the status quo will favour the contractor.

Where the Court is unable to decide whether the uncompensatable disadvantage to each party differs significantly, it is permissible for the court to investigate the merits of the respective cases, but only to the extent that there is no credible dispute regarding the evidence.

The Court must exercise caution when applying existing principles to the special circumstances of public procurement cases. Granted, on the one hand, regard may be had to special contexts in which public procurement cases arise and the possible damage not only to the public interest which may result from delaying the award of a public contract, but also to other contractors.[3] But on the other hand regard must be had to the overriding principle set out in Article 1 of the Remedies Directive, to ensure that the decisions of public bodies are reviewed effectively and as rapidly as possible.

It is submitted that if an interlocutory injunction is denied at every turn because of the public interest or the interests of third party contractors or because damages will always be an adequate remedy, interim relief will prove to be effectively a non-remedy and the object of Article 1 of the Remedies Directive will not have been attained.

Appropriate use of the balance of convenience test

In the context of public procurement, judicial reluctance to investigate the merits of a case when considering the grant of an interlocutory injunction would demonstrate the inappropriateness of the balance of convenience test in all but those cases in which a contractor wishes to prevent the award of

---

[1] Per Lord Diplock, *American Cyanamid Co v Ethicon Ltd* [1975] AC 396 at 408–409, HL.
[2] Per Hoffman J, as he then was, in *Films Rover International Ltd v Cannon Film Sales Ltd* [1987] 1 WLR 670 at 680.
[3] Article 2(4) of the Remedies Directive, supra.

a contract, not because he has been improperly excluded, but because he complains that the public body was mistaken when deciding which was the most economically advantageous tender.

The balance of convenience test was developed in the context of an application for an interlocutory injunction where the legal rights of the parties depend on facts that are in dispute and the evidence available to the court is both incomplete and cannot be tested orally.

Thus it was said that 'it was no part of the court's function at [the stage of an application for an interlocutory injunction] to try to resolve conflicts of evidence on affidavit as to facts on which the claims of either party may ultimately depend nor to decide difficult questions of law which call for detailed argument and mature consideration. These are matters to be dealt with at trial'.[1]

As we have already seen, originating summons procedure allows the court to dispose of a public procurement case at trial on the basis of affidavit evidence alone. In the majority of public procurement cases where the issue is whether the correct awards procedure has been selected, or whether a contractor was justifiably excluded, the material facts will be undisputed and before the court in a complete form and the construction of the Regulations ought to be straightforward. Thus, it is submitted the court ought to consider the merits of the case and proceed to deal with the case as if it were a final hearing or order an expedited trial.[2] Further, there is Court of Appeal authority in the case of *Fellowes & Son v Fisher*[3] and the case of *Newsweek Inc v BBC*[4] which supports the adoption of such a course in appropriate cases. If such a course is adopted in public procurement cases, it will have the advantage of achieving the overriding objective of the directive of ensuring that the decisions of public bodies are reviewed effectively and as rapidly as possible. Furthermore one potential bar to a contractor seeking interim relief, namely that he should give an undertaking in damages, will fall away.

Impact of ECJ public procurement decisions on question of public interest and interim relief

By Article 83(2) of the ECJ s Rules of Procedure, an applicant for interim relief must state the circumstances giving rise to urgency and the factual and legal grounds establishing a prima facie case. In order to establish urgency an applicant must show that the interim measure is necessary to avoid serious and irreparable damage to the applicant.

In the case of *Dundalk*,[5] the ECJ found that the factual and legal grounds giving rise to a prima facie case had been established, namely that the Dundalk Urban District Council proposed to discriminate unfairly in favour of an Irish contractor and to award a public contract in breach of Article 30 of the EEC Treaty.

On the question of urgency the Commission argued that Community law and contractors excluded from the tendering process would suffer irreparable

---

[1] *American Cyanamid Co v Ethicon Ltd* [1975] AC 396 at 407G-H.
[2] In the case of *General Building and Maintenance plc v Greenwich Borough Council* (1993) 92 LGR 21, precisely because this situation arose the parties agreed to allow the court to determine the case as if it were a final hearing.
[3] [1976] QB 122.
[4] [1979] RPC 441.
[5] Case 45/87 [1988] ECR 4929.

harm unless the contract award was suspended. The Irish government contended that excluded contractors might have an alternative remedy in damages. The President of the ECJ ruled that notwithstanding the damage to the Commission as the guardian of the interests of the Community, it was also necessary on an application for interim relief to weigh all the interests at stake. Interim relief was refused on the grounds that existing health and safety concerns would be aggravated if the contract were delayed and so the balance of interests was against the granting of interim relief. However, the President indicated that the decision might have been otherwise but for the issue of public health and safety.

In the case of *La Spezia*,[1] the ECJ awarded the Commission interim relief where, prima facie, it appeared that the public body proposed to conclude a public works contract for the construction of an incinerator for the disposal of solid waste without first publishing a notice in the Official Journal. On the question of urgency it was argued that the Commission and contractors alike would suffer immediate and serious damage. For the public body it was argued that public health interests were so pressing that they outweighed other considerations. The court found that damage to contractors' interests would be irreparable since at the time there was no remedy in damages. Moreover the public body did not find favour in arguing that the public interest required the new incinerator to be built as a matter of urgency. The court found that the public body was itself responsible for bringing about the situation in which the incinerator was urgently required.

In the *Lottomatica* case,[2] the court granted the Commission interim measures suspending the award of a lottery concession. The court found that if interim measures were not granted and subsequently breach of the public procurement regime were shown, the damage would be irremediable. Therefore, the court held the Commission's interests outweighed any competing argument that the national interest required the concession to be let in order to eradicate clandestine gambling and to preserve substantial revenues for the government.

In the *Van Hool* case[3] the court refused the Commission interim measures where it had failed to act promptly with regard to a breach of the regime. However, the court expressly cited damage to the interests of contractors deprived of the opportunity to tender as a matter which it would take into account.

Conclusion

In both *Dundalk* and *La Spezia* the Commission expressly contended that contractors who had been unable to tender would suffer serious and irreparable damage. At the time the public procurement regime had not yet specifically provided contractors with an independent remedy in damages, and in each case the court only cited irreparable damage to the Commission, in its ruling. The position changed in the *Van Hool* case when the court acknowledged that damage caused to contractors was a relevant factor. Moreover. when *Van Hool* was decided the Remedies Directive had come into force and contractors had a remedy in damages. It would appear that the existence of a contractor's remedy in damages expressly canvassed by the Irish

[1] Case 194/88R [1988] ECR 4547.
[2] Case C-272/91R: [1995] 2 CMLR 504.
[3] Case C-87/94R: [1994] ECR I-1395.

Government in *Dundalk* would not have prevented the court from granting interim measures had not public health considerations been so pressing. Doubtless it will be argued that in each case the court was concerned primarily with the damage that would be caused to the Commission if interim measures were not granted. Thus, since the existence of a remedy in damages for contractors does not detract from the harm suffered by the Commission, which of course cannot sue for damages when Community law is breached, the cases do not lend support to the view that interim measures ought to be available to contractors even where they have a remedy in damages. But it is submitted that in *Van Hool* the court accepted that contractors might still suffer serious and irreparable harm notwithstanding any remedy in damages. Furthermore, it is clear that where an applicant can show, prima facie, that there has been a breach of the public procurement regime and there is the potential for serious and irreparable harm, only rarely will a public body be able successfully to contend that, notwithstanding the alleged breach, interim relief should be refused in the public interest. The court stated in *Van Hool* that to permit otherwise would be to allow public bodies to set up their own default in order to excuse a breach of the regime.

Final relief

The nature of final relief provided in the Regulations is discretionary in that the court may either set aside all or part of the contract awards procedure or award damages or do both. However, where a public contract has been concluded in breach of the Regulations the court may only award damages.

The Regulations[1] provide as follows:

'the Court may if satisfied that a decision or action taken by a contracting authority was in breach of the duty owed [under the Regulations]—

order the setting aside of that decision or action or order the contracting authority to amend any document, or
award damages to a [contractor] who has suffered loss or damage as a consequence of the breach, or
do both of those things.

...the Court shall not have power to order any remedy other than an award of damages in respect of a breach of duty owed [under the Regulations] if the contract in relation to which the breach occurred had been entered into.

For the reasons which are dealt with below, contractors will face very real difficulties when seeking to prove loss or damage arising out of a breach of the Regulations. Thus, it is submitted that as a rule contractors will be best served by a court order setting aside all or part of any contract awards procedure which discriminates against them, thereby ensuring either that the contract is re-let in accordance with the Regulations, that they are re-admitted to any bids procedure from which they have been unlawfully excluded or otherwise ensuring their equality of opportunity with regard to the contract's award.

However, it is important to note that by giving the court discretion over the form of any final relief, it will be possible in exceptional circumstances

---

[1]   Reg 29(5)(b) SI 1995/201.

for a public body to persuade the court to allow a public contract to be concluded even where it is proven that the award was made in breach of the Regulations.

Thus a contractor will not be able in all circumstances to insist that a public contract be re-let in accordance with proper contracts awards procedures, where to do so would cause unacceptable delay and harm to the public interest.

It is, however, submitted that the court's discretion in this matter must be exercised sparingly. For otherwise public bodies will be able to rely on their own default to defeat the object of the Regulations, and award contracts without fear that they will be interfered with.

Where a contract is allowed to proceed in spite of a breach of the Regulations, it is submitted that a contractor ought to be awarded damages as a matter of course and not simply in the exercise of the Court's discretion. Otherwise, a contractor will be without any remedy at all and the object of the Remedies Directive, that contractors should have an effective remedy for breach of the Community regime, will not have been attained.

Damages

The two most easily identifiable types of loss or damage will be the expense involved in submitting a tender and the amount of any anticipated profit which would have been earned if the contract had been won and successfully completed. It is conceivable that a contractor could also claim for loss of business reputation and even exemplary damages where the public body has acted in bad faith.

Where a contractor has been unable to submit a tender because a public body has not given proper notice of its intention to let a public contract, the contractor will not have incurred any expense in submitting a tender. In such circumstances the contractor's only claim for substantial damages will be for loss of profit. In all other circumstances, where a contractor has been unlawfully excluded from the bids procedure prior to the contract's award stage, or where he has been unsuccessful at the final stage, he will have incurred expense in submitting a tender or in seeking an invitation to tender. Thus a contractor may choose whether to seek recovery of his expenses or for loss of profits.

In reality, the problem is that in both cases, only one tenderer, the successful one out of all the various competing tenderers, stands to make any profit and, moreover, the same tenderer will be the only one to recoup the expense of submitting a tender and then only if the cost of tendering had been included in his bid price. It follows that if a contractor were to recover the cost of submitting a tender or all of his anticipated profit, he would have to show, on the balance of probabilities, that he would have won the contract.

Thus, in every case a contractor will face very real difficulties in seeking to recover either the full cost of tendering or the total amount of lost profit as a result of a breach of the Regulations. for it will be open to the public body to show that the complainant would not have won the contract in any event. The task will be relatively simple if the contract's award criterion is based on the offer which offers the lowest price. However, where the contract is awarded on the basis of the offer most economically advantageous to the contracting authority a contractor will have to discharge a heavy evidential burden.

In all cases it will be for the contractor to show that he would have won the contract. Thus, he will not have proved his case if he merely shows that his tender when matched against the award criteria was a good tender. For there is likely to be any number of other good tenders from which the public body would have been free to select the successful tender. In such circumstances, it will not be possible to show that the public body would have been obliged to select the complainant's tender. Indeed there may be circumstances in which the public body may contend that it would not have awarded any contract at all.

Ordinarily it will be extremely difficult for a contractor to show that his tender should be or should have been regarded as the best, by reason of the many different criteria which a public body may use to select the offer which is most economically advantageous to it. It would not be surprising to find that one tender was superior when judged against one or other of the contract's award criteria, but deficient in some other respect when compared to the tender most favoured by the public body.

Loss of a chance

A solution to the difficulty may be that where a contractor can prove that he has lost the opportunity of being awarded a contract either because the contract was not advertised or for some reason he was excluded from the bids procedure or because his tender was not considered on the equal footing prescribed by the Regulations, he should be awarded substantial damages in the form of either a proportion of the expense he has incurred in submitting a tender or alternatively a proportion of the profit he could have expected had he won the contract.

There are no decided cases in the UK which give guidance on how damages should be assessed for breach of the public procurement regime because it provides contractors with an entirely novel cause of action. However, in civil proceedings generally, whether they are measured in contract or in tort, damages may be recoverable for loss of a chance.[1]

In cases concerning professional negligence, where solicitors have deprived their clients of the opportunity to recover damages by failure to prosecute legal claims within the limitation period, the courts have awarded substantial damages where it has been shown that the original claim had some prospect of succeeding. If some prospect of success can be shown, damages may be awarded in proportion to the chances of success.[2]

Ordinarily, the measure of damages will take as its starting point the most that the claimant was likely to recover and thereafter a discount is made to reflect the various contingencies which might have served to reduce the claim. Nevertheless, the application of the principles concerning the award of damages for loss of a chance in public procurement cases will be fraught with difficulty.

It is an accepted proposition of law that where the nature of the damage claimed is contingent on the will of the wrongdoer, damages are assessed

---

[1] *Chaplin v Hicks* [1911] 2 KB 786, CA; *Hotson v East Berkshire Area Health Authority* [1987] AC 750, CA.
[2] *Kitchen v Royal Air Forces Association* [1958] 1 WLR 563, CA.

on the assumption that, where there are several options open to the wrongdoer, he would have acted in the way most favourable to him.[1]

In those cases where the contract is to be awarded on the basis of the offer the most economically advantageous to the public body, success obviously depends on the discretion of the public body. However, it is submitted that public bodies will not be heard to say simply that in each case the complainant would not have been awarded the contract. Their discretion must be exercised in accordance with the Regulations and so the court will retain some control.[2] But, doubtless, the contingent nature of a contractor's claim, depending as it does on the will of the public body, will ensure that claims are routinely and perhaps heavily discounted.

In *The Mihalis Angelos*[3] the plaintiff only recovered nominal damages in a case where a contract had been wrongfully repudiated in circumstances in which it was inevitable that the contract would have been lawfully repudiated within a matter of days. Thus, it may be open to a public body to defend a case brought by a contractor for the loss of a chance on the basis that, even if the Regulations had been properly complied with, the contractor would not have been awarded the contract.

For example, a contractor may have been excluded for some unlawful reason, but it transpires that he could have been excluded for another valid reason. Such an example presents no problems in itself and, as already stated, when claiming for the loss of a chance, a contractor must establish that he had some prospect of success.

However the situation is more complicated where a public body does not seek to justify the exclusion, but instead argues that in all other respects the contract was properly awarded and invites the court to draw a direct comparison between the plaintiff's tender and the successful bid, on the assumption that the public body would have been justified in declining to award the contract to the plaintiff in any event.

It is submitted that the court should assess the plaintiff's prospects of success as at the date of the unlawful action which denied him the chance of completing his tender. It would be wrong to deny a plaintiff substantial damages merely on the basis of hindsight,[4] for had the plaintiff been in contention at the time when the contract was awarded it might have affected the decision.

But where a contractor complains that he has been unable to tender because the public body failed to give notice of the intended contract, he must show that he would have tendered, if he is to recover substantial damages. In the case of *Sykes v Midland Bank Executor and Trustee Co*[5] the plaintiff entered into a property transaction, having been negligently advised by its solicitors that the property could be re-let. The Court of Appeal declined to award substantial damages after it transpired that the plaintiff would not have the opportunity of reletting the property on the basis that, even if correctly advised, the plaintiff had not shown that it would not have entered into the transaction.

Where a contractor's sole complaint is that he should have been awarded the contract because his tender was the most economically advantageous to

---

[1]   *Kaye Steam Navigation Co Ltd v W & R Barnett Ltd* (1932) 48 TLR 440; *Withers v General Theatre Corpn* [1933] 2 KB 536, CA and see generally the discussion in *McGregor on Damages* (15th ed) at paras 366 and 367.

[2]   *Abrahams v Herbert Reiach Ltd* [1922] 1 KB 477, CA; *Paula Lee Ltd v Robert Zehil & Co Ltd* [1983] 2 All ER 390.

[3]   [1971] 1 QB 164, CA.

[4]   See the Scottish case, *Yeoman's Executrix v Ferries* 1967 SLT 332.

[5]   [1971] 1 QB 113, CA.

the public body or offered the lowest price, he cannot be said to have been deprived of the opportunity to tender and the claim will not fall to be assessed proportionally on the basis of a loss of a chance. Instead it will stand or fall on an all-or-nothing basis, depending on whether his bid surpassed the successful bidder's.

Nominal damages and costs

The foregoing discussion of damages concerns the recovery of substantial damages. As an alternative, the court may award nominal damages to a contractor where breach of the Regulations is proved, but where otherwise the amount of any loss or damage is unclear. Since all that is required under the Regulations for a breach to be actionable is that the contractor 'risks suffering' loss or damage in consequence of a breach, an award of merely nominal damages will have a practical function in that it should entitle a contractor to the costs of the action in the context of a public procurement case.

Ordinarily, a failure to prove substantial damages would entail either no award of costs or having to pay the costs of the other side. But the position is different in public procurement cases, for two reasons. First, in many cases the principal claim for breach of the Regulations will be for the setting aside of all or part of the contract's award procedure. Thus, on the issue of costs, success or failure in the action will not depend on an award of damages, but on whether a breach is proved. Furthermore, only in exceptional circumstances should the contract's award procedure be permitted to continue undisturbed where a breach has been proven. Where a public body is permitted to proceed in spite of its breach it should be ordered to pay the contractor's costs as a matter of course. Secondly the Community's purpose in enacting the Remedies Directive was to give the regime the teeth that it otherwise lacked and to give contractors the role, which the Commission was unable to fulfil by itself, of policing the public procurement regime themselves. Therefore it is submitted that in all but the most frivolous cases, a contractor's purpose in bringing an action will be the creditable one of determining his rights under the regime and in seeking to uphold Community law for which he should be awarded costs.

Conclusion

The form of any final relief in public procurement cases is ultimately in the discretion of the Court. Whereas a contractor should be entitled to have all or part of the procedures leading to the award of a public contract set aside, there may be circumstances in which the need to safeguard the public interest will discount that possibility. The circumstances in which the public interest will take precedence over the rights of a contractor when seeking interim relief apply equally on an application for final relief. However, an application for interim relief may well be denied on the basis that a contractor has an adequate remedy in damages.

The foregoing discussion of damages in the context of public procurement cases highlights the difficulties which contractors will have to overcome in order to obtain substantial damages. In most cases the issue of damages will focus on whether the contractor can demonstrate that he has suffered substantial damage as a result of the loss of a chance to tender for a public contract on the footing of the Regulations.

Where a public body is intent on awarding a public contract without first advertising its intention to do so, a contractor has clearly lost an opportunity to submit a tender, and unless the contract is re-let in accordance with the Regulations, his alternative remedy in damages may be so speculative that he is only likely to obtain nominal damages in respect of his loss. He may not have tendered at all or in time. Any number of other contractors may have tendered along with him, thus reducing his prospects of success. The public body may not even have defined the criteria under which the contract should have been awarded.

Again there are many imponderables which will reduce the likelihood of a contractor recovering substantial damages where he has been unlawfully excluded prior to the contract's award stage or where he has been forced to abandon his bid because of the imposition of unlawful technical specifications. If a contractor is obliged to seek a remedy in damages and the contract has subsequently been let, he may be required to compare his tender with that of the successful one,[1] which may have been further elucidated, such that it would not be possible to compare like with like. In such circumstances a contractor risks only being able to recover nominal damages or having his damages so substantially discounted that they cannot be said to reflect his real loss or damage given the difficulties of its estimation.

An award of nominal damages may be useful to a contractor when seeking to argue costs, but otherwise it will not be adequate compensation for the loss of the opportunity to win a valuable public contract and to enhance his record of performing public contracts. It is suggested that a contractor's remedy in damages will only be adequate in those circumstances where a contractor's completed tender has been considered by a public body at the final stage of the contract's award procedure, and the court has available to it all the material necessary for an assessment of a contractor's claim for loss arising out of a breach of the Regulations.

Remedies under the Utilities Regulations[2]

Contractors may bring court proceedings for interim and final relief for breach of the Utilities Regulations in the same circumstances in which an action can be maintained for breach of the Public Works, Supply and Services Regulations. The procedure does not differ at all. However, in one important respect the conditions governing the award of substantial damages may have been improved by Regulation 30(7).

> 'where in proceedings under this regulation the Court is satisfied that a [contractor] would have had a real chance of being awarded a contract if that chance had not been adversely affected by a breach of the duty owed to him by the utility pursuant to the [Regulations] the [contractor] shall be entitled to damages amounting to his costs in preparing his tender and in participating in the procedure leading to the award of the contract.'

---

[1] See discussion of *The Mihalis Angelos*, above.
[2] SI 1992/3279.

Thus, in contrast to an action for recovery of the costs of submitting a tender under the Public Works, Supplies and Services Regulations, a contractor will not be required to show that he would have won the contract. Instead, the contractor will only be required to show that but for the breach, he would have had a real chance of winning. Furthermore the inclusion of this additional entitlement is without prejudice to any other claim for damages arising out of a breach of the Utilities Regulations.

A consequence of this additional remedy may well be to reduce the availability of interim relief to contractors who have submitted tenders. Indeed they might also be persuaded not to seek final orders setting aside contracts awards procedures at all. On the other hand the potential liability of a utility may be increased where several contractors claim for the loss of a real chance.

However, the addition of a remedy for loss of a real chance will be of no help to a contractor who has been unable to tender through lack of notice of intention to award a contract. His only claim in damages can be for a proportion of his potential lost profit. Thus, his principal remedy will continue to be for an order setting aside the contracts award procedure, if the contract has not already been concluded.

Conciliation

In addition to bringing an action for breach of the Utilities Regulations, a contractor may also take advantage of the conciliation procedure provided by the Utilities Remedies Directive 92/13.[1] The conciliation procedure has been incorporated by reference in Regulation 31.

The procedure is initiated by a request from the contractor addressed to the EU Commission and the utility must consent to its operation. The costs of the conciliation are borne equally by both parties and either of them may terminate the procedure at any time.

A conciliator is drawn from a panel set up by the Commission. The parties can object to the conciliator and also designate one further conciliator apiece. In turn, the conciliators may also appoint up to two experts each to assist them. The parties are entitled to make both written and oral representations. Further, every other contractor who participated in the contract's award procedure is entitled to make representations at his own cost. The conciliators are required to report to the Commission on their findings and on any result achieved.

Attestation

The Utilities Regulations do not implement the attestation procedures provided for by the Directive. By Article 3 'Member States shall give contracting entities the possibility of having recourse to an attestation system in accordance with Articles 4 to 7'.

Thus the UK has failed to implement a mandatory provision of the Directive. Potentially, the omission exposes the UK to Artlcle 169 proceedings brought by the Commission and also to an action by any party who can show loss as a result. However, it is difficult to see how such loss might arise. An

---

[1]   OJ No L76, 23 March 1992, p 14.

attestation could not provide utilities with proof against claims brought by contractors.

Theoretically, utilities might argue that through their inability to gain an attestation they have lost the opportunity of attracting foreign bids from contractors who would only tender if they had the assurance given by an attestation. Moreover, foreign contractors might claim that they have had to forgo tendering for UK utility contracts, because the omission of attestation procedures deprives them of the certainty that their marketing strategies require.

CHAPTER 14

Remedies for Infringement of the Government Procurement Agreement

Joseph Dalby

Private remedies in international law are few and far between, and this is equally so in the realm of public procurement. It is true that in some states with a 'monist' approach to international law, rights in international conventions and treaties are conferred directly on the individual as part of that state's body of private international law. In most cases, however, international law requires ratification and implementation by national legislators before it can be said to take direct effect. (The exception is, of course, the law of the European Community which, alone amongst customs unions, is able to create laws which bind individuals and states alike.)

So when speaking of public procurement in international law, one is looking for a set of rules which transcend national boundaries and legislators, but which offer guarantees and conditions which are nonetheless accessible by private individuals.

The problem is that procurement in international law has less of the neat structures and legal certainties which have come to characterise European and hence national law. There is, for a start, very little precedent upon which one can usefully demonstrate the procedures for challenging awards. Indeed, in the past access to justice via international channels was very restricted. In addition there were very practical problems of making effective use of rights conferred by international law at a national level on account of the difficulties in litigating across borders, differences in law and culture and, in some jurisdictions, a lack of judicial independence and therefore certainty as to the outcome.

In the future, however, with greater emphasis on international trade both precedent and ease of access should improve. The difference is marked by the World Trade Organisation ('WTO') and in particular a (new) Agreement on Government Procurement. Both emerged from completion of the Uruguay Round on the General Agreement on Tariffs and Trade ('GATT') which ushered in a new way of regulating international trade. As regards the procurement regime, it is not one which resembles others you can read about in this book; however anyone endeavouring to protect or enforce their rights must realise that they are at the mercy of international politics – an environment in which negotiation and so-called horse-trading are substitutes for transparency and adversarial hearings. That said, some semblance of fairness and order is provided by general principles of international law and the rules found in the GATT Final Act which recognises that international trade must provide for accessible and effective remedies if it is to be a success.

OVERVIEW OF THE GATT AND THE WTO

The General Agreement on Tariffs and Trade is the largest multi-lateral trade agreement of all time. Not even a contemporised comparison of the combined trade routes of colonial times comes close. Yet even the GATT – which is becoming something of an outdated term – will and must give way to a forum whose aspirations and potential dwarf its own, as we know it.

The GATT is a continual process of trade improvement punctuated by agreements concluded after rounds of multilateral trade negotiations dealing with packages of measures as opposed to single issues. The first round opened in 1946 with just 23 members. The object of each round is progressively to diminish and then eradicate customs tariffs, thus freeing national markets to worldwide competition. The first round led to concessions worth $10 billion, about one-fifth of world trade at the time.

Subsequent rounds built on the initial success by attracting more and more members, more and more markets for goods and with them more complex issues. Growth was certainly a result, but so was the burden of the whole system. Each round required further elaboration of procedures to cover up loopholes, deal with worldwide recession and further liberalise trade. The Tokyo Round of 1973 was the first attempt to reform the trading system. Then came the Uruguay Round, beginning in 1986, which had 105 nations participating, later increasing to 117. It was of such immense size that the decision was taken to replace the now conventional concept of long, arduous rounds of negotiations with a permanent and continuous rolling programme of trade liberalisation.

Enter the World Trade Organisation ('WTO'). As a concept it was conceived in the heady, institutional atmosphere of the mid to late 1940s as a specialised agency of the then newly-formed United Nations Organisation. Rejected for lack of political commitment at the time, the GATT became a separate multilateral instrument, founded in 1948 along with the World Bank and the International Monetary Fund to regulate the world economy.

The agreement to form the WTO – and to sign the results of the Uruguay Round – was made in Marrakesh, Morocco, in April 1994. The WTO was formally established on 1 January 1995.

The Uruguay Round

The Uruguay Round ('UR') was significant in many respects. Primarily there was a need to continue the GATT tradition of liberalising trade because a failure to do so was widely regarded as catastrophic. On the other hand, there was a need to embrace the increasing services sector – which accounts for 20% of world trade – and regulate intellectual property rights, especially in respect of the boom market of computer software. In spite of so many competing fundamentals and nations, a complex matrix of agreements was finally agreed in December 1993. The Final Act comprised some 29 individual legal texts and a further 25 ministerial declarations.

The object of the UR is to reduce tariff barriers by at least a third within five years so that they stand at an average of 3.5% – compared with 1940 when they stood at 40%. In some areas they will be zero, but tariff rates will not be the same across the board. Account is taken of what each party can reduce. The main areas in which reductions have been achieved are construction and agricultural machinery, steel, beer, medical equipment, pharmaceuticals, toys, paper, furniture and distilled spirits. Overall, over 40% of all EU imports are duty free.

The Uruguay Round also simplified non-tariff barriers by rationalising and minimising custom procedures, including information requirements, valuations, and inspections. This includes health and safety regulations and quality standards.

It is estimated that the conclusion of the Uruguay Round will engender $3 trillion of world trade. This is a figure that is easy to claim, but hard to prove. Hard also to know who will share in it. It will not be divided equally but rather concentrated amongst the developed nations of the world who will, at the same time, be the nations primarily responsible for wealth creation of others. Of these, the USA and the EU are the leaders in world trade. It was not for nothing that the stumbling blocks of the UR surfaced in the North Atlantic. The voices of the many smaller nations, including those emanating in the Pacific Rim, do not count for much at this stage.

Procurement and the GATT

Procurement is singled out for special treatment because of the considerable wealth it creates. In command and capital economies alike, the state is the single biggest purchaser of goods and services; thus procurement rules have become an important feature of the Rounds. The last Government Procurement Agreement brought about ECU 30 million additional public business. The present one expects to engender ECU 350 billion as well as major savings through economies of scale, greater efficiency and more competitive bidding. The regime mirrors the one operating in the EU.

THE AGREEMENT ON GOVERNMENT PROCUREMENT

The Agreement on Government Procurement ('GPA') was originally drawn up because it was recognised that there was a need for an effective multilateral framework of rights and obligations with respect to laws, regulations, procedures and practices regarding government procurement with a view to achieving greater liberalisation and expansion of world trade and improving the international framework for the conduct of world trade.

It was also recognised that governments should not maintain laws which afford protection to domestic products and services at the expense of foreign ones, nor should they discriminate between different foreign products, services or suppliers.

The present agreement has been signed by 23 nations: Canada, the EC 15; Hong Kong, Israel, Japan, Korea, Norway, Switzerland, and the USA. Other parties are free to join at any time. Particular note should be taken of the application of the GPA as regards the US and the EU. Under a separate agreement on government procurement, concluded in the form of an exchange of letters, the EC and the US have agreed that their respective Appendix 1 entries (see below) in the GPA should be amended as between each other. Essentially the agreement extends the principles of the GPA to certain states and cities in the US otherwise not included in the GPA for the exclusive benefit of EC undertakings. As an aside, it is nowhere suggested that these concessions breach the fundamental rules which central to the GPA and mentioned below.

Scope

The Agreement applies to any law, regulation, procedure or practice regarding any procurement achieved by any contractual means. It covers both services, including construction, and supplies in five utility sectors: water, ports, airports, electricity and urban transport.

Remedies

The GPA also provides for the enforcement of remedies. Yet these relate solely to those rights and procedures which it creates itself. It is therefore a stand-alone regime. Countries that sign up to the GPA agree to adapt their internal procurement procedures to those of the GPA. Whilst this may lead to improved enforcement procedures at a national (or European) level, those changes should be seen purely in their domestic context, for they neither preclude nor usurp the role of the GPA as a conduit for resolving disputes.

For a complaint to be brought under the aegis of the GPA, there are two important pre-conditions. First the purchasing entity must be one covered by the agreement. Second, the procurement contract in question must be of a value which is not less than the relevant threshold.

The number and type of entities covered by the GPA (and listed in Appendix 1 therein) are too numerous and diverse to list here. Each contracting state has put forward those entities which it is willing to be subject to the GPA regime. These are grouped into three categories: central government entities, sub-central government entities, and other entities.

Likewise with regard to the types of contracts which are covered – on condition, that is, that they are offered by a listed procuring entity – each state has drawn from a Universal List of Services those services which it is content to expose to the rigour of the GPA. It will be noted that the GPA only refers to services; however, this includes construction services, which of course relate to works contracts.

Finally, thresholds have been assigned to each category of entity and service. These are expressed as Special Drawing Rights (with SDR I = ECU 1.1). This has resulted in a slight lowering in the respective thresholds in the EU directives by about 1%. A directive giving effect to these changes is due for adoption shortly. At the time of writing there is some dispute as to whether the proposed directive will actually take EC law further than required by GATT/WTO. One school of thought is that the EC procurement directives already provide for the fundamental principles of the directive.

The thresholds used in the GPA are as follows:

Central government:	services:	SDR 130,000
	works:	SDR 5,000,000
Sub-central government:	services:	SDR 200,000
	works:	SDR 5,000,000
Other entities:	services:	SDR 400,000
	works:	SDR 5,000,000

In determining the value of contracts it is necessary to take into account all forms of remuneration, including any premiums, fees, commission and interest receivable. States expressly declare that selection of the valuation method by the entity will not be used with the intention of avoiding the application of the GPA. Special provision is made for the award of more than one contract, contracts in parts and fixed-term contracts.

Grounds for complaint

The two most central features of the agreement are the fundamental principles of 'national treatment and non-discrimination' and 'rules of origin'. If experience of the old regime is anything to go by, these will often form the basis of a 'cause of action' under the aegis of the GPA. This said, the Agreement envisages that these are not the sole grounds for complaint by providing that the challenge procedures explained below can be invoked for 'a breach of this Agreement'. Thus, one should also have in mind breaches of procedure (mentioned briefly below) including failing to award a contract according to the GPA regime as described above.

With respect to non-discrimination, Article III provides that

'each Party [ie each state signatory] shall provide immediately and unconditionally to the products, services and suppliers of other Parties offering products or services of the Parties, treatment no less favourable than that accorded to domestic products, services and suppliers, or that accorded to products, services and suppliers of any other Party.'

By extension, locally-established suppliers are not to be discriminated against on the grounds that they either have foreign affiliation or ownership or on the basis of the country of production of the goods or services being supplied. As for local enterprises without any foreign connection, their interests are not expressly provided for. Thus, technically, reverse discrimination could be said to exist under the GPA. For a remedy in such a situation, recourse should be had to European and national law.

The term 'rules of origin' refers to provisions which serve to distinguish foreign products or services from domestic ones for a variety of reasons when a state does not want to give equal treatment to foreign products and services. It is to overcome these rules of origin that the Most Favoured Nation clause concept was devised so as to ensure that every state was treated on the same terms as a state's most favoured nation.

Rules of origin can manifest themselves as technical requirements, economic evaluation or custom classifications, or any combination of these. However so defined or applied, these sorts of requirements often come under the category of quantitative restrictions and measures having equivalent effect under Article 30 of the EC Treaty, which are of course prohibited.

Under Article IV of the GPA,

'A Party shall not apply rules of origin to products or services imported or supplied for different purposes of government covered by this Agreement from other Parties, which are different from the rules of origin applied in the normal course of trade to imports or supplies of the same products or services from the same Parties.'

The two principles set out under Articles III and IV, fundamental as they are, permeate the whole agreement. Thus technical specifications must not create obstacles to international trade; tendering procedures must not be applied in a discriminatory manner; in the process of qualifying suppliers, entities shall not discriminate among suppliers of other parties or between domestic suppliers and suppliers of other parties; to ensure optimum effective international competition under selective tendering procedures, entities shall invite tenders from the maximum number of domestic and foreign suppliers; in determining the time-limit for the preparation of tenders, entities shall take account of the normal time for transmitting tenders by mail from foreign points. These rules are, however, not without exceptions: under the GPA, special or differential treatment may be applied for developing countries.

Thereafter tendering procedures under the GPA are similar to those under European Union law. Thus, contracts can be awarded by way of open, selective or limited procedures. Invitations to participate have to be published, but may only take the form set out in the GPA. Entities may be permitted to negotiate in order to identify the strengths and weaknesses of particular tenders, but all aspects of the tender process must be regular and transparent.

These then are the parameters and ground rules which contracting states must implement into their national laws and regulations and which will form the substantive grounds for complaint. If implemented properly by the contracting states, the regime established by the GPA should lead to an open and competitive world market for all government contracts over the financial thresholds. However, a problem-free regime is not anticipated. Those who come across difficulties or who wish to challenge the award of a government contract may avail themselves of the challenge procedures which the GPA provides.

There are two forms of challenge procedures, examined below. First is the Dispute Resolution System for contracting states, and the challenge system for suppliers. The second form will be looked at from a national and EC perspective.

CHALLENGING GPA CONTRACTS AT THE INTERNATIONAL LEVEL

There is no direct right of recourse or locus standi for private individuals and undertakings within the legal structure established under the GPA or the WTO. The WTO is a forum for contracting states to air their grievances and seek resolution of and compensation for disputes.

Under the GPA,

'if any Party [that is, a contracting state] considers that any benefit accruing to it, directly or indirectly, under this Agreement is being nullified or impaired, or that the attainment of any objective of this Agreement is being impeded as a result of the failure of another Party or Parties to carry out its obligations under the Agreement, or by the application by another Party or Parties of any measure, whether or not it conflicts with the provisions of the Agreement, it may with a view to reaching mutually satisfactory resolution of the matter, make written representation or proposals to the other Party or Parties which it considers to be concerned. Such action will be promptly notified to the Dispute Settlement Body of the DSU. Any Party thus approached shall give sympathetic consideration to the representation or proposals made to it.'

In short, this clause enables a member state to raise not only complaints of a general nature, either about the application or implementation of the GPA, but also (by virtue of the words 'directly or indirectly') complaints about a specific award by a procuring entity in another contracting state. In this latter scenario the state can pursue a complaint on behalf of an aggrieved supplier.

The form and procedure for this means of redress is contained in Article XXII of the GPA, from which the above cause of action clause is taken. This provision begins with a reminder of the fact that this level of dispute resolution is very much for states alone in that the specific dispute resolution rules found in the GPA are subject to the Understanding on Rules and Procedures Governing the Settlement of Disputes under the WTO Agreement (referred to as the Dispute Settlement Understanding ('DSU')) – that is the dispute resolution procedure under the parent agreement.

The DSU is conventionally regarded as a two-stage procedure, the stages of which are, to confuse matters, sometimes referred to in parallel, and sometimes separately. Either way the two components are, on the one hand, consultation, good office, conciliation and mediation – often described as the conciliation and negotiation approach – and on the other, panel proceedings – often described as the adjudication approach. Purists would argue that the real dispute resolution procedure is only to be found in panel proceedings, and whilst in theory that might be correct, it should not be forgotten that disputes at the international level are resolved just as much through diplomacy and negotiation (sometimes called 'horsetrading') as by open argument. In this light the conciliation/negotiation stage is equal in its importance and role to the second stage.

The DSU system serves to preserve the rights and obligations of the WTO members under the WTO Agreements and is administered by the Dispute Settlement Body. Its first priority is to bring about the withdrawal of measures inconsistent with these agreements, an objective which is reinforced by the sanctions of compensation and suspension of obligations. Thus, in the context of the GPA, a contracting state which is particularly flagrant and repetitive in its breaches of the principle of open and fair competition in the awarding of procurement matters may ultimately face suspension not just from the GPA but also from the WTO.

Under the GPA also there exists the two-staged handling of disputes by way of negotiation and then before panel proceedings. This is clearly indicated in the cause of action clause set out in full above: a complaint must in the first instance be raised with the relevant party.

That may be easier said than done because bringing a complaint to the attention of an allegedly errant state involves two significant assumptions. It implies that the aggrieved supplier has, first, the wherewithal to approach, and second, the ability and the case to convince, its home state – that is the state in which the supplier is established – that it has been discriminated against in a tender administered by a procuring entity of another contracting state.

The art of persuading government ministers to take up a particular cause has become known as lobbying. As a service lobbying has always existed, but only recently, in Europe, has it become a fashionable – even honourable – profession. There is not room enough here to explain the art in detail, but it is essentially litigation by more subtle and informal means: the government official might be regarded as a judge who needs to be convinced of the merits of a case. Fortunately, however, the official is not there to adjudicate but simply to judge whether a supplier has a grievance that the state should take up. In this regard it might be said that a state has a vested interest in taking up complaints on behalf of aggrieved suppliers against other contracting states to the GPA, since it is in the interests of the state that its own suppliers win contracts in other states, if necessary by challenging an award which is believed to be irregular. That is not to say that advice and representation should not be sought from professionals with experience (and connections) in handling cases before government officials.

Thereafter, once the case has been taken up by the home state the matter should be brought to the attention of the contracting state whose procuring entity is said to have acted irregularly. A complaining supplier is likely to have little or no involvement in the dialogue between states, but at the very least it should be kept in close touch with its home government department, and supplied with the appropriate information and documentation necessary to prosecute the complaint. As required by Article XXII the contracting state alleged to be in breach of the GPA should give 'sympathetic consideration to the representations or proposals made to it'. Clearly, this offers no guarantee of a solution and will depend upon whether the state is prepared to support and defend the way in which its procuring entity handled the tender in issue. Assuming that it is, then it is open to the state of the aggrieved supplier to initiate proceedings before a panel of experts in government procurement.

This is done by way of request made to the Dispute Settlement Body ('DSB'). The DSB has sole authority to establish panels and adopt their reports or the reports of Appellate Bodies also established by itself. It can also make recommendations or give rulings on a matter, and maintain surveillance of implementation of rulings and recommendations. Finally it can authorise the suspension of concessions and other obligations under the GPA or alternative remedies when withdrawal of measures found to be in contravention of the GPA is not possible.

The DSB will establish a panel by appointing (usually three) persons qualified in the area of government procurement and issuing its terms of reference. The GPA provides that the terms of reference should be:

> 'To examine, in the light of the relevant provisions of this agreement and of (any other Agreement cited by the parties to the dispute), the matter referred to the DSB by (name of party) in document ... and to make such findings as will assist the DSB in making the recommendations or in giving the rulings provided for in the Agreement.'

Under the old GATT, panels were convened in just three cases. The first, in 1984, arose out of a complaint from the USA against the EEC about the latter's practice of excluding value-added tax from the contract price of EC member state government purchases in relation to the determination of whether such purchases fell under the GPA.[1] In that case the panel found against the EEC. In the second, the EC complained against the US about the latter's 'Buy America' policy and the manner in which the US National Science Foundation procured a sonar mapping system.[2] Again the panel found for the complainant. In the final case, the US successfully complained that Norway

[1]   Panel on Value-Added Tax and Threshold, Ref GPR/21, 26 June 1984.
[2]   United States – Procurement of a Sonar Mapping System, Ref GPR.DS1/R, 23 April 1992.

had violated the GPA in the way the city of Trondheim procured toll collection equipment.[1]

Clearly, examples of the panel in action are few and far between and so those interested in knowing more about how a panel deals with particular arguments (not that its treatment of the law is binding) are confined to these three cases.

The panel acts as a tribunal of fact, whose findings are delivered to the DSB to act upon. It should be kept well in mind that, just as with the appointment of an arbitrator, the panel is bound to act within its terms of reference. Thus an aggrieved supplier must ensure that it makes clear from the start the full extent of its grievances so that all allegations are included amongst the issues into which the panel must enquire.

Once the panel is appointed and its terms of reference known, it will receive a document with details of the matter referred to it. It will then meet with the parties, and meet again however many times it requires, although the need to report within four months (or if there is a delay, seven months) will naturally limit the number of these meetings. In any event, it will usually be required of panels to give the fullest possible opportunity for the parties to present their evidence and arguments, and, if possible, develop a mutually satisfactory solution, but at the same time the panel make every effort to accelerate the proceedings as much as possible.

Once all argument has been heard the panel will deliberate in private and then draw up its report. This is divided into five parts: the introduction (comprising terms of reference, the basic allegations, and the dates when the panel met with the parties); the factual aspects based on respective versions presented to the panel by the parties; the main arguments in law and fact of the parties; the findings of the panel in fact with reference to the GPA, supported by its own reasoning, and finally, the panel's conclusions on whether the procuring entity did or did not comply with the GPA, and if not, to what extent the complaint has been proved. It will then recommend to the DSB to take the measures necessary to ensure that the entity concerned conducts government procurement in accordance with its findings. It appears to be standard practice for the panel to make this general recommendation rather than to particularise measures which should be taken. The specific detail is left to the DSB to which the report is submitted.

Unfortunately, if past performance of the GPA is anything to go by, the availability of remedial measures is likely to be scarce. Nowhere in the GPA is there enumerated the remedies applicable in cases of violations, and it appears that complainants must look to private international law for a remedy because the GATT/WTO as a whole does not provide for remedies which are any more effective. The DSB might order reparation and restitutio in integrum, but these depend upon compliance by the state concerned, which will only be forthcoming if the ultimate threat of suspension is likely to be enforced. An alternative way of overcoming the shortage of defined remedies in international law is for the complaining state to ask for specific or sufficient remedies. Otherwise the most that the DSB can come close to guaranteeing is the non-repetition of a violation by the state in breach, which for the supplier

---

[1] Norway – Procurement of Toll Collection Equipment for the City of Trondheim, Ref GPR.DS2/R, 28 April 1992. For a study of the Trondheim case see Mavrodis, Petro C, 'Government Procurement Agreement. The Trondheim case: the remedies issue' Aussenwirtschaft (1993) 48/01.

that envisages considerably more opportunities to tender in the state concerned may be something worth having.

CHALLENGING GPA CONTRACTS AT THE NATIONAL LEVEL

In the past, dispute resolution under the GATT and GPA was an international affair. Certainly the few cases heard under the old regime witnessed complaints on the part of aggrieved suppliers or prospective suppliers being brought before a specially constituted ad-hoc panel by the supplier's home state against the host state said to have been in breach of the terms of the old GPA.

The new regime is much more sophisticated, in that it envisages that a claim can be brought by the aggrieved supplier against the procuring entity before a local court or tribunal, in addition to the forum for disputes between contracting states.

These national challenge procedures are not spelt out in detail in the GPA. It merely provides for the framework which contracting states must apply and meet within their own jurisdictions. The GPA does, however, envisage two stages to the resolution of a complaint under the aegis of the Agreement. The first stage is consultation:

'in the event of a complaint by a supplier that there has been a breach of the Agreement in the context of a procurement, each Party shall encourage the supplier to seek resolution of its complaint in consultation with the procuring entity. In such instances the procuring entity shall accord impartial and timely consideration to any such complaint, in a manner that is not prejudicial to obtaining corrective measures under the challenge system.' (Article XX).

There is nothing to indicate that consultation is a pre-requisite to a challenge – least of all for the supplier who, its seems, could proceed to direct action straightaway. It thus leaves the supplier with the option of seeking amicable redress at a local level – with the added attraction that such consultation is without prejudice to later action.

The challenge procedure itself is contained in Article XX of the GPA. The Article states that each party shall provide non-discriminatory, timely, transparent and effective procedures enabling suppliers to challenge alleged breaches of the Agreement arising in the context of procurement in which they have, or have had, an interest. Each party is to provide its challenge procedures in writing and make them generally available. To that singular requirement is added certain other conditions with regard to initiating a procedure, the composition and procedures of the court and the available remedies.

First, the option is left to contracting states to require that a supplier initiate a challenge procedure and notify the procuring entity within specified time-limits. These time-limits must run from the time at which the basis of the complaint is known or reasonably should have been known and should not be less than 10 days.

Second, the challenge should be heard by a court or 'impartial and independent review body with no interest in the outcome of the procurement and the members of which are secure from external influence during the term of the appointment'. 'Court' implies one which is properly constituted by law with the powers of such, whereas the facility of creating a review body enables contracting states to cordon off GPA disputes to a special forum. However, Article E adds that this review body must observe certain characteristics. These characteristics are essentially devised to make the tribunal accountable and observe the principles of natural justice. Hence, participants must have a right to be heard or be represented, present witnesses and documents, have access to all proceedings which can take place in public and have the tribunal put into writing the reasons for its opinion or decision.

Finally, the challenge procedures must provide for rapid interim measures to correct breaches of the Agreement and to preserve commercial opportunities, such as assessment and a possibility for a decision on the justification of the challenge, and a correction of the breach of the Agreement or compensation for the loss or damages suffered which may be limited to costs for tender preparation or protest.

The overall duty to give effect to these requirements is one which rests on the contracting state under national law. In the case of the EC this is to be brought about via amendment to existing directives which in turn must be implemented in the national laws of the Member States. However, since the Member States have signed up to the GPA in their own right it could be argued that the duty impacts on them directly.

The question remains whether the GPA itself is of any legal relevance in what will otherwise be national proceedings. In other words, do the provisions have direct effect – to borrow the terminology of the Court of Justice of the European Community?

In this regard, the answer turns on how national law treats international agreements and in particular whether the legal tradition of the state in question is monist or dualist. That is to say, does an international agreement, to which the state is a party, become 'law' simply on accession or signature (the monist doctrine) or does it need to be ratified as a piece of substantive legislation in the normal way before it can become law (the dualist approach)? International law recognises both approaches and thus it cannot be argued that suppliers in a dualist state are being disadvantaged compared with those in a monist state. The question is of particular relevance should, however, a contracting state fail to facilitate an accessible and effective remedy. In this situation, the only course open to the aggrieved supplier is to have the host state take the dispute to the DSB.

In conclusion, therefore, an aggrieved supplier must look to national provisions implementing the essence of Article XX for a remedy. Should this fail to bring satisfaction, then there may be an avenue to pursue a claim indirectly through the Dispute Settlement Procedures.

CHALLENGING GPA PROCUREMENT PROCEDURES – EC

European Community membership of the WTO arises out of its exclusive competence to deal with common commercial policy (under Article 113 of the EC Treaty). It was therefore the European Commission which participated in negotiations, and signed on the Community's behalf, although representatives of the Member States also signed. Under Article IX of the GATT Final Act, the EC may vote on behalf of its Member States in the Ministerial Council and the General Council of the WTO. In these fora, as an exception to the principle that each member of the WTO has one vote, the EC 'shall have a number of votes equal to the number of the member states which are members of the WTO'.

The participation of the EC in the WTO and GPA offers an interesting and useful dimension. As the richest trading block involved, and with a locus standi before the institutions of the GATT and WTO, the EC offers considerable weight and influence in the determination of disputes under the GPA Dispute Settlement Procedures. Its support in these, if forthcoming, will be additional to that which will hopefully be available to a complainant from its own national government. The way to enlist the support of the Community would be to contact the Commission directly. A complaint should be directed by the Secretariat-General, but any action taken would be by the External Affairs Directorate General of the Commission, via the Delegation Office in the state concerned.

However, the EC's participation is also interesting in that a complaint falling to be resolved by a national court concerning an award covered by the GPA might also fall to be considered by the European Community institutions. Here one must briefly consider whether the openings normally available can be accessed here.

Although the GPA has not been formally entered into Community law the Court has ruled[1] that the Community is bound by GATT. However, this is not to say that the GPA or any provision in the GATT/WTO Agreement has direct effect. The Court has consistently held[2] that the GATT does not contain provisions of such a nature as to confer on individuals rights which they can rely on before national courts in order to challenge the application of conflicting national provisions. This is because it takes the view that the GATT is based on the principle of negotiations undertaken on the basis of reciprocal and mutually advantageous arrangements, characterised by the great flexibility of its provisions, in particular those conferring the possibility of derogation, the measures to be taken when confronted with exceptional difficulties and the settlement of conflicts between the contracting states. Most of all the possibility of a contracting party withdrawing or being suspended from the agreement ultimately renders it conditional and insufficiently precise for the purposes of direct effect. From this one can essentially derive that the EC is a dualist 'state' since accession to an international agreement is not on its own sufficient to make it law.

On the other hand, the Court has also held that it has exclusive jurisdiction to interpret GATT in EC law[3] and the lack of direct effect does not affect the EC's obligation to ensure that the provisions of GATT are observed in its relationship with third non-Member States which are parties to GATT.[4]

From the jurisprudence it is established that a national court can refer a case to the ECJ for a preliminary ruling on the interpretation of a GATT/WTO Agreement/GPA provision. However it is uncertain whether an aggrieved supplier from outside the EC could bring a direct action against a Community institution before the Court of Justice – bearing in mind that the EC institutions are also covered by the GPA. There is no precedent directly

[1] In *International Fruit Co NV v Commission*: 41/70 [1971] ECR 411.
[2] Most recently in case C-469/93 *Amministrazione delle Finanze dello Stato v Chiquita Italia SpA* [1995] ECR I-4533, ECJ.
[3] See case 267-269/81 *Amministrazione delle Finanze dello Stato v Societa Petrolifera Italiana SpA* [1983] ECR 801.
[4] See case 266/81 *Societa Italiana per l'Oleodotto Transalpino v Ministero delle Finanze* [1983] ECR 731.

on this point, but a significant amount of academic thinking,[1] and on balance it must be considered arguable that a direct action would lie before the Court of Justice.

CONCLUSION

For many, if not most, the GPA rules, and especially the dispute resolution system at the GATT level, will be too far removed from the standard perceptions and expectation of government procurement.

On the other hand, for major undertakings that are very much concerned with the type of infrastructure projects covered by the GPA and who welcome the increased liberalisation in government procurement, the right to take part in a tender, the rules by which tender proceedings must be carried out, and the ability to challenge awards which appear to be irregular, will be real and bring very realisable benefits. For these large undertakings, connections with governmental departments in the home state and the resources to pursue challenge procedures in the host state are the necessary means of enforcing the rights under the GPA.

In any event, the shortcomings of the regime, particularly the availability of exercisable remedies, and all the vagaries of international diplomacy, make the GPA procurement rules a largely untested and uncertain forum to enforce one's rights.

---

[1] For an overview see Castillo de La Torre, Fernando, 'The Status of GATT in EC Law, Revisited' (1994) WT 53.

APPENDIX

EC Directives

COUNCIL DIRECTIVE 89/665/EEC OF 21 DECEMBER 1989 ON THE COORDINATION OF THE LAWS, REGULATIONS AND ADMINISTRATIVE PROVISIONS RELATING TO THE APPLICATION OF REVIEW PROCEDURES TO THE AWARD OF PUBLIC SUPPLY AND PUBLIC WORKS CONTRACTS.

THE COUNCIL OF THE EUROPEAN COMMUNITIES,
Having regard to the Treaty establishing the European Economic Community, and in particular Article 100a thereof,
Having regard to the proposal from the Commission,
    In cooperation with the European Parliament,
    Having regard to the opinion of the Economic and Social Committee,
    Whereas Community Directives on public procurement, in particular Council Directive 71/305/EEC of 26 July 1971 concerning the coordination of procedures for the award of public works contracts, as last amended by Directive 89/440/EEC, and Council Directive 77/62/EEC of 21 December 1976 coordinating procedures for the award of public supply contracts, as last amended by Directive 88/295/EEC, do not contain any specific provisions ensuring their effective application;
    Whereas the existing arrangements at both national and Community levels for ensuring their application are not always adequate to ensure compliance with the relevant Community provisions particularly at a stage when infringements can be corrected;
    Whereas the opening-up of public procurement to Community competition necessitates a substantial increase in the guarantees of transparency and non-discrimination; whereas, for it to have tangible effects, effective and rapid remedies must be available in the case of infringements of Community law in the field of public procurement or national rules implementing that law;
    Whereas in certain Member States the absence of effective remedies or inadequacy of existing remedies deter Community undertakings from submitting tenders in the Member State in which the contracting authority is established; whereas, therefore, the Member States concerned must remedy this situation;
    Whereas, since procedures for the award of public contracts are of such short duration, competent review bodies must, among other things, be authorised to take interim measures aimed at suspending such a procedure or the implementation of any decisions which may be taken by the contracting authority; whereas the short duration of the procedures means that the aforementioned infringements need to be dealt with urgently;

Whereas it is necessary to ensure that adequate procedures exist in all the Member States to permit the setting aside of decisions taken unlawfully and compensation of persons harmed by an infringement;

Whereas, when undertakings do not seek review, certain infringements may not be corrected unless a specific mechanism is put in place;

Whereas, accordingly, the Commission, when it considers that a clear and manifest infringement has been committed during a contract award procedure, should be able to bring it to the attention of the competent authorities of the Member State and of the contracting authority concerned so that appropriate steps are taken for the rapid correction of any alleged infringement;

Whereas the application in practice of the provisions of this Directive should be re-examined within a period of four years of its implementation on the basis of information to be supplied by the Member States concerning the functioning of the national review procedures,

HAD ADOPTED THIS DIRECTIVE:

Article 1

1.   The Member States shall take the measures necessary to ensure that, as regards contract award procedures falling within the scope of Directives 71/305/EEC and 77/62/EEC and 92/50/EEC, decisions taken by the contracting authorities may be reviewed effectively and, in particular, as rapidly as possible in accordance with the conditions set out in the following Articles, and, in particular, Article 2(7) on the grounds that such decisions have infringed Community law in the field of public procurement or national rules implementing that law.

2.   Member States shall ensure that there is no discrimination between undertakings claiming injury in the context of a procedure for the award of a contract as a result of the distinction made by this Directive between national rules implementing Community law and other national rules.

3.   The Member States shall ensure that the review procedures are available, under detailed rules which the Member States may establish, at least to any person having or having had an interest in obtaining a particular public supply or public works contract and who has been or risks being harmed by an alleged infringement. In particular, the Member States may require that the person seeking the review must have previously notified the contracting authority of the alleged infringement and of his intention to seek review.

Article 2

1.   The Member States shall ensure that the measures taken concerning the review procedures specified in Article 1 include provision for the powers to:
(a) take, at the earliest opportunity and by way of interlocutory procedures, interim measures with the aim of correcting the alleged infringement or preventing further damage to the interests concerned, including measures to suspend or to ensure the suspension of the procedure for the award of a public contract or the implementation of any decision taken by the contracting authority;
(b) either set aside or ensure the setting aside of decisions taken unlawfully, including the removal of discriminatory technical, economic or financial

specifications in the invitation to tender, the contract documents or in any other document relating to the contract award procedure;

(c) award damages to persons harmed by an infringement.

2. The powers specified in paragraph 1 may be conferred on separate bodies responsible for different aspects of the review procedure.

3. Review procedures need not in themselves have an automatic suspensive effect on the contract award procedures to which they relate.

4. The Member States may provide that when considering whether to order interim measures the body responsible may take into account the probable consequences of the measures for all interests likely to be harmed, as well as the public interest, and may decide not to grant such measures where their negative consequences could exceed their benefits. A decision not to grant interim measures shall not prejudice any other claim of the person seeking these measures.

5. The Member States may provide that where damages are claimed on the grounds that a decision was taken unlawfully, the contested decision must first be set aside by a body having the necessary powers.

6. The effects of the exercise of the powers referred to in paragraph 1 on a contract concluded subsequent to its award shall be determined by national law.

Furthermore, except where a decision must be set aside prior to the award of damages, a Member State may provide that, after the conclusion of a contract following its award, the powers of the body responsible for the review procedures shall be limited to awarding damages to any person harmed by an infringement.

7. The Member States shall ensure that decisions taken by bodies responsible for review procedures can be effectively enforced.

8. Where bodies responsible for review procedures are not judicial in character, written reasons for their decisions shall always be given. Furthermore, in such a case, provision must be made to guarantee procedures whereby any allegedly illegal measure taken by the review body or any alleged defect in the exercise of the powers conferred on it can be the subject of judicial review or review by another body which is a court or tribunal within the meaning of Article 177 of the EEC Treaty and independent of both the contracting authority and the review body.

The members of such an independent body shall be appointed and leave office under the same conditions as members of the judiciary as regards the authority responsible for their appointment, their period of office, and their removal. At least the President of this independent body shall have the same legal and professional qualifications as members of the judiciary. The independent body shall take its decisions following a procedure in which both sides are heard, and these decisions shall, by means determined by each Member State, be legally binding.

Article 3

1. The Commission may invoke the procedure for which this Article provides when, prior to a contract being concluded, it considers that a clear and manifest infringement of Community provisions in the field of public procurement has been committed during a contract award procedure falling within the scope of Directives 71/305/EEC and 77/62/EEC.

2. The Commission shall notify the Member State and the contracting

authority concerned of the reasons which have led it to conclude that a clear and manifest infringement has been committed and request its correction.

3.   Within 21 days of receipt of the notification referred to in paragraph 2, the Member State concerned shall communicate to the Commission:

(a) its confirmation that the infringement has been corrected; or

(b) a reasoned submission as to why no correction has been made; or

(c) a notice to the effect that the contract award procedure has been suspended either by the contracting authority on its own initiative or on the basis of the powers specified in Article 2(1)(a).

4.   A reasoned submission in accordance with paragraph 3(b) may rely among other matters on the fact that the alleged infringement is already the subject of judicial or other review proceedings or of a review as referred to in Article 2(8). In such a case, the Member State shall inform the Commission of the result of those proceedings as soon as it becomes known.

5.   Where notice has been given that a contract award procedure has been suspended in accordance with paragraph 3(c), the Member State shall notify the Commission when the suspension is lifted or another contract procedure relating in whole or in part to the same subject matter is begun. That notification shall confirm that the alleged infringement has been corrected or include a reasoned submission as to why no correction has been made.

Article 4

1.   Not later than four years after the implementation of this Directive, the Commission, in consultation with the Advisory Committee for Public Contracts, shall review the manner in which the provisions of this Directive have been implemented and, if necessary, make proposals for amendments.

2.   By 1 March each year the Member States shall communicate to the Commission information on the operation of their national review procedures during the preceding calendar year. The nature of the information shall be determined by the Commission in consultation with the Advisory Committee for Public Contracts.

Article 5

Member States shall bring into force, before 1 December 1991, the measures necessary to comply with this Directive. They shall communicate to the Commission the texts of the main national laws, regulations and administrative provisions which they adopt in the field governed by this Directive.

Article 6

This Directive is addressed to the Member States.

Done at Brussels, 21 December 1989.

COUNCIL DIRECTIVE 92/13/EEC OF 25 FEBRUARY 1992
COORDINATING THE LAWS, REGULATIONS AND
ADMINISTRATIVE PROVISIONS RELATING TO THE APPLICATION
OF COMMUNITY RULES ON THE PROCUREMENT PROCEDURES
OF ENTITIES OPERATING IN THE WATER, ENERGY, TRANSPORT
AND TELECOMMUNICATIONS SECTORS.

THE COUNCIL OF THE EUROPEAN COMMUNITIES,
Having regard to the Treaty establishing the European Economic Community,
and in particular Article 100a thereof,
  Having regard to the proposal from the Commission,
  In cooperation with the European Parliament,
  Having regard to the opinion of the Economic and Social Committee,
  Whereas Council Directive 90/531/EEC of 17 September 1990 on the
procurement procedures of entities operating in the water, energy, transport
and telecommunications sectors lays down rules for procurement procedures
to ensure that potential suppliers and contractors have a fair opportunity
to secure the award of contracts, but does not contain any specific provisions
ensuring its effective application;
  Whereas the existing arrangements at both national and Community levels
for ensuring its application are not always adequate;
  Whereas the absence of effective remedies or the inadequacy of existing
remedies could deter Community undertakings from submitting tenders;
whereas, therefore, the Member States must remedy this situation;
  Whereas Council Directive 89/665/EEC of 21 December 1989 on the
coordination of the laws, regulations and administrative provisions relating
to the application of review procedures to the award of public supply and
public works contracts is limited to contract award procedures within the
scope of Council Directive 71/305/EEC of 26 July 1971 concerning the
coordination of procedures for the award of public works contracts, as last
amended by Directive 90/531/EEC, and Council Directive 77/62/EEC of
21 December 1976 coordinating procedures for the award of public supply
contracts, as last amended by Directive 90/531/EEC;
  Whereas the opening-up of procurement in the sectors concerned to
Community competition implies that provisions must be adopted to ensure
that appropriate review procedures are made available to suppliers or
contractors in the event of infringement of the relevant Community law or
national rules implementing that law;
  Whereas it is necessary to provide for a substantial increase in the guarantees
of transparency and non-discrimination and whereas, for it to have tangible
effects, effective and rapid remedies must be available;
  Whereas account must be taken of the specific nature of certain legal orders
by authorising the Member States to choose between the introduction of
different powers for the review bodies which have equivalent effects;
  Whereas one of these options includes the power to intervene directly in the
contracting entities' procurement procedures such as by suspending them, or by
setting aside decisions or discriminatory clauses in documents or publications;
  Whereas the other option provides for the power to exert effective indirect
pressure on the contracting entities in order to make them correct any
infringements or prevent them from committing infringements, and to prevent
injury from occurring;
  Whereas claims for damages must always be possible;

Whereas, where a claim is made for damages representing the costs of preparing a bid or of participating in an award procedure, the person making the claim is not be required, in order to obtain the reimbursement of his costs, to prove that the contract would have been awarded to him in the absence of such infringement;

Whereas the contracting entities which comply with the procurement rules may make this known through appropriate means; whereas this requires an examination, by independent persons of procurement procedures and practices applied by those entities;

Whereas for this purpose an attestation system, allowing for a declaration on the correct application of the procurement rules, to be made in notices published in the *Official Journal of the European Communities,* is appropriate;

Whereas the contracting entities should have the opportunity of having recourse to the attestation system if they so wish; whereas the Member States must offer them the possibility of doing so; whereas they can do so either by setting up the system themselves or by allowing the contracting entities to have recourse to the attestation system established by another Member State; whereas they may confer the task of carrying out the examination under the attestation system to persons, professions or staff of institutions;

Whereas the necessary flexibility in the introduction of such a system is guaranteed by laying down the essential requirements for it in this Directive; whereas operational details should be provided in European Standards to which this Directive refers;

Whereas the Member States may need to determine operational details prior to, or in addition to, the rules contained in European Standards;

Whereas, when undertakings do not seek review, certain infringements may not be corrected unless a specific mechanism is put in place;

Whereas, accordingly, the Commission, when it considers that a clear and manifest infringement has been committed during a contract award procedure, should be able to bring it to the attention of the competent authorities of the Member State and of the contracting entity concerned so that appropriate steps are taken for the rapid correction of that infringement;

Whereas it is necessary to provide for the possibility of conciliation at Community level to enable disputes to be settled amicably;

Whereas the application in practice of this Directive should be reviewed at the same time as that of Directive 90/531/EEC on the basis of information to be supplied by the Member States concerning the functioning of the national review procedures;

Whereas this Directive must be brought into effect at the same time as Directive 90/531/EEC;

Whereas it is appropriate that the Kingdom of Spain, the Hellenic Republic and the Portuguese Republic are granted adequate additional periods to transpose this Directive, taking account of the dates of application of Directive 90/531/EEC in those countries,

HAS ADOPTED THIS DIRECTIVE:

Chapter 1   Remedies at national level

Article 1

1. The Member States shall take the measures necessary to ensure that decisions taken by contracting entities may be reviewed effectively and, in

particular, as rapidly as possible in accordance with the conditions set out in the following Articles and, in particular, Article 2 (8), on the grounds that such decisions have infringed Community law in the field or procurement or national rules implementing that law as regards:

(a) contract award procedures falling within the scope of Council Directive 90/531/EEC; and

(b) compliance with Article 3 (2) (a) of that Directive in the case of the contracting entities to which that provision applies.

2. Member States shall ensure that there is no discrimination between undertakings likely to make a claim for injury in the context of a procedure for the award of a contract as a result of the distinction made by this Directive between national rules implementing Community law and other national rules.

3. The Member States shall ensure that the review procedures are available, under detailed rules which the Member States may establish, at least to any person having or having had an interest in obtaining a particular contract and who has been or risks being harmed by an alleged infringement. In particular, the Member States may require that the person seeking the review must have previously notified the contracting entity of the alleged infringement and of his intention to seek review.

Article 2

1. The Member States shall ensure that the measures taken concerning the review procedures specified in Article 1 include provision for the powers:
either

(a) to take, at the earliest opportunity and by way of interlocutory procedure, interim measures with the aim of correcting the alleged infringement or preventing further injury to the interests concerned, including measures to suspend or to ensure the suspension of the procedure for the award of a contract or the implementation of any decision taken by the contracting entity; and

(b) to set aside or ensure the setting aside of decisions taken unlawfully, including the removal of discriminatory technical, economic or financial specifications in the notice of contract, the periodic indicative notice, the notice on the existence of a system of qualification, the invitation to tender, the contract documents or in any other document relating to the contract award procedure in question;

or

(c) to take, at the earliest opportunity, if possible by way of interlocutory procedures and if necessary by a final procedure on the substance, measures other than those provided for in points (a) and (b) with the aim of correcting any identified infringement and preventing injury to the interests concerned; in particular, making an order for the payment of a particular sum, in cases where the infringement has not been corrected or prevented.

Member States may take this choice either for all contracting entities or for categories of entities defined on the basis of objective criteria, in any event preserving the effectiveness of the measures laid down in order to prevent injury being caused to the interests concerned;

(d) and, in both the above cases, to award damages to persons injured by the infringement.

Where damages are claimed on the grounds that a decision has been taken unlawfully, Member States may, where their system of internal law so requires and provides bodies having the necessary powers for that purpose, provide that the contested decision must first be set aside or declared illegal.

2.   The powers referred to in paragraph 1 may be conferred on separate bodies responsible for different aspects of the review procedure.

3.   Review procedures need not in themselves have an automatic suspensive effect on the contract award procedures to which they relate.

4.   The Member States may provide that, when considering whether to order interim measures, the body responsible may take into account the probable consequences of the measures for all interests likely to be harmed, as well as the public interest, and may decide not to grant such measures where their negative consequences could exceed their benefits. A decision not to grant interim measures shall not prejudice any other claim of the person seeking these measures.

5.   The sum to be paid in accordance with paragraph 1(c) must be set at a level high enough to dissuade the contracting entity from committing or persisting in an infringement. The payment of that sum may be made to depend upon a final decision that the infringement has in fact taken place.

6.   The effects of the exercise of the powers referred to in paragraph 1 on a contract concluded subsequent to its award shall be determined by national law. Furthermore, except where a decision must be set aside prior to the award of damages, a Member State may provide that, after the conclusion of a contract following its award, the powers of the body responsible for the review procedures shall be limited to awarding damages to any person harmed by an infringement.

7.   Where a claim is made for damages representing the costs of preparing a bid or of participating in an award procedure, the person making the claim shall be required only to prove an infringement of Community law in the field of procurement or national rules implementing that law and that he would have had a real chance of winning the contract and that, as a consequence of that infringement, that chance was adversely affected.

8.   The Member States shall ensure that decisions taken by bodies responsible for review procedures can be effectively enforced.

9.   Whereas bodies responsible for review procedures are not judicial in character, written reasons for their decisions shall always be given. Furthermore, in such a case, provision must be made to guarantee procedures whereby any allegedly illegal measures taken by the review body or any alleged defect in the exercise of the powers conferred on it can be the subject of judicial review or review by another body which is a court or tribunal within the meaning of Article 177 of the Treaty and independent of both the contracting entity and the review body.

The members of the independent body referred to in the first paragraph shall be appointed and leave office under the same conditions as members of the judiciary as regards the authority responsible for their appointment, their period of office, and their removal. At least the President of this independent body shall have the same legal and professional qualifications as members of the judiciary. The independent body shall take its decisions following a procedure in which both sides are heard, and these decisions shall, by means determined by each Member State, be legally binding.

Chapter 2   Attestation

Article 3

The Member States shall give contracting entities the possibility of having recourse to an attestation system in accordance with Articles 4 to 7.

Article 4

Contracting entities may have their contract award procedures and practices which fall within the scope of Directive 90/531/EEC examined periodically with a view to obtaining an attestation that, at that time, those procedures and practices are in conformity with Community law concerning the award of contracts and the national rules implementing the law.

Article 5

1.   Attestors shall report to the contracting entity, in writing, on the results of their examination. They shall satisfy themselves, before delivering to the contracting entity the attestation referred to in Article 4, that any irregularities identified in the contracting entity's award procedures and practices have been corrected and measures have been taken to ensure that those irregularities are not repeated.

2.   Contracting entities having obtained that attestation may include the following statement in notice published in the *Official Journal of the European Communities* pursuant to Articles 16 to 18 of Directive 90/531/EEC:

> 'The contracting entity has obtained an attestation in accordance with Council Directive 92/13/EEC that, on ...., its contract award procedures and practices were in conformity with Community law and the national rules implementing that law.'

Article 6

1.   Attestors shall be independent of the contracting entities and must be completely objective in carrying out their duties. They shall offer appropriate guarantees of relevant professional qualifications and experience.

2.   Member States may identify any persons, professions or institutions whose staff, called upon the act as attestors, they regard as fulfilling the requirements of paragraph 1. For these purposes, Member States may require professional qualifications, at least at the level of a higher education diploma within the meaning of Directive 89/48/EEC, which they regard as relevant, or provide that particular examinations of professional competence organised or recognised by the State offer such guarantees.

Article 7

The provisions of Articles 4, 5 and 6 shall be considered as essential requirements for the development of European standards on attestation.

Chapter 3   Corrective mechanism

Article 8

1.   The Commission may invoke the procedures for which this Article provides when, prior to a contract being concluded, it considers that a clear and manifest infringement of Community provisions in the field of procurement has been committed during a contract award procedure falling within the scope of Directive 90/531/EEC or in relation to Article 3(2)(a) of that Directive in the case of the contracting entities to which that provision applies.

2.   The Commission shall notify the Member States and the contracting entity concerned of the reasons which have led it to conclude that a clear and manifest infringement has been committed and request its correction by appropriate means.

3.   Within 30 days of receipt of the notification referred to in paragraph 2, the Member States concerned shall communicate to the Commission:
(a) its confirmation that the infringement has been corrected; or
(b) a reasoned submission as to why no correction has been made; or
(c) a notice to the effect that the contract award procedure has been suspended
     either by the contracting entity on its own initiative or on the basis of
     the powers specified in Article 2(1)(a).
4.   A reasoned submission in accordance with paragraph 3(b) may rely among other matters on the fact that the alleged infringement is already the subject of judicial review proceedings or of a review as referred to in Article 2(9). In such a case, the Member State shall inform the Commission of the result of those proceedings as soon as it becomes known.

5.   Where notice has been given that a contract award procedure has been suspended in accordance with paragraph 3(c), the Member State concerned shall notify the Commission when the suspension is lifted or another contract procedure relating in whole or in part to the same subject matter is begun. That new notification shall confirm that the alleged infringement has been corrected or include an reasoned submission as to why no correction has been made.

Chapter 4   Conciliation

Article 9

1.   Any person having or having had an interest in obtaining a particular contract falling within the scope of Directive 90/531/EEC and who, in relation to the procedure for the award of that contract, considers that he has been or risks being harmed by an alleged infringement of Community law in the field of procurement or national rules implementing that law may request the application of the conciliation procedure provided for in Articles 10 and 11.

2.   The request referred to in paragraph 1 shall be addressed in writing to the Commission or to the national authorities listed in the Annex. These authorities shall forward requests to the Commission as quickly as possible.

Article 10

1.   Where the Commission considers, on the basis of the request referred to in Article 9, that the dispute concerns the correct application of Community law, it shall ask the contracting entity to state whether it is willing to take part in the conciliation procedure. If the contracting entity declines to take part, the Commission shall inform the person who made the request that the procedure cannot be initiated. If the contracting entity agrees, paragraphs 2 to 7 shall apply.

2.   The Commission shall propose, as quickly as possible, a conciliator drawn from a list of independent persons accredited for this purpose. This list shall be drawn up by the Commission, following consultation of the Advisory Committee for Public Contracts or, in the case of contracting entities the activities of which are defined in Article 2 (2) (d) of Directive 90/531/EEC, following consultation of the Advisory Committee on Telecommunications Procurement.

Each party to the conciliation procedure shall declare whether it accepts the conciliator, and shall designate an additional conciliator. The conciliators may invite not more than two other persons as experts to advise them in their work. The parties to the conciliation procedure and the Commission may reject any expert invited by the conciliators.

3.   The conciliators shall give the person requesting the application of the conciliation procedure, the contracting entity and any other candidate or tenderer participating in the relevant contract award procedure the opportunity to make representations on the matter either orally or in writing.

4.   The conciliators shall endeavour as quickly as possible to reach an agreement between the parties which is in accordance with Community law.

5.   The conciliators shall report to the Commission on their findings and on any result achieved.

6.   The person requesting the application of the conciliation procedure and the contracting entity shall have the right to terminate the procedure at any time.

7.   Unless the parties decide otherwise, the person requesting the application of the conciliation procedure and the contracting entity shall be responsible for their own costs. In addition, they shall each bear half of the costs of the procedure, excluding the costs of intervening parties.

Article 11

1.   Where, in relation to a particular contract award procedure, an interested person within the meaning of Article 9, other than the person requesting the conciliation procedure, is pursuing judicial review proceedings or other proceedings for review within the meaning of this Directive, the contracting entity shall inform the conciliators. These shall inform that person that a request has been made to apply the conciliation procedure and shall invite that person to indicate within a given time limit whether he agrees to participate in that procedure. If that person refuses to participate, the conciliators may decide, acting if necessary by a majority, to terminate the conciliation procedure if they consider that the participation of this person is necessary to resolve the dispute. They shall notify their decision to the Committee and give the reasons for it.

2.   Action taken pursuant to this Chapter shall be without prejudice to:

(a) any action that the Commission or any Member State might take pursuant of Articles 169 or 170 of the Treaty or pursuant to Chapter 3 of this Directive;

(b) the rights of the persons requesting the conciliation procedure, of the contracting entity or of any other person.

Chapter 5   Final provisions

Article 12

1. Not later than four years after the application of this Directive, the Commission, in consultation with the Advisory Committee for Public Contracts, shall review the manner in which the provisions of this Directive have been implemented and, in particular, the use of the European Standards and, if necessary, make proposals for amendments.

2. Before 1 March each year the Member States shall communicate to the Commission information on the operation of their national review procedures during the preceding calendar year. The nature of the information shall be determined by the Commission in consultation with the Advisory Committee for Public Contracts.

3. In the case of matters relating to contracting entities the activities of which are defined in Article 2 (2) (d) of Directive 90/531/EEC, the Commission shall also consult the Advisory Committee on Telecommunications Procurement.

Article 13

1. Member States shall take, before 1 January 1993, the measures necessary to comply with this Directive. The Kingdom of Spain shall take these measures not later than 30 June 1995. The Hellenic Republic and the Portuguese Republic shall take these measures not later than 30 June 1997. They shall forthwith inform the Commission thereof.

When Member States adopt these measures, they shall contain a reference to this Directive or shall be accompanied by such reference on the occasion of their official publication. The methods of making such a reference shall be laid down by the Member States.

2. Member States shall bring into force the measures referred to in paragraph 1 on the same dates as those (laid down in Directive 90/531/EEC).

3. Member States shall communicate to the Commission the texts of the main provisions of domestic law which they adopt in the field governed by this Directive.

Article 14

This Directive is addressed to the Member States.
   Done at Brussels, 25 February 1992.

Index